Red Flag Unfurled

Red Flag Unfurled

History, Historians,
and the Russian Revolution

RONALD GRIGOR SUNY

VERSO
London • New York

To my daughters,
Sevan Siranoush Suni and Anoush Tamar Suni,
who have been through it with me

First published by Verso 2017
© Ronald Grigor Suny 2017

"The Empire Strikes Out" by permission of Oxford University Press, USA

1 3 5 7 9 10 8 6 4 2

Verso
UK: 6 Meard Street, London W1F 0EG
US: 20 Jay Street, Suite 1010, Brooklyn, NY 11201
versobooks.com

Verso is the imprint of New Left Books

ISBN-13: 978-1-78478-564-2
ISBN-13: 978-1-78478-567-3 (US EBK)
ISBN-13: 978-1-78478-566-6 (UK EBK)

British Library Cataloguing in Publication Data
A catalogue record for this book is available from the British Library

Library of Congress Cataloging-in-Publication Data
Names: Suny, Ronald Grigor, author.
Title: Red flag unfurled : history, historians, and the Russian Revolution /
  Ronald Grigor Suny.
Description: Brooklyn, NY : Verso Books, 2017. | Includes index.
Identifiers: LCCN 2017027209 (print) | LCCN 2017026935 (ebook) | ISBN
  9781784785642 (hardback) | ISBN 9781784785673 (US ebook) | ISBN
  9781784785666 (UK ebook) | ISBN 9781784785673 (E-book)
Subjects: LCSH: Soviet Union—History—Revolution, 1917–1921—Historiography.
  | Soviet Union—History—Revolution, 1917–1921—Influence.
Classification: LCC DK265.A553 .S74 2017 (ebook) | LCC DK265.A553 (print) |
  DDC 947.084/1072—dc23
LC record available at https://lccn.loc.gov/2017027209

Typeset in Monotype Sabon by Hewer Text Ltd, Edinburgh
Printed and bound by CPI Group (UK) Ltd, Croydon, CR0 4YY

Contents

Introduction: Making History and the Historian

Every history is embattled in some sense, but perhaps none more than the history of Russia, particularly that of the Soviet Union. The history of the USSR in particular is public property in a way that histories of most other countries are not. As the American humorist Will Rogers said, "Russia is a country that no matter what you say about it, it's true. Even if it's a lie, it's true. If it's about Russia."[1] Everyone is entitled to their own opinion, and since the cause for which the USSR stood no longer holds its former potency, there appears less incentive to try to tell the story in its full complexity and moral ambiguity. The market appreciates the simplified anti-Communist version, complete with the dramas and tragedies of Stalinism, the Gulag and the Terror. The central metaphor for the Soviet experiment is the prison camp, and the central figure is neither the state's founder, Vladimir Lenin, nor the well-intentioned reformer who unraveled the system, Mikhail Gorbachev, but Stalin, the heir of the revolution and, for many, its gravedigger. While academic historians might still engage in subtle and elaborate explanations of the ambitions, successes, and failings of the Soviet regime, their publications find a small professional audience, while most popular accounts range from indictments to flat-out condemnations. The monster must be killed over and over again, for, like the killer in slasher films, it may rise again, perhaps in a new form, authoritarianism-light, capitalist but statist, headed by a small, fit, dour policeman.

"The past," it is said, "is another country; they do things differently there."[2] For someone like me, who started studying the Soviet Union over

---

1 Will Rogers, *The Papers of Will Rogers, Volume V: The Final Years, August 1928–August 1935*, edited by Steven K. Gragert and M. Jane Johansson (Norman: University of Oklahoma Press, 1995), p. 512.

2 First line of L. P. Hartley's novel *The Go-Between* (1953) (London: Penguin Books, 2000).

half a century ago, at the beginning of the 1960s, the present seems to be another planet! It is not the world we anticipated. Then the objects of our study, the Soviet Union and Communist regimes in East Central Europe, were alive if not well, and few imagined that Lenin's utopian vision, even after its descent into Stalinist nightmare, would collapse so abruptly at a moment of neo-liberal triumph. In those heady years when change really meant change, the interest in varieties of socialism and the analytical potential of Marxist approaches, particularly in the emerging field of social history, invigorated a generation of scholars, not only to attempt to understand the mysterious "Second World," but to question the ortho-doxies and complacency of Cold War scholarship and even Western liber-alism. When I was a young professor at Oberlin College, a liberal oasis in northeastern Ohio, a senior professor of religion came into my modest office, past the larger-than-life-size poster of Lenin on the door, and asked me, "Is it true that you are a Marxist?" In those youthful days, confident in my radicalism, I assured him I was. "How quaint!" he said. "You know," he continued, "you on the Left believe in the goodness of man and therefore are always disenchanted, while we who believe in Original Sin expect the worst and are never disappointed by what happens."

For the Left, in so far as a Left actually existed in the United States, and for liberals as well, certainly the next few decades were ones of disap-pointment and disenchantment. The last spasm of hope for many of us came with the Gorbachev experiment in radical reform from above that ended only too quickly, in the catastrophic collapse, not only of Soviet Communism but of any real "third way" alternatives to the triumph of neo-liberal economics and, eventually, neo-conservative politics. The Soviet studies profession limped along, trying to find its feet in a much-disparaged field called "area studies." Sovietology was discarded on the trash bin of history; economics of non-capitalist societies evaporated as a field of study; though, it should be noted, other disciplines revived—history benefiting from the newly opened archives and anthropology and sociology now able to benefit from field work in regions hitherto closed to investigation.

A new teleology shaped Soviet historiography, since, for many histori-ans, failure and collapse appeared to be written into the story, even into the genetic code of the revolution. More consequentially than how Soviet socialism was interpreted, the end of Communism and the Soviet empire in East Central Europe dragged down virtually any socialist alternative to

Western capitalism. Almost every form, from mild European Social Democracy to Third World revolutionary movements, was weakened or discredited. To be sure, the erosion of the post–World War II Social Democratic moment was already underway long before 1991, as neo-liberal capitalism in advanced countries subverted unions and welfare programs in aid of a transnational competition that has been sanctified and naturalized as the inevitable, agentless force of history known under the anodyne rubric "globalization." But the collapse of the USSR appeared to confirm the perversity of Marxism as political practice and a view of history. The principal critical analysis of capitalism and imperialism, the major opponent of Western capitalism in both Western socialist parties and in the Soviet support of national liberation movements and Communist parties—Marxism—was swept from politics in much of Europe and the United States, driven into universities where, enfeebled, it would occasionally be taught to freshmen through a process of inoculation: give them one short text to read, preferably a pretty dense one, and they will be immune to Marx for life.

In the absence of significant secular revolutionary or reformist alternatives to the "new world order" of Western capitalism and democracy, unanticipated new forces, much more conservative and religious, appeared, first in Iran in the revolution of the ayatollahs in 1979, in the Muslim Brotherhood movements in Egypt and elsewhere, in the mujahidin resistance to the Soviet intervention in Afghanistan, which metastasized into the jihadist radical Islamic movements of the present. A Green Menace replaced the Red. Enrollments in Russian and Soviet history courses dropped while professors scrambled to find hotter, more relevant topics to teach.

The conflation of the USSR with socialism, that served liberalism and conservatism so well, became the new common sense. The Soviet Union had in fact set itself up as the guardian of the faith, and liberals, conservatives, and Stalinists alike easily conceived of socialism as consonant with the practices and achievements of the USSR. Stalin incorporated his own version of Marxism even while he defanged Marx, eliminating the critical power of Marxism and transforming it into a legitimizing ideology for a repressive regime. For most post-Soviet Western observers of the USSR, Marxism was equivalent to what was done in Marx's name in the last century. For a few, however, the original project of a critical analysis of society and economics, over which Marx had labored in the British

3

Library, retained its power as an external standpoint from which to view the hegemonic social forms and practices of our time while preserving a cluster of values, norms, and practices that exposed what needed to be changed. Although it appeared unlikely in 1991, it seems in our current conjuncture of capitalist crisis a quarter century after the collapse of Soviet "communism" that Marx's alternative vision of the common good, freed of the memories and legacies of the Soviet past, has in the new century acquired an unanticipated potency. Once again it is time to think about what is left (in both senses of the word) of Marx.

Communism in its Leninist or Stalinist forms is a historical fact, no longer an active threat to the capitalist world, and has lost its sting. Moreover, historians have done a good job unraveling the mysteries and myths of Soviet history and the relationship of what was done in Marx's name by the one great power where his ideas were least appropriate. It is reasonable to expect that Marx would have been the most fervent critic, from the Left, of the disempowering of the working class and the exploit-ative character of the Soviet regime, as were many Western and (to their personal detriment) Soviet Marxists of the time. Russia was conceivably the worst place to attempt to build the kind of socialism that Marx had envisioned coming after capitalism had exhausted all its potential.

An understanding of Marx and the varieties of Marxism would seem to be indispensable to the subject of this book: the history as written by Western historians of the first great state that self-confidently proclaimed itself the bearer of his vision. Yet most Western historians of the Soviet Union never embraced Marxism as their principal mode of historical interpretation. For much of the Cold War period, 1945 to 1991, Marxism was dismissed as an ideology, in the sense of a partisan, unscientific approach that obscured or distorted more than it illuminated. One paid a price in the American academy particularly if one took Marx too seri-ously, or unwisely proclaimed that one was a Marxist. Better not to tell.

An Excursion into Autobiography

Marx warned his readers that they had to ask who educated the educator. In that spirit, I shall indulge in some auto-ethnography. I was born in Philadelphia of Armenian parents, my mother American-born, my father came from "the other side." George (Gurken) Suny's family had emigrated from the Russian Empire after the Russian Revolution and the Bolshevik invasion of Georgia, and Arax Kesdekian's had come to the United States before the Genocide of 1915—my mother's father from the central Turkish town of Yozgat, my mother's mother from Diarbakır, now a major city in Kurdistan. Most of their family who had remained in the Ottoman lands were massacred during World War I, though a few escaped to Iraq and made their way, eventually with our help, to the United States. There were stories, traumatic memories, but the family did not dwell on these matters or foster in their children a hatred of Turks and Kurds.

From my father I heard stories of his boyhood in Tiflis (Tbilisi, now the capital of independent Georgia), his memories of the revolution and the coming of the Bolsheviks. But the most constant theme through his tales was the enormous affection and respect for his father, the ethnomusicologist and composer, Grikor Mirzaian Suni. This fascinating, contradictory "maestro" (*varpet* in Armenian) combined high culture with an un-Armenian bohemianism and a dedication to revolution, Marxism, and Soviet Armenia. "Suni," as he was always called, had died the year before I was born, but his legacy was stamped on me early in the 1950s when, provoked by my father, I gave a report to my seventh-grade class on the achievements of the Soviet Union: the victory over fascism, the rebuilding of dozens of cities after the war, the number of steel mills . . . The teacher in those frigid days of the Cold War was shocked, and wanted to know where I had come up with such ideas. My classmates rewarded me with the epithet "Comrade Suny" for the rest of my school years. A skinny, shy kid, I now had a kind of identity that I wore (and defended) proudly. For my father and me (but not in the same way for my mother and sister), the Soviet Union was an ideal against which the inadequacies of capitalist America, into which I seemed not to fit particularly well, were judged.

Part of that misfit came as well from the other side of my family, the side we socialized with almost exclusively. My mother's mother, Azniv (noble, in Armenian), was a woman of saintly simplicity and kindness, whose world was bounded by the Armenian community in Philadelphia, and her love for her people and for the land (historic Armenia, eastern Turkey today) from which her family had been driven was simply part of her nature, unconscious, assumed, and unquestioned. She told me of the death of her sister whose throat had been cut during the 1894–96 massacres of Armenians in the Ottoman Empire. But much more impressive was her confidence that we Armenians were a special people, privileged to speak a language that had not only been the first language of human beings, spoken before the Tower of Babel, but still the lingua franca of heaven. Thus began my life-long struggle with the intricacies of a language assumed to be my "mother tongue." Grandma always insisted that my sister and I "marry Armenian," and she made it clear that *"menk hai enk,"* (we are Armenian), but *"anonk amerikatsi en"* (they are American). The Americans, it was understood, were *odar* (foreign). Here we were in America, and we considered the Americans, at least those who were not Armenian, to be foreigners! Thus, from an early age I had a double sense of distance from the society and the nation in which I actually lived, as an Armenian and a person of the Left.

Armenians, whose self-representation is often that of the victim and martyr, in the United States were an "invisible diaspora," not particularly persecuted and often not seen at all. There was always great delight when someone notable turned out to be Armenian or something Armenian was recognized by others. I felt no essential conflict between my Armenian and American identities, both of which were simply available for use in different situations and complemented each other almost everywhere, with no need to choose between them. American was different from what we considered Armenian, but it was accepting and inclusive, and as long as one tried to fit in, to conform, West Philadelphia and its suburbs in the 1950s were safe, secure, comfortable homes. It was not until my freshman year in college that I first heard an *odar* refer to me, the son of an immigrant, as a "foreigner."

For most of my growing-up years, the opportunity to both be a part of and yet stand apart from either of my "national" identities gave me a freedom from unquestioning American patriotism—particularly during the Cold and Vietnam Wars—as well as from the congested nationalism of the Armenian community. My parents gave my sister and me wide choice in defining ourselves, never forcing on us the stamp of ethnicity. Eventually Linda married a Greek, learned modern Greek, and for some time distanced herself from things Armenian. In our family, being different was something worth preserving, even celebrating. Outside there were limits, of course. As a naïve, idealistic seventeen-year-old, I wrote a commencement speech about the need for non-conformity which was gently rejected as "too controversial."

When it came time to make the decisive choice of what career to select—in my case between theater and the academy—the decision to go to graduate school in history was deeply shaped by the need to know more about the Soviet Union. Socialism remained in my young adulthood a utopia that first-hand knowledge of the actualities of the Soviet system did not tarnish. For me, as for many who drifted from Old to New Left, the USSR was no longer the model of socialism but a distorted or degenerate failure to realize the emancipatory promise of Marxism. Still, when I finally arrived in the Soviet Union in 1964, I experienced no disillusionment, only a concrete confirmation that socialism lay in the future. I was traveling with my father's brother from relatives in Tashkent to others in Leningrad on the day that Nikita Khrushchev fell from power. Our plane was pulled down in Cheliabinsk, where we waited for hours until released to go on to Leningrad. There was no news about Khrushchev's removal on radio or television, my thoughts were that if only I were in New York I could find out what was happening.

The people I met in the Soviet Union the next year, when I was an exchange student with Moscow and Erevan State universities, seemed to live a more authentic life than my compatriots back home: struggling, to be sure, with the material poverty of the early Brezhnev years, but at the same time maneuvering through the restrictions on public life and preserving a rich interior, private life marked by a deep humanism, a sense of social justice, and faith in a better future. That mid-1960s moment, living with students at the university dormitories, was my first and most durable experience of a non-capitalist world, a place free of commercialism and concern for money, marked by a rough equality. My enthusiasm for the Soviet experience was not shared by most of my fellow American exchange students who complained incessantly about the petty discomforts—no toilet paper, for example—that plagued our daily lives. Upset when I discovered I was being followed by plainclothes police, I confided in one of my fellow students, only to find out soon afterwards that he had betrayed my confidence and reported me to the American Embassy. When I applied to stay a second year on the exchange, the Soviets agreed but the Americans refused.

I reveled in the warmth of close Russian and Armenian friends, who helped in dozens of different ways to ease the material and bureaucratic difficulties of Soviet life. These friendships were deep, reinforcing, and have been maintained until the present. The mid-1960s were still a time when many intellectuals and most ordinary people supported the gradual reforms evident since the death of Stalin, maintained their belief in progress toward socialism, and remained both curious toward and suspicious of the West. Much of that immediate post-Khrushchevian affection for the system on the part of those I knew would soon disappear. Inequities and corruption grew in the next decades, along with social pessimism and inertia. Still, my own take was that the USSR was fundamentally a healthy society, that was struggling to overcome the legacy of Stalinism, but required radical reform to open its constricted public sphere. In my first published article (in a New Left journal published by Oberlin College students), I wrote about the need for a "bourgeois democratic revolution" in the USSR, more openness and protections for those in the embryonic civil society struggling to emerge. Paradoxically, the greatest sense of distance I felt in the Soviet Union was in Armenia itself, where I was received as a long-lost relative but was immediately aware of how different I was from the "we" that insisted I was one of them.

At Oberlin College in the late 1960s and through the 1970s, I was the young firebrand professor, the "Red-in-Residence" on that isolated Ohio campus, a self-proclaimed "Marxist" (who was just beginning to struggle through *Capital*, the *Economic and Philosophical Manuscripts*, and the *Grundrisse*). The Marxism of that time was that of the young Marx along with the socialist humanism of Erich Fromm, Herbert Marcuse, György Lukács, and Leszek Kolakowski, providing a compelling theoretical tradition that informed my work on Soviet history. Intellectually, the most innovative writing was by the new social historians, particularly British Marxist labor historians, and again I found a standpoint outside the society in which I lived from which to observe, analyze, and advocate. Teaching and scholarship, even in northeastern Ohio, was, I believed, a kind of political activity that required the most meticulous scholarly engagement: faithful attention to the evidence, as neutral and objective as possible a construction of narrative and analysis, and awareness that one came to the work with values of one's own. "Truth was revolutionary" (in Régis Debray's phrase), and honest scholarship on the USSR was essential for the activist Left, which all too often was overly apologetic or content to be just plain ignorant. We were confident that the student anti-war agitation and the civil rights movement were merely the first steps toward a more radical restructuring of American society. These were infectious thoughts, and I was an active participant, even from the precarious perch of an untenured assistant professor. The History Department slapped my wrists firmly when they refused to put me up for tenure, but in the best traditions of that liberal college the faculty pressured reconsideration.

Without much self-reflection, I wrote about class and nationality, which now seems to have come out of my own life experience as a leftist Armenian in America. After more than a decade as a Soviet historian at Oberlin, I moved to the University of Michigan, where I was appointed to a chair in modern Armenian history. I became a "professional Armenian," that is, I taught Armenian history largely to Armenian students, lectured to the Armenian community, and tried to elevate a rather parochial sub-field to the standards of the discipline. My interests in Transcaucasia and nationality problems in the Soviet Union continued to be marginal among mainline Russianists, until the explosion of national resistance in 1988. Suddenly, I was given my "fifteen minutes of fame," as I glided from radio to television to appearances in Washington as the "expert on the Caucasus."

The promise presented by the reforms of Mikhail Gorbachev was extraordinarily consequential for those of us in Soviet Studies who had argued against the demonization of the Soviet Union and for a more "détentist" approach in foreign policy. At that effervescent moment of the late 1980s, "actually-existing socialism" seemed about to become modern and humane, against the pessimistic predictions of most of the Sovietological community, which was convinced either of the perma-nence of the Stalinist infrastructure or the inevitability of collapse. Gorbachev's failure, in part because of the emergence of separatist nationalisms, had a catastrophic effect on the identities that I had formed over much of my life. The Soviet Union disappeared; Armenia became independent; socialism was (at least temporarily) thrown on the trash heap of history. When someone innocently congratulated me that now I had a country, I told him coldly, rashly, no, I have lost my country. I remember with sadness my father's query to me shortly before his death, would socialism come back again? I told him, not in the short run, though as long as capitalism existed there would be some kind of social-ist opposition.

But just as the reality of the Soviet Union did not diminish the ideal of a more egalitarian, socially just, and participatory social order beyond "actually-existing democracy," so its disappearance did not scour the political landscape of alternatives or bring history to an end. America had not changed as we had wanted in the 1960s, and the post-Soviet

Union metamorphosed into something more like what we hoped to avoid. But the optimism and security of family and children, of satisfying work, prevented political despair. Indeed, my marriage to Armena Marderosian (an Armenian to be sure!) kept me afloat, even when tragedy—the death of our first child, Grikor—nearly drowned us. For a decade, I shifted identities slightly, from Soviet and Armenian historian to Soviet and post-Soviet political scientist (at the University of Chicago), interested in nations and nationalisms, and then back to history (returning to Michigan). I continue to search for new places from which to observe. I remain a foreigner, an *odar*, in my native land, but that distance seems to be a propitious place to look beyond the political limits that the present offers us, and explore how I and my colleagues in Soviet history have understood the country we seek to explain.

So, What Is Left of Marx and Socialism?

Historians of my generation grew up in the Cold War decades in a world divided between (what Marxists call) bourgeois democracy, on one side, and statist socialism, on the other, and the dichotomy between a utopia of exclusively political rights versus a utopia of social and economic rights. We learned from the Soviet and East European experiments the bitter lesson that there is no real socialism without political democracy, and some of us concluded from our own political experience in countries polarized between the very wealthy and the rest that there is no real democracy without some kind of socialism. Perhaps not for most of those in the Soviet historical profession, but for a minority of practitioners Marx remained an inspiration, a provider of questions rather than a priori answers.

Marx himself was many things in his life—a post-Hegelian radical searching for the source of the expected German revolution; an Enlightenment rationalist who believed in naturalistic explanations of social and natural phenomena, rather than in supernatural or religious causes; a social scientist with a deep faith in empirical research; a moral philosopher, a secular humanist, who thought he could provide a factual, real-world basis for such normative categories as exploitation, inequality, and emancipation; a historical sociologist *avant la lettre* who believed he had discovered the laws of social motion in the class struggle as well as the instrument of human liberation from capital, the proletariat. Here one might argue that science was superseded by eschatology, and that in its futurism, Marxism became a religion done up in scientific drag.[3] For scholars today, Marx is most importantly a poser of questions, the formulator of a vast research program that he himself had too little time to realize. His questions, his critiques, his values, and his moral vision remain part of a legacy that encompasses a powerful specter still haunting global capitalism and bourgeois democracy at the beginning of the twenty-first century. Those questions, critiques, and values continue to inspire people in many parts of the world who without them would be even more disempowered before the onslaught of global capitalism and American hegemony.

Whether or not they were Marxist in orientation themselves, the generation of historians that was educated in the 1960s and entered the Soviet studies profession in the 1970s had a particularly intense engagement with Marx and Marxist historiography. Theirs was a moment of exploration of the new social history that came out of Britain and France, some of it overtly socialist history, the replacement of the older emphasis on structure with a gravitation toward appreciation of human agency, experience, culture, and later of discourse and the problem of meaning. All those influences—whether Eric Hobsbawm's revealing study of primitive rebels, E. P. Thompson's concern with experience, the feminists' radical deconstruction of naturalized identities, the scholars of nationalism's constructivist assault on primordialized communities—had the cumulative effect of historicizing what had been taken for granted, undermining what common sense told us had always been the way it was now. They gave one a sense that intellectual work was more than academic, and could have real effects on the real world; that scholarship, even in its need to be apolitical or extra-political, as neutral, objective, and evidence-based as possible, had a politics that could not be denied. Our generation rejected a Marxism that reduced ideas and politics to economics, dismissed the base/superstructure model of determination, and echoed Engels who in his last letters repeatedly denied that he and Marx were economic determinists.

This generation puzzled over the "relative autonomy" of politics and the state, was infatuated at first with the young Marx and the problem of alienation and the fulfillment of human potential. From the notion of an

---

3   For the distinction between the religious and scientific in Marx, I am indebted to an unpublished paper by my late friend Alex Szejman, "What Is Left of Marxism?"

early and late Marx, many tried to integrate the humanist utopianism of the 1844 manuscripts with the materialist structural analysis of *Capital*; we trudged through the *Grundrisse* with Hobsbawm's assistance, looked to Louis Althusser and Antonio Gramsci and György Lukács for aid (and comfort), and tried to find substitute proletariats—African-Americans, women, Chinese or Vietnamese peasants—when the White working class of America put on their hard hats and joined Richard Nixon and his racist "Southern Strategy." Perhaps the moment of realization for me that the American Left was in trouble was when at the University of California, Berkeley, I heard the writer Imamu Amear Baraka, the former LeRoi Jones, reduced to quoting from the selected works of Enver Hoxha and the Albanian Communist newspaper *Zëri i Popullit*. It was an exhilarating journey that ended up with becoming a tenured radical (first at Oberlin and later at the University of Michigan and the University of Chicago) just as the "revolution" turned into Reaganism. Disappointment, yes; discouragement and disillusionment, no—at least not for many of us. Marx, if he gives you anything, provides an appreciation of contradictions and a sense of historical progression (not necessarily progress, as it turned out) that guards against mistaking the present for the future, within a radical historicist sense that all that seems natural is historically constructed, constantly changing and being replaced. "All that is solid melts into air, all that is holy is profaned."

Marx's view of history, unlike liberal modernization theory, did not end with capitalism or legitimize the present as the best of all possible worlds. Even in his appreciation of the power and productivity of capitalism, he aimed to subvert and supersede bourgeois society in the interest of a more egalitarian, socially just, and democratic form of society. This vision certainly contains within it a utopia, as does any politics except conservative acceptance of the way the world exists at any one time. That utopia, that different and better future which the overwhelming one-dimensionality of the liberal political imagination renders ridiculous, retains enormous power, even for those who would not think to align themselves with Marx, as an immanent critique of the limits, mystifications, apologetics, and deceptions of bourgeois democracy and market capitalism. Utopia, in other words, might be thought of not in the usual sense of an impossible dream, but rather as a far-off goal toward which one directs one's political desires, even if the ultimate objective might never be reached. My personal goal, for instance, might be perfect health, immortality. Even though I know neither is possible, that does not stop me from going to the gym for a workout.

For those who embrace its positive meaning, socialism is a utopia—not in the sense of an unattainable goal but rather in the sense of a direction toward which people might point their political desires. The political goal, whether reachable or not, is the empowerment of all the people, social justice, and equality (not only of opportunity, as liberals believe, but of reward, as much as is practically possible). Socialism stands opposed to the proposition so central to classical liberal (now conservative) economic ideology, that individual greed will magically produce the greatest good for the greatest number and that capitalism is the end of history. Moreover, by resurrecting a politics aimed at the common good, socialism—in contrast to liberalism but closer to some forms of conservatism, religion, and nationalism—seeks the restoration of a social solidarity fractured by the individualizing effects of competitive market relations. That utopia remains a telos for socialist politics.

Historians and other scholars also operate in a utopian context. As a discipline, history provides what knowledge we can have about how the present was made and what human beings might or might not do in the future. It contributes both to how we understand what nations and societies are, and to the intellectual constitution of our imagination of political communities, which could not exist without the narratives that make up national and social histories. Even as historians seek to render an objective understanding of the past and propose a critique of what they consider to be "mythological" formulations, they are forced to accept that they too are products of historical pasts and historically constituted presents. The educator was educated somewhere and at some time. Accuracy and balance may be the closest we can come to objectivity and neutrality. None of us is without political commitments; some of us are more engaged than others; but those commitments and engagements can contribute to the seriousness with which we do history.

In the essays that follow the reader may feel the tension between the utopian goals of objective, neutral history and the influences of the temporal, spatial, and political contexts that shape the historian. In no historiography is this more palpable than in the history of Russia, the Soviet Union, and Communism. As produced both in the USSR and the West, that body of work has proven almost impossible to free from the tension between the historian's noble ideal of objectivity and the partisan political arena in which that history has been written. Both in the case of Western historians of the Soviet Union, as well as their more constrained Soviet counterparts, partisan frames and political preferences have been particularly difficult to eliminate. Not only was the USSR the principal enemy of democratic and capitalist Europe and America, but post-Soviet Russia inherited many of the images and negative constructions that had marked the Soviet Union. The essays in this book, written and revised over four decades, review much of the historiography that has shaped understandings of Russia, the Soviet Union, and Communism. Overcoming obstacles that historians of other countries were not required to face, Sovietologists and Soviet historians created a body of writing that could not be written in the USSR. The achievements by serious researchers have been exemplary contributions to our knowledge of a world that was difficult to penetrate and whose authorities obstructed both domestic and foreign critical investigations of its history. Foundational in how the West constructed its understanding of the socialist alternative, the history and historians examined in this book were at once products of their own world and producers of the imaginary of that world regarding its principal alternative.

Most of the chapters in this book deal with the Soviet Union and how it was understood, imagined, and constructed by Western historians and social scientists. The first chapter—"Back and Beyond: Reversing the Cultural Turn?"—deals more broadly with the nature of history and how new paradigms, like nationalism, social history, and the cultural turn shaped the ways historians think and work. This chapter delineates the wider professional and intellectual universe in which historians of Russia and the Soviet Union operated. When most of these essays first appeared, they were meant to throw light on the intense discussions that at the time determined and divided us in the Soviet field. The hundredth anniversary of the revolution that gave birth to Leninism, Stalinism, Gorbachev, and the Soviet Union seems a good time to re-examine how we who made it our life's work to examine and interpret the USSR learned about what went on, and why, across the ideological divide.

PART I

History and Historians

CHAPTER ONE

Back and Beyond: Reversing the Cultural Turn?

In social science, if you are not "bringing (something) back"—class, the state, whatever—you are probably already moving "beyond"—beyond Orientalism, beyond identity, and now beyond the cultural turn.[1] For those of us who made the cultural or linguistic or historical turn not so long ago, it is dismaying that all our efforts to catch up and bring back are still leaving us behind. Or are they? Back and beyond are metaphors for movement through space and time, in this case an intellectual journey from one practice of social analysis to another, abandoning certain ways of thinking and including, often reintroducing, others. The presumption is that travel is indeed broadening, not to mention deepening, and that experienced analysts will want to enrich their investigations with whatever insights, tools, and data can be gathered along the way.

From the heights of political history, the move in the late 1960s and 1970s was to step down into society and include new constituencies in the narrative (or get rid of narrative altogether). From social history, with its often functionalist or mechanistic forms of explanation, the shift was to plunge even deeper into the thick webs of significance that make up culture. In the narrative proposed by *Beyond the Cultural Turn*, "the new

---

1   My gratitude for advice and suggestions goes to Julia Adams, Geoff Eley, Matthew Evangelista, Elise Giuliano, Gary Herrigel, Erin Jenne, Stathis Kalyvas, Valerie Kivelson, David Laitin, Linda Myrsiades, Kathleen Much, and Lucan Way. Much of this article was written at the Center for Advanced Study in the Behavioral Sciences, Stanford, CA, where I was a fellow in 2001–02. I would like to thank the Center, the William and Flora Hewlett Foundation, and the University of Chicago for support during that year. An earlier version of this chapter was published in the *American Historical Review* (December 2002), pp. 1476–99.

For "backs" and "beyonds," see Peter B. Evans, Dietrich Rueschemeyer, and Theda Skocpol (eds.), *Bringing the State Back In* (Cambridge: Cambridge University Press, 1985); Scott G. McNall, Rhonda F. Levine, and Rick Fantasia (eds.), *Bringing Class Back In: Contemporary and Historical Perspectives* (Boulder, CO: Westview Press, 1991); Fred Dallmayr (ed.), *Beyond Orientalism: Essays on Cross-Cultural Encounters* (SUNY Press, 1996); Rogers Brubaker and Frederick Cooper, "Beyond 'identity'," *Theory and Society* XXIX (2000), pp. 1–47.

cultural history took shape in the 1980s as an upstart critique of the established social-economic and demographic histories."[2] The turn began, many would argue, with Edward Thompson's introduction of a notion of culture into labor history, the bastion of Marxist social history, and Clifford Geertz's redefinition of culture in anthropology, a move that proved particularly seductive to historians.[3] At the same time that all this moving was going on among historians and anthropologists, and to a lesser extent among historical sociologists, it found little resonance among political scientists, as the self-proclaimed "core" of the discipline moved closer to economics, formal modeling, game theory, and rational choice. Old fault lines hardened, between disciplines and within disciplines, even as appeals to interdisciplinarity sounded. Yet, at the same time, social science could not go back, for the various turns had created heightened awareness of and sensitivity to matters of agency and subjectivity, contingency, the constructed nature of social "reality," textuality, and the need for self-reflexivity on the part of the investigator.

In this chapter, I trace, first, some of the genealogy of the cultural turn, particularly in Marxist social history and in the aftermath of Geertz's essays; second, I outline what I believe are the principal approaches and insights of the cultural interpretivists; and, finally, I explore the relative absence of this kind of work within political science, with the exception of a few political theorists and constructivist international-relations theorists.

Marxism and the Moves Within Social History

For many of my generation, the coming of age in the 1960s was both politically and professionally connected with an initiation into the new forms of Marxism (often unacknowledged as such) that were disrupting the academy. The momentary revival of an intellectual Marxism, particularly among historians, derived, on the one hand, from the hot wars into which the Cold War establishment had taken young Americans and, on the other,

---

2   Richard Biernacki, "Method and Metaphor After the New Cultural History," in Victoria E. Bonnell and Lynn Hunt (eds.), *Beyond the Cultural Turn: New Directions in the Study of Society and Culture* (Berkeley, Los Angeles, and London: University of California Press, 1999), p. 62.

3   E. P. Thompson, *The Making of the English Working Class* (1963; Harmondsworth, 1968); Clifford Geertz, *The Interpretation of Culture: Selected Essays* (New York: Basic Books, 1973).

from the exciting achievements of British social historians—Eric J. Hobsbawm, George Rudé, and Edward Thompson were the most important—that expanded the focus of historians of the modern era in both topics and methods. Given the realities of American academic life, at a moment when the market for scholars was shrinking, social history in the United States was never as openly socialist as it was in Britain, but the research agenda that celebrated revolution, the working class, pre-capitalist forms of community, and alternatives to the dominant and seemingly immovable social order was closely allied and deeply indebted to the British Marxists. What made this alliance possible was that both historiography and intellectual Marxism were undergoing transformations that permitted divergent and open-ended explorations. What made it necessary was that Marxism as it existed failed to answer the most important questions it itself posed: How does class formation take place? What are the sources of consciousness? What makes a revolutionary situation? Why nation and not class? Thompson called these "the real silences of Marx."[4]

At the beginning of the new millennium, Marxism appeared to have lost both its inspirational power and the confidence with which its loyalists had been able to defend the vilest acts as political necessities. Still, for many in the generation of the 1960s, a particular form of humanist and critical Marxism, along with a variety of forms of liberalism, defined the principal lines of political choice. Western Marxism, primarily outside the circles of Communist parties (but also sometimes within, as in Britain and Italy), was in a constant struggle with the looming presence of the Soviet Union and unable to ignore the often perverse influence of actually-existing socialisms. More concerned with the defeats of socialism in its more democratic form in the West than with the successes of Soviet socialism, Western Marxism, despite the plurality of different theoretical positions and practices, was to some extent a Marxism of despair.[5]

---

4 E. P. Thompson, *The Poverty of Theory and Other Essays* (London: Merlin Press, 1978), p. 362.

5 Perry Anderson, *Considerations on Western Marxism* (London: Verso, 1976). Much of what follows is a reconstruction of personal and generational experience remembered through readings of Anderson's works—besides *Considerations*, his *Arguments Within English Marxism* (London: Verso, 1980); *In the Tracks of Historical Materialism* (London: Verso, 1983); *The Origins of Postmodernity* (London: Verso, 1998)—and Geoff Eley's *Forging Democracy: The History of the Left in Europe, 1850–2000* (New York and Oxford: Oxford University Press, 2002).

In the late 1950s and 1960s, significant intellectual defections from Soviet-style Communist parties in the West (for instance, E. P. Thompson and the "New Left" leaving the Communist Party of Great Britain) and an appeal by some to the socialist humanism of the young Marx turned attention to Marx's early "Economic and Philosophical Manuscripts" and the newly translated *Grundrisse*. With the appearance of the New Left, Western Marxists—György Lukács, Karl Korsch, the Frankfurt School, various strains of Trotskyism, and, most notably, Antonio Gramsci—were able to renew and refine earlier discussions of critical Marxism. Among Communist parties, Khrushchev's liberalization permitted national roads to socialism, and a healthy pluralism and lively discussion re-entered the petrified official Marxism of the Stalinist era. On one side of the discussion were those influenced by the structuralist Marxism of Louis Althusser, which was highly critical of socialist humanism and attempted to return the discussion to the great economic works, *Capital* and *Pre-Capitalist Economic Formations*.[6]

Althusser interrogated the relation between structure and subject in history and society—a theoretical conundrum central to the problem of class formation. Already in Marx, there was an unsteadiness, an oscillation between structural causality and human agency; between the contradiction of the forces of production and the relations of production in *Capital*, on the one hand, and his more political analyses of class, particularly in his historical works, such as *The Eighteenth Brumaire of Louis Napoleon*. Lenin's later attempt to deal with this problem on the practical level, through the agency of the party, combating at one and the same time the passivity of Second International reformism and revisionism *and* the multifaceted spontaneity of the "masses" themselves, left the New Left unimpressed as they searched for more communitarian and less elitist forms of organization. For much of the short twentieth century, Marxists divided between those who emphasized the primacy of structure (including Nikolai Bukharin, and later Althusser) and those who emphasized human agency (including many Trotskyists and Marxist humanists). With the triumph among French intellectuals of Claude Lévi-Strauss and Structuralism in the 1960s, Marxists like Althusser eliminated the subject, "save as the illusory effects of ideological structures,"

---

6 Althusser's two major studies—*Pour Marx* and *Lire le Capital*—both appeared in 1965.

radically rejecting any volition of the individual or collective.[7] "History," Althusser claimed, "is a process without a subject." Men and women are simply the "supports of the means of production." Althusser's former student Michel Foucault carried the flag into post-structuralism and described Marxism itself as an involuntary effect of an old-fashioned Victorian episteme. His erasure of the subject and elevation of discourse contributed powerfully to what would be termed the "cultural turn."

Although there are many ways to tell the story of structure and agency and the revival of culture, the discussion that took place with the appearance of the influential work of E. P. Thompson offers a bridge from the moment of social history to the fascination with cultural studies. For Thompson, Althusser's structuralism represented an outmoded kind of Marxism, one in which "process is fate," and he and his comrades sought to revive an alternative tradition in which men and women are the "ever-baffled and ever-resurgent agents of an unmastered history." Rather than a process without a subject, Thompson argued, history is the arena in which humans transmute structure into process. Through experience (Thompson's key term) individuals make themselves into social classes, groups conscious of differences and antagonisms and conflicting interests. In his famous formulation—"Classes arise because men and women, in determinative productive relations, identify their antagonistic interests, and come to struggle, to think and to value in class ways: thus the process of class formation is a process of self-making, although under conditions which are 'given'"[8]—Thompson presented human beings as part-subjects, part-objects in history, voluntary agents of involuntary determinations. What seemed so transparently to have been resolved by Marx—either in the version of the "bottom line," that in the final instance it's the economy, stupid, or in the formula of "man making history but not under conditions chosen by himself"—were now seen to contain theoretical and methodological ambiguities.

Thompson's introduction of the concept of experience as the mediation through which "structure is transformed into process and the subject re-enters into history" implied a further "necessary middle term"— culture.[9] "For people do not experience their own experience as ideas,

---

7 Anderson, *In the Tracks of Historical Materialism*, p. 38.
8 Thompson, *The Poverty of Theory*, pp. 297–8.
9 Ibid., p. 362.

within thought and its procedure . . . They also experience their own experience as *feeling*, and they handle their own feelings within their culture, as norms, familial and kinship obligations and reciprocities, as values or (through more elaborated forms) within art or religious beliefs."[10] Thompson's beautifully crafted account of working-class experience in England up to 1832 presented class formation as the product both of the objective advent of the factory system *and* of the self-constitution of class by workers themselves. Agency took the form of a collective experience that was converted into broad social consciousness by workers themselves. In an often-quoted introductory paragraph, he tells us,

> Class happens when some men, as a result of common experiences (inherited or shared), feel and articulate the identity of their interests as between themselves, and as against other men whose interests are different from (and usually opposed to) theirs. The class experience is largely determined by the productive relations in which men are born—or enter involuntarily. Class consciousness is the way in which the experiences are handled in cultural terms: embodied in traditions, value-systems, ideas and institutional forms. If the experience appears as determined, class consciousness does not . . . class is defined by men as they live their own history, and, in the end, this is its only definition.[11]

Here, Thompson held on to a notion of interest as latent, given by the structure of social relations, and to be realized fully through experience. Thompson, of course, never abandoned the materialism that had always been part of Marxism. In his later studies of the eighteenth century, he proposed that class in the sense he used it in earlier works is a nineteenth-century phenomenon and that the more universal category is class struggle.

> People find themselves in a society structured in determined ways (crucially, but not exclusively, in productive relations), they experience exploitation (or the need to maintain power over whom they exploit), they identify points of antagonistic interest, they commence to struggle

---

10 Ibid., p. 363.
11 Thompson, *The Making of the English Working Class*, pp. 9–10.

around these issues, and in the process of struggling they discover themselves as classes, they come to know this discovery as class consciousness.[12]

Here, very clearly, Thompson exposes his own objectivist side. Class exists immanently as a template into which experiences arrange people. Not so much a construction, as it would become later with post-structuralism, class is a discovery.

For Thompson, experience as well was sometimes something external to the subject, something that "walks in without knocking at the door and announces deaths, crises of subsistence, trench warfare, unemployment, inflation, genocide. People starve: their survivors think in new ways about the market. People are imprisoned: in prison they meditate in new ways about the law."[13] Historical events, actualities, teach lessons that are true about the real world. As Perry Anderson points out (critically), for Thompson experience was many different things: the actual living through events by participants and the effects they have on people; "the mental and emotional response, of an individual or of a social group, to inter-related events or the many repetitions of the same kind of event"; and the process of learning from such events, "a subjective alteration capable of modifying ensuing objective actions."[14] Thompson conflated these different aspects (or kinds) of experience, maintaining what he calls a dialogue between social being and social consciousness. But he was particularly interested in how experience as lived life was processed, understood, and represented. Foreign to his thinking was any notion of an ahistorical, acultural idea of a rational interest somehow independent of affect, values, and cultural norms.

Although Thompson's turn toward culture and consciousness, in many ways like Geertz's emphasis on signification, would lead successive scholars to play down or ignore altogether the material, structural, "objective" side of social determination, both of these authors retained a focus on the material. In his essay "The Peculiarities of the English," a polemic against Anderson and fellow Marxist Tom Nairn, Thompson

---

12   E. P. Thompson, "Eighteenth-Century English Society: Class Struggle Without Class?" *Social History* III, 2 (May 1978), p. 147; *The Making of the English Working Class,* p. 151.

13   Thompson, *The Poverty of Theory,* p. 201.

14   Ibid., p. 199; Anderson, *Arguments Within English Marxism,* p. 26.

argued that the growing moderation of English workers in mid-century was the product of their progressive imbrication into the fabric of English society. Their very successful entry and the improvement of their well-being made them less revolutionary. Here structure, rather than agency, is paramount. Thompson wrote: "Let us look at history *as* history—men placed in actual contexts which they have not chosen, and confronted by indivertible forces, with an overwhelming immediacy of relations and duties and with only a scanty opportunity for inserting their own agency."[15] Thompson suggested that the relative determinative power of agency and structure shift though history, so that one or the other may take on greater power at different conjunctures. In the period of *The Making*, that is, up to 1832, workers faced an unconsolidated capitalism, an embryonic industrial society, with the ideological structures of liberalism and political economy not yet securely in place. Here the political opening was available and certain lessons had not yet been learned, whereas later workers had already undergone certain experiences, successes and failures; structures had become consolidated; ideological hegemony of the middle class was gaining strength; and the very successes of workers in ending the earlier social apartheid and integrating within the new social order entangled them in unanticipated ways and reduced their aspirations toward revolutionary destructuring.

Along with his elevation of consciousness and culture—what Marxists often dismissively referred to as "superstructure"—and his repositioning of agency, E. P. Thompson embraced Marxism, not as an all-encompassing explanatory theory, but as a tradition of historical materialist, empirical inquiry. What was most exciting was the sense that the seemingly one-dimensional "natural" world of capitalist economics was itself a product of specific histories, and people who would become its victims stood up against it with values and passions that survived from an older form of social organization. Rejecting the reductionism of earlier Marxists, Thompson and other theorists, like Raymond Williams, reminded us of the radical historicism in Marxism.

While some Marxist sociologists, like Erik Olin Wright, took the objectivist road, and materialist understandings of interest found their

---

15 E. P. Thompson, "The Peculiarities of the English" [first published in *The Socialist Register* (1965)]; *The Poverty of Theory*, p. 69.

way into political science through economics, many historians and historical sociologists took the implications of Thompson's work further to
explore the origins and evolution of consciousness, culture, and historical
contextualization. The important interventions by Gareth Stedman
Jones, William H. Sewell Jr., and Joan Wallach Scott, among others, in
the late 1970s and early 1980s shifted the analytical focus from the material to the linguistic and marked a turning away from the sociology of
earlier social history toward a greater association with anthropology.[16]
Borrowing from the work of feminist historians, Scott faulted Thompson
for taking experience for granted, as simply existing out there busily
determining consciousness, and insisted that experience itself is being
constituted, contested, and given meaning all the time. Interests themselves, like identities, must be understood to be discursively articulated
and constituted. Experience should not be "seen as the objective circumstances that condition identity; identity is not an objectively defined sense
of self defined by needs and interests. Politics is not the collective coming
to consciousness of similarly situated individual subjects. Rather politics
is the process by which plays of power and knowledge constitute identity
and experience."[17] Moving on from Thompson, historians became
increasingly interested, not in the "facts" of experience itself, but in how
"experience" was experienced by historical actors.

The very questions Marxism raised about consciousness and ideology,
the inexplicable power of nationalism, and the particular kinds of oppression visited on women and experienced in the family led to new ways of
answering that moved beyond anything conventionally included within
Marxism. For some, the limits of Marxism encouraged expanding the
boundaries of the tradition, for others the constraints of Marxism
provoked rejection and defection. First, the influence of Foucault and the
growing interest in language that flowed from Saussure through

---

16 William H. Sewell, Jr., *Work and Revolution in France: The Language of Labor
from the Old Regime to 1848* (Cambridge: Cambridge University Press, 1980); Gareth
Stedman Jones, *Languages of Class: Studies in English Working-Class History, 1832–
1982* (Cambridge: Cambridge University Press, 1983); Geoff Eley, "Is All the World a
Text? From Social History to the History of Society Two Decades Later," in Terrence J.
McDonald (ed.), *The Historic Turn in the Human Sciences* (Ann Arbor: University of
Michigan Press, 1996), pp. 195–200.

17 Joan W. Scott, *Gender and the Politics of History* (New York: Columbia
University Press, 1988), p. 5.

structuralism into post-structuralism, the new emphasis on meaning and discourse, fundamentally changed the direction of much research by Marxist (now perhaps post-Marxist) historians and social scientists. The direction of the arrow of determination shifted from the material to the realm of discourse, culture, and language. Second, Marxism as a potent, totalizing grand narrative was undermined by the post-modernist suspicion of all such master narratives with their ideas of progress, their teleological certainty, and their resistance to anomalies and ambiguities.[18] Third, at a moment of confusion and doubt among Marxists, even before the disappearance of European state socialisms, scholars replaced the focus on class (at least for a time) with a concern for other social collectivities. The most important were nation and gender. Feminist historians and theorists rapidly moved from an inclusivist women's history driven by a commitment to recover and include women in the existing narratives, to questioning those narratives themselves, and ultimately to a deep interrogation of the category "woman." Once the earlier confidence of Marxist and social historians in the primacy of the social was shattered, culture and discourse appeared to offer possibly richer forms of explanation.

From the Geertzian Revolution to the Cultural Turn

The cultural turn is neither the same as the linguistic or historical turn nor coterminous with post-structuralism or post-modernism, but it has overlapped temporally and intellectually with a number of concerns shared by all of them. The attention to language and its deep structures preceded the renewed interest in history within American social science in the 1980s and 1990s, a profound reversal of the post-1945 rejection of history from political science and sociology particularly.[19] The cultural turn, it should be noted, was neither the same as "bringing culture back in" (though it certainly entailed that as well) nor the belief that "culture matters," a stance that would lead in a quite different direction (and a

18 A powerful critical intervention into the discussion of Marxist totality came from within the fold in the persons of Ernesto Laclau and Chantal Mouffe, *Hegemony and Socialist Strategy: Towards a Radical Democratic Politics*, trans. Winston Moore and Paul Cammack (London: Verso, 1985).

19 Terrence J. McDonald, "Introduction," in McDonald (ed.), *The Historic Turn*, pp. 2–5.

different implied politics) from the cultural turn.[20]

One might tell the story of the evolving, revolving "cultural turn" from a number of key texts—Hayden White's *Metahistory: The Historical Imagination in Nineteenth-Century Europe* (1973), Michel Foucault's *Discipline and Punish: The Birth of the Prison* (1975, translated into English, 1977); or from the seminal works of Roland Barthes, Pierre Bourdieu, Jacques Derrida, Thomas Kuhn, Richard Rorty, Marshall Sahlins, or Raymond Williams.[21] But—again from both generational and personal experience—the most influential text was probably Clifford Geertz's *The Interpretation of Cultures: Selected Essays* (1973). Few come away from this book indifferent to its challenge or unaffected by its lapidary language. The program of Geertz (and others like White) was to reject positivist approaches to understanding human experience and to insist on the centrality of meaning, the historically and culturally specific constructions of understanding and feeling. As Sherry Ortner puts it,

> Geertz's battle against various forms of functionalist and mechanistic perspectives (regardless of their theorists of origin—Emile Durkheim, Karl Marx, Sigmund Freud, and so on) was important . . . because it challenges a view of society as a machine, or as an organism, a view in which complex human intentions and complex cultural formations are reduced to their effects on that social machine or social organism.[22]

Or in Geertz's own description of his research program: "Believing, with Max Weber, that man is an animal suspended in webs of significance he himself has spun, I take culture to be those webs, and the analysis of it to be therefore not an experimental science in search of law but an

---

20 For examples of culture without the cultural turn, see Samuel P. Huntington, *The Clash of Civilizations and the Remaking of World Order* (New York: Simon & Schuster, 1996); Lawrence E. Harrison and Samuel P. Huntington (eds.), *Culture Matters: How Values Shape Human Progress* (New York: Basic Books, 2000).

21 For an excellent account of the influence of the linguistic and cultural turns on history, see Peter Novick's concluding chapters in *That Noble Dream: The "Objectivity Question" and the American Historical Profession* (Cambridge: Cambridge University Press, 1988).

22 Sherry B. Ortner, "Thick Resistance: Death and the Cultural Construction of Agency in Himalayan Mountaineering," in Ortner (ed.), *The Fate of "Culture": Geertz and Beyond* (Berkeley, Los Angeles, and London: University of California Press, 1999), p. 137.

interpretive one in search of meaning."[23] To be opposed were all forms of "objectivism" and "reductionism"—something against which Marxists and social historians were then struggling.

In his essay "The Concept(s) of Culture," which is all the more brilliant for its transparency, William H. Sewell, Jr. remembers facing the limits of social history and what has been called "the revelation of anthropology":

> I experienced the encounter with cultural anthropology as a turn from a hardheaded, utilitarian, and empiricist materialism—which had both liberal and *marxisant* faces—to a wider appreciation of the range of human possibilities, both in the past and in the present. Convinced that there was more to life than the relentless pursuit of wealth, status, and power, I felt that cultural anthropology could show us how to get at that "more."[24]

Geertz provided a way to understand meaning as something not buried deep in the mind but visible externally in public practices, rituals, and symbols. "Culture is public because meaning is."[25] A culture could be read like a text, and so could past societies. As he wrote in *Local Knowledge*,

> The trick is not to get yourself into some inner correspondence of spirit with your informants. Preferring, like the rest of us, to call their souls their own, they are not going to be altogether keen about such an effort anyhow. The trick is to figure out what the devil they think they are up to . . . [The ethnographer does this by] searching out and analyzing the symbolic forms—words, images, institutions, behaviors—in terms of which, in each place, people actually represented themselves to them-

---

23   Clifford Geertz, *The Interpretation of Cultures: Selected Essays* (New York: Basic Books, 1973), p. 5.

24   William H. Sewell, Jr., "The Concept(s) of Culture," in Bonnell and Hunt (eds.), *Beyond the Cultural Turn*, pp. 35–6. The phrase "revelation of anthropology" comes from Gayle Rubin, "The Traffic in Women: Notes on the 'Political Economy' of Sex," in Rayna R. Reiter (ed.), *Toward an Anthropology of Women* (New York, 1975), p. 157, and is quoted by Sewell in "Geertz, Cultural Systems, and History: From Synchrony to Transformation," in Ortner (ed.), *The Fate of "Culture"*, p. 37.

25   Geertz, "Thick Description: Toward an Interpretive Theory of Culture," in *The Interpretation of Cultures*, p. 12.

selves and to one another.[26]

At the same time that he provided a method and direction for new research—"sorting out the structures of signification"—Geertz challenged historians and social scientists to be wary of what passed for "data." "What we call our data are really our own constructions of other people's constructions of what they and their compatriots are up to."[27] And the work of social scientists, in his case anthropological writings, "are themselves interpretations, and second and third order ones to boot . . . They are, thus, fictions; fictions, in the sense that they are 'something made,' 'something fashioned'—the original meaning of *fictio*—not that they are false, unfactual, or merely 'as if' thought experiments."[28] Therefore, social science was to be more interpretative than simply observational, more like the work of literary critics than that of cipher clerks.

With the fallout from Geertz's theoretical essays and the almost simultaneous influence of literary and linguistic studies on history, the principal elements were in place for what would later be recognized as a "cultural turn" in history and social science. We should remember that the turn kept turning, but it might be instructive at this point to ask: What was specific about the cultural turn? What exactly have been its contributions? And what is to be gained precisely by going beyond it?

First and most fundamentally, the cultural turn opposes explanations that follow from social naturalism, or what George Steinmetz has called "foundationalist decontextualization."[29] Rather than making some ahistorical and essentialist assumptions about human nature—humans are instrumentally rational, aggressive, or territorial; women are nurturing; Armenians are good merchants—or positing primordial or transhistorical institutions—individuality, the market, the nation—as fundamental to human society, culturalism and historicism argue that there are no timeless, decontextualized, ahistorical or "natural" characteristics or institutions. Things that appear to be most natural to human

---

26 Clifford Geertz, "'From the Native's Point of View': On the Nature of Anthropological Understanding," in his *Local Knowledge: Further Essays in Interpretive Anthropology* (New York: Basic Books, 1983), p. 58.

27 Geertz, "Thick Description," p. 9.

28 Ibid., p. 15.

29 George Steinmetz, *State/Culture: State-Formation after the Cultural Turn* (Ithaca and London: Cornell University Press, 1999), pp. 20–1.

society—market economies, the state, the nation, society itself—are historical constructions made by human actors who in turn are reconstituted by the very products of their making. Culturalists, therefore, are deeply suspicious of hard, fixed, essential social categories—class, nation, gender—and propose considering a more radical understanding of identities as fluid, multiple, fragmented, and constantly in need of hard work to sustain.[30]

Second, whereas the linguistic and historical turns share this general proposition, they place the weight of explanation on language and history, while the cultural turn emphasizes the constitutive power of culture broadly understood. Culture is seen as a "category of social life," different from though not unrelated to the economy, society, or politics. Culture is not simply derivative of other spheres, as more objectivist approaches might have it, nor is it reducible to material or other non-cultural causes. The ordinary uses of the word "culture" are multiple and contested, but culturalists are intensely interested in the problem of meanings that are not limited by the strictly linguistic and the processes through which they are made. Most fruitfully, culture may be thought of as "a system of symbols possessing a real but thin coherence that is continually put at risk in practice and therefore subject to transformation."[31] Culturalism proposes the autonomy and power of culture, even while it is deeply committed to historicization. Understanding comes with cultural, spatial, and temporal contextualization. But—here following Thompson—history is never just lived, but made. Similarly, many accept the constitution of social forms and knowledge by language, but are reluctant to limit constitution to language alone. Although the world might be read like a text, it is not the same as a text.

Third, culture itself was, like all other categories and identities, to be "problematized" (a favorite activity of those invested in the turn). From a holistic or unified idea of culture as a self-sustaining system, in which all the parts work toward an integrated whole (something akin to the Marxist notion of totality), anthropologists would shift increasingly toward a

---

30 The literature on identities is now enormous. My own brief discussion can be found in "Provisional Stabilities: The Politics of Identities in Post-Soviet Eurasia," *International Security* XXIV, 3 (Winter 1999/2000), pp. 139–78, particularly pp. 144–6.

31 Sewell, "The Concept(s) of Culture," p. 52.

notion of culture as a contested area in which meaning was changeable, conflicted, and inflected with politics. Culture as "a coherent system of symbols and meanings" gave way in the work of many scholars to a notion of culture as practice.[32] What looked far more coherent, constant, and integrated in the classical ethnographies of Bronislaw Malinowski, Margaret Mead, Ruth Benedict, and even Clifford Geertz is now thought of as "worlds of meaning" that are normally "contradictory, loosely integrated, contested, mutable, and highly permeable."[33] Culture, like society, is a field of play with borders far less clear than in earlier imaginations, internal harmonies less apparent, in which actors and groups contend for position and power, sometimes in institutions, sometimes over control of meaning. In its full flower the cultural turn holds that culture "is not an object to be described, neither is it a unified corpus of symbols and meanings that can be definitively interpreted. Culture is contested, temporal, and emergent."[34]

Anthropology in the post-colonial globalized world no longer enjoys the imagined luxury of studying isolated, uncontaminated "primitive" societies far from the invading influence of modernity.[35] A new generation of ethnographers has turned its attention back to the metropole and investigation of more complex societies in the first and second worlds. Likewise, other categories are no longer seen as fixed, given, and stable. Society, nation, gender, politics, the economy, and identities are recon-

---

32 Ibid., pp. 44–7. Sewell argues that "the presumption that a concept of culture as a system of symbols and meanings is at odds with a concept of culture as practice is perverse. System and practice are complementary concepts: each presupposes the other" (p. 47). But he warns that "the network of semiotic relations that make up culture is not isomorphic with the network of economic, political, geographical, social, or demographic relations that make up what we usually call a 'society'" (p. 49).

33 Ibid., p. 53. Besides the stress on coherence of culture, three other critiques of the original Geertzian program are worth noting: his relative lack of emphasis on power and dominance, his tendency to attach a particular culture to a particular group, and his commitment to the notion of the ethnographer's rapport with the "natives" and reluctance to move toward hyperreflexivity. These critiques are made respectively in the essays by Sherry B. Ortner, Lila Abu-Lughod, and George E. Marcus in Ortner (ed.), *The Fate of "Culture"*.

34 James Clifford and George E. Marcus (eds.), *Writing Culture: The Poetics and Politics of Ethnography* (Berkeley, Los Angeles, and London: University of California Press, 1986), p. 19.

35 Eric Wolf, *Europe and the People Without History* (Berkeley, Los Angeles, and London: University of California Press, 1982).

ceived as arenas of contestation, of difference rather than harmony.[36]

Fourth, the cultural turn shares with Foucault a suspicion of the stable, rational, sovereign subject. It emphasizes agency, but the nature of the agent is under reconsideration. As Terrence McDonald puts it, "Agency and the agent . . . have taken on critical importance at precisely the same time that the concept of the agent has been evacuated of much of its content. Rather than a colossus bestriding the pages of history, the agent must now emerge from those pages."[37] The historical agent can no longer simply be deduced "from a putative map of social structures and accompanying subject positions," but must be understood in the contexts of power and discourse, constituted structures as well as historic conjunctures and events.[38] The injunction against reductionisms of any kind has led some cultural interpretivists to suspect the kinds of explanations from "exogenous" factors, like economics, ideologies, or even psychological drives or human nature. And the emphasis on the self-constituting agent, or the problem of subjectivity and the mutual constitution of actor and structure, leads cultural interpretivists to question the paradigms of positivism and hold back from seeking causal explanations. This reluctance puts them at odds with those social scientists, particularly in political science, whose fundamental reason to do science is the search for causality.[39] Even before the cultural turn, but more intensively after it, scholars have turned their attention to the constitution of social phenomena, particularly to those previously so emphatically naturalized: identity, interests, and power.

Fifth, the cultural turn has increasingly moved from the elaboration of systems of meaning, in the Geertzian sense, to an exploration of regimes of domination, of power, reflecting the influence of Foucault and

---

36   On problematizing and pluralizing politics, see Jodi Dean, "Introduction: The Interface of Political Theory and Cultural Studies," in Dean (ed.), *Cultural Studies and Political Theory* (Ithaca and London: Cornell University Press, 2000), p. 3.

37   McDonald, "Introduction," p. 6.

38   Ibid.

39   For a thorough discussion of the difference between the two types of social inquiry—causal processes, in which one independent agent, temporally preceding an effect, makes that effect occur; and constitutive processes, in which ideas or social structures "create phenomena . . . that are conceptually or logically dependent on those ideas or structures, that exist only 'in virtue of' them"—see Alexander Wendt, *Social Theory of International Politics* (Cambridge: Cambridge University Press, 1999), especially pp. 47–138 (p. 88).

feminism. The cultural turn embeds politics in everyday life, in the ways in which meaning is constructed and actors are either empowered or constrained. "Foucault's concept of the disciplinary society," Geoff Eley writes, "profoundly shifts our understanding of politics, carrying the analysis of power away from the core institutions of the state in the national-centralized sense toward the emergence of new individualizing strategies 'that function outside, below, and alongside the State apparatuses, on a much more minute and everyday level'."[40] This radically alternative conception of power—in Keith Baker's succinct formulation—"included emphases on power as constituted by regimes of truth rather than by the exercise of political will, as polymorphous and pervasive rather than unitary, as productive rather than repressive, as internal rather than external to the subject, as subjectivizing rather than subjecting."[41] Identity, discourse, and affect are all brought into play in explaining political choice, not only in the micropolitics of everyday life, but at the level of the state itself.

Sixth, the cultural turn exposed the art and artifice of historical metanarratives, with their usual starting point in the Enlightenment and their grand tours from tradition to modernity. The problem was not so much that the grand narratives were right or wrong but that they had been taken as true, as accurate reflections of an actual past, and as bases of analysis and further elaboration, rather than as highly selective and convenient frames for understanding. The cultural turn saw all social scientific accounts as constructed narratives, selected from available evidence, akin to other fictions, and told by narrators situated in specific time and place.[42]

Stories are necessary to make sense out of the raw material of lived experience. Gone is the omniscient, objective observer, and in his place is a weaver of a new historical or ethnographic web woven with the threads and according to the conventions of particular disciplines. The great

---

40 Eley, "Is All the World a Text?", p. 217. Eley is quoting here from Michel Foucault, "Body/Power," in Colin Gordon (ed.), *Power/Knowledge* (Brighton: The Harvester Press, 1980), p. 60.

41 Keith Michael Baker, "A Foucauldian French Revolution?," in Jan Goldstein (ed.), *Foucault and the Writing of History* (Oxford, UK, and Cambridge, MA: Blackwell Publishers, 1994), p. 194.

42 Karen Halttunen, "Cultural History and the Challenge of Narrativity," in Bonnell and Hunt (eds.), *Beyond the Cultural Turn*, p. 166.

stories of the past—the rise of the bourgeoisie or the working class, the struggle of nations toward consciousness and freedom, the progressive emancipation of humankind from ignorance and superstition—were now seen precisely to be stories more or less plausible and resonant in so far as they played by the rules of disciplinary games and appealed to disciplinary communities. As Margaret R. Somers puts it, "Within a knowledge culture, narratives . . . not only convey information but serve epistemological purposes. They do so by establishing veracity through the integrity of their storied form. This suggests that in the first instance the success or failure of truth claims embedded in narratives depends less on empirical verification and more on the logic and rhetorical persuasiveness of the narrative."[43]

Seventh, by foregrounding the involvement of the investigator in the investigation, the cultural turn accepts the inability to achieve either full objectivity, the distance from the object of study for which the historians had longed, or the rapport so ardently imagined by classical anthropology. The observer/analyst is situated in both time and place, is educated in a particular way, and comes with her own subjectivity. She is involved despite herself, or because of herself, and is now free to reflect on her own position. Self-reflexivity parallels the whole constructivist thrust of the cultural turn, bringing the constitution of both structure and agent back to the observer/analyst. As the introduction to an influential collection explains, the ethnographers represented in the volume "see culture as composed of seriously contested codes and representations; they assume that the poetic and the political are inseparable, that science is in, not above, historical and linguistic processes . . . Their focus on text making and rhetoric serves to highlight the constructed, artificial nature of cultural accounts." The "historical predicament of ethnography" is precisely that "it is always caught up in the invention, not the representation, of cultures."[44] Any attempt to represent and explain culture must by necessity be historicist and self-reflexive.

The list of stances and preferences of those having turned can be further extended, as can the new fields of inquiry that cultural interpretivists have opened up. The concern with the body and the self, and the

---

43 Margaret R. Somers, "The Privatization of Citizenship: How to Unthink a Knowledge Culture," in Bonnell and Hunt (eds.), *Beyond the Cultural Turn*, p. 129.

44 Clifford and Marcus (eds.), *Writing Culture*, p. 2.

whole question of the production of subjectivities, come to mind. While some historians and sociologists returned to the creation of new mega-historical narratives, only very partially informed by insights from cultural studies, others, particularly cultural historians, explored micro-history, a style of work in which the full context of a historical moment can be grasped.[45] The image of historians in the mind of some social scientists has been of laborers toiling in the fields of data collection, whereas in fact the cultural turn has granted a general permission to historians to practice their own kind of intellectual imperialism, expanding the range of legitimate topics. If politics is profoundly culturally constructed, and culture is fraught with political meanings and practice, and both are produced in time, then historians can easily move past the disciplinary border guards at the softening edges of anthropology, sociology, economics, and political science.

Discourse and representations, of course, are central to the cultural turn, but in recent years some culturalists have pulled back from the desire to replace older materialist accounts with purely discursive ones. A noticeable trend, reflected unevenly in *Beyond the Cultural Turn*, was not so much an abandonment of the ground gained by the turn toward discourse, language, and culture, but a reassessment of the place of the material and the structural, or what is often referred to as "the social." An oversimplified materialist or structural determination is not to be replaced by an equally one-sided cultural or discursive determination.[46]

---

45 For new macrohistories, one might look at Michael Mann, *The Sources of Social Power*, 4 vols. (Cambridge: Cambridge University Press, 1986–2013); Hendrik Spruyt, *The Sovereign State and Its Competitors: An Analysis of Systems Change* (Princeton: Princeton University Press, 1994); and Eric Hobsbawm's series of histories: *The Age of Revolution, 1789–1848* (London: Weidenfeld & Nicolson, 1962); *The Age of Capital, 1848–1875* (New York: Charles Scribner's Sons, 1975); *The Age of Empire, 1875–1914* (New York: Pantheon Books, 1987); and *The Age of Extremes: A History of the World, 1914–1991* (New York: Pantheon, 1995). Among the most influential micro-histories are Carlos Ginzburg, *The Cheese and the Worms: The Cosmos of a Sixteenth-Century Miller*, trans. John and Anne Tedeschi (Baltimore: Johns Hopkins University Press, 1980); Natalie Zemon Davis, *The Return of Martin Guerre* (Cambridge and London: Harvard University Press, 1983); and Emmanuel Le Roy Ladurie, *Montaillou: The Promised Land of Error*, trans. Barbara Bray (New York: George Braziller, 1978).

46 Insistence on the materiality of symbols and "the cultural" was long ago recognized by the cultural Marxists, like Raymond Williams and Stuart Hall, and can even be found in Gramsci and Althusser, in their discussions of ideology. Here is a telling example of how going beyond looks suspiciously like a bringing back. I am grateful to Geoff

The turn back to the material and social is evident in Sewell's writings, notably in an essay on Geertz where he retrieves the materiality of the anthropologist's location of symbolization in the evolution of the human mind. "If Geertz is right as I [Sewell] firmly believe he is, semiotic systems are not unworldly or ghostly or imaginary; they are as integral to the life of our species as respiration, digestion, or reproduction. Materialists, this suggests, should stop worrying and love the symbol."[47] "Beyond," here, is in part a return, a going back, but even going back or beyond involves the journeys that one has already made and the consequent learning that has taken place. As Dorothy says, and Salman Rushdie reminds us: "There's no place like home."[48]

Where Does That Leave Political Science?

As a discipline, political science has hardly been touched by the cultural turn. The few influenced by the hermeneutic direction implicit in the linguistic, historical, and cultural turns have found themselves at a "separate table" within comparative politics, one set far from those engaged in rational-choice or game-theoretic work, a bit closer to those interested in new institutionalist and historical approaches, and closest to political theorists and international relations scholars of a constructivist bent.[49]

Eley both for pointing to the relevant texts of the 1970s and for his memory of the reception of Gramsci, Althusser, and Laclau and Mouffe in Britain.

47 Sewell, "Geertz, Cultural Systems, and History," p. 45.

48 Salman Rushdie, *The Wizard of Oz* (London: British Film Institute, 1992), p. 57. Rushdie's concluding on Dorothy's journey is a nice metaphor for some of the points being made in this chapter: "So Oz finally *became* home; the imagined world became the actual world, as it does for us all, because the truth is that once we have left our childhood places and started to make up our lives, armed only with what we have and are, we understand that the real secret of the ruby slippers is not that 'there's no place like home', but rather that there is no longer any such place *as* home: except, of course, for the home we make, or the homes that are made for us, in Oz: which is anywhere, and everywhere, except the place from which we began."

49 The metaphor comes from Gabriel Almond, "Separate Tables: Schools and Sects in Political Science," *PS: Political Science and Politics* XXI (1988), pp. 828–42. Almond distinguished four schools or separate tables of political science along two dimensions, one methodological, the other ideological, and a large, eclectic "cafeteria" of liberal moderates in the middle. The four tables were: a soft left of critical theorists, inspired by Frankfurt school Marxism, opposed to a positivist, value-free political science and committed to a unity of theory and praxis; a hard right largely associated with rational choice work; a soft right around the anti-historicist political theory of Leo Strauss and his followers; and a hard left of quantitative dependency and world-system

The resistance of those who see themselves to be both the core and the future of the discipline to the approaches and preferences of cultural interpretivists begins with a specific view of science, and a commitment to a particular politics that has informed much of political science. From its inception, American political science has held "aspirations to be both truly scientific and a servant of democracy, aspirations abetted by deep faith that these two enterprises went hand in hand."[50] But this basically liberal agenda contains within it an irreconcilable tension between asserting the importance of political agency, so fundamental to democratic citizenship, and providing "full causal accounts of politics, usually on the model of natural sciences that deny any conscious agency to the phenomena they study."[51]

Historically, political science, a field bound more by the object of its study, that is politics, than by any consensus on the method of study, has engaged with a subject that even the most naturalistic and materialist investigators would agree is, unlike natural sciences, constituted by the activities and self-understandings of human actors, among them political scientists.[52] In its initial phase of professionalization between the two world wars, political science stressed objective study, free from ideological preferences and values, and elaborated a naturalistic view of political behavior as determined by specific environments rather than universal laws. Empirical particularistic studies, accurate description and measurement of observable phenomena, were seen to be the basis for a truly objective science of politics. Leaders in the field, like Charles E. Merriam

---

theorists and econometricians. His plea in this essay is for a return to objective social science, while recognizing the need for a multiplicity of methods. What is striking in reading his review is how rapidly in the last few decades his tables have been abandoned and occupied by new schools of thought.

50 Rogers M. Smith, "Science, Non-Science, and Politics," in McDonald (ed.), *The Historic Turn in the Human Sciences*, p. 127.

51 Ibid.

52 John S. Dryzek and Stephen T. Leonard, "History and Discipline in Political Science," *American Political Science Review* LXXXII, 4 (December 1988), p. 1250. "The very existence of these objects—say a bureaucracy, army, monetary system, political party, monarchy, capitalist economy, socialist state, or democracy—is contingent on the subscription by social agents to some particular beliefs or theories. There is no analog to this in the natural sciences, where the objects—however they may be conceptualized—are not constituted by theories. They exist quite independently of whatever the scientist may *say* about them." This statement appears to me to be too dichotomous in a post-Kuhnian epoch, not allowing any social constitution of natural science's objects.

of the University of Chicago, eschewed rationalistic explanations, a priori reasoning, theories dependent on innate drives or instincts, or elaborate system-building. The meaning of political behavior was to be discovered in how politics operated in practice.

Edward Purcell has eloquently told the story of how this objectivism and an appreciation of cultural differences led researchers increasingly toward a moral neutrality and relativism that contradicted their personal commitment to democracy.[53] Their empirical findings confirmed that elite groups were able to dominate the majority of the population in democratic polities, and studies of public opinion and voting behavior undermined claims that humans were informed judges of their own interests. Eventually, the shock of the Great Depression, the struggle against Nazism, and the Cold War confrontation with the Soviet Union stimulated a re-evaluation of democratic theory and encouraged a more positive evaluation of the actual practices of American democracy.

In the years following World War II the discipline grew enormously and found links to public influence and power. Challenged by McCarthyism, political scientists sought shelter behind their claims to objectivity and neutrality. Yet celebratory theories of pluralism and cultural consensus dominated the analyses of American politics. Elites still ran things, they argued, but no single elite group dominated in the free-for-all of contested politics and all groups could compete. Without examining the barriers of class, race, and gender that gave coherence to this congenial system, the critical edge of political studies diminished. Students of politics joined in the general anti-Communist patriotism of the day, developing the theory of totalitarianism that neatly homogenized Stalinism and Hitlerism and contrasted the T-model with Western democracy. Across the social sciences "Marx was replaced by Freud, the word 'capitalism' dropped out of social theory after the war, and class became stratification."[54] When Robert A. Dahl and Charles E. Lindblom requested clearance to teach a course on planning in the late 1940s, the Yale

53   Edward A. Purcell, Jr., *The Crisis of Democratic Theory: Scientific Naturalism and the Problem of Value* (Lexington, KY: University of Kentucky Press, 1973).

54   Thomas Bender, "Politics, Intellect, and the American University, 1945–1995," in Thomas Bender and Carl E. Schorske (eds.), *American Academic Culture in Transformation: Fifty Years, Four Disciplines* (Princeton: Princeton University Press, 1997), p. 29.

economics department asked that they label it "Critique of Planning" instead.[55] And the group of social scientists at the University of Chicago who chose the term "behavioral sciences" to describe their endeavor did so consciously, in order to appear neutral and not confuse congressional funders who "might confound social science with socialism."[56]

Political science suffered from science envy, and the so-called Behavioral Revolution of the 1950s was an effort to emulate, once again, the certainty, even predictability, of the natural sciences. Rather than a radical new departure, the revolution was a re-emphasis on scientific methods and a turn away from historical, philosophical, or descriptive approaches. Once again "is" instead of "ought" would be the principal concern of the investigator; the object of study would be observed and observable behavior; the method would be rigorous, empirical, and theoretically informed; and the aim was to be significant generalizations and empirically testable theories.[57] Among the dominant approaches to the study of politics and society were sociological theory descended from Max Weber, Emile Durkheim, and Vilfredo Pareto; culture and personality theory indebted to anthropologists like Margaret Mead and Ruth Benedict; and social psychological theory that led to numerous surveys and small group experiments. Political scientists took beliefs, ideas, values, and feelings seriously, and by the early 1960s the investigation of political culture was considered by many to be fundamental to an understanding of comparative politics.[58]

Although some reviewers believe that mid-century "political science produced almost no general scientific propositions of a high degree of conclusiveness," the intense discussions within the discipline—between historical political theory and "the new science of politics," on questions of values and political culture, for example—prepared the ground for a critical reaction in the late 1960s. The mobilization of the disenfranchised undermined the positive consensus about American politics, questioned

55 Charles E. Lindblom, "Political Science in the 1940s and 1950s," in Bender and Schorske (eds.), *American Academic Culture*, p. 264.

56 John G. Gunnell, *The Descent of Political Theory: The Genealogy of an American Vocation* (Chicago: University of Chicago Press, 1993), p. 218.

57 This description is a paraphrase of David Truman's characterization of behavioralism, as reported in Gunnell, *The Descent of Political Theory*, p. 222.

58 Gabriel A. Almond, *A Discipline Divided: Schools and Sects in Political Science* (Newbury Park, CA: Sage Publications, 1990), pp. 122–3.

assumptions about liberalism and actually-existing democracy, and inspired new interest in justice and egalitarianism. While Marxism and critical theory remained on the margins, younger scholars were fascinated by the social structural work of Barrington Moore, the critique of modernization theory presented by dependency theory, new comparative studies of capitalism and labor, and a left turn in political theory.[59]

Ironically, at the moment when Western Marxists were abandoning economic determinist models of explanation, and historians wrestled with anthropology and literary criticism, many political scientists found new value in a view of human and group choice borrowed from economics. Much of political science had emphasized the predatory activities of elites, the established structures and procedures of modern politics, the determining effects of political culture, or the complexity of political decision-making that makes the agency of citizens difficult if not impossible, whereas new departures toward rational choice theory centered the individual and his or her choices.[60] Rational choice theory (closely related to social or public choice) and its associate game theory offered students of politics a theory that claimed to explain politics across time and space as the result of strategic, rational, goal-maximizing behavior within given

59   Among the key texts were Barrington Moore, *Social Origins of Dictatorship and Democracy: Lord and Peasant in the Making of the Modern World* (Boston: Beacon Press, 1966); David Greenstone, *Labor in American Politics* (New York: Alfred A. Knopf, 1969); Theodore J. Lowi, *The End of Liberalism: Ideology, Policy, and the Crisis of Public Authority* (New York: W. W. Norton, 1969); Walter Dean Burnham, *Critical Elections and the Mainsprings of American Politics* (New York: W. W. Norton, 1970); Sheldon Wolin, *Politics and Vision: Continuity and Innovation in Western Political Thought* (Boston: Little, Brown, 1960); and Andre Gunder Frank, *Capitalism and Underdevelopment in Latin America: Historical Studies of Chile and Brazil* (New York: Monthly Review Press, 1969).

60   For reviews of the evolution of professional political science, see Almond, "Separate Tables"; Bernard Crick, *The American Science of Politics* (Berkeley: University of California Press, 1959); Robert A. Dahl, "The Behavioral Approach in Political Science: Epitaph for a Monument to a Successful Protest," *American Political Science Review* LV, 4 (December 1961), pp. 763–72; Dryzek and Leonard, "History and Discipline in Political Science," pp. 1245–60; William Mitchell, "Virginia, Rochester, and Bloomington: Twenty-five Years of Public Choice and Political Science," *Public Choice* LVI (1988), pp. 101–19; David Ricci, *The Tragedy of Political Science* (New Haven: Yale University Press, 1984); Raymond Seidelman, *Disenchanted Realists: Political Science and the American Crisis, 1884–1984* (Albany: State University of New York, 1985); and Smith, 'Science, Non-Science, and Politics."

structures and institutions.[61] This methodological individualism questions the sufficiency of structuralist explanations, with their emphasis on
constraints, and focuses instead on the choice of strategies adopted by
actors to achieve their goals.[62] The model does not account for the formation of goals (first order preferences), but is interested in the institutions
and structures that shape strategies (second order preferences). The
theory assumes only that people choose the means most likely to bring
about their desired ends, that they can order their priorities, and that they
hold consistent preferences.[63] When theorists in this tradition looked at
parties, nations, or classes, they treated them as unitary actors capable of
rationally calculating their preferences and strategies toward utility maximization, in the manner of individuals. Although not all political science
succumbed to rational choice theory, methodological individualism
proved to be a muscular challenger to both the political culture approach
and the post-behavioralist "inclination to stress institutional
phenomena."[64] And in many ways rational choice appears to be at the
opposite pole in the discipline from cultural interpretivist approaches.

The question for political science has not been *whether* to deal with

---

61   A useful distinction is made by Jeffrey Friedman between public choice theory,
usually favored by economists, which argues that political actors, like economic actors,
have a propensity to pursue their material interests; and rational choice theory, which
argues that "regardless of what sort of ends people pursue, they do so through strategic,
instrumentally rational behavior." The two approaches are often conflated and confused,
and this conflation may account for the notion that rational choice arguments are inherently conservative. Jeffrey Friedman, "Introduction: Economic Approaches to Politics,"
in Friedman (ed.), *The Rational Choice Controversy: Economic Models of Politics
Reconsidered* (New Haven and London: Yale University Press, 1995), p. 2. Game theory
is the exploration of how actors make decisions if their actions and outcomes depend on
the actions of others.

62   "Political science finds itself sitting uneasily between economics where choice
under constraint is paramount, and sociology and anthropology where constraint by
structures or culture is fundamental." Ira Katznelson and Helen V. Milner, "American
Political Science as Normative Realism: The Discipline's State and the State of the
Discipline," in Katznelson and Milner (eds.), *Political Science: The State of the Discipline*
(New York: Norton Publishing for the American Political Science Association, 2002),
p.16.

63   Barbara Geddes, "Uses and Limitations of Rational Choice," in Peter H. Smith
(ed.), *Latin America in Comparative Perspective: New Approaches to Methods and
Analysis* (Boulder, CO: Westview Press, 1995), p. 83.

64   Theodore J. Lowi, in *American Political Science Review* LXXXII, 3 (September
1988), p. 885.

culture. Political scientists had followed American anthropology into an appreciation of the diversity of cultural forms in the 1920s and had generally adopted its relativist and value-neutral approach, and from the 1950s they carried that interest further into political culture. The question was *how* to deal with culture. Some political scientists consider political systems to be products of and limited by their cultures, with an elective affinity of one to the other, and still others treat culture as an instrument available for elites to use politically. There is no consensus on whether culture is just a piece of information to be considered or an independent explanatory variable.

Rational choice has taken several different approaches to deal with the inconvenience of culture. At one end, transhistorical and deductive notions of human preferences ignore cultural specificities and determinations. Here analysts assume that all people want either wealth, status, or power and that other motivations can be reduced to these fundamental preferences. Others within the tradition recognize the importance of culture. Shared symbols, they argue, create a field of communication and trust and solve coordination and collective action problems. Cultural systems are political resources that can be employed by political entrepreneurs to mobilize otherwise divided populations without paying the start-up costs of organization. Yet, critics point out, reducing culture or constructions of identity to instrumental decisions, calculated strategic choices, loses much of the texture, complexity, and richness of actual politics. Such simplifications have led to a stark polarization in the discipline. As Lisa Wedeen argues,

> Insofar as individualism presupposes agents who are forward-looking strategists forever calculating costs and benefits, there will be a serious ontological and epistemological divide between most rational choice and interpretivist theorists. Interpretivists, in my view, can rightly claim that individualist assumptions prevent rational choice scholars from asking important questions about politics, not the least of which is how we come to know that people maximize their interests, if they do.[65]

---

65 Lisa Wedeen, "Conceptualizing Culture: Possibilities for Political Science," *American Political Science Review* XCVI, 4 (December 2002), p. 717.

The reductionist psychology of rational choice theory has been a source of debate and discussion within political science from its earliest appearance. The early neo-institutionalists were among the most effective critics, raising the point that although self-interest certainly permeates politics, actual human action "is often based more on discovering the normatively appropriate behavior than on calculating the return expected from alternative choices. As a result, political behavior, like other behavior, can be described in terms of duties, obligations, roles, and rules."[66] Rational choice theorists have responded by introducing culture, values, and morals and then considering their instrumental employment. "To share a culture," David D. Laitin writes,

> means to share a language or a religion or a historiography. Very rarely do these cultural systems coincide perfectly within a large society. People must often choose which among their religious group, language group, and so on will be their primary mode of cultural identification. This choice is often guided by instrumental reasoning, based on the potential resources available for identifying yourself . . . Once a cultural group organizes politically, the common symbolic system makes for efficient collective action.[67]

For Laitin, culture is "Janus-faced," that is, "people are both guided by the symbols of their culture and instrumental in using culture to gain wealth and power." But this claim leads us to ask: How do we know when actions will be guided by values within the terms of a culture or instrumental in terms that transcend time, place, and culture, like wealth and power? It appears that rational choicers would like to have it both ways: people may be guided by preferences that are historical and cultural, but their ultimate ends and the real nature of human actions—goal maximization—are transhistorical, ultimately the same in all contexts. And one cannot help but notice that the most prevalent preferences posited by rational choice are ones that have come to dominate modern capitalist Western societies. Certainly wealth, material well-being, or power is a

---

66 James March and Johan Olsen, "The New Institutionalism: Organizational Factors in Political Life," *American Political Science Review* LXXVIII, 3 (September 1984), p. 744.

67 David D. Laitin, "Political Culture and Political Preferences," *American Political Science Review* LXXXII, 2 (June 1988), p. 591.

strong motivation for many, but interpretivists propose that such motivations are always culture-bound and historically derived. Status, security, respect, and love also function frequently, but the most interesting questions to ask are precisely about what meanings are attached to such concepts, and under what conditions they drive people to act. For historians deeply located in different times and cultures, what may seem the most strategic choice is precisely the one that is most inflected (infected?) by culture or values in a historic setting.

The difficulty, of course, is finding out what preferences are, how they are formed, and how actors calculate what is rational. Laitin attempts to solve this problem outside the theory by turning to Geertzian ethnography: "Only with a keen understanding of the meanings embedded in shared symbols—the first face of culture—can one adduce cultural preferences without tautologically claiming that preferences can be derived from the behavior of actors who are assumed to be rational."[68] It is here that cultural interpretivists might make the greatest contribution. People act on the basis of preferences and toward desired goals, but the preferences, goals, and strategies are provided and given meaning within a cultural system. Culturalists contend that a large part of politics is the struggle over meaning and the right to be authorized to speak. For culturalists, language not only expresses but also constitutes the political world. Derived from neither social position nor ideology, language itself helps to shape perception of position, interests, ideologies, and the meanings attached to the social and political world.[69] Interests and identities, even what might constitute strategic choices, are themselves part of a political process of constructing meanings. The process of constructing meaning, agents, and even the very notion of rationality, something central to cultural interpretivist explorations, is largely left out in normal rational choice work.

Cultural interpretivists can certainly admit that, in certain circumstances, people operate strategically to maximize their interests, as they conceive them, and even that material or power incentives influence

---

68   David D. Laitin, *Culture and Hegemony: Politics and Religious Change Among the Yoruba* (Chicago: University of Chicago Press, 1986), p. 16.

69   For an example of this process of linguistic and symbolic constitution of modern political rhetoric and understandings, see Lynn Hunt, *Politics, Culture, and Class in the French Revolution* (Berkeley and Los Angeles: University of California Press, 1984).

human action in many contexts. But that is only part of the story. Interpretivists are suspicious of any strict separation of culture and politics, identities and interests. In an exemplary essay on early-modern familial states, Julia Adams generously accepts the contributions of rational-choice analysts, who have demonstrated the transhistorical structural factors compelling rulers to pursue economic resources, but goes on to show how a culturalist approach opens the issues of who the rulers were, what their values consisted of, and how the identities, values, and emotional commitments of rulers shaped their preferences and actions. Her argument "insists on the socially malleable boundaries of self, originally formed in the family, the cultural component of identity, and the historically specific role of affect for early modern elite political actors."[70] Among her patrimonial rulers it is familial concerns, their identities and discourses, that structured choices. Identities and emotional attachments take on causal weight, as Adams argues that they led to resistance to change, even when change might have been economically advantageous.

Adams employs the useful distinction between "thin" and "thick" versions of rational choice theory: thin versions "are agnostic about actors' goals and values, whereas 'thicker' versions try to specify actors' desired ends, at least as exogenously given constraints." In either case, however, the ultimate ends or goals are "exogenously determined, and random with respect to the general theory, at the same time that they are held to be contingent on a universal means to an end [in this case]—revenue—that must itself be a goal if any higher-order ends are to be realized."[71] Although rational choice is agent-centered, actors, for all their importance, are conceived in fundamental ways as being independent of their historical and cultural context.

Rational choice has made significant contributions within political science (not to mention within economics), but in a whole range of political behavior, such as ethnic politics and nationalist movements, its value is limited. If we think about ethnic violence, a theory of instrumental rationality works best under two conditions. When there is total breakdown of the state, a "security dilemma" is created in which groups defined

---

70 Julia Adams, "Culture in Rational-Choice Theories of State-Formation," in Steinmetz (ed.), *State/Culture*, p. 114.
71 Ibid., p. 100.

as ethnic or national may perceive a threat from neighbors and take pre-emptive action. In a second case, there may be a "bandwagon" story in which individuals will join a nationalist movement or follow a leader when they perceive the real possibility of victory. But instrumental ration-ality fails to explain why such movements get started in the first place, or why people are ready to die or kill for such symbolic goods as the site of a defeat 500 or 1000 years ago. Rationality makes sense as a means to reach a goal, but both means and goals are very often constituted by reli-gious, historical, or cultural values that have little to do with material or status improvement. Cost-benefit analyses do not help much with the kinds of ends set by cultures, which can require self-sacrifice, pain, and even death.[72] Both preference formation and strategic choices, then, must be considered within cultures and historic time. Rational choicers are ready to concede that culture and history, reason and emotion, help deter-mine first order preferences. I am suggesting that they also determine second order preferences—institutions and structures—and the very strategies that actors adopt.

The added value offered by the cultural turn is exceptionally apparent in the study of nations and nationalism. Senses of mortality and desire for immortality, of the ethnic group or nation as kinship or the family writ large, of the conviction unquestioned that this group above all others is a part of nature rather than of choice, are fundamental to the bonds of solidarity that people forge in ethnic and national communi-ties. These affective ties—the promise of redemption from oblivion, the remedy for anonymity and meaningless mortality—must be taken seri-ously if we are to understand why, in the very process of constructing and imagining certain communities, the effort of construction is so emphatically denied.[73] A critical question is why constructed identities and fabricated histories are held sacred as sources of primordial allegiances.[74]

---

72 Ashutosh Varshney, "Cultures and Modes of Rationality," *APSA–Comparative Politics Newsletter* (Summer 1997), pp. 18–21.

73 Yael Tamir, "The Enigma of Nationalism," *World Politics* XLVII (April 1995), pp. 418–40; Margaret Canovan, *Nationhood and Political Theory* (Cheltenham, UK, and Brookfield, US: Edward Elgar, 1996), pp. 68–9.

74 For an investigation of this question, see Suny, "Constructing Primordialism: Old Histories for New Nations," *Journal of Modern History* LXXIII, 4 (December 2001), pp. 862–96.

Finally, the cultural turn strongly warns against seeing cultural units, nations or classes, as unitary and internally homogeneous. Treating them as unitary actors with coherent identities and interests leads to essentialist conclusions about group behavior. Here there may be an unrecognized affinity between rational individualism and cultural constructivism: many practitioners of both these approaches are suspicious of relying on the idea of the group and seek to disaggregate the seeming solidarity of the collective.[75] And all across political science, sociology, history, and anthropology scholars recognize that it is through culture that we apprehend the world and construct the imaginative concepts with which to understand our place within it. Culture both limits and empowers; it gives agency and constrains it. Culture defines goals, guides us toward achieving them, and misguides us often as to what might be in our "interest."

Roads Less Traveled
Many of the insights and stances of the cultural turn—the inherently unstable nature of categories, the problem of reflexivity, the preference for deep texture and thick description over parsimony, and the Foucauldian extension of power out from the state into the realm of disciplinary discourses and onto the body itself—provide fascinating openings for research by social scientists interested in politics. The very sphere of politics has been widened. (Just think of the job opportunities this offers!) Not only does Foucault's micropolitics become a locus for investigation, not only is the personal political and the body a site for politics, but fundamental assumptions about interests, the state, and the power and limits of political language now have to be interrogated.

Rather than flee from Foucault's imprecisions and obscurities, political scientists should borrow what they can from his difficult but fecund mind. The concept of discourse as a field of knowledge with its own practices and rules contributes a powerful new frame for thinking about politics,

---

75 In recent years a number of rational choice practitioners have made conciliatory moves toward integrating formal, rationalist methodologies and traditional or cultural interpretivist approaches. See, for example, Barry R. Weingast, "Formal Theory and Comparative Politics," *APSA–Comparative Politics Newsletter* (Winter 1997); Robert H. Bates and Rui J. P. De Figueiredo Jr., "The Politics of Interpretation: Rationality, Culture, and Transition," *Politics and Society* XXVI, 4 (December 1998), pp. 603–42; and David D. Laitin, *Identity in Formation: The Russian-Speaking Populations in the Near Abroad* (Ithaca, NY: Cornell University Press, 1998).

47

but at the same time discursive analysis would benefit from more precise critical examination and empirical grounding. There is much here for political science to do in understanding the state, the less institutionalized forms of politics, and the languages and representations of power.[76] The insights from the cultural turn give us some purchase on the web of disciplinary and power relations that make up a political regime, the web in which subjects and citizens are caught, of which they may or may not be aware, and against which they may or may not be able to resist. At the same time the state can be brought back in along with culture. In an exciting departure, the authors of the essays in *State/Culture: State-Formation after the Cultural Turn*, edited by sociologist George Steinmetz, seek to reverse the idea of culture as a product of the state and elaborate culture's constitutive role in state formation—not only in the Weberian application exclusively to non-Western states but in the core countries of northwestern Europe.[77] Without deciding beforehand the power of discursive or cultural "constraints" on actors' abilities, or accepting what interests or identities are out there, political scientists might expand the range of possible preferences and motivations, rationally calculated and emotional, that people may have and explore how particular subjectivities are constituted.

The cultural turn, however, comes with its own politics and political costs. The radical doubting of cultures (and national cultures as the moment of congruence of culture and politics) challenges the dominant discourses of politics in the modern world. If cultures can no longer be assumed to be coherent, bounded entities in the real world, then their claims to self-determination, autonomy, and possibly statehood cannot be said to derive unproblematically from the need to represent a particular culture politically. The claims of nationalists that national cultures run back in time to a primordial originating moment and that culture was, is, or should be isomorphic with a territory (the "homeland") have

---

76 For examples of political scientists who both borrow from Foucault and other post-structuralists and expand the legitimate space of political science, see Lisa Wedeen, *Ambiguities of Domination: Politics, Rhetoric, and Symbols in Contemporary Syria* (Chicago and London: University of Chicago Press, 1999); and Anne Norton, *Republic of Signs: Liberal Theory and American Popular Culture* (Chicago and London: University of Chicago Press, 1993).

77 See, particularly, Steinmetz's introduction, Steinmetz (ed.), *State/Culture*, pp. 1-49.

been subjected to critical, subversive historical analysis. Moreover, the very idea of constructedness of nations, like that of cultures in general, and the central importance of belief, representation, and imagination in making cultures and nations, both challenge the more positivist theories of ethnic conflict and open the possibility for new constructions of national identity that could lead less predictably to conflict or cooperation. Here is an opportunity for a reconceptualization of a problem in political science. Indeed, the historicization and cultural formation of nations and nationalism were most significantly taken up by a political scientist, Benedict Anderson, but one who for all of his influence in broader social science, history, and literary studies remained marginal to the mainstream of political science.[78]

The deconstructive thrust of the cultural turn, however, need not lead us into a completely indeterminate world without any coherences or temporal solidarities whatsoever. Even as cultural interpretivists disaggregate the assumed wholeness of societies, cultures, and nations, there is an awareness that a certain "thin coherence" (the term is Sewell's) remains.[79] Sherry Ortner suggests where anthropology may be on this point at the present:

People are spinning what Geertz called "webs of meaning" all the time, with whatever cultural resources happen to be at hand. Thus, even if culture(s) were never as whole and consistent and static as anthropologists portrayed them in the past, and even if, as many thinkers now claim, there are fewer and fewer in the way of distinct and recognizable "cultures" in the contemporary world (though I am less sure about that), the fundamental assumption that people are always trying to make sense of their lives, always weaving fabrics of meaning, however fragile and fragmentary, still holds.[80]

---

78 Benedict Anderson, *Imagined Communities: Reflections on the Origin and Spread of Nationalism* (London: Verso, 1983, 1991).

79 Sewell argues that a culture must have some semiotic coherence, but it is a "thin coherence" that allows for linguistic and symbolic instabilities within a culture and, therefore, cultural change. What look within a culture (and often to outside observers) like indisputable truths and stable practices are likely to be unstable and dubious over time. Sewell, "Concept(s) of Culture," pp. 49–50.

80 Ortner, "Introduction," in Ortner (ed.), *The Fate of "Culture"*, pp. 9–10.

Thin coherence and weaving fabrics of meaning also imply a (not-so-new) political program of deconstruction that holds that the social reality of any society is only one possibility among many. History and anthropology have often promised us an open world, a world (in Sewell's words) "contingent rather than necessary," in which

> there exist forms of life radically different from ours that are nonetheless fully human . . . In the pasts they study, historians find worlds, structured differently from ours, worlds where people's motives, senses of honor, daily tasks, and political calculations are based on unfamiliar assumptions about human society and the cosmic order . . . History, like anthropology, specializes in the discovery and display of human variety, but in time rather than space.[81]

The most potent moment for this act of discovery is probably in the study of origins, the very moment in more essentialist theories used to naturalize present phenomena. Pierre Bourdieu suggests that "There is no more potent tool for rupture than the reconstruction of genesis: by bringing back into view the conflicts and confrontations of the early beginnings and therefore all the discarded possibles, it retrieves the possibility that things could have been (and still could be) otherwise. And, through such a practical utopia, it questions the 'possible' which, among all others, was actualized."[82] This, of course, was precisely what the projects of Thompson and Geertz were all about—recovery of alternative worlds that held up visions, not of why we had arrived at where we were, but of where we might have gone.

In a way, we have come back from beyond. For the same idea of possible futures other than the present was what compelled people to turn to Marxism. Although a deep pessimism about the possibility of socialism followed in the wake of the collapse of Soviet-style systems and the global hegemony of market capitalism, there has been a revival of the kind of radical historicism that marked the best of the Marxist tradition—the view that all social formations (capitalism included) have their own

---

81 Sewell, "Geertz, Cultural Systems, and History," in Ortner (ed.), *The Fate of "Culture"*, pp. 37–8.

82 Pierre Bourdieu, "Rethinking the State: Genesis and Structure of the Bureaucratic Field," in Steinmetz (ed.), *State/Culture*, p. 57.

history and evolution, their birth, maturity, and death, and their replacement by other forms. This revival has taken place not on materialist grounds but in the array of approaches loosely labeled post-structuralist and post-modern. In his conclusion to *Beyond the Cultural Turn*, one of the most influential voices in that turn, Hayden White, proposes:

> A modernist social science must be directed to the study of those aspects of social reality that attest to human beings' capacities to make and remake that reality, not merely adjust to it. And it seems to me that the significance of the cultural turn in history and the social sciences inheres in its suggestion that in "culture" we can apprehend a niche within social reality from which any given society can be deconstructed and shown to be less an inevitability than only one possibility among a host of others.[83]

This new historicization of capitalism and the dominant social forms, the attempt to be self-reflexive about the very order in which you live and work, is reminiscent of earlier Marxist attempts to become self-conscious about the bourgeois world. The relativization and historicization of capitalism allow for the retention of hope for development beyond. But any optimism must be tempered by the post-modernist sensitivity to the arbitrariness of any progressive master narratives that give easy confidence in a democratic, egalitarian, socially just future.

---

83 Hayden White in the afterword to Bonnell and Hunt (eds.), *Beyond the Cultural Turn*, p. 316.

CHAPTER TWO

Reading Russia and the Soviet Union in the Twentieth Century: How the "West" Wrote Its History of the USSR

From its very beginnings, the historiography of Russia in the twentieth century has been much more than an object of coolly detached scholarly contemplation.[1] Many observers saw the USSR as the major enemy of Western civilization, the principal threat to the stability of nations and empires, a scourge that sought to undermine the fundamental values of decent human societies. For others, the Soviet Union promised an alternative to the degradations of capitalism and the fraudulent claims of bourgeois democracy, represented the bulwark of Enlightenment values against the menace of fascism, and preserved the last best hope of colonized peoples. In the Western academy, the Soviet Union was most often imagined to be an aberration in the normal course of modern history, an unfortunate detour from the rise of liberalism that bred its own evil

---

1   My gratitude is extended to Robert V. Daniels, Georgi Derluguian, David C. Engerman, Peter Holquist, Valerie Kivelson, Terry Martin, Norman Naimark, Lewis Siegelbaum, David Stone, Josephine Woll, and members of the Russian Studies Workshop at the University of Chicago for critical readings of earlier versions of this chapter. This essay discusses primarily the attitudes and understandings of Western observers, more precisely the scholarship and ideational framings of professional historians and social scientists, about the Soviet Union as a state, a society, and a political project. More attention is paid to Anglo-American work, and particularly to American views, since arguably they set the tone and parameters of the field through much of the century. This account should be supplemented by reviews of other language literatures, e.g., Laurent Jalabert, *Le Grand Débat. Les universitaires français—historiens et géographes—et les pays communistes, de 1945 à 1991* (Toulouse: Groupe de Recherche en Histoire Immédiate, Maison de la Recherche, Université Toulouse Le Mirail, 2001); and Lennart Samuelson, "Interpretations of Stalinism: Historiographical Patterns Since the 1930s and the Role of the 'Archival Revolution' in the 1990s," in Marko Kangaspuro and Vesa Oitiinen (eds.), *Discussing Stalinism: Problems and Approaches* (Helsinki: Aleksanteri Institute, University of Helsinki, 2015), pp. 11–41.

A version of this essay was published in Ronald Grigor Suny (ed.), *Cambridge History of Russia, Volume III: The Twentieth Century* (Cambridge: Cambridge University Press, 2006), pp. 5–64.

opposite, traveling its very own *Sonderweg* that led eventually (or inevitably) to collapse and ruin. The very endeavor of writing a balanced narrative required a commitment to standards of scholarship suspect to those either militantly opposed to or supportive of the Soviet enterprise. At times, as in the years just after the revolution or during the Cold War, scholarship too often served other masters than itself. While much worthy analysis came from people deeply committed to or critical of the Soviet project, a studied neutrality was difficult (though possible) in an environment in which one's work was always subject to political judgment.

With the opening of the Soviet Union and its archives to researchers from abroad, beginning in the Gorbachev years, professional historians and social scientists produced empirically grounded and theoretically informed works that avoided the worst polemical excesses of earlier years. Yet, even those who claimed to be unaffected by the battles of former generations were themselves the product of what went before. The educator still had to be educated. While the end of the Cold War and the collapse of the Soviet Union permitted a greater degree of detachment than had been possible before, the Soviet story—itself so important an ingredient in the self-construction of the modern "West"—remains one of deep contestation.

The Prehistory of Soviet History

"At the beginning of [the twentieth century]," wrote Christopher Lasch in his study of American liberals and the Russian Revolution,

> people in the West took it as a matter of course that they lived in a
> civilization surpassing any which history had been able to record. They
> assumed that their own particular customs, institutions and ideas had
> universal validity; that having showered their blessings upon the coun-
> tries of western Europe and North America, those institutions were
> destined to be carried to the furthest reaches of the earth, and bring
> light to those living in darkness.[2]

---

2 Christopher Lasch, *The American Liberals and the Russian Revolution* (New York and London: Columbia University Press, 1962; paperback edition: McGraw Hill, 1972), p. 1. All references in this chapter are from the latest edition listed, unless otherwise noted.

Those sentences retain their relevance at the beginning of the twenty-first century. Western, particularly American, attitudes to and understandings of Russia and the Soviet Union unfolded in the last hundred years within a broad discourse of optimism about human progress, that relied on the comforting thought that capitalist democracy represented the best possible solution to human society, if not the "end of history." Within that universe of ideas, Russians were constructed as people fundamentally different from Westerners, with deep, largely immutable national characteristics. Ideas of a "Russian soul" or an essentially spiritual or collectivist nature guided the interpretations and policy prescriptions of foreign observers. This tradition dates back to the very first travelers to Muscovy. In his *Notes Upon Russia (1517–1549)*, Sigismund von Herberstein wrote, "The people enjoy slavery more than freedom," an observation echoed by Adam Olearius in the seventeenth century, who saw Russians as "comfortable in slavery" and requiring "cudgels and whips" to make them work. Montesquieu and others believed that national character was determined by climate and geography, and the harsh environment in which Russians lived had produced a barbarous and uncivilized people, ungovernable, lacking discipline, lazy, superstitious, subject to despotism, yet collective, passionate, poetical and musical. The adjectives differed from writer to writer, yet they clustered around the instinctual and emotional pole of human behavior rather than the cognitive and rational. Race and blood, more than culture and choice, decided what Russians were able to do. In order to make them civilized and modern, it was often asserted, force and rule from above was unavoidable. Ironically, the spokesmen of civilization justified the use of violence and terror on the backward and passive people of Russia as the necessary means to modernity.

The most influential works on Russia in the early twentieth century were the great classics of nineteenth-century travelers and scholars, like the Marquis de Custine, Baron August von Haxthausen, Donald Mackenzie Wallace, Alfred Rambaud, Anatole Leroy-Beaulieu, and George Kennan, the best-selling author of *Siberia and the Exile System*.[3]

---

3 Marquis de Custine, *Journey for Our Time: The Journals of Marquis de Custine*, ed. and trans. Phyllis Penn Kohler (1843; New York: Pellegrini and Cudahy, 1951); Baron August von Haxthausen, *The Russian Empire: Its People, Institutions and Resources*, 2 vols., trans. Robert Farie (1847; London: Chapman and Hall, 1856); Sir Donald Mackenzie Wallace, *Russia on the Eve of War and Revolution*, ed. and intro. Cyril E. Black (1877; New York: Random House, 1961); Alfred Rambaud, *The History of Russia*

France offered the most professional academic study of Russia, and the influential Leroy-Beaulieu's eloquent descriptions of the patience, submissiveness, lack of individuality, and fatalism of the Russians contributed to the ubiquitous sense of a Slavic character that contrasted with the Gallic, Anglo-Saxon, or Teutonic. American writers, like Kennan and Eugene Schuyler, subscribed equally to such ideas of nationality, but rather than climate or geography as causative, they emphasized the role of institutions, like tsarism, in generating a national character that in some ways was mutable.[4] Kennan first went to Russia in 1865, became an amateur ethnographer, and grew to admire the courageous revolutionaries ("educated, reasonable, self-controlled gentlemen, not different in any essential respect from one's self") that he encountered in Siberian exile.[5] For his sympathies, the tsarist government banned him from Russia, placing him in a long line of interpreters whose exposures of Russian life and politics would be so punished.[6]

Russia as an autocracy remained the political "other" of Western democracy and republicanism, and it was with great joy and relief that liberals, including President Woodrow Wilson, greeted the February Revolution of 1917 as "the impossible dream" realized. Now the new Russian government could be enlisted in the Great War to make "the world safe for democracy."[7] But the Bolshevik seizure of power in Petrograd turned the liberal world upside down. For Wilson's Secretary of

---

from the Earliest Times to 1877, trans. Leonora B. Lang, 2 vols. (1878; New York: Hovendon Company, 1886); Anatole Leroy-Beaulieu, *The Empire of the Tsars and the Russians*, 3 vols., trans. Zénïade A. Ragozin (New York: Knickerbocker Press, 1902); George F. Kennan, *Siberia and the Exile System*, 2 vols. (New York: Century, 1891).

4 David C. Engerman, *Modernization from the Other Shore: American Intellectuals and the Romance of Russian Development* (Cambridge, MA: Harvard University Press, 2003), pp. 28–53.

5 Ibid., p. 37.

6 For a thorough account of American views and images of Russia at the end of the nineteenth and beginning of the twentieth centuries, see V. I. Zhuravleva, *Ponimanie Rossii v SShA: Obrazy i Mify* (Moscow: Rossiiskii Gosudarstvennyi Gumanitarnyi Universitet, 2012).

7 On American views of Russia and the revolution, see Lasch, *The American Liberals and the Russian Revolution*; and N. Gordon Levin, Jr., *Woodrow Wilson and World Politics: America's Response to War and Revolution* (Oxford: Oxford University Press, 1968); Peter G. Filene, *Americans and the Soviet Experiment, 1917–1933* (Cambridge: Harvard University Press, 1967); Peter G. Filene (ed.), *American Views of Soviet Russia, 1917–1965* (Homewood, IL: The Dorsey Press, 1968).

State, Robert Lansing, Bolshevism was "the worst form of anarchism," "the madness of famished men."[8] In the years immediately following the October Revolution, the first accounts of the new regime reaching the West were by journalists and diplomats. The radical freelance journalist John Reed, his wife and fellow radical Louise Bryant, Bessie Beatty of the *San Francisco Bulletin*, the British journalist Arthur Ransome, and Congregational minister Albert Rhys Williams all witnessed events in 1917 and conveyed the immediacy and excitement of the revolutionary days to an eager public back home.[9] After several trips to Russia, the progressive writer Lincoln Steffens told his friends, "I have seen the future and it works." Enthusiasm for the revolution propelled liberals and social-ists further to the left, and small Communist parties emerged from the radical wing of Social Democracy. From the right came sensationalist accounts of atrocities, debauchery, and tyranny, leavened with the repeated assurance that the days of the Bolsheviks were numbered. *L'Echo de Paris* and the London *Morning Post*, as well as papers through-out Western Europe and the United States, wrote that the Bolsheviks were "servants of Germany" or "Russian Jews of German extraction."[10] The *New York Times* so frequently predicted the fall of the Communists that two young journalists, Walter Lippmann and Charles Merz, exposed their misreadings in a long piece in *The New Republic*.[11]

---

8 Arno J. Mayer, *Politics and Diplomacy of Peacemaking: Containment and Counterrevolution at Versailles, 1918–1919* (New York: Alfred P. Knopf, 1967), p. 260. See also his *Political Origins of the New Diplomacy, 1917–1918* (New Haven: Yale University Press, 1959).

9 John Reed, *Ten Days that Shook the World* (New York: Boni & Liveright, 1919); Louise Bryant, *Six Months in Russia: An Observers Account of Russia Before and During the Proletarian Dictatorship* (New York: George H. Doran, 1918); Bessie Beatty, *The Red Heart of Russia* (New York: Century, 1918); Arthur Ransome, *Russia in 1919* (New York, 1919); *The Crisis in Russia* (New York, 1921); Albert Rhys Williams, *Through the Russian Revolution* (New York: Boni & Liveright, 1921). See also the accounts in Filene, *Americans and the Soviet Experiment*; Filene (ed.), *American Views of Soviet Russia*; Lasch, *The American Liberals and the Russian Revolution*.

10 Walter Laqueur, *The Fate of the Revolution: Interpretations of Soviet History from 1917 to the Present* (London: Macmillan, 1967; rev. ed. New York and London: Collier Books, 1987), p. 8.

11 "Thirty different times the power of the Soviets was definitely described as being on the wane. Twenty times there was news of a serious counter-revolutionary menace. Five times was the explicit statement made that the regime was certain to collapse. And fourteen times that collapse was said to be in progress. Four times Lenin and Trotsky were planning flight. Three times they had already fled. Five times the Soviets were

The Western reaction to the Bolsheviks approached panic. Officials and advisors to the Wilson administration spoke of Russia as drunk, the country as mad, taken over by a mob, the people victims of an "outburst of elemental forces," "sheep without a shepherd," a terrible fate for a country in which "there were simply too few brains per square mile."[12] Slightly more generously, the American ambassador David Francis told the State Department that the Bolsheviks might be just what Russia needed: strong men for a people that do not value human life and "will obey strength . . . and nothing else."[13] To allay fears of domestic revolution the American government deported over 200 political radicals in December 1919 to the land of the Soviets on the *Buford*, an old ship dubbed "the Red Ark." The virus of Bolshevism seemed pervasive, and powerful voices raised fears of international subversion. The arsenal of the Right included the familiar weapon of anti-Semitism. In early 1920, Winston Churchill told demonstrators that the Bolsheviks "believe in the international Soviet of the Russian and Polish Jews."[14] Baron N. Wrangel opened his account of the Bolshevik revolution with the words "The sons of Israel had carried out their mission; and Germany's agents, having become the representatives of Russia, signed peace with their patron at Brest-Litovsk."[15]

Western reading publics, hungry for news and analyses of the enigmatic social experiment underway in Soviet Russia, turned to journalists and scholars for information. The philosopher Bertrand Russell, who had accompanied a delegation of the British Labour Party to Russia in 1919, rejected Bolshevism for two reasons: "the price mankind must pay to achieve communism by Bolshevik methods is too terrible; and secondly, . . . even after paying the price I do not believe the result would be what the

---

'tottering.' Three times their fall was 'imminent' . . . Twice Lenin had planned retirement; once he had been killed; and three times he was thrown in prison." Walter Lippmann and Charles Merz, "A Test of the News," *The New Republic* (Supplement), August 4, 1920; cited in Engerman, *Modernization from the Other Shore*, pp. 198–9.

12 Quotations from Engerman, *Modernization from the Other Shore*, pp. 94, 95.

13 Ibid., p. 98.

14 *The Times* (London), January 5, 1920; cited in E. Malcolm Carroll, *Soviet Communism and Western Opinion, 1919–1921*, ed. by Frederic B. M. Hollyday (Chapel Hill: University of North Carolina Press, 1965), p. 13.

15 *From Serfdom to Bolshevism: The Memoirs of Baron N. Wrangel, 1847–1920*, trans. Brian and Beatrix Lunn (Philadelphia: J. B. Lippincott, 1927), p. 291.

Bolsheviks profess to desire."[16] Other radical dissenters included the anarchist Emma Goldman, who spent nearly two years in Bolshevik Russia only to break decisively with the Soviets after the repression of the Kronstadt mutiny in March 1921.[17]

The historian Bernard Pares (1867–1949) had begun visiting Russia regularly from 1898, and reported on the beginnings of parliamentarianism in Russia after 1905. As British military observer to the Russian army he remained in the country from the outbreak of World War I until the early days of the Soviet government. After service as British commissioner to Admiral Kolchak's anti-Bolshevik White government, Pares taught Russian history at the University of London, where he founded *The Slavonic Review* in 1922 and directed the new School of Slavonic Studies. A friend of the liberal leader Pavl Miliukov and supporter of constitutional monarchy in Russia, by the 1930s Pares had become more sympathetic to the Soviets and an advocate of Anglo-Russian rapprochement. Like most of his contemporaries, Pares believed that climate and environment shaped the Russians. "The happy instinctive character of clever children," he wrote, "so open, so kindly and so attractive, still remains; but the interludes of depression or idleness are longer than is normal."[18] In part because of his reliance on the concept of "national character," widely accepted among scholars, journalists, and diplomats, Pares's influence remained strong, particularly during the years of the Anglo-American–Soviet alliance. But with the coming of the Cold War, he, like others "soft on communism," was denounced as an apologist for Stalin.[19]

In the United States the most important of the few scholars studying Russia were Archibald Cary Coolidge (1866–1928) at Harvard and Samuel Northrup Harper (1882–1943) of the University of Chicago. For Coolidge, the variety of "head types" found among Slavs was evidence that they were a mixture of many different races, and while autocracy might be repugnant to the "Anglo-Saxon," it appeared to be appropriate for

16 Bertrand Russell, *The Practice and Theory of Bolshevism* (London, 1920; New York: Simon & Schuster, 1964), p. 101.

17 Emma Goldman, *My Disillusionment in Russia* (New York: Doubleday, Page & Co., 1923; London: C. W. Daniel, 1925).

18 Sir Bernard Pares, *Russia Between Reform and Revolution: Fundamentals of Russian History and Character*, ed. and intro. Francis B. Randall (New York: Schocken Books, 1962), p. 3. The book was first published in 1907.

19 On Pares, see Laqueur, *The Fate of the Revolution*, pp. 173–5.

Russians.[20] After working with Herbert Hoover's American Relief Administration (ARA) during the famine of 1921–22, he concluded that the famine was largely the result of the peasants' passivity, lethargy, and Oriental fatalism, not to mention the "stupidity, ignorance, inefficiency and above all meddlesomeness" of Russians more generally.[21] The principal mentor of American experts on the Soviet Union in the interwar period, Coolidge trained the first generation of professional scholars and diplomats. One of his students, Frank Golder (1877–1927), also worked for Hoover's ARA and was an early advocate of Russia's reconstruction, a prerequisite, he felt, for ridding the country of the "Bolos." Golder went on to work at the Hoover Institution of War, Peace, and Revolution at Stanford University, building up important collections of documents that make up the major archive for Soviet history in the West.[22]

Samuel Harper, the son of William Rainey Harper, the President of the University of Chicago, shared the dominant notions of Russian national character, which for him included deep emotions, irregular work habits, apathy, lethargy, pessimism, and lack of "backbone."[23] Harper was a witness to Bloody Sunday in 1905 and, like his friend Pares, a fervent defender of Russian liberals who eventually succumbed to the romance of communism. Russians may have been governed more by emotion and passion than reason, he argued, but they possessed an instinct for democracy. In 1926, he accepted an assignment from his colleague, chairman of the political science department at Chicago, Charles E. Merriam (1874–1953), arguably the most influential figure in American political science between the wars, to study methods of indoctrinating children with the love of the state. Russia, along with fascist Italy, was to be the principal laboratory for this research. Merriam was fascinated with the successes of civic education in Mussolini's Italy, while other political scientists saw virtues in Hitler's Germany.[24] For Merriam, creating patriotic loyalty to the state was a technical problem, not a matter of culture, and the Soviet

---

20 Engerman, *Modernization from the Other Shore*, pp. 60–1.
21 Ibid., p. 110.
22 Terence Emmons and Bertrand M. Patenaude (eds.), *War, Revolution, and Peace in Russia: The Passages of Frank Golder, 1914–1927* (Stanford: Hoover Institution Press, 1988).
23 Ibid., p. 65.
24 Ido Oren, *Our Enemies and US: America's Rivalries and the Making of Political Science* (Ithaca, NY: Cornell University Press, 2003), pp. 47–90.

Union, which had rejected nationalism and the traditional ties to old Russia, was a "striking experiment" to create "de novo a type of political loyalty to, and interest in a new order of things."[25] In *The Making of Citizens* (1931), he concluded that the revolution had employed the emotions generated by festivals, the Red Flag, the *Internationale*, and mass meetings and demonstrations effectively to establish "a form of democratic nationalism."[26]

To study what they called "civic education," something akin to what later would be known as "nation-building," Harper and Merriam traveled to Russia together in 1926. Guided by Maurice Hindus, an influential journalist sympathetic to the Soviet experiment, Harper visited villages where he became enthusiastic about the Bolshevik educational program. Impressed by Soviet efforts to modernize the peasantry, he supported their industrialization drive.[27] This led eventually to estrangement from the State Department specialists on Russia with whom Harper had worked for over a decade. In the mid-1930s, he wrote positively about constitutional developments in the USSR, and his 1937 book, *The Government of the Soviet Union*, made the case for democratic, participatory institutions in the Soviet system. His book appeared the very same year that Stalin's show trials reached their zenith, carrying away the Communist elite whom the dictator saw as potential political threats. Harper rationalized the Moscow trials and never publicly criticized Stalin. When Harper defended the Nazi–Soviet Pact of 1939 as a shrewd maneuver, students abandoned his classes and faculty colleagues shunned him. Only after the Soviets became allies of the United States in 1941 did he enjoy a few twilight years of public recognition, even appearing with Charlie Chaplin and the poet Carl Sandburg at a mass "Salute to our Russian Ally."[28]

Seeing the Future Work

Through the interwar years, the Soviet Union offered many intellectuals a vision of a preferred future outside and beyond capitalism. Contained

---

25 Ibid., pp. 59–60.

26 Ibid., p. 61; Charles E. Merriam, *The Making of Citizens: A Comparative Study of Methods of Civic Training* (Chicago: University of Chicago Press, 1931), p. 222.

27 Samuel N. Harper, *The Russia I Believe In: The Memoirs of Samuel N. Harper, 1902–1941*, ed. Paul V. Harper (Chicago: University of Chicago Press, 1945).

28 Oren, *Our Enemies and US*, pp. 111–16.

within the hope and faith in the USSR and communism, however, were the seeds of disillusionment and despair. Writers made ritualistic visits to Moscow and formed friendships with other political pilgrims. In November 1927, novelist Theodore Dreiser accepted an invitation to tour the USSR, and his secretary remembered an evening at the Grand Hotel with Dorothy Thomas, Sinclair Lewis, Scott Nearing, and Louis Fischer, followed by a visit to *New York Times* correspondent Walter Duranty.[29] By the early 1930s, many "Russianists" had moved decisively to the left. The sociologist Jerome Davis, who taught at Dartmouth and Yale, advocated recognition of the USSR and was ultimately fired from Yale for condemning capitalism.[30] Paul Douglas, a distinguished University of Chicago labor economist, enthusiastically but mistakenly predicted that Soviet trade unions would soon overtake the Communist Party as the most powerful institution in the country.[31] Robert Kerner, a Russian historian at the University of Missouri, gave up what he had called "racial metaphysics" (he said he had studied the Slavs as the "largest white group in the world") to investigate environmental and historical factors, work that culminated in his *The Urge to the Sea* (1942). The epitome of professional Russian history in the interwar period, Geroid Tanquary Robinson of Columbia University, was attracted to radical thought early in his life and dedicated his scholarship to a re-evaluation of the much-maligned Russian peasantry. His magnum opus, *Rural Russia Under the Old Regime* (1932), the first substantial historical work by an American scholar that was based on extensive work in the Soviet archives, challenged the prevalent notion of peasant lethargy and passivity. Influenced by the "New Historians" who turned to the study of everyday life and borrowed insights from the other social sciences, he worked to distinguish professional historical writing, which looked to the past to explain the present (or other pasts), from journalism or punditry, which used the past and present to project into and predict the future.

"Collectively," writes David C. Engerman, these new professional experts on Russia—Harper, Kerner, Davis, Douglas, Robinson, Vera Micheles Dean, and Leo Pasvolsky—"offered more reasons to support

---

29 Ruth Epperson Kennell, *Theodore Dreiser and the Soviet Union, 1927–1945* (New York: International Publishers, 1969), pp. 25–6.

30 Engerman, *Modernization from the Other Shore*, pp. 132–6.

31 Ibid., p. 136. He later turned to politics and was elected Democratic senator from Illinois.

Soviet rule than to challenge it."[32] They played down ideology as they elevated national, geographic, or even racial characteristics. Russia, they believed, had affected communism much more than communism Russia. The small cohort of American diplomats (George Kennan, Charles "Chip" Bohlen, Loy Henderson, and the first ambassador to the USSR, William Bullitt) who manned the new US embassy in Moscow after recognition of the Soviet Union in 1933 shared similar attitudes. Kennan reported that in order to understand Russia he "had to weigh the effects of climate on character, the results of century-long conflict with the Asiatic hordes, the influence of medieval Byzantium, the national origins of the people, and the geographic characteristics of the country."[33] Influenced by the German sociologist Klaus Mehnert's study of Soviet youth, Kennan noted how young people were carried away by the "romance of economic development" to the point that they were relieved "to a large extent of the curses of egotism, romanticism, daydreaming, introspection, and perplexity which befall the young of bourgeois countries."[34] To demonstrate the continuity and consistency of the Russian character of life, Kennan sent home an 1850 diplomatic dispatch, passing it off as if it were current![35]

In the years of the First Five-Year Plan, Western writing reached a crescendo of praise for the Soviets' energy and sacrifice, their idealism and attendant suffering endured in the drive for modernization. The post–World War I cultural critique of unbridled capitalism developed by American thinkers like John Dewey and Thorstein Veblen encouraged many intellectuals to consider the lessons that capitalist democracies might learn from the Soviets. Western leftists and liberals hoped that engineers, planners, and technocrats would be inspired by Soviet planning to discipline the anarchy of capitalism. In "An Appeal to Progressives," contrasting the economic breakdown in the West with the successes of Soviet planned development, the critic Edmund Wilson (1895–1972) proclaimed that American radicals and progressives "must take Communism away from the Communists . . . asserting emphatically that their ultimate goal is the ownership of the means of production by the

32 Ibid., p. 152.
33 Engerman, *Modernization from the Other Shore*, p. 258.
34 Ibid., p. 255; Klaus Mehnert, *Die Jugend in Sowjetrussland* (Berlin: S. Fischer, 1932), pp. 34–9.
35 Engerman, *Modernization from the Other Shore*, p. 260.

government and an industrial rather than a regional representation."[36] The educator George Counts (1889–1974) waxed rhapsodic about the brave experiment in the USSR and its challenge to America, though within a few years he turned into a leading anti-Communist. As economist Stuart Chase put it in 1932, "Why should the Russians have all the fun of remaking the world?"[37] John Dewey expressed the mood of many when he wrote that the Soviet Union was "the most interesting [experiment] going on upon our globe—though I am quite frank to say that for selfish reasons I prefer seeing it tried out in Russia rather than in my own country."[38]

Even the evident negative aspects of a huge country in turmoil did not dampen the enthusiasm for Stalin's revolution from above. Popular historian Will Durant (1885–1981) traveled to Russia in 1932, witnessed starvation, but was still able to write, "The challenge of the Five-Year Plan is moral as well as economic. It is a direct challenge to the smugness and complacency which characterize American thinking on our own chaotic system." Future historians, he predicted, would look upon "planned social control as the most significant single achievement of our day."[39] That same year the Black writer Langston Hughes (1902–1967), already interested in socialism, visited the USSR with other writers to produce a documentary. Inspired by what he saw—a land of poverty and hope, with much struggle but no racism or economic stratification—he wrote a poem, "One More 'S' in the U. S. A.," for his comrades. Decades later the anti-Communist Senator Joseph McCarthy brought him before his committee to discuss publicly his political involvement with Communists.[40]

Journalism occupied the ideological frontline. With the introduction of by-lines and a new emphasis on conceptualization and interpretation instead of simple reportage, newspapermen (and they were almost all men) evaluated and made judgments. Reporters became familiar figures

---

36 Edmund Wilson, "An Appeal to Progressives," *New Republic* LXV (January 14, 1931), pp. 234–8; Filene, *American Views*, pp. 76–7.

37 Engerman, *Modernization from the Other Shore*, p. 165.

38 Ibid., p. 184.

39 Will Durant, *The Tragedy of Russia: Impressions from a Brief Visit* (New York: Simon & Schuster, 1933), p. 21; Filene, *American Views*, p. 89.

40 Langston Hughes, *I Wonder as I Wonder: An Autobiographical Journey* (New York: Rinehart, 1956).

in popular culture, and as celebrities back home, those posted in Russia gradually became identified with one political position or another. Of the handful of American correspondents in Moscow, Maurice Hindus (1891–1969) stood out as a sympathetic observer of the country about which he wrote. Unlike those who relied on Soviet ideological pronouncements or a reading of the Marxist classics as a guide to understanding what was going on in Russia, Hindus chose to "be in the country, wander around, observe and listen, ask questions and digest answers to obtain some comprehension of the sweep and meaning of these events."[41] He befriended Western men and women of letters, like John Dewey and George Bernard Shaw (whom he guided through the USSR on a celebrated trip), and once was prevailed upon by F. Scott Fitzgerald's psychiatrist to allay the novelist's fears of a coming Communist revolution in America. To his critics, Hindus was naïve, apologetic, and even duplicitous. One of his fellow correspondents, the disillusioned Eugene Lyons (1898–1985), considered Hindus to be one of the most industrious of Stalin's apologists.[42] Whatever his faults or insights, Hindus developed and popularized a particular form of reporting on the Soviet Union—one emulated later with enormous success by Alexander Werth, Hedrick Smith, Robert Kaiser, David Shipler, Andrea Lee, Martin Walker, David Remnick, and others—that combined personal observations, telling anecdotes and revealing detail to provide a textured picture of the USSR that supplemented and undercut more partisan portraits.[43]

The *Christian Science Monitor*'s William Henry Chamberlin (1897–1969) came as a socialist in 1922, and left in 1934 as an opponent of Soviet communism. In those twelve years, he researched and wrote a classic two-volume history of the Russian Revolution that, along with Trotsky's account, remained for nearly a quarter of a century the principal narrative of 1917 and the civil war.[44] The *Nation*'s Louis Fischer (1890–1977) was an early Zionist, who became disillusioned when he served in the

---

41   Maurice Hindus, *A Traveler in Two Worlds*, intro. by Milton Hindus (Garden City: Doubleday, 1971), p. 311.

42   Eugene Lyons, *Assignment in Utopia* (New York: Harcourt Brace, 1937).

43   For a more extensive review of Hindus's work, see my foreword to Maurice Hindus's 1931 book *Red Bread: Collectivization in a Russian Village* (Bloomington and Indianapolis: Indiana University Press, 1988).

44   William Henry Chamberlin, *The Russian Revolution, 1917–1921* (New York: Macmillan, 1935; New York: Grosset & Dunlap, 1965).

Jewish Legion in Palestine and came to Russia in 1922 to find "a brighter future" in the "kingdom of the underdog." His two-volume study of Soviet foreign policy, *The Soviets in World Affairs* (1930), was a careful rebuttal to the polemics about Soviet international ambitions. Lyons was very friendly to the Soviets when he arrived in Moscow at the end of 1927 and wrote positively about Stalin in a 1931 interview, before he turned bitterly against them with his *Assignment in Utopia* (1937). Duranty, the acknowledged dean of the Moscow press corps, stayed for a decade and a half, won a Pulitzer Prize in 1932, refused to recognize the great famine in Ukraine of that year, and often justified what he observed with the phrase, "You can't make an omelet without breaking eggs."[45]

Several European journalists were more critical earlier than the Americans. Malcolm Muggeridge of the *Manchester Guardian* reported on the famine months before his American counterparts; and Paul Scheffer of the *Berliner Tageblatt* was refused re-entry after he wrote about the violence of mass collectivization. One of the most dramatic defections was by Max Eastman, a leftist celebrity, formerly the bohemian editor of the radical journal *Masses*, who had enjoyed notoriety as the representative of the Left Opposition in America and promoted Trotsky's line in *Since Lenin Died* (1925) and *Leon Trotsky: Portrait of a Youth* (1926). The translator of Trotsky's extraordinary *History of the Russian Revolution* (1932), he attacked Stalin's cultural policies in *Artists in Uniform* (1934). By the mid-1930s his doubts about Marxism led him to conclude that Stalinism was the logical outcome of Leninism, a position that Trotsky rejected.[46] In time, Eastman became a leading anti-Communist, even defending the necessity of "exposing" Communists during the McCarthy years.[47]

---

45 Engerman, *Modernization from the Other Side*, pp. 199–243; S. J. Taylor, *Stalin's Apologist: Walter Duranty: The New York Times's Man in Moscow* (New York and Oxford: Oxford University Press, 1990). See also the later controversy over rescinding Duranty's Pulitzer Prize: Jacques Steinberg, "Times Should Lose Pulitzer from 30's, Consultant Says," *New York Times*, October 23, 2003; "Word for Word/The Soft Touch: From Our Man in Moscow, In Praise of Stalinism's Future," ibid., October 26, 2003.

46 Alan M. Wald, *The New York Intellectuals: The Rise and Decline of the Anti-Stalinist Left from the 1930s to the 1980s* (Chapel Hill, NC: University of North Carolina Press, 1987), pp. 112–18, 154–6.

47 Ibid., p. 273. Eastman himself denied that he was ever a "follower" of Trotsky, though he was closely associated with the opposition to Stalin and Stalinism. See his "Biographical Introduction" to Max Eastman, *Reflections on the Failure of Socialism* (New York: Grosset & Dunlap, 1955), pp. 7-20.

The great ideological and political struggles that pitted liberals against conservatives, socialists against communists, the left and center against fascists intensified with the coming of the Great Depression. Like a litmus test of one's political loyalties, one's attitude toward the Soviet Union separated people who otherwise might have been allies. Communists by the 1930s were unquestioning supporters of Stalinism and the General Line. Their democratic critics included liberals and Europe's Social Democrats, among whom the exiled Mensheviks used their contacts within the country to contribute knowledgeable analyses in their journals and newspapers, most importantly *Sotsialisticheskii vestnik* (Socialist Herald). To their left were varieties of Trotskyists, most agreeing with Trotsky that the Soviet Union had suffered a Thermidorian reaction and become a degenerated workers' state.[48] For Trotsky the USSR was ruled, not by a dictatorship of the proletariat, but by "a hitherto unheard-of apparatus of compulsion," an uncontrolled bureaucracy dominating the masses.[49] Stalin's personal triumph was that of the bureaucracy, which perfectly reflected his own "petty bourgeois outlook," and his state had "acquired a totalitarian-bureaucratic character."[50] Impeccably Marxist, Trotsky provided an impressive structuralist alternative to the more common accounts based on national character or rationalization of the Soviet system as an effective model of statist developmentalism.

Along with Menshevik and Trotskyist critics of Stalinism, and Communist enthusiasts for Stalinism, an array of intellectuals, often referred to as "fellow-travelers," were swept along by the exciting transformations taking place in the USSR. Frightened by the virulent anti-Communism and violence of the fascists and Nazis, they buried their doubts about the evident poverty and brutality in the Soviet Union, at least for a while, and lauded the achievements (*dostizheniia* as the Russians exalted every success) of the Soviet system. The popular French writer Romain Rolland (1866–1944), author of the multivolume *Jean Christophe*, praised the Stalinist "revolution-from-above" of the First Five-Year Plan and accepted the invitation of his friend, Maxim Gorky, to visit the USSR in 1935. He was "fascinated with Stalin as an intellectual

---

48   Leon Trotsky, *The Revolution Betrayed: What Is the Soviet Union and Where Is It Going?*, trans. Max Eastman (1937; New York: Pathfinder Press, 1972), pp. 19, 47, 61.
49   Ibid., p. 52.
50   Ibid., pp. 93, 97, 108.

man of action, a kind of philosopher-king who bridged the old divide between thought and action."[51] Even when he was plagued by doubts about the state terror of the late 1930s and the Nazi–Soviet Pact, Rolland kept his personal pledge to Stalin, whom he addressed as "dear comrade," that it was his duty to defend the heroic victories of the Soviet Union.[52] On the French Left, however, Rolland was outflanked in his sympathy for the Soviets by the French Communist biographer of Stalin, Henri Barbusse (1873–1935), whose "authorized biography" dueled with the critical account by ex-Communist Boris Souvarine (1895–1984).[53]

In the second half of the 1930s, the threat posed by fascism intensified the personal, political, and psychological struggles of the politically minded and politically active. While some continued to embrace Stalinism, even as it devoured millions of its own people, as the best defense against the radical Right, others denounced the great experiment as a grand deception. The show trials of 1936–38 swept away loyal Bolsheviks, many of whom had been close comrades of Lenin, for their alleged links to an "anti-Soviet Trotskyite" conspiracy. John Dewey, novelist James T. Farrell, and other intellectuals formed the American Committee for the Defense of Leon Trotsky, and the "Dewey Commission" traveled to Coyoacan, Mexico, to interrogate Trotsky. It concluded that none of the charges leveled against Trotsky and his son was true.[54] But equally eminent intellectuals—among them Dreiser, Fischer, playwright Lillian Hellman, artist Rockwell Kent, author Nathaniel West, and journalist Heywood

51   Michael David-Fox, *Crossing Borders: Modernity, Ideology, and Culture in Russia and the Soviet Union* (Pittsburgh: University of Pittsburgh Press, 2015), p. 173.

52   Ibid., p. 175.

53   Henri Barbusse, *Stalin, Un monde nouveau à travers un homme* (Paris: Editions Carrefour, 1935); *Stalin: A New World Seen Through One Man*, trans. Vyvyan Beresford (London: Macmillan, 1935); Boris Souvarine, *Staline. Aperçu historique du bolchévisme* (Paris: Plon, 1935); *Stalin: A Critical Survey of Bolshevism*, trans. C. L. R. James (New York: Alliance, 1939). Souvarine continued to update his Stalin biography; the last version was *Staline. Aperçu historique du bolchévisme* (Paris: IVREA, 1992). See also Jean-Louis Panné, *Boris Souvarine. Le premier désenchanté du communisme* (Paris: Robert Laffont, 1993).

54   *The Case of Leon Trotsky: Report of Hearings on the Charges Made Against Him in the Moscow Trials by the Preliminary Commission of Inquiry* (New York: Merit Publishers, 1937); *Not Guilty: Report of the Commission of Inquiry into the Charges Made Against Leon Trotsky in the Moscow Trials* (New York: Harper & Brothers, 1938). See also Alan Wald, "Memories of the John Dewey Commission: Forty Years Later," *Antioch Review* (1977), pp. 438–51.

Broun—denounced the Commission's findings and urged American liberals not to support enemies of the USSR, "a country recognized as engaged in improving conditions for all its people" that should "be permitted to decide for itself what measures of protection are necessary against treasonable plots to assassinate and overthrow its leadership and involve it in war with foreign powers."[55] Confusion and self-delusion about the USSR affected even the American ambassador to Moscow, the political appointee Joseph E. Davies. The ambassador attended the trial of the prominent Communist Nikolai Bukharin, who was innocent of all charges of treachery, and left convinced that Old Bolsheviks had committed terrible, treasonous crimes.[56]

Stalin himself delivered the body blow to the faithful with the August 1939 non-aggression pact with Nazi Germany. Fellow travelers found it hard to travel down this road, and Communist parties around the world hemorrhaged members. The *New Republic*, which had supported the Soviet Union for decades, reversed itself when Stalin attacked Finland. Many who had resisted the concept of "totalitarianism," which collapsed Stalinism and Nazism into a single analytical category, suddenly saw merit in this formulation. In 1940 Edmund Wilson published *To the Finland Station*, an excursion through the prehistory and history of Marxism in thought and in power.[57] Once a Communist, later an admirer of Trotsky, Wilson questioned the sureties of his earlier faith and ended up with praise for Marxism's moral and social vision, while rejecting the authoritarianism and statism of the Soviet model.[58] Arthur Koestler (1905–1983), the son of Hungarian Jews, explored his loss of faith in the Communist movement in his novel *Darkness at Noon* (1940). Basing his hero on Bukharin, Koestler told the story of an idealistic Soviet leader, Rubashov, who agrees to confess to imaginary crimes as his last contribution to the revolutionary cause. Along with George Orwell's dystopian novels, Koestler's exploration into the mind of a Bolshevik would become one of the defining literary portraits in the anti-Communist arsenal in the post-war years.

---

55   "An Open Letter to American Liberals," *Soviet Russia Today* VI (March 1937), pp. 14–15; Filene, *American Views*, p. 119.

56   Joseph E. Davies, *Mission to Moscow* (New York: Simon & Schuster, 1941), pp. 269–72.

57   Edmund Wilson, *To the Finland Station: A Study in the Writing and Acting of History* (Garden City, NY: Doubleday, 1940; Anchor Books, 1953).

58   Wald, *The New York Intellectuals*, pp. 157–63.

With the Nazi invasion of the USSR in June 1941, attitudes shifted once again, spawning an outpouring of writing on Russia and the Soviet Union. Some 200 books were published in the United States in 1943–45 alone. Ambassador Davies's memoir, *Mission to Moscow* (December 1941), sold 700,000 copies and was memorialized in a splashy Hollywood film that lauded Soviet achievements, "convicted" those charged at the Moscow trials, justified the Soviet attack on Finland, and portrayed Stalin as a benignly avuncular patriarch. A grotesque piece of war propaganda, playing fast and loose with historical fact, the film was widely panned in the press, and leading "progressive" intellectuals, including Dewey, Dwight Macdonald, Wilson, Eastman, Sidney Hook, Farrell, and the leader of the Socialist Party of America, Norman Thomas, signed public protests against it. Four years after the film's opening in 1943, Warner Brothers reacted to the onset of the Cold War by ordering all release prints destroyed.[59]

One of the most important and influential scholarly works of the period was by the Russian-born émigré sociologist Nicholas S. Timasheff (1886–1970), whose *The Great Retreat* showed in detail how the Soviet state had abandoned its original revolutionary program and internationalist agenda in the mid-1930s and turned into a traditional Great Power.[60] Instead of the radical leveling of social classes of the early 1930s, Stalinism introduced new hierarchies based on wage differentials, education, party affiliation and loyalty to the state. This Great Retreat represented the triumph of the "national structure," Russian history, and the needs and desires of the people over "an anonymous body of international

---

59 Clayton R. Koppes and Gregory D. Black, *Hollywood Goes to War: How Politics, Profits and Propaganda Shaped World War II Movies* (New York: The Free Press, 1987; Berkeley and Los Angeles: University of California Press, 1990), pp. 185–221. Other pro-Soviet films of the war years included: *North Star*, written by Lillian Hellman; *Song of Russia*; *Days of Glory*; *Counter-Attack*; *Three Russian Girls*; and *Boy from Stalingrad*.

60 Nicholas S. Timasheff, *The Great Retreat: The Growth and Decline of Communism in Russia* (New York: E. P. Dutton, 1946). An earlier reference to "the Great Retreat" can be found in C. L. R. James, *World Revolution, 1917–1936: The Rise and Fall of the Communist International* (New York: Pioneer Publishers, 1937). Born in Trinidad, James (1901–1989) emigrated to Britain where he became a leading Trotskyist. Best known for his study of the Haitian Revolution, *The Black Jacobins* (1938), he was also the translator of Boris Souvarine's biography of Stalin into English.

workers."[61] Rather than betraying the revolution, the Retreat signaled its
nationalization and domestication, the victory of reality and "objective
facts" over utopianism and radical experimentation. The book appeared
in 1946, just after the highpoint of Soviet–American cooperation, clearly
a reflection of the Yalta spirit of the immediate pre–Cold War years.
Timasheff predicted that the revolutionary years were over; faith in the
Marxist doctrine had faded, and a future development toward democracy
was possible. Here he echoed his collaborator, fellow Russian-born sociologist Pitirim Sorokin (1889–1968) of Harvard, who in his *Russia and
the United States* (1944) proposed that Russia and the United States were
meant to be allies, not enemies, and that the two societies were indeed
converging along the lines of all other highly industrialized societies.
This "convergence thesis" would eventually become standard in the
modernization literature of the 1950s, and both in its introduction and its
elaboration formed part of a general political recommendation for understanding, tolerance, patience, and entente between the Soviet Union and
the Western powers.

The Cold War and Professional Sovietology

In late 1945, American public opinion was generally positive about the
Soviet Union. A *Fortune* poll in September showed that only a quarter of
the population believed that the USSR would attempt to spread communism into Eastern Europe. By July 1946, more than half of those polled
felt that Moscow aimed to dominate as much of the world as possible.[62]
Within government and in the public sphere, opposing formulations of
the Soviet Union contended with one another. Vice-president and later
Secretary of Commerce Henry A. Wallace used the Russian character to
explain why a "get tough with Russia" policy would only result in tougher
Russians. Others like Walter Lippmann warned that not recognizing
Soviet interests in Eastern Europe would lead to a "cold war." But far
more influential, and eventually hegemonic, were the views of a number
of State Department specialists, most importantly George Kennan, who
did not trust the Soviet leadership.

In 1946, Kennan sent his famous "Long Telegram" from Moscow,

61   Ibid., pp. 361–2.
62   John Lewis Gaddis, *The United States and the Origins of the Cold War, 1941–
1947* (New York and London: Columbia University Press, 1972), p. 321.

reiterating that Russian behavior was best explained by national characteristics. The inherent, intractable, immutable traits of the Russians as "Asiatics" required the use of countervailing force to contain the Soviets' aggressive tendencies. When he published his views in *Foreign Affairs*, famously signing the article "X," Kennan abruptly shifted his position from considering Marxism largely irrelevant to emphasizing the importance of Marxist doctrine. "The political personality of Soviet power as we know it today," he wrote, "is the product of ideology and circumstances: ideology inherited by the present Soviet leaders from the movement in which they had their political origin, and circumstances of the power which they now have exercised for nearly three decades in Russia."[63] Soviet ideology included the idea of the innate antagonism between capitalism and socialism and the infallibility of the Kremlin as the sole repository of truth. Though his explanation had changed from national character to ideology, Kennan's prescription for US foreign policy remained the same: the USSR was a rival, not a partner, and the United States had no other course but containment of Russian expansive tendencies.[64]

Under the imperatives of the American government's apprehension about Soviet expansionism, a profession of "Sovietologists" began to form, primarily in the United States. In 1946, the first American center of Russian studies, the Russian Institute, was founded at Columbia University, soon to be followed by the Russian Research Centre at Harvard (1948). The first "area studies" centers in the United States became prototypes for a new direction in social science research, bringing together various disciplines to look intensively at a particular society and culture. A generation of scholars, many of whom had had wartime experience in the military or in intelligence, worked closely with governmental agencies and on official projects sponsored by the Central Intelligence Agency or the military. Most importantly, the Air Force funded the Harvard Interview Project, questioning thousands of Soviet émigrés and producing valuable information on daily life and thought in the USSR, as well as guides for target selection and psychological warfare. In 1950, the Institute for the Study of the USSR was founded in Munich. Secretly funded by the CIA

---

63 'X' (George F. Kennan), "The Sources of Soviet Conduct," *Foreign Affairs* XXV (July 1947), p. 566.

64 The point about the shift from national character to ideology is made convincingly by Engerman, *Modernization from the Other Shore*, pp. 264–71.

until it was closed in 1971, the Institute produced numerous volumes and journals by émigré writers that confirmed the worst expectations of Western readers. More interesting to scholars was the American government-sponsored journal *Problems of Communism*, edited from 1952 to 1970 by a skeptical scion of the Polish Jewish Bund, Abraham Brumberg, which managed to condemn the Soviet Union as a totalitarian tyranny while avoiding the worst excesses of anti-Communist hysteria.

American scholars, particularly political scientists and sociologists, were caught in a schizophrenic tension between their disciplinary identity as detached scientists and their political commitment to (and often financial dependency on) the American state. The benefits of working in tandem with the interests of the state were enormous; the dangers of non-conformity were omnipresent. Two of the founders of Columbia's Russian Institute, Soviet legal expert John N. Hazard and Soviet literature specialist Ernest J. Simmons, were named by Senator McCarthy in 1953 as members of the "Communist conspiracy."[65] The intellectual historian H. Stuart Hughes was dismissed as associate director of Harvard's Russian Research Center when a trustee of the Carnegie Corporation, a major funder of the Center, complained that Hughes supported the 1948 Henry Wallace presidential campaign.[66] In Britain, the most prominent historian of Russia, E. H. Carr, reported in 1950 that "it had become very difficult . . . to speak dispassionately about Russia except in a 'very woolly Christian kind of way' without endangering, if not your bread and butter, then your legitimate hopes of advancement," and the Marxist historian Eric J. Hobsbawm affirmed that "there is no question that the principle of freedom of expression did not apply to communist and Marxist views, at least in the official media."[67]

The Totalitarian Model
With the collapse of the Grand Alliance, the more sympathetic renderings of Stalin's USSR, popular during the war, gave way to the powerful image

---

65 Stephen F. Cohen, *Rethinking the Soviet Experience: Politics and History Since 1917* (New York and Oxford: Oxford University Press, 1985), p. 17.

66 Charles Thomas O'Connell, "Social Structure and Science: Soviet Studies at Harvard" (Ph.D. diss., UCLA, 1990); Martin Oppenheimer, "Social Scientists and War Criminals," *New Politics* VI, 3 (new series) (Summer 1997), pp. 77–87.

67 Both citations are from Eric Hobsbawm, *Interesting Times: A Twentieth-Century Life* (London: Allen Lane, 2002), p. 183.

of "Red Fascism" that melded the practices of Nazi Germany with those of the Soviet Union.[68] In order to conceptualize these terror-based, one-party ideological regimes, political scientists elaborated the concept of "totalitarianism." Carl Friedrich (1901–1984) and Zbigniew Brzezinski formulated the classic definition of totalitarianism, with its six systemic characteristics: a ruling ideology, a single party typically led by one man, a terroristic police, a communications monopoly, a weapons monopoly, and a centrally directed economy.[69] Such states, with their mass manipulation, suppression of voluntary associations, violence, and expansionism, were contrasted with liberal democratic, pluralistic societies. Because such systems were able so effectively to suppress internal dissension, many theorists concluded they would never change unless overthrown from outside.

The T-model dominated scholarship, particularly in political science, through the 1950s and well into the 1960s, a time when the academy was intimately involved in the global struggle that pitted the West against the Soviet Union, its "satellite" states, and anti-colonial nationalism. The model of a gargantuan prison state, "a huge reformatory in which the primary difference between the forced labor camps and the rest of the Soviet Union is that inside the camps the regimen is much more brutal and humiliating," was compelling—both because high Stalinism matched much of the image of a degenerated autocracy, and because Soviet restrictions and censorship eliminated most other sources, like travelers, journalists, and scholars with in-country experience.[70] The image of an imperialist totalitarianism, spreading its red grip over the globe, was at one and the same time the product of Western anxieties and the producer of inflated fears. George Orwell (1903–1950), already well-known for his satire on Soviet politics, *Animal Farm* (1945), produced the most effective literary vision of totalitarianism in his popular novel *1984* (1949). Its

---

68   Les K. Adler and Thomas G. Paterson, "Red Fascism: The Merger of Nazi Germany and Soviet Russia in the American Image of Totalitarianism, 1930's–1950's," *American Historical Review* LXXV, 4 (April 1970), pp. 1046–64.

69   Carl J. Friedrich and Zbigniew K. Brzezinski, *Totalitarian Dictatorship and Autocracy* (Cambridge, MA: Harvard University Press, 1956; revised ed., New York: Frederick A. Praeger, 1966), p. 22. See also Carl J. Friedrich (ed.), *Totalitarianism* (Cambridge, MA: Harvard University Press, 1954; New York: Grosset & Dunlap, 1964).

70   Merle Fainsod, *How Russia Is Ruled* (Cambridge, MA: Harvard University Press, 1953), p. 482.

hero, Winston Smith, tries valiantly to revolt against the totally adminis-
tered society presided over by Big Brother, but by novel's end he has been
ground into submission and spouts the doublespeak slogans of the
regime. The political philosopher Hannah Arendt (1906–1975), a refugee
from Nazism, provided the most sophisticated and subtle interpretation
of *The Origins of Totalitarianism*, which she connected to anti-Semitism,
nationalism, pan-national movements, imperialism, and the replacement
of class politics by mass politics.[71]

Scholars explained the origins and spread of totalitarianism in various
ways. Arendt linked totalitarianism with the coming of mass democracy;
Waldemar Gurian saw the source in the utopian ambitions of leftist politicians; Stefan Possony tied it to the personality of Lenin; Robert C.
Tucker to the personality of Stalin; and Nathan Leites employed psycho-
analytic concepts to write about the psychopathology of the Bolshevik
elite, distinguished primarily by paranoia. The anthropologists Geoffrey
Gorer and Margaret Mead reverted to the ever-handy notion of national
character, in this case patterns of inbred submissiveness to authority
caused by the peasant practice of swaddling Russian infants.[72] In 1947
Mead, then the most famous anthropologist in the United States,

> secured funding from the Air Force's new think tank, the Rand
> Corporation, to set up a Studies in Soviet Culture Project, recruiting
> Gorer [her lover at the time] to run it. Gorer had never been to Russia
> and didn't speak the language, but ignorance only made his work
> easier. He quickly discovered the key that would unlock the Russian

---

71 Hannah Arendt, *The Origins of Totalitarianism* (New York: Harcourt, Brace,
1951). For a history of the concept of totalitarianism, see Abbott Gleason,
Totalitarianism: The Inner History of the Cold War (New York and Oxford: Oxford
University Press, 1995).

72 This catalogue of causes is indebted to Alfred Meyer, "Coming to Terms with
the Past," *Russian Review* XLV, 4 (October 1986), p. 403; Waldemar Gurian, *Bolshevism:
An Introduction to Soviet Communism* (Notre Dame, IN: University of Notre Dame
Press, 1956); Stefan Possony, *Lenin: The Compulsive Revolutionary* (Chicago: Henry
Regnery, 1964); Robert C. Tucker, *Stalin As Revolutionary, 1879–1929* (New York: W. W.
Norton, 1973); Margaret Mead, *Soviet Attitudes Toward Authority: An Interdisciplinary
Approach to Problems of Soviet Character* (New York: McGraw-Hill, 1951); Nathan
Leites, *The Operational Code of the Politburo* (New York: McGraw-Hill, 1951); *A
Study of Bolshevism* (Glencoe, IL: Free Press, 1953); Geoffrey Gorer and John Rickman,
The People of Great Russia: A Psychological Study (New York: Chanticleer Press, 1950).

psyche: swaddling. Russian children, bound and swaddled in infancy, would naturally turn into paranoid and authoritarian adults, with repressed longings for warm-water harbors.[73]

Russians, it was concluded in one study, were not quite like other human beings. "They endure physical suffering with great stoicism and are indifferent about the physical sufferings of others . . . [Therefore] No techniques are yet available for eradicating the all-pervasive suspicion which Great Russians, leaders and led alike, feel towards the rest of the world. This suspicion springs from unconscious and therefore irrational sources and will not be calmed, more than momentarily, by rational actions."[74]

The positive vision of "civic education" put forth in the 1920s gave way to the image of "brain-washing." In 1949 George Counts (1907–1974), who eighteen years earlier had written *The Soviet Challenge to America* (1931), now co-authored with Nucia Lodge *The Country of the Blind: The Soviet System of Mind Control* (1949). The totalitarian approach turned an apt if not wholly accurate description into a model, complete with predictions of future trajectories. The concept exaggerated similarities and underestimated differences between quite distinct regimes, ignoring the contrast between an egalitarian, internationalist doctrine (Marxism) that the Soviet regime failed to realize and the inegalitarian, racist and imperialist ideology (fascism) that the Nazis implemented only too well. Little was said about the different dynamics in a state capitalist system with private ownership of property (Nazi Germany), and those operating in a completely state-dominated economy with almost no production for the market (Stalin's USSR); or about how an advanced industrial economy geared essentially to war and territorial expansion (Nazi Germany) differed from a program for modernizing a backward, peasant society and transforming it into an industrial, urban one (Stalinist Soviet Union). The T-model led many political scientists and historians to deal almost exclusively with the state, the center and the top of the political pyramid, and make deductions from a supposedly fixed ideology, while largely ignoring social dynamics and the shifts and

73 Thomas Meaney, "The Swaddling Thesis," a review of Peter Mandler, *Return from the Natives: How Margaret Mead Won the Second World War and Lost the Cold War* (New Haven: Yale University Press, 2013), in *London Review of Books*, March 6, 2014, p. 34.

74 Gorer and Rickman, *The People of Great Russia*, pp. 189, 191–2.

improvisations that characterized both Soviet and Nazi policies. Even more pernicious were the predictive parallels: since Nazi Germany had acted in an expansionist, aggressive way, it could be expected that another totalitarian regime would also be aggressive and expansionist. Indeed, during the Cold War, Western media and governments fostered the notion that the USSR was poised and ready to invade Western Europe. Any concessions to Soviet communism were labeled "appeasement," a direct analogy to Western negotiations with the Nazis in the 1930s.

Ironically, not only changing reality but the findings of specific studies belied the model. The most influential text, Merle Fainsod's *How Russia Is Ruled*, the key text in the field for over a decade, appeared within months of Stalin's death and saw little evidence that the Soviet system would change. Yet later when Fainsod (1907–1972) used an extraordinary cache of Soviet archives captured by the German invaders to write a ground-breaking study, *Smolensk Under Soviet Rule* (1958), he exposed a level of complexity that made "generalizing processes" like "urbanisation, industrialisation, collectivisation, secularisation, bureaucratisation, and totalitarianisation ... seem rather pallid and abstract."[75] His younger colleague, Barrington Moore, Jr. (1913–2005), asked the important question regarding the relationship between Leninist ideology and the actual policies and products of the Soviet regime under Stalin, and concluded that the Bolshevik ideology of ends—greater equality, empowerment of working people, internationalism—had been trumped by the Bolshevik ideology of means—"the need for authority and discipline." The "means have swallowed up and distorted the original ends." Instead of "humane anarchism," the very elasticity of Communist doctrine allowed for the entry of nationalism, pragmatism, and inequalities that ultimately used anti-authoritarian ideas to justify and support an authoritarian regime.[76] In a second book, Moore shifted from a language of

---

75 Merle Fainsod, *Smolensk Under Soviet Rule* (Cambridge, MA: Harvard University Press, 1958; Rand Corporation, 1958; Vintage Books, 1963), p. 446. For a Russian look at the effect of the Smolensk archive on American Sovietology, see Evgenii Kodin, *'Smolenskii arkhiv' i amerikanskaia sovetlogiia* (Smolensk: SGPU, 1998).

76 Barrington Moore, Jr., *Soviet Politics—The Dilemma of Power: The Role of Ideas in Social Change* (Cambridge, MA: Harvard University Press, 1950; New York: Harper Torchbook, 1965), pp. 1–12, 402–5, 430. See also his *Terror and Progress: Some Sources of Change and Stability in the Soviet Dictatorship* (Cambridge, MA: Harvard University Press, 1954; New York: Harper Torchbook, 1966).

authority to the then current vocabulary of totalitarianism and elaborated a set of possible scenarios for the USSR, ranging from a rationalist technocracy to a traditionalist despotism. The Soviet state would continue to require terror, however, if it meant to remain a dynamic regime.[77]

As the Cold War consensus of the 1950s gave way to a growing discomfort with American policy, especially when containment of the Soviet threat turned into the military intervention in Vietnam, the Soviet Union itself was evolving away from Stalinism. Nikita Khrushchev ended the indiscriminate mass terror, loosened the state's hold on the population, and opened small windows to the West. Increasingly, the regime attempted to govern through material satisfaction of popular needs and encouraged popular initiative. Persuasion and delivering material goods replaced the punishing terror of Stalinism. The monolithic Soviet empire in Eastern Europe showed signs of what was called "polycentrism," a variety of "roads to socialism," with somewhat increased autonomy, if not real independence, from the Kremlin. And, after nearly two decades of T-model dominance, the first serious critiques of totalitarianism appeared, first from political scientists and later from historians.

In 1965, Princeton political scientist and former diplomat Robert C. Tucker attempted to refine the concept of totalitarianism by analyzing the personalities of the dictators. He concluded that the system of totalitarianism was not the cause of the massive violence of the late 1930s, rather, terror was in large part an expression of the needs of the dictatorial personality of Stalin.[78] In a more radical vein, Herbert J. Spiro and Benjamin R. Barber claimed that the concept of totalitarianism was the foundation of "American Counter-Ideology" in the Cold War years. Totalitarianism theory had played an important role in the reorientation of American foreign policy by helping "to explain away German and Japanese behavior under the wartime regimes and thereby to justify the radical reversal of alliances after the war." A purported "logic of totalitarianism" provided an all-encompassing explanation of Communist behavior, which led to suspicion of liberation movements in Third World, a sense that international law and organizations were insufficiently strong

---

77   Moore, *Terror and Progress*, pp. xiii–xiv, 173–4, 179–231.

78   Robert C. Tucker, "The Dictator and Totalitarianism," *World Politics* XVII, 4 (July 1965), pp. 555–83.

to thwart totalitarian movements, and a justification of "the consequent necessity of considering the use of force—even thermonuclear force—in the settlement of world issues."[79] Totalitarian theory was a deployed ideological construction of the world that denied its own ideological nature, at a time when leading American thinkers proclaimed "the end of ideology."[80]

Scholars had to shift their views or jigger with the model. For Merle Fainsod in 1953, terror had been the "linchpin of modern totalitarianism," but ten years after Stalin's death he revised that sentence to read: "Every totalitarian regime makes some place for terror in its system of controls." In 1956, Brzezinski wrote that terror is "the most universal characteristic of totalitarianism."[81] But, in 1962, he reconsidered: terror is no longer essential; the USSR is now a "voluntarist totalitarian system" in which "persuasion, indoctrination, and social control can work more effectively."[82] Yet, in that same year, Harvard political scientist Adam B. Ulam insisted that "the essence of the Soviet political system" lies not in "transient aberrations arising out of willful and illegal acts of individuals," but is, rather, "imposed by the logic of totalitarianism." Given the immutable laws that follow from that logic, "in a totalitarian state terror

79   Herbert J. Spiro and Benjamin R. Barber presented a paper on totalitarianism at the 1967 meeting of the American Political Science Association. The quotations here are from the published version, "Counter-Ideological Uses of 'Totalitarianism,'" in *Politics and Society* I, 1 (November 1970), pp. 3–21 (p. 9); see also Herbert J. Spiro, "Totalitarianism," *International Encyclopedia of the Social Sciences* (New York: Macmillan and Free Press, 1968–1976), XVI, pp. 106b–112b. At the invitation of William G. Rosenberg of the University of Michigan I presented a paper on the panel, "Uses of the Soviet Past—A Critical Review," at the 1970 meeting of the American Association for the Advancement of Slavic Studies. The response from many in the audience to the paper, "The Abuses of the Soviet Past," which primarily criticized the totalitarian model, was hostile, even accusatory. I decided not to pursue this line of inquiry in print until many years later.

80   On the end of ideology discussion, see Daniel Bell, *The End of Ideology: On the Exhaustion of Political Ideas in the Fifties* (Glencoe, IL: The Free Press, 1960; Cambridge, MA: Harvard University Press, 2000); and Nils Gilman, *Mandarins of the Future: Modernization Theory in Cold War America* (Baltimore: Johns Hopkins University Press, 2003), pp. 56–62, 109–10.

81   Zbigniew K. Brzezinski, *The Permanent Purge—Politics in Soviet Totalitarianism* (Cambridge, MA: Harvard University Press, 1956), p. 27.

82   Zbigniew K. Brzezinski, *Ideology and Power in Soviet Politics* (New York: Praeger, 1962), pp. 80, 88–9.

can never be abolished entirely."[83] When the evidence of the waning of terror appeared to undermine that argument, Ulam spoke of a "sane pattern of totalitarianism, in contrast to the extreme of Stalin's despotism" and "claimed that terror was "interfering with the objectives of totalitarianism itself."[84] But since Stalinism itself had earlier been seen as the archetype of totalitarianism, and terror its essence, Ulam inadvertently laid bare the fundamental confusion and contradictions of the concept.

From the mid-1960s, a younger generation of historians, many of them excited by the possibilities of a "social history" that looked beyond the state to examine society, were traveling to the Soviet Union through expanded academic exchange programs. The luckiest among them were privileged to work in heavily restricted archives, but all of them saw firsthand the intricacies, complexities, and contradictions of everyday Soviet life that fit poorly with the totalitarian image of ubiquitous fear and rigid conformity. Stimulated by the idea of a "history from below," social historians pointed out that by concentrating on the political elite and the repressive apparatus, the totalitarian approach neglected to note that in the actual experience of these societies the regime was unable to achieve the full expectation of the totalitarian model, that is, the absolute and total control over the whole of society and the atomization of the population. What was truly totalitarian in Stalinism or Nazism were the intentions and aspirations of rulers like Hitler or Stalin, who may have had ambitions to create a society in which the party and the people were one, and in which the interests of all were harmonized and all dissent destroyed. But the control of so-called totalitarian states was never so total as to turn the people into "little screws" (*vintiki*, Stalin's word) to do the bidding of the state. Despite all the limitations of the model, scholars writing in this tradition illuminated anomalous aspects of the Stalinist and post-Stalinist regimes that contradicted the fundaments of the totalitarianism paradigm. At the same time, though less widely regarded, critics of liberalism and market society, from the Marxists of the Frankfurt

---

83 Adam B. Ulam, "The Russian Political System," in Samuel H. Beer and Adam B. Ulam (eds.), *Patterns of Government: The Major Political Systems of Europe*, 2nd ed. rev. (New York: Random House, 1962), pp. 670, 656, 646; cited in Spiro and Barber, "Counter-Ideological Uses," pp. 13–14.

84 Ulam, "The Russian Political System," p. 646; Spiro and Barber, "Counter-Ideological Uses," p. 19.

School to post-modernist cultural theorists, took note of the "totalitarian" effects of modernity more generally—of technology, industrialism, commercialism, and capitalism—which were excluded from the original model.[85]

The Modernization Paradigm

The Cold War American academy celebrated the achievements of American society and politics, which had reached an unprecedented level of stability and prosperity. Historians of the "consensus school" held that Americans were united by their shared fundamental values; political scientists compared the pluralistic, democratic norm of the United States to other societies, usually unfavorably. America was "the good society itself in operation," "with the most developed set of political and class relations," "the image of the European future," a model for the rest of the globe.[86] Western social science worked from an assumed Western master narrative brought to bear on non-Western societies: they too were expected to evolve as had Western Europe from theocratic to secular values, from status to contract, from more restricted to freer capitalist economies, from *Gemeinschaft* to *Gesellschaft*, in a word, from tradition to modernity.

Elaborating ideas from the classical social theorists Emile Durkheim and Max Weber, modernization theory proposed that societies would progressively assume greater control over nature and human suffering through developments in science, technology, mass education, economic growth, and urbanization. While Marxism may also be understood as a theory of modernization, complete with its own theory of history that reached beyond capitalism to socialism, what might be called "liberal modernization theory" was elaborated in opposition to Marxism and claimed that the best road to modernity lay through capitalism (though

---

85 Key texts for the Marxists are: Max Horkheimer and Theodor W. Adorno, *Dialectic of Enlightenment* (New York: Seabury Press, 1972), originally published as *Dialektik der Aufklärung* (New York: Social Studies Association, 1944); Herbert Marcuse, *Soviet Marxism: A Critical Analysis* (New York: Columbia University Press, 1958); *One-Dimensional Man* (Boston: Beacon Press, 1964); and *Negations* (Boston: Beacon Press, 1968). For post-modernist critics, see Zygmunt Bauman, *Modernity and the Holocaust* (Ithaca, NY: Cornell University Press, 1989); and his *Intimations of Postmodernity* (London and New York: Routledge, 1992).

86 From Seymour Martin Lipset, *Political Man: The Social Bases of Politics* (Garden City, NJ: Doubleday, 1960), as cited in Oren, *Our Enemies and US*, p. 126.

not necessarily through democracy as well), with no necessary transcendence to a post-capitalist socialism.[87] Since the modern was usually construed to be American liberal capitalist democracy, this powerful, evolving discourse of development and democracy legitimized a new post-colonial role for the developed world vis-à-vis the underdeveloped. The West would lead the less fortunate into prosperity and modernity, stability and progress, and the South (and later the East) would follow.

Modernizationists divided between optimists, who held that all people had the capacity to reach Western norms if they had the will or managed the transition properly, and pessimists, who believed that not all non-Western cultures were able to modernize and reach democracy. For an optimist like Gabriel Almond (1911–2002), one of the most prominent comparative politics scholars of his generation, human history was generally seen to be progressive, leading upward, inevitably, to something that looked like the developed West.[88] Classic works such as Seymour Martin Lipset's *Political Man: The Social Bases of Politics* (1960) and Almond and Sidney Verba's *The Civic Culture* (1963) considered a democratic political culture with civic values of trust and tolerance, crucial prerequisites for democracy that would somehow have to be instilled in modernizing societies. Democracy, development, and anti-communism were values that went together. As in the years following World War I, so during the Cold War, poverty was not only undesirable but a positive danger, precisely because it enflamed minds and could potentially lead to communism.

The Soviet Union presented the modernizationists with an anomalous example of a perverse road to modernity that looked very seductive to anti-imperialist revolutionaries. With American scholarship intimately linked to the global struggle against Soviet communism, the modernization paradigm both provided an argument for the universal developmental pattern from traditional society to modern, a path that the Third

---

87 The classic statement on the priority of order over democracy in the process of development can be found in Samuel P. Huntington, *Political Order in Changing Societies* (New Haven: Yale University Press, 1968). Huntington saw the USSR and other Soviet-style states as examples of a high level of development and social stability. On modernization theory, see Gilman, *Mandarins of the Future: Modernization Theory in Cold War America*.

88 Gabriel Almond, *Political Development: Essays in Heuristic Theory* (Boston: Little, Brown, 1970), p. 232.

World was fated to follow, and touted the superiority and more complete modernity of capitalist democracy American-style. A team of researchers and writers at MIT's Center for International Studies (CENIS) worked in the modernization mode, developing analyses of the deviant Soviet road. CENIS, a conduit between the university community and the national government, had been established with CIA funding and was directed by Max Millikan, former assistant director of the intelligence agency. No specialist on the Soviet Union, the MIT economic historian Walt Whitman Rostow (1916–2003) published *The Dynamics of Soviet Society* (1952), in which he and his team argued that Soviet politics and society were driven by the "priority of power." Where ideology came into conflict with the pursuit of power, ideology lost out.[89] After being turned over to the CIA and the State Department, and vetted by Philip E. Mosley (1905–1972) of Columbia's Russian Institute and others before it was declassified and published, Rostow's study was released to the public as a work of independent scholarship.[90]

In his later and much more influential book, *The Stages of Economic Growth: A Non-Communist Manifesto* (1960), Rostow proposed that peoples moved from traditional society through the preconditions for take-off, to take-off, on to the drive to maturity, and finally to the age of high mass-consumption. He trumpeted that Russia, "as a great nation, well endowed by nature and history to create a modern economy and a modern society," was in fact developing parallel to the West.[91] But traditional society gave way slowly in Russia, and its take-off came only in the mid-1890s, thirty years after the United States, and its drive to maturity in

---

89   W. W. Rostow and Alfred Levin, *The Dynamics of Soviet Society* (New York: W. W. Norton, 1952; Mentor Books, 1954), p. 89.

90   Allan A. Needell, "Project Troy and the Cold War Annexation of the Social Sciences," in Christopher Simpson (ed.), *Universities and Empire: Money and Politics in the Social Sciences During the Cold War* (New York: The New Press, 1998), p. 23; Bruce Cumings, "Boundary Displacement: Area Studies and International Studies During and After the Cold War," in ibid., pp. 167–8. Then at Harvard, historian Robert V. Daniels worked on the project at MIT because Harvard had a rule against classified research and farmed such work out to other institutions. Daniels disagreed with Rostow's single factor analysis—that the pursuit of power was a complete explanation—and eventually broke with Rostow over authorial credit before the commercial publication of the book. [Personal communication with the author, March 19, 2004.]

91   W. W. Rostow, *The Stages of Economic Growth: A Non-Communist Manifesto* (Cambridge: Cambridge University Press, 1960), p. 104.

the first five-year plans. Its growth was remarkable, but there was no need for alarm in the West, for its growth was built on under-consumption. Communism, which for Rostow was "a disease of the transition," "is likely to wither in the age of high mass-consumption."[92]

Most Sovietologists shared the general assumptions of modernization theory, and the most fervent adherents of the totalitarian concept made valiant attempts to preserve the T-model in the face of the challenge from the more dynamic modernization paradigm, or to reconcile the two. In a 1961 discussion, Brzezinski distinguished between the "totalitarian breakthrough" of Stalinism that destroyed the old order and created the framework for the new and the post-terror totalitarianism of the Khrushchev period.[93] The latter looked much more like the corporate system described by John Armstrong (1922–2010) in his study of Ukrainian bureaucrats, managed by the "Red Executives" analyzed by David Granick (1926–1990) and Joseph Berliner (1921–2001).[94] Brzezinski pointed out that Soviet ideology was no longer about revolution but the link that legitimized the rule of the party by tying it to the project of technical and economic modernization. Whereas Brzezinski argued that "indoctrination has replaced terror as the most distinctive feature of the system," Alfred G. Meyer (1920–1998) went further: "acceptance and internalization of the central principles of the ideology have replaced both terror and frenetic indoctrination." In what he called "spontaneous totalitarianism," Meyer noted that "Soviet citizens have become more satisfied, loyal, and co-operative."[95] The USSR was

92 Ibid., pp. 163, 133. Rostow later became a key advisor to President Lyndon Baines Johnson and an architect of the American intervention in Vietnam.

93 Zbigniew Brzezinski, "The Nature of the Soviet System," *Slavic Review* XX, 3 (October 1961), pp. 351–68.

94 David Granick, *The Red Executive: A Study of the Organization Man in Russian Industry* (Garden City, NY: Doubleday, 1960); Joseph S. Berliner, *Factory and Manager in the USSR* (Cambridge: Harvard University Press, 1957).

95 Brzezinski, "The Nature of the Soviet System"; Alfred G. Meyer, "USSR, Incorporated," *Slavic Review* XX, 3 (October 1961), pp. 369–76. Among the most influential authorities on modernization theory as applied to the Soviet Union was Princeton's Cyril E. Black, who edited *The Transformation of Russian Society: Aspects of Social Change Since 1861* (Cambridge, MA: Harvard University Press, 1960), and later organized the team that published Cyril E. Black, Marius B. Jansen, Herbert S. Levine, Marion J. Levy, Jr., Henry Rosovsky, Gilbert Rozman, Henry D. Smith, II, S. Frederick Starr, *The Modernization of Japan and Russia: A Comparative Study* (New York: Free Press, 1975).

simply a giant "company town" in which all of life is organized by the company.

The two models, however, differed fundamentally. The T-model was based on sharp differences between communist and liberal societies, while the modernization paradigm proposed a universal and shared development. For many writing in the modernization mode, the Soviet Union appeared as less aberrant than in the earlier model, a somewhat rougher alternative program of social and economic development. While some writers expected that the outcome of modernization would be democratic, more conservative authors were willing to settle for stability and order rather than representation of the popular will. For Samuel P. Huntington (1927–2008), a critic of liberal modernization theory, Communists were not only good at overthrowing governments but at making them. "They may not provide liberty, but they do provide authority; they do create governments that can govern."[96]

By the 1960s, it was evident to observers from the Right and Left that the Soviet Union had recovered from the practice of mass terror, was unlikely to return to it, and was slowly evolving into a modern, articulated urban society sharing many features with other developed countries. In the years when modernization theory, and its kissing cousin, convergence theory, held sway, the overall impression was that the Soviet Union could become a much more benign society and tolerable enemy than had been proposed by the totalitarian theorists.[97] Later conservative critics would read this rejection of exceptionalism as a failure to emphasize adequately the stark differences between the West and the Soviet Bloc, and to suggest a "moral equivalence" between them.

---

96 Huntington, *Political Order in Changing Societies*, p. 8; Gilman, *Mandarins of the Future*, pp. 228–34.

97 Among works in the "modernization school" that continued to subscribe to the language of totalitarianism, one might include Raymond A. Bauer, Alex Inkeles and Clyde Kluckhohn, *How the Soviet System Works: Cultural, Psychological and Social Themes* (Cambridge, MA: Harvard University Press, 1956; New York: Vintage Books, 1961); Alex Inkeles and Raymond A. Bauer, *The Soviet Citizen: Daily Life in a Totalitarian Society* (Cambridge, MA: Harvard University Press, 1961). Moshe Lewin, *Political Undercurrents of Soviet Economic Debates: From Bukharin to the Modern Reformers* (Princeton: Princeton University Press, 1974) uses a modified modernization framework but without the liberal telos. For an account that rejects the convergence thesis, see Zbigniew Brzezinski and Samuel Huntington, *Political Power: USA/USSR* (New York: Viking Press, 1964).

Deploying the anodyne language of social science, modernization theory seemed to some to apologize for the worst excesses of Soviet socialism and excuse the violence and forceful use of state power as a necessary externality of development. Social disorder, violence, even genocide could be explained as part of the modernization process. If Mustafa Kemal Atatürk was acceptable as a modernizer, why not Lenin or Stalin?[98]

Alternatives

Even though government and many scholars were deeply invested in an unmodulated condemnation of all Soviet policies and practices from the late 1940s through much of the 1960s, no single discourse ever dominated Russian/Soviet studies. A number of influential scholars—E. H. Carr (1892–1982), Isaac Deutscher (1907–1967), Theodore von Laue (1916–2000), Alec Nove (1915–1994), Moshe Lewin (1921–2010), Alexander Dallin (1924–2000), and Robert C. Tucker (1918–2010)—offered alternative pictures of the varieties of Bolshevism and possible trajectories. Edward Hallett Carr was a British diplomat, a journalist, a distinguished realist theorist of international relations, an advocate of appeasement in the 1930s, a philosopher of history, and the prolific author of a multi-volume history of the Soviet Union, 1917–29.[99] Even in the 1930s, when Carr had been sympathetic to the Soviet project, what he called "the Religion of the Kilowatt and the Machine," he was critical of Western Communists and "fellow travelers," like the British Marxist economist Maurice Dobb (1900–1976) and the Fabian socialists Beatrice and Sidney Webb, who ignored the "darker sides of the Soviet regime" and defended

---

98 In a famous essay (April 1962) in the journal *Encounter*, economic historian Alec Nove asked, "Was Stalin Really Necessary?" And he concluded that the "whole-hog Stalin . . . was not 'necessary', but the possibility of a Stalin was a necessary consequence of the effort of a minority group to keep power and to carry out a vast social-economic revolution in a very short time. And *some* elements were, in those circumstances, scarcely avoidable." *Was Stalin Really Necessary? Some Problems of Soviet Political Economy* (London: Allen & Unwin, 1964), pp. 17–39, p. 32. See also James Millar and Alec Nove, "A Debate on Collectivization: Was Stalin Really Necessary?" *Problems of Communism* XXV (July–August 1976), pp. 49–66.

99 Jonathan Haslam, *The Vices of Integrity: E. H. Carr, 1892–1982* (London and New York: Verso, 1999); E. H. Carr, *A History of Soviet Russia*, 14 vols. (London and Basingstoke: Macmillan, 1950–1978).

them "by transparent sophistry."[100] During World War II, at the moment when the Soviet army and popular endurance halted the Nazi advance, Carr "revived [his] initial faith in the Russian revolution as a great achievement and a historical turning-point." "Looking back on the 1930s," he later wrote, "I came to feel that my preoccupation with the purges and brutalities of Stalinism had distorted my perspective. The black spots were real enough, but looking exclusively at them destroyed one's vision of what was really happening."[101] For more than thirty years, Carr worked on his Soviet history as a story of a desperate and valiant attempt to go beyond bourgeois capitalism in a country where capitalism was weak, democracy absent, and the standard of living abysmally low. Politically, Carr was committed to democratic socialism, to a greater equality than was found in most capitalist societies. He believed in public control and planning of the economic process, and a stronger state exercising remedial and constructive functions.[102] Shortly before his death, he glumly remarked to his collaborator Tamara Deutscher: "The left is foolish and the right is vicious."[103]

His volume on the Bolshevik revolution appeared in 1950 and challenged the dominant émigré historiography on the October revolution as a sinister coup d'état. Carr stood between the Mensheviks, who thought that bourgeois democracy could have been built in Russia, and the Bolsheviks, who took the risk of seizing power in a country ill-prepared for "a direct transition from the most backward to the most advanced forms of political and economic organization . . . without the long experience and training which bourgeois democracy, with all its faults, had afforded in the west."[104] Turning later to the 1920s, Carr eschewed a struggle-for-power tale for a narrative that placed the feuding Bolsheviks within the larger economic and social setting. He tied Stalin's victories

---

100   R. W. Davies, "Introduction" to Edward Hallett Carr, *The Russian Revolution, From Lenin to Stalin (1917–1929)* (London: Palgrave, 2003), pp. xvi–xvii; Maurice Dobb, *Soviet Economic Development Since 1917* (London: Routledge, 1948); Beatrice and Sidney Webb, *Soviet Communism: A New Civilisation?*, 2 vols. (London: Longmans, Green, 1935).

101   Cited in Davies, "Introduction," p. xvii.

102   Ibid., p. xviii.

103   Tamara Deutscher, "E. H. Carr—A Personal Memoir," *New Left Review* 137 (January-February 1983), p. 85.

104   E. H. Carr, *A History of Soviet Russia: The Bolshevik Revolution, 1917–1923*, I (London: Macmillan, 1950: Pelican Books, 1966), p. 111.

over Trotsky, Zinoviev, and Bukharin to his ability to sense and manipulate opportunities that arose from the play of social forces. Still later, Carr argued that collectivization was unavoidable, given Russia's limited resources for industrialization, and on this issue he differed from his collaborator, R. W. Davies (b. 1925), who had become convinced that industrialization at a modest pace had been possible within the framework of the New Economic Policy.[105] Carr's work was criticized for its sense of inevitability that tended to justify what happened as necessary and to avoid alternative possibilities.[106] Yet in its extraordinary breadth and depth (a study of twelve momentous years in fourteen volumes), Carr's history combined a sensitivity to political contingency, as in his analysis of Stalin's rise, and an attention to personality and character, as in his different assessments of Lenin and Stalin, with attention to structural determinations, like the ever-present constraints of Russian backwardness.

Carr's friend, Isaac Deutscher, was a life-long rebel: a Jew who broke with religious orthodoxy and wrote poetry in Polish; a bourgeois who joined the outlawed Communist Party of Poland; a Communist who in 1932 was expelled from the party for his anti-Stalinist opposition; a Trotskyist who remained independent and critical of the movement; and finally a historian who produced some of the most important works on Soviet history in his day, but was shunned by academia.[107] In exile in England, both from his native Poland and the Communist milieu in which he had matured, Deutscher turned first to journalism and then to a

---

105   Davies, "Introduction," p. xxxiv.

106   Carr's critics were often impressed by his industriousness and command of the material, but wary of his stances toward the Soviet Union. Historian James Billington wrote: "The work is scrupulously honest and thorough in detail, but the perspective of the whole remains that of a restrained but admiring recording angel of the Leninist Central Committee." *World Politics* (April 1966), p. 463. And even his good friend Isaac Deutscher thought Carr too much the political instead of social historian, who "is inclined to view the State as the maker of society rather than society the maker of the State." *Soviet Studies*, VI (1954–1955), p. 340; Isaac Deutscher, *Heretics and Renegades and Other Essays* (Indianapolis and New York: Bobbs-Merrill, 1969), p. 95; cited in Davies, "Introduction," p. xxx.

107   Tamara Deutscher, "On the Bibliography of Isaac Deutscher's Writings," *Canadian Slavic Studies* III, 3 (Fall 1969), pp. 473–89. See also the reminiscences in David Horowitz (ed.), *Isaac Deutscher: The Man and His Work* (London: MacDonald, 1971); and David Caute, *Isaac and Isaiah: The Covert Punishment of a Cold War Heretic* (New Haven: Yale University Press, 2013).

biography of Stalin, which appeared in 1949.[108] A "study [of] the politics rather than the private affairs of Stalin," this monumental work by "an unrepentant Marxist" challenged the liberal and conservative orthodoxies of the Cold War years and sought to rescue socialism from its popular conflation into Stalinism.[109] Deutscher laid out a law of revolution in which "each great revolution begins with a phenomenal outburst of popular energy, impatience, anger, and hope. Each ends in the weariness, exhaustion, and disillusionment of the revolutionary people ... The leaders are unable to keep their early promises ... [The revolutionary government] now forfeits at least one of its honourable attributes—it ceases to be government by the people."[110] As in Trotsky's treatment, so in Deutscher's: Stalin had been hooked by history. He became "both the leader and the exploiter of a tragic, self-contradictory but creative revolution."[111]

A year later, Deutscher reviewed a powerful collection of memoirs by six prominent former Communists, the widely-read *The God That Failed*, edited by the British socialist Richard Crossman. At that time, a parade of former Communists—among them André Malraux, Ruth Fischer, and Whittaker Chambers—had become public eyewitnesses of the nature of the movement and the USSR, all the more credible and authentic in the eyes of the public by virtue of their experience inside and break with the Party. Within a few years, those who stayed loyal to Communist parties would be regarded by much of the public, particularly in the United States, as spies for the Soviet Union. Deutscher was pained, not so much by the apostasies of the ex-Communists, as by their embrace of capitalism. While he saw the ex-Communist as an "inverted Stalinist," who "ceases to oppose capitalism" but "continues to see the world in black

---

108   Isaac Deutscher, *Stalin, A Political Biography* (Oxford: Oxford University Press, 1949; Vintage paperback edition: New York, 1960; second edition: Oxford-New York, 1966). Page references to Deutscher are from the second edition.

109   Ibid, p. xv. "Unrepentent Marxist" comes from one of Deutscher's most severe critics, Leopold Labedz. See his two-part article, "Deutscher as Historian and Prophet, I," *Survey*, no. 41 (April 1962), pp. 120–44; "Deutscher as Historian and Prophet, II," ibid., XXIII, no. 3 (104) (Summer 1977–1978), pp. 146–64. For a more balanced critique of Deutscher's work, see J. I. Gleisner, "Isaac Deutscher and Soviet Russia," Centre for Russian and East European Studies, University of Birmingham, Discussion Papers, Series RC/C, no 5, March 1971.

110   Deutscher, *Stalin*, pp. 173–5.

111   Ibid., p. 569.

and white, [though] now the colours are differently distributed," Deutscher believed that the god was not bound to fail.[112] Himself a passionate opponent of Stalinism, Deutscher sought to distance what the Soviet Union had become from what the Bolsheviks had originally intended and from the possibility of a different socialism. His idealism and utopian aspiration distinguished him from Carr's pragmatism and realism. His three-volume biography of Trotsky at once celebrated the intellectual and revolutionary, and soberly revealed his faults and frailties.[113] Summing up his interpretation of the failure of socialism in the Soviet Union, he wrote: "In the whole experience of modern man there had been nothing as sublime and as repulsive as the first Workers' State and the first essay in 'building socialism.'"[114] "There can be no greater tragedy than that of a great revolution's succumbing to the mailed fist that was to defend it from its enemies. There can be no spectacle as disgusting as that of a post-revolutionary tyranny dressed up in the banners of liberty."[115]

In the small world of British Sovietology, Carr, the Deutschers, R. W. Davies (b. 1925), and Rudolf Schlesinger (1901–1969), the Marxist founder of Glasgow's Institute of Soviet and East European Studies and the journal *Soviet Studies*, stood on one side. On the other were the liberal Oxford philosopher Isaiah Berlin (1909–1997), London School of Economics historian Leonard Schapiro (1908–1983), Hugh Seton Watson (1916–1984), David Footman (1895–1983), and much of the academic establishment. Carr was extremely critical of Schapiro's *Origins of the Communist Autocracy* (1955), and fought with Berlin over its publication.[116] Never receiving the appointment he desired at Oxford, Carr ended up back at his own alma mater, Trinity College, Cambridge, at the age of sixty-three. His collaborator, Davies, became a leading figure at the Centre for Russian and East European Studies of the University of Birmingham, established in 1963, and it was to Birmingham that Moshe Lewin came to teach Soviet history in 1968.

---

112 Deutscher, *Heretics and Renegades*, p. 15.

113 Isaac Deutscher, *The Prophet Armed: Trotsky 1879–1921*; *The Prophet Unarmed: Trotsky 1921–1929*; *The Prophet Outcast: Trotsky 1929–1940* (New York and London: Oxford University Press, 1954, 1959, 1963).

114 Ibid., p. 510.

115 Deutscher, *Heretics and Renegades*, p. 12.

116 Haslam, *The Vices of Integrity*, pp. 157–65.

A socialist Zionist from his youth, Lewin escaped from his native Vilno ahead of the advancing Germans, thanks to peasant Red Army soldiers who disobeyed their officer and winked him aboard their retreating truck. In the wartime USSR, he worked on collective farms, in a mine and a factory before entering a Soviet officers' school. He then returned to Poland and later emigrated to Israel. Upset with the direction that the Israeli state took during the 1950s, he began studying history, moving on to Paris where he worked with Roger Portal and was deeply influenced by the social-historical *Annales* school and by his friend, the sociologist Basile Kerblay. After teaching in Paris and Birmingham, he moved to the University of Pennsylvania in 1978, where he and Alfred Rieber organized a series of seminars that brought a generation of younger historians from the study of imperial Russia to the post-1917 period.

Lewin considered himself a "historian of society," rather than simply of a regime. "It is not a state that has a society but a society that has a state."[117] His *Russian Peasants and Soviet Power* (1966) was the first empirical study of collectivization in the West, and it was followed by his influential study, *Lenin's Last Struggle* (1967).[118] In sprawling essays on Stalinism he enveloped great social processes in succinct and pungent phrases: "quicksand society," "ruling class without tenure."[119] Lewin resurrected a Lenin who learned from his errors and tried at the end of his life to make serious readjustments in nationality policy and the nature of the bureaucratic state. Although he failed in his last struggle, Lenin's testament remained a demonstration that there were alternatives to Stalinism within Bolshevism. Lewin's reading of Leninism challenged the view of Bolshevism as a single consistent ideology that supplied ready formulae for the future. For Lewin, Bukharin offered another path to economic development; but once Stalin embarked on a war against the peasantry, the massive machinery of repression opened

---

117 Personal communication with the author, March 13, 2004.

118 Moshe Lewin, *La paysannerie et le pouvoir soviétique, 1928–1930* (La Haye: Mouton, 1966); *Russian Peasants and Soviet Power: A Study of Collectivization*, trans. Irene Nove (Evanston: Northwestern University Press, 1968); *Le dernier combat de Lénine* (Paris: Minuit, 1967); *Lenin's Last Struggle* (New York: Random House, 1968; Ann Arbor: University of Michigan Press, 2005).

119 Moshe Lewin, *The Making of the Soviet System: Essays in the Social History of Interwar Russia* (New York: Pantheon Books, 1985); *Russia, USSR, Russia: The Drive and Drift of a Superstate* (New York: The New Press, 1995).

the way to a particularly ferocious, despotic autocracy and mass terror.[120]

From Political Science to Social History

By the time Lewin arrived in the United States, in the late 1970s, the privileges of material resources, state support, and perceived national interest had made the American sovietological establishment the most prolific and influential purveyor of information on the Soviet Union and its allies outside the USSR. A veritable army of government employees, journalists, scholars, and private consultants were hard at work analyzing and pronouncing on the Soviet Union. In a real sense, the view of the other side forged in America not only shaped the policy of one great superpower, but determined the limits of the dialogue between "West" and "East." While the interpretations produced by American journalists and professional Sovietologists were by no means uniform, the usual language used to describe the other great superpower was consistently negative—aggressive, expansionistic, paranoid, corrupt, brutal, monolithic, stagnant. Exchange students going to the USSR for a year of study routinely spoke of "going into" and "out of" the Soviet Union, as into and out of a prison, instead of the conventional "to" and "from" used for travel to other countries. Language itself reproduced the sense of Russia's alien nature, its inaccessibility and opaqueness.

Before the 1960s few professional historians in American universities studied Russia; until the 1980s fewer still ventured past the years of revolution. The doyen of Russian imperial history at Harvard, Michael Karpovich (1888–1959), stopped at the fall of tsarism in February 1917, "announcing that with that event Russian history had come to an end."[121] He and his colleague, the economic historian Alexander Gerschenkron (1904–1978), celebrated the cultural and economic progress that the late tsarist regime had made but which had been derailed with the wrong turn taken by the Bolsheviks. Marc Raeff (1923–2008) at Columbia, the eloquent author of original studies of imperial Russian intellectuals and officials, was equally suspicious of the ability seriously to study history after the divide of 1917. George Vernadsky (1887–1973) at Yale focused

---

120   Moshe Lewin, *Political Undercurrents in Soviet Economic Debates*; and *Le siècle soviétique* (Paris: Fayard/*Le Monde diplomatique*, 2003); originally written in English and published later as *Russia's Twentieth Century: The Collapse of the Soviet System* (London: Verso, 2005).

121   Meyer, "Coming to Terms with the Past," p. 403.

primarily on early and medieval Russia, and emphasized Russia's unique Eurasian character. Given that most archives in the Soviet Union were either closed or highly restricted to the few exchange students who ventured to Moscow or Leningrad beginning in the late 1950s, what history of the post-revolutionary period was written before the 1970s was left almost entirely to political scientists, rather than historians. Robert Vincent Daniels's study of Communist oppositions in Soviet Russia in the 1920s, an exemplary case of historically informed political science, presented the full array of socialist alternatives imagined by the early revolutionaries and argued that the origins of Stalinist totalitarianism lay in the victory of the Leninist current within Bolshevism over the Leftist opposition, "the triumph of reality over program." Stalin typified "practical power and the accommodation to circumstances" that won out over "the original revolutionary objectives," which proved "to be chimerical."[122]

Russian studies in the United States ranged from more liberal, or what might be called "détentist," views of the USSR to fervently anti-Communist interpretations that criticized mainstream Sovietology from the Right. With Karpovich's retirement from the Harvard chair, the leading candidates were two of his students, Martin Malia (1924–2004) and Richard Pipes (b. 1923), who in the next generation would become, along with Robert Conquest (1917–2015) of the Hoover Institution, the leading representatives of conservative views in the profession. Harvard gave the nod to Pipes, whose first major work was an encyclopedic study of the non-Russian peoples during the revolution and civil war that portrayed the Bolshevik revolution and the Soviet state as a fundamentally imperial arrangement, a colonial relationship between Russia and the borderlands.[123] Using the activities and proclamations of nationalist leaders or

122 Robert Vincent Daniels, *The Conscience of the Revolution: Communist Opposition in Soviet Russia* (Cambridge, MA: Harvard University Press, 1960), pp. 4–5.

123 Richard Pipes, *The Formation of the Soviet Union: Communism and Nationalism, 1917–1923* (Cambridge, MA: Harvard University Press, 1954; revised ed., 1980). Similar views of Russian/Soviet imperialism were expressed in other works of the time: Walter Kolarz, *Russia and Her Colonies* (New York: Frederick A. Praeger, 1952); Olaf Caroe, *Soviet Empire: The Turks of Central Asia and Stalinism* (New York: Macmillan, 1953); Robert Conquest, *The Soviet Deportation of Nationalities* (London: Macmillan, 1960), reprinted and expanded as *The Nation Killers: The Soviet Deportation of Nationalities* (London: Macmillan, 1970); Hugh Seton-Watson, *The New Imperialism* (Chester Springs, PA: Dufour Editions 1962); and outside of scholarship: U. S. Congress, Senate Committee on the Judiciary, *The Soviet Empire* (Washington, D.C., 1958; revised edition, 1965).

writers as indicators of the attitudes of whole peoples, he played down the widespread support for socialist programs, particularly in the early years of the revolution and Civil War, and touted the authenticity and legitimacy of the nationalists' formulations in contrast to the artificiality of the Communists' claims.

Robert Conquest, born in the year of the revolution, was a poet, novelist, political scientist, and historian. Educated at Oxford, he joined the British Communist Party in 1937 but left the party after the Nazi–Soviet Pact. While serving in the Information and Research Department (IRD) of the Foreign Office (1948 to 1956), a department known to the Soviets but kept secret from the Western public, he promoted and produced "research precisely into the areas of fact then denied, or lied about by Sovietophiles."[124] Even George Orwell supplied the IRD with "a list of people he knew whose attitudes to Stalinism he distrusted," among them E. H. Carr and Charlie Chaplin.[125] In the late 1960s, Conquest edited seven volumes of material from IRD on Soviet politics, without acknowledgement that the books' source was a secret government agency or that the publisher, Frederick A. Praeger, was subsidized by the CIA. His first major book of scholarship (he was already known for his poetry and science fiction) was a carefully detailed study of the political power struggle from the late Stalin years to Khrushchev's triumph.[126] But far more influential was his mammoth study of the Stalin terror in 1968, which, like Alexander Solzhenitsyn's *Gulag Archipelago* some years later, stunned its readers with gruesome details of the mass killings, torture, imprisonment, and exiling of millions of innocent victims.[127] No elaborate theories for the purges were advanced, only the simple argument that "Stalin's personal drives were the motive force of the Purge."

For Conquest, Stalinism was the apogee of Soviet communism, and the secret police and the terror its underlying essence. In another widely-read

---

124   Robert Conquest, "In Celia's Office," *Hoover Digest* (1999), no. 2; hoover.stanford.edu, p. 3.

125   Ibid.

126   Robert Conquest, *Power and Politics in the USSR: The Struggle for Stalin's Succession, 1945–1960* (London: Macmillan, 1961).

127   Robert Conquest, *The Great Terror: Stalin's Purge of the Thirties* (London: Macmillan, 1968); *The Great Terror: A Reassessment* (New York: Oxford University Press, 1990). In subsequent editions, Conquest adjusted some of his arguments and the excessively high numbers of victims of Stalin's repressions. See *The Great Terror: A Reassessment. 40th Anniversary Edition* (Oxford: Oxford University Press, 2008).

book he argued that the Ukrainian famine of 1931–33 was a deliberate, state-initiated genocide against the Ukrainian peasantry.[128] Most scholars rejected this claim, seeing the famine as following from a badly conceived and miscalculated policy of excessive requisitioning of grain, but not as directed specifically against ethnic Ukrainians. Disputes about his exaggerated claims of the numbers of victims of Stalin's crimes went on until the Soviet archives forced the field to lower its estimates.[129] Yet for all the controversy stirred by his writing, Conquest was revered by conservatives, enjoyed a full-time research position at the Hoover Institution from 1981, and was "on cheek-kissing terms" with British Prime Minister Margaret Thatcher and American Secretary of State Condoleezza Rice.[130]

Interest in the Soviet Union exploded in the United States with the Soviet launching of the first artificial earth satellite, Sputnik, in October 1957. A near hysteria about the USA falling behind the USSR in technology, science, and education led to a pouring of funding into Soviet and East European studies. Yet the focus of attention remained on regime studies and foreign policy. In the 1960s, political scientists focused on the distribution of power within the Soviet elite and the processes of decision-making. Well within the larger paradigm of totalitarianism, Kremlinology looked intently for elite conflict, even peering at the lineup on the Lenin Mausoleum to detect who was on top. Slow to revise their models of the USSR, scholars underestimated the significance of Khrushchev's de-Stalinization reforms, emphasizing instead the dysfunctional and brutal aspects of a regime seen as largely static and unchanging. Moscow's resort to military force in the Soviet Bloc—suppressing the workers' revolt in East Germany in 1953, the revolution in Hungary in

---

128   Robert Conquest, *The Harvest of Sorrow: Soviet Collectivization and the Terror-Famine* (New York and Oxford: Oxford University Press, 1986).

129   This subject remains highly controversial. For example, Conquest estimated 15 million deaths in the collectivization and famine, while a study based on archival records by R. W. Davies and S. G. Wheatcroft lowers that figure to 5,700,000. The total number of lives destroyed by the Stalinist regime in the 1930s is closer to 10–11 million than the 20–30 million estimated earlier. From 1930 to 1953, over 3,778,000 people were sentenced for counterrevolutionary activity or crimes against the state; of those, 786,000 were executed; at the time of Stalin's death, there were 2,526,000 prisoners in the USSR and another 3,815,000 in special settlements or exile. Ronald Grigor Suny, *The Soviet Experiment: Russia, the USSR, and the Successor States* (New York and Oxford: Oxford University Press, 2011), p. 287.

130   Conquest, "In Celia's Office," p. 2.

1956, and the "Prague Spring" in Czechoslovakia in 1968—only confirmed the images of a redeployed and only slightly modified Stalinism. But increasingly the evident differences, and even rivalries, between Communist regimes, as well as the growing variation and contention within East Bloc countries led some observers to question the idea of Communism as monolithic, unchanging, and driven simply by ideology or a single source of power.

Sovietology stood somewhat distant from mainstream political science, which employed an empiricism and observation that was impossible for students of the USSR. The "behavioralist revolution" in political science in the 1960s was palely reflected in Soviet studies and was soon replaced by policy analysis, comparative case studies, and the deployment of concepts borrowed from Western studies such as corporatism, pluralism, interest groups, and civil society. Turning to the study of the Soviet Union as a "political system," a "process of interaction between certain environmental influences and the consciously directed actions of a small elite group of individuals working through a highly centralized institutional structure," scholars now emphasized the environmental, cultural, and historically-determined constraints on the Soviet leaders, rather than their revolutionary project to transform society or their total control over the population.[131] They investigated how decisions were made; which interest groups influenced policy choices and were to have their demands satisfied; how popular compliance and the legitimacy of the regime was sustained in the absence of Stalinist terror; and whether the system could adapt to the changing international environment. By looking at institutions and how they functioned, many Sovietologists noted the structural similarities and practices the Soviet system shared with other political systems.[132]

A particularly influential methodology in Soviet studies—and in which Sovietology made an impact on mainstream political science—was the political culture approach. The concept possessed a long pedigree, going

---

131   Richard Cornell (ed.), *The Soviet Political System: A Book of Readings* (Englewood Cliffs, NJ: Prentice Hall, 1970), p. 3.

132   For Alfred G. Meyer, a bureaucratic model of the USSR was needed to supplement the outdated totalitarian model. See his "The Comparative Study of Communist Political Systems," *Slavic Review* XXVI, 1 (March 1967), pp. 3–12. For Meyer, an important difference was "that Communist systems are sovereign bureaucracies, whereas other bureaucracies exist and operate within larger societal frameworks."

back at least to René Fülöp-Miller's *The Mind and Face of Bolshevism* (1928) and Harper's work on civic training, if not to earlier work on national character.[133] In part a reaction against the psychocultural studies of the 1940s that had attributed political attitudes of a national population to child-rearing and family practices (e.g., the swaddling thesis), political culture studies held that political systems were affected by political attitudes and behaviors that made up a separate cultural sphere available for analysis.[134] Beliefs, values, and symbols provided a subjective orientation to politics that defined the universe in which political action took place.[135] Associated with Frederick Barghoorn (1911–1991), Robert C. Tucker, and the British political scientists Stephen White and Archie Brown, political culture focused on consistencies in political behavior and attitudes over the *longue durée*.[136] Tucker's "continuity thesis," for example, connected Stalin's autocracy to tsarism, the Communist party to the pre-Revolutionary nobility, and collectivization to peasant serfdom. Harvard medievalist Edward Keenan (1935–2015) carried this path-dependent version of political culture even further in a determinist direction when he explored the influence of what he called "Muscovite political folkways" on the Soviet Union. As impressive as such megahistorical connections appear, the political culture approach faltered when it tried to explain change over time or the precise mechanisms that carried the culture from generation to generation over centuries.[137]

133 René Fülöp-Miller, *Geist und Gesicht des Bolschewismus: Darstellung und Kritik des kulturellen Lebens in Sowjet-Russland* (Zurich: Amalthea-Verlag, 1926); *The Mind and Face of Bolshevism: An Examination of Cultural Life in Soviet Russia* (London and New York: G. P. Putnam's Sons, 1927); Samuel N. Harper, *Civic Training in Soviet Russia* (Chicago, 1929): *Making Bolsheviks* (Chicago, 1931).

134 Ruth Benedict, *The Chrysanthemum and the Sword: Patterns of Japanese Culture* (New York: Houghton Mifflin Harcourt, 1946); Margaret Mead, *Soviet Attitudes Toward Authority: An Interdisciplinary Approach to Problems of Soviet Character* (New York: McGraw-Hill, 1951); Nathan Leites, *The Operational Code of the Politburo* (New York: McGraw-Hill, 1951); *A Study of Bolshevism* (New York: Free Press, 1953); Gorer and Rickman, *The Peoples of the USSR*.

135 Lucian Pye and Sidney Verba (eds.), *Political Culture and Political Development* (Princeton: Princeton University Press, 1965), p. 513; Robert C. Tucker, *Political Culture and Leadership in Soviet Russia: From Lenin to Gorbachev* (New York: W. W. Norton, 1987), p. 3.

136 Frederick C. Barghoorn, *Politics in the USSR* (Boston: Little, Brown, 1966, 1972); Stephen White, *Political Culture in Soviet Politics* (London: Macmillan, 1979); Archie Brown, *Political Culture and Communist Studies* (Armonk, NY: M. E. Sharpe, 1985).

137 For an alternative look at early Russian political culture, see Valerie A. Kivelson, *Autocracy in the Provinces: The Muscovite Gentry and Political Culture in the Seventeenth Century* (Stanford: Stanford University Press, 1996).

Tucker supplemented political culture with studies of the dictator and turned to psychohistory as a way to understand Stalin. Influenced by Karen Horney's *Neurosis and Human Growth*, particularly her concept of the "neurotic character structure," Tucker argued that the Stalin cult was Stalin's own "monstrously inflated vision of himself."[138] Stalin's personality, combined with the nature of Bolshevism, the Soviet regime's historical situation in the 1920s, and "a tradition of autocracy and popular acceptance of it," were the keys to understanding the USSR. Despite Tucker's attempt to explain history through personality, psychohistory had little resonance in the profession. Most historians were unimpressed by an approach that underplayed ideas and circumstances and treated historical figures as neurotic or psychopathic.[139] Rather than Freud, it was Marx and Weber that influenced the next generation of historians, as they turned from a focus on personality and politics to the study of society, ordinary people, large structures and impersonal forces.

The First Revisionism: 1917

The political and social turmoil of the 1960s—civil rights struggles, opposition to the Vietnam War, student challenges to the university, and resistance to imperial dominance, whether Western colonialist or Communist—had a profound effect on the academy in general, historical writing in particular, and Sovietology even more specifically. Young scholars in the late 1960s questioned, not only the Cold War orthodoxies about the Manichean division of free world from slave, but also the usually unquestioned liberal assumptions about valueless social science. While detachment and neutrality were valued as methodology, the concern for a history with relevance to the politics of one's own time and place gave rise to a deep skepticism about the histories that had been written to date. "Social history," "radical history," and "history from below" were in their earliest formations challenges to the political narratives and state-centered histories of earlier years. They were self-consciously "revisionist."

The Cold War convictions that Soviet expansionism had forced a reluctant United States to turn from isolationism to a global

---

138   Robert C. Tucker, "A Stalin Biographer's Memoir," in Baron and Pletsch (eds.), *Introspection in Biography*, pp. 251–2; Tucker, "Memoir of a Stalin Biographer," *University: A Princeton Magazine* (Winter 1983), p. 2.

139   Psychohistorical methodologies are more prevalent in pre-Soviet than Soviet historiography.

containment policy, that the Cold War was almost entirely the fault of Stalin's territorial and political ambitions, and that, if left unchecked by Western power, Communism would conquer the world, were seriously challenged in the 1960s by a revisionist scholarship on the origins of the Cold War. Moderate revisionists allotted blame for the division of the world to both superpowers, while more radical revisionists proposed that the United States, in its dedication to "making the world safe for free market capitalism," was the principal culprit. The historians who wrote the new Cold War histories were almost exclusively historians of American foreign policy, with only limited knowledge of Soviet history and no access to Soviet archives. No parallel history from the Soviet side would be available until the end of the Cold War. Yet the revisionist undermining of the orthodox liberal consensus profoundly affected many young scholars who were then able to interrogate hitherto axiomatic foundational notions about the Soviet Union and the nature of communism.

Beginning in the late 1960s, younger historians of Russia, primarily in the United States, began to dismantle the dominant political interpretation of the 1917 revolution, with its emphasis on the power of ideology, personality, and political intrigue, and to reconceptualize the conflict as a struggle between social classes. The older interpretation, largely synthesized by anti-Bolshevik veterans of the revolution, had argued that the Russian Revolution was an unfortunate intervention that ended a potentially liberalizing political evolution of tsarism from autocracy through constitutional reforms to a Western-style parliamentary system. The principal agents in this interpretation were personalities and parties, Lenin and the Bolsheviks most importantly, who took power in a conspiratorial coup d'état, deceiving their plebian followers as to their real intentions.

The social historians writing on 1917 in the 1970s and 1980s proposed a more structuralist appreciation of the movements of social groups, in a displacement of the former emphasis on leaders and high politics. By looking below the political surface at the actions and aspirations of workers and soldiers, they revealed a deep and deepening social polarization between the top and bottom of Russian society that undermined the Provisional Government by preventing the consolidation of a political consensus—Menshevik leader Iraklii Tsereteli's concept of an all-national unity of the "vital forces" of the country—so desired by moderate socialists and liberals. Rather than being dupes of radical intellectuals, workers articulated their own concept of autonomy and lawfulness at the factory level, while peasant soldiers developed a keen sense of what kind of war (and for what regime) they were willing to fight. More convincingly than any of their political opponents, the Bolsheviks pushed for a government of the lower classes institutionalized in the soviets, advocated workers' control over industry and an end to the war. By the early fall of 1917, a coincidence of lower-class aspirations and the Bolshevik program resulted in elected Leninist majorities in the soviets of both Petrograd and Moscow, and the strategic support of soldiers on the northern and western fronts. But, after a relatively easy accession to power, the Bolsheviks, never a majority movement in peasant Russia, were faced by dissolution of political authority, complete collapse of the economy, and disintegration of the country along ethnic lines. As Russia slid into civil war, the Bolsheviks embarked on a program of regenerating state power that involved economic centralization and the use of violence and terror against their opponents.

The political/personality approach of the orthodox school, revived later in Pipes's multi-volume treatment, usually noted the social radicalization but offered no explanation of the growing gap between the propertied classes (*tsensovoe obshchestvo*) and the *demokratiia* (as the socialists styled their constituents), except the disgust of workers, soldiers, and sailors with the vacillations of the moderate socialists, and the effectiveness of Bolshevik propaganda.[140] Historians of Russian labor described the growing desperation of workers after the inflationary erosion of their wage gains of the early months of the revolution and the lockouts and closures of factories. The parallel radicalization of soldiers turned the ranks against officers as the government and the moderate leadership of the soviets failed to end the war. As the revolutionary year progressed, propertied society and the liberal intelligentsia grew increasingly hostile toward the lower classes and the plethora of committees and councils, which they believed undermined legitimately constituted authority. Taken together, these works demonstrated that the Bolsheviks came to power in 1917 with considerable popular support in the largest cities of the empire.

---

140 Richard Pipes, *The Russian Revolution* (New York: Alfred A. Knopf, 1990); *Russia Under the Bolshevik Regime* (New York: Alfred A. Knopf, 1993); *Three Whys of the Russian Revolution* (London: Pimlico, 1998).

What remained a matter of dispute was the degree, consistency, durability, and meaning of that support.

While the "political conspiratorial" interpretation, dominant in the West for the first fifty years of Soviet power, implied the illegitimacy of the Communist government and contained within it a powerful argument for political opposition to the Soviet regime, the revisionists were accused of rationalizing, even justifying, the actions of the Bolsheviks. Conservative historians, like Malia and Pipes, rejected the notion that the revolution "had gone wrong" in the years after Lenin or been "betrayed" by Stalin, and argued instead that "Stalin was Lenin writ large, and there cannot be a democratic source to return to."[141] In the late 1980s and 1990s Soviet intellectuals, disillusioned by the economic and moral failures of the Soviet system, found these views, as well as the concept of totalitarianism, consonant with their own evolving alienation from Marxism-Leninism. When Gorbachev proposed a rereading of Soviet history but tried to limit the critique to Stalinism, daring intellectuals opened (after 1987) a more fundamental attack on the legacy of the revolution. The interpretation of the October seizure of power as either a coup d'état without popular support or as the result of a fortuitous series of accidents in the midst of the "galloping chaos" of the revolution re-emerged, first among Soviet activists and politicians, journalists and publicists, and later in the West in the discussion around the publication of Pipes's own study of the revolutions of 1917.[142] Yet most Western specialists writing on the revolution considered the thesis that the revolution was popular, both in the sense of involving masses of people and broad support for Soviet power (if not the Bolshevik party itself), "incontrovertible."[143] By

---

141 Martin Malia, "The Hunt for the True October," *Commentary* XCII, 4 (October 1991), pp. 21–2. Pipes makes a similar argument: "The elite that rules Soviet Russia lacks a legitimate claim to authority . . . Lenin, Trotsky, and their associates seized power by force, overthrowing an ineffective but democratic government. The government they founded, in other words, derives from a violent act carried out by a tiny minority." Richard Pipes, "Why Russians Act Like Russians," *Air Force Magazine* (June 1970), pp. 51–5; cited in Louis Menasche, "Demystifying the Russian Revolution," *Radical History Review*, no. 18 (Fall 1978), p. 153.

142 Pipes's history of the Russian Revolution was first published in Russian translation in three volumes, an edition of 100,000 copies, in 1994–97 and sparked intense discussion in Russia.

143 Terence Emmons, "Unsacred History," *The New Republic*, November 5, 1990, p. 36.

the 1980s, despite the resistance of Pipes and a few others, the revisionist position had swept the field of 1917 studies, and the term "revisionism" migrated to characterize a group of social historians investigating the vicissitudes of the working class and the upheavals of the Stalin years.

The Fate of Labor History: From Social to Cultural

Social history was never a unified practice, either in its methodologies or its interests, but rather a range of approaches, from social "scientific" quantification to cultural anthropologies, concerned with the expansion of the field of historical inquiry.[144] The major effect of the turn to the social was the broadening of the very conception of the political, in two important ways. First, borrowing from the insights of feminism and the legacy of the New Left that the "personal is political," politics was now seen as deeply embedded in the social realm, in aspects of everyday life far beyond the state and political institutions.[145] The turn toward social history reduced the concern with labor politics, but "politics in the broader sense—the power relations of various social groups and inter-ests—intruded in the lives of Russian workers too directly and persis-tently to be ignored."[146] Second, the realm of politics was recontextual-ized within society, so that the state and political actors were seen as constrained by social possibilities and influenced by actors and processes outside political institutions.[147] Not surprisingly, this rethinking of power relations would eventually involve consideration of cultural and discur-sive hegemony and exploration of "the images of power and authority, the popular mentalities of subordination."[148]

---

144 This section on labor history is indebted to the work that Lewis H. Siegelbaum and I did in the organization of a conference at Michigan State University on Russian labor history, that culminated in our edited volume *Making Workers Soviet: Power, Class, and Identity* (Ithaca: Cornell University Press, 1994).

145 Geoff Eley, "Edward Thompson, Social History and Political Culture: The Making of a Working-class Public, 1780–1850," in Harvey J. Kaye and Keith McClelland (eds.), *E. P. Thompson: Critical Perspectives* (Philadelphia: Temple University Press, 1990), p. 13.

146 Ziva Galili, "Workers, Strikes, and Revolution in Late Imperial Russia," *International Labor and Working-Class History*, no. 38 (Fall 1990), p. 69.

147 Here, the work of Moshe Lewin has been particularly influential, integrating political history with his own brand of historical sociology.

148 The phrase is E. P. Thompson's, quoted in Eley, "Edward Thompson, Social History and Political Culture," p. 16.

The great wave of interest in the Russian working class crested in the last decades of the Soviet experience, only to crash on the rocks of state socialism's demise. Some labor historians in Britain and the United States challenged Soviet narratives of growing class cohesion and radical consciousness in the years up to the revolution with counter-stories of decomposition, fragmentation, and accommodation, while others elaborated a grand march of labor not far removed from the Soviet account of a trajectory from peasant to peasant-worker to hereditary proletarian. In the latter narrative, the Russian worker moved from the world of the village to the factory, encountering along the way more "conscious" worker activists and Social Democratic intellectuals, who enlightened the worker to his true interests and revolutionary political role. Workers' experience involved the unfolding of an immanent sense of class, the "discovery" of class and the eventuality, even inevitability, of revolutionary consciousness (under the right circumstances or with the strategic intervention of radical intellectuals). Categories, as well as narrative devices, were drawn either from sources themselves saturated with Marxist understandings or directly from Soviet works.

The classic picture of Soviet labor in the 1930s had been provided by the former Menshevik Solomon Schwarz, who wrote in 1951 about the draconian labor laws that had essentially tied workers to factories and eliminated their ability to resist.[149] By the 1980s, the focus shifted from an emphasis on state intervention and repression to the nature of the work process and the informal organization of the shop-floor. Several accounts, eventually dubbed "revisionist," related the enthusiasm of workers for the exertions of rapid industrialization of the early 1930s. Young skilled workers joined the "offensives" against "bourgeois" specialists, moderate union leaders, and others dubbed "enemy." This group of workers in particular, standing between their older, skilled co-workers disoriented by the industrialization drive and peasant migrants to the factories, were committed to the notion of building socialism.[150] Tens of thousands of radicalized workers left for the countryside to "convince" the peasants to

---

149   Solomon Schwarz, *Labor in the Soviet Union* (New York: Praeger, 1951).

150   Sheila Fitzpatrick, *Education and Social Mobility in Soviet Russia, 1921–1934* (Cambridge: Cambridge University Press, 1979); Hiroaki Kuromiya, *Stalin's Industrial Revolution: Politics and Workers, 1928–1932* (Cambridge: Cambridge University Press, 1988).

join the collective farms.[151] Rather than successfully "atomizing" the working class, the state, powerful as it appeared, was limited in its ability to coerce workers. With working hands scarce, workers found areas of autonomy in which they could "bargain" with the state, and factory bosses had to compete with one another for skilled labor. Even as they lost the ability to act in an organized fashion, workers were able to affect the system in thousands of small ways.[152] Shop-floor studies and micro-histories undermined the overly simple political interpretation of Stalinist society and, more particularly, the totalitarian model, in which an all-powerful state rendered an atomized population completely impotent.

Social history was often uncomfortable with its pedigree in Marxism and a base-substructure model of explanation. Following the pioneering work in other historiographies by E. P. Thompson, William H. Sewell, Jr., Gareth Stedman Jones, Joan Wallach Scott, and others, Russian historians began to pay more attention to language, culture, and the available repertoire of ideas.[153] Investigating class formation in the post-Thompsonian period involved not only exploring the structures of the capitalist mode of production or the behavior of workers during protests and strikes, but also the discourses in which workers expressed their sense of self, defined their "interests," and articulated their sense of power or, more likely, powerlessness. Whatever the experience of workers might have been, the availability of an intense conversation about class among the intellectuals closest to them provided images and language with which to articulate and reconceive their position. While structures and social positions, or even "experience," influence, shape, and limit social actors, they do not lead to action or create meaning in and of themselves. The discourses, cultures, and universes of available

---

151 Lynne Viola, *The Best Sons of the Fatherland: Workers in the Vanguard of Soviet Collectivization* (Oxford: Oxford University Press, 1987).

152 Lewis Siegelbaum, *Stakhanovism and the Politics of Productivity in the USSR, 1935–1941* (Cambridge: Cambridge University Press, 1988); Donald Filtzer, *Soviet Workers and Stalinist Industrialization: The Formation of Modern Soviet Production Relations, 1928–1941* (Armonk, NY: M. E. Sharpe, 1986).

153 E. P. Thompson, *The Making of the English Working Class* (London: Victor Gollancz, 1963); Gareth Stedman Jones, *Languages of Class: Studies in English Working Class History, 1832-1982* (Cambridge: Cambridge University Press, 1983); William H. Sewell, Jr., *Work and Revolution in France: The Language of Labor from the Old Regime to 1848* (Cambridge: Cambridge University Press, 1980); Joan Wallach Scott, *Gender and the Politics of History* (New York: Columbia University Press, 1988).

meanings through which actors mediate their life experience all had to be added into the mix.[154]

The Study of Stalinism: The Next Revisionism
The term "Stalinism" has its own genealogy, beginning in the mid-1920s even before the system that would bear its name yet existed. Trotsky applied the word to the moderate "centrist" tendencies within the party, stemming from the "ebbing of revolution" and identified with his opponent, Stalin.[155] By 1935, Trotsky's use of Stalinism gravitated closer to the Marxist meaning of "Bonapartism" or "Thermidor," "the crudest form of opportunism and social patriotism."[156] Even before Trotsky's murder in August 1940, Stalinism had become a way of characterizing the particular form of social and political organization in the Soviet Union, distinct from capitalism but, for Trotskyists and other non-Communist radicals, not quite socialist. Not until the falling away of the totalitarian model, however, did scholars bring the term Stalinism into social science discussion as a sociopolitical formation to be analyzed in its own right. For Robert C. Tucker Stalinism "represented, among other things, a far-reaching Russification of the already somewhat Russified earlier (Leninist) Soviet political culture."[157] For his younger colleague at Princeton, Stephen F. Cohen, "Stalinism was not simply nationalism, bureaucratization, absence of democracy, censorship, police repression, and the rest in any precedented sense . . . Instead Stalinism was excess, extraordinary extremism, in each."[158] Taking a more social historical perspective, Lewin saw Stalinism as a deeply contradictory phenomenon:

154 For work that reflects the interest in language, discourse, and representation, see Orlando Figes and Boris Kolonitskii, *Interpreting the Russian Revolution: The Language and Symbols of 1917* (New Haven: Yale University Press, 1999); Mark D. Steinberg, *Voices of Revolution, 1917* (New Haven and London: Yale University Press, 2001); his *Proletarian Imagination: Self, Modernity, and the Sacred in Russia, 1910–1925* (Ithaca, NY: Cornell University Press, 2002); Katerina Clark, *Petersburg: Crucible of Cultural Revolution* (Cambridge, MA: Harvard University Press, 1995), and her *Moscow, the Fourth Rome: Stalinism, Cosmopolitanism, and the Evolution of Soviet Culture, 1931–1941* (Cambridge, MA: Harvard University Press, 2011).
155 Robert H. McNeal, "Trotskyist Interpretations of Stalinism," in Robert C. Tucker (ed.), *Stalinism: Essays in Historical Interpretation* (New York: W. W. Norton, 1977), p. 31.
156 Ibid., p. 34.
157 Tucker, "Introduction: Stalinism and Comparative Communism," in Tucker (ed.), *Stalinism*, p. xviii.
158 Cohen, "Bolshevism and Stalinism," in Tucker (ed.), *Stalinism*, p. 12.

The Stalinist development brought about a different outcome: as the country was surging ahead in economic and military terms, it was moving backwards, compared to the later period in tsarism and even the NEP, in terms of social and political freedoms. This was not only a specific and blatant case of development without emancipation; it was, in fact, a retreat into a tighter-than-ever harnessing of society to the state bureaucracy, which became the main social vehicle of the state's policies and ethos.[159]

Stalinism was now a way of describing a stage of development of non-capitalist statist regimes in developing countries dominated by a Leninist party, as well as an indictment of undemocratic, failed socialist societies.

A key question dividing Soviet studies was the issue of continuity (or rupture) between the regimes of Lenin and Stalin. Was Stalinism implicit in original Marxism or the Leninist version, or had there been alternatives open to the Bolsheviks? Along with Tucker and Lewin, Cohen was one of the major opponents of the view that saw Stalin as the logical or even inevitable outcome of Leninism. While it had its roots in earlier experiences, Stalinism was qualitatively different from anything that went before or came after.[160] Original Bolshevism had been a diverse political movement in which Leninism was but one, albeit the dominant, strain. In the years of the New Economic Policy (1921–28) the Bolsheviks, far from united in their plans for a future socialist society, presided over a far more tolerant and pluralistic social order than would follow after Stalin's revolution from above. Stalin's policies of 1929–33 rejected the gradualist Bukharinist program of slower but steady growth within the framework of NEP, and in its place built a new state that "was less a product of Bolshevik programs or planning than of desperate attempts to cope with the social pandemonium and crises created by the Stalinist leadership itself in 1929–33."[161]

The cohort of social historians of Stalinism that emerged in the 1980s

159   Lewin, "The Social Background of Stalinism," in Tucker (ed.), *Stalinism*, p. 126.

160   Stephen F. Cohen, *Rethinking the Soviet Experience: Politics and History Since 1917* (New York and Oxford: Oxford University Press, 1985), p. 48.

161   Ibid., p. 64. See also Cohen, *Bukharin and the Bolshevik Revolution: A Political Biography, 1888–1938* (New York: Alfred A. Knopf, 1973).

was not particularly interested in broad synthetic interpretations of Stalinism or Marxist-inspired typologies. Their challenge was directed against the top-down, state intervention into society approach, and proposed looking primarily at society, while at the same time disaggregating what was meant by society. They looked for initiative from below, popular resistance to the regime's agenda, as well as sources of support for radical transformation.[162] Some stressed the improvisation of state policies, the chaos of the state machinery, the lack of control in the countryside. Others attempted to diminish the role of Stalin. As they painted a picture quite different from the totalitarian vision of effective dominance from above and atomization below, these revisionists came under withering attack from more traditional scholars, who saw them as self-deluded apologists for Stalin at best and incompetent, venal falsifiers at worst.[163]

For Sheila Fitzpatrick, the standard Trotskyist formulation of the bureaucracy standing over and dominating society was far too simplistic, for the lower echelons of the bureaucracy were as much dominated as dominating.[164] Fascinated by the upward social mobility into the elite that characterized early Soviet society, she introduced Western audiences to the *vydvizhentsy* (those thrust upward from the working class).[165] Rather than seeing an evolution away from the promise of proletarian revolution, Fitzpatrick contended that the accomplishment of the revolution was the upward mobility of former workers who occupied key party and state positions in significant numbers. The dictatorship of the proletariat was an absurd and undeliverable promise that the Bolsheviks could not possibly fulfill: "The oxymoron of a 'ruling proletariat,' appealing though it might be to dialectical thinkers, was not realizable in the real world."[166] Workers, in her view, had

---

162   For a bold attempt to find initiative for state policies from below, see Sheila Fitzpatrick (ed.), *Cultural Revolution in Russia, 1928–1931* (Bloomington, IN, and London: Indiana University Press, 1978).

163   See, for example, Richard Pipes, *Vixi, Memoirs of a Non-Belonger* (New Haven and London: Yale University Press, 2003), pp. 126, 221–3, 242.

164   Sheila Fitzpatrick, "New Perspectives on Stalinism," *Russian Review* XLV, 4 (October 1986), p. 361–2.

165   Sheila Fitzpatrick, *Education and Social Mobility in the Soviet Union, 1921–1934* (Cambridge: Cambridge University Press, 1979).

166   Sheila Fitzpatrick, 'The Bolshevik Dilemma: Class, Culture and Politics in the Early Soviet Years,' *Slavic Review* XLVII, 4 (Winter 1988), pp. 599–613.

become "masters" of Russian society by moving into the old masters' jobs.[167]

Along with the collectivization of peasant agriculture and the vicious dekulakization campaigns, the principal subject of inquiry for revisionist historians in the 1980s was the Great Terror of the late 1930s. Earlier, political scientists, such as Brzezinski, had proposed that purging was a permanent and necessary component of totalitarianism in lieu of elections.[168] Solzhenitsyn, whose fiction and quasi-historical writing on the "Gulag Archipelago" had enormous effect in the West, particularly in France, saw the purges as simply the most extreme manifestation of the amorality of the Marxist vision, and the mass killings of the late 1930s, labeled in Russian *Ezhovshchina*, as an inherent and inevitable part of the Soviet system.[169] Tucker and Conquest saw the Great Purges as an effort "to achieve an unrestricted personal dictatorship with a totality of power that [Stalin] did not yet possess in 1934."[170] Initiation of the Purges came from Stalin, who guided and prodded the arrests, show trials, and executions forward, aided by the closest members of his entourage. Similarly, Lewin argued that the purges were the excessive repression that Stalin required to turn a naturally oligarchic bureaucratic system into his personal autocracy. Here personality and politics merged. Stalin could not "let the sprawling administration settle and get encrusted in their chairs and habits," which "could also encourage them to try and curtail the power of the very top and the personalized ruling style of the chief of the state—and this was probably a real prospect the paranoid leader did not relish."[171]

Revisionists explained the Purges as a more extreme form of political infighting. High-level personal rivalries, disputes over the direction of the

---

167   Sheila Fitzpatrick, *The Russian Revolution, 1917–1932* (Oxford and New York: Oxford University Press, 1984), p. 8; 2nd edition (1994), pp. 9–13. In the second edition, published after the collapse of the Soviet Union, Fitzpatrick speaks of the revolution as a mix of illusions and disillusions, euphoria, madness, and unrealized expectations (pp. 8–9).

168   Brzezinski, *The Permanent Purge.*

169   Alexander Solzhenitsyn, *The Gulag Archipelago, 1918–1956: An Experiment in Literary Investigation* (various editions, 1973–78).

170   Robert C. Tucker, "Introduction: Stalin, Bukharin, and History as Conspiracy," in Tucker and Cohen (eds.), *The Great Purge Trial* (New York: Grosset & Dunlap, 1965), p. xxix; Conquest, *The Great Terror*, p. 62.

171   Lewin, *The Making of the Soviet System*, p. 309.

modernization program, and conflicts between center and periphery were at the base of the killing. J. Arch Getty argued that "the Ezhovshchina was rather a radical, even hysterical, *reaction* to bureaucracy. The entrenched officeholders were destroyed from above and below in a chaotic wave of voluntarism and revolutionary Puritanism."[172] Dissatisfaction with Stalin's rule and with the harsh material conditions was palpable in the mid-1930s, wrote Gabor T. Rittersporn, and the purges were fed by popular discontent with corruption, inefficiency, and the arbitrariness of those in power.[173] Several writers focused on the effects of the purges rather than the causes, implying that intentions may be read into the results. A. L. Unger, Kendall E. Bailes, and Fitzpatrick showed how a new "leading stratum" of Soviet-educated "specialists" replaced the Old Bolsheviks and "bourgeois specialists."[174] The largest numbers of beneficiaries were promoted workers and party rank-and-file, young technicians, who would make up the Soviet elite through the post-Stalin period until Gorbachev took power. Stalin, wrote Fitzpatrick, saw the old party bosses less as revolutionaries than "as Soviet boyars (feudal lords) and himself as a latter-day Ivan the Terrible, who had to destroy the boyars to build a modern nation state and a new service nobility."[175] The Russian historian Oleg Khlevniuk, perhaps the most deeply invested in and knowledgeable about the archival sources, turned the lens back to focus on Stalin as the demiurge of the Great Terror.[176] Fear of the impending war and suspicion about internal and external enemies working together fed into Stalin's obsessively distrustful disposition, and made the pathological bloodletting of the late 1930s seem perversely reasonable in the eyes of many.

---

172   J. Arch Getty, *Origins of the Great Purges: The Soviet Communist Party Reconsidered, 1933–1938* (Cambridge: Cambridge University Press, 1985), p. 206.

173   Gabor T. Rittersporn, *Stalinist Simplifications and Soviet Complications: Social Tensions and Political Conflicts in the USSR, 1933–1953* (Chur, Switzerland: Harwood, 1991).

174   A. L. Unger, "Stalin's Renewal of the Leading Stratum: A Note on the Great Purge," *Soviet Studies* XX, 3 (January 1969), pp. 321–30; Kendall E. Bailes, *Technology and Society Under Lenin and Stalin: Origins of the Soviet Technical Intelligentsia, 1917–1941* (Princeton: Princeton University Press, 1978), pp. 268, 413; Fitzpatrick, "Stalin and the Making of a New Elite," *Slavic Review*, XXXVIII, 3 (September 1979), pp. 377–402.

175   Fitzpatrick, *The Russian Revolution*, p. 159.

176   Oleg V. Khlevniuk, *Stalin: A New Biography of a Dictator* (New Haven: Yale University Press, 2015), pp. 150–62.

Soviet power, however, could never rule by terror alone. In Weberian terms, the regime needed to base itself on more than raw power; it needed to create legitimated authority with a degree of acquiescence or even consent from the people. Social historians were able to record both displays of enthusiasm and active, bloody resistance. Lynn Viola recorded over 13,700 peasant disturbances and more than 1000 assassinations of officials in 1930 alone, while Jeffrey Rossman uncovered significant worker resistance in the textile industry under Stalin, protests accompanied by the rhetoric of class struggle and commitment to the revolution.[177] Sarah Davies read through police reports (*svodki*) to discover that popular opinion in Stalin's Russia was contradictory and multivalent, borrowing the themes set down by the regime and sometimes turning them in new directions.[178] Workers, for example, favored the affirmation action measures during the First Five-Year Plan that gave them and their families privileged access to education but were dismayed at the conservative "Great Retreat" of the mid-1930s. Davies's Russians did not fit the stereotype of a downtrodden people fatally bound by an authoritarian political culture. Given half a chance, as during the elections of 1937, Soviet citizens brought their more democratic ideas to the political process. Along with grumbling about the lack of bread and alienation from those with privileges, ordinary Soviets retained a faith in the revolution and socialism and preserved a sense that the egalitarian promise of 1917 had been violated. Class resentment and suspicion of those in power marched along with patriotism and a sense of social entitlement.

From Above to Below, From Center to Periphery

Revisionism's assault on older interpretations of Communism during the years of détente (roughly 1965 to 1975) gained such wide acceptance within the academy in the late 1970s and early 1980s that conservatives felt beleaguered and marginalized in the profession. Yet representatives of earlier conceptualizations still had the greater resonance outside the

---

177 Lynn Viola, *Peasant Rebels Under Stalin: Collectivization and the Culture of Peasant Resistance* (New York: Oxford University Press, 1996), pp. 105, 136, *passim*; Jeffrey Rossman, "The Teikovo Cotton Workers' Strike of April 1932: Class, Gender, and Identity Politics in Stalin's Russia," *Russian Review* LVI, 1 (January 1997), pp. 44–69.

178 Sarah Davies, *Popular Opinion in Stalin's Russia: Terror, Propaganda and Dissent, 1934–1941* (Cambridge: Cambridge University Press, 1997).

circles of specialists, within the public sphere, and in government. Zbigniew Brzezinski served as National Security Advisor to President Jimmy Carter (1977–81) and was instrumental in the turn toward a harder line toward the Soviet Union, which after the Soviet intervention in Afghanistan in December 1979 escalated into a covert war aiding Muslim militants against the Kabul government and the Soviets.[179] Richard Pipes was appointed in 1976 as head of Team-B to counter a CIA report on Soviet weaponry and later spent two years early in the administration of Ronald Reagan (1981–83) on the National Security Council as resident expert on the USSR. Pipes proudly took credit for toughening the anti-Soviet line of President Reagan, already a dedicated anti-Communist but prone at times to sentimentality.[180] As a historian primarily of tsarist Russia, he brought back to Washington views based on ideas of national character and culture that had long been abandoned by professional historians.[181]

Political history had often meant little more than the story of great men, monarchs and warriors, while social history was by its nature inclusive, bringing in workers, women, and ethnic minorities. As more women entered the field, gender studies gained a deserved respectability. Gail Lapidus's pioneering study was followed by monographs on women workers, the women's liberation movement, Soviet policies toward women, and the baleful effects of a liberation that kept them subordinate and subject to the "double burden" of work outside and inside the home.[182] Just as it had once been acceptable for historians to treat all

179   Jeffrey St. Clair and Alexander Cockburn, "How Jimmy Carter and I Started the Mujahideen," *Counterpunch*, January 15, 1998, counterpunch.org.

180   Pipes, *Vixi*, pp. 163–8.

181   Of Russians he wrote: "Centuries of life under a harsh and capricious climate and an equally harsh and capricious government had taught them to submit to fate. At the first sign of trouble they withdraw like turtles into their shells and wait for the danger to pass. Their great strength lies in their ability to survive even under the most adverse conditions; their great weakness is their unwillingness to rebel against adversity. They simply take misfortune in stride; they are much better down than up. If they no longer can take it, they drink themselves into a stupor." Ibid., pp. 239–40; see also, pp. 62–3.

182   Among the earliest works by Western scholars on Russian and Soviet women were Gail Warshofsky Lapidus, *Women in Soviet Society: Equality, Development, and Social Change* (Los Angeles and Berkeley: University of California Press, 1979); her *Women, Work, and the Family in the Soviet Union* (Armonk, NY: M. E. Sharpe, 1982); Dorothy Atkinson, Alexander Dallin, and Gail Warshofsky Lapidus (eds.), *Women in*

humankind as if it were male, so the study of imperial Russia and the Soviet Union was long treated unapologetically as if these empires were homogeneously Russian. For the first several decades, émigrés with strong emotional and political affiliations with nationalist movements and personal experiences with the brutalities of Stalinism were the principal writers on non-Russians. Their studies, so often pungently partisan and viscerally anti-Communist, were relegated to a peripheral, second-rank ghetto within Soviet studies and associated with the right-wing politics of the "captive nations." Usually neglected by "Russian" historians, the non-Russian peoples were treated as if they were of a single mind. Differences and conflicts within them were effaced, and emphasis was placed on the political repression of natural, inevitable nationalist ambitions. Since studying many nationalities was prohibitively costly and linguistically unfeasible, one nationality (the Ukrainian, in the case of the Harvard Project on the Soviet Social System) was chosen to stand in for the rest.

In Friedrich and Brzezinski's totalitarian model, nationalities were largely unmentioned, not seen as potential "islands of separateness"—along with family, church, universities, writers and artists—that might threaten the Soviet system. But, in time, both émigrés and American-born scholars began to think of the non-Russian nationalities as possible "sources of cleavage" in the Soviet system and, therefore, of significance. Alex Inkeles and Raymond Bauer noted that "national and ethnic membership constitutes a basis for loyalties and identifications which cut across the lines of class, political affiliation, and generation."[183] In the wake of the dismantling of the totalitarian model, more empirical and historical studies focused on non-Russians. Zvi Gitelman, like Gregory J. Massell, told a story of Communist failure "to combine modernization and ethnic maintenance," largely because of the poor fit between the developmental plans of the Party and the reservoir of traditions and interests of the ethnic population. Secularized Jewish Communists set

---

Russia (Stanford: Stanford University Press, 1977); Richard Stites, *The Women's Liberation Movement in Russia: Feminism, Nihilism, and Bolshevism, 1860–1930* (Princeton: Princeton University Press, 1978); Barbara Evans Clements, *Bolshevik Feminist: The Life of Alexandra Kollontai* (Bloomington and Indianapolis: Indiana University Press, 1979); and Barbara Alpern Engel, *Mothers and Daughters: Women of the Intelligentsia in Nineteenth Century Russia* (New York: Cambridge University Press, 1983).

183   Inkeles and Bauer, *The Soviet Citizen*, p. 339.

out to destroy the old order among the Jews, Bolshevize Jewish workers, and reconstruct Jewish life on a "socialist" basis, but as successful as they were in eliminating Zionism and Hebrew culture and encouraging Yiddish culture, they failed to "eradicate religion, so firmly rooted in Jewish life."[184] In Central Asia the failure to mobilize women as a "surrogate proletariat" with which to overturn the patriarchal social regime led to a curious accommodation with traditional society.[185]

Much Sovietological work on nationalities and nationalism accepted uncritically a commonsensical view of nationality as a relatively observable, objective phenomenon based on a community of language, culture, shared myths of origin or kinship, perhaps territory. Nationalism was seen as the release of denied desires and authentic, perhaps primordial, aspirations. This "Sleeping Beauty" view of nationality and nationalism contrasted with a more historicized view that gravitated toward a postmodernist understanding of nationality as a constructed category, an "imagined community." This "Bride of Frankenstein" view of nationality and nationalism asserted that, far from being a natural component of human relations, something like kinship or family, nationality and the nation are created (or invented) in a complex political process in which intellectuals and activists play a formative role. Rather than the nation giving rise to nationalism, it is nationalism that gives rise to the nation. Rather than primordial, the nation is a modern sociopolitical construct. By the 1990s, this "modernist" view of the construction of nations within the Soviet empire began to appear in a number of studies in the Soviet field.[186]

184 Zvi Gitelman, *Jewish Nationality and Soviet Politics: The Jewish Sections of the CPSU, 1917–1930* (Princeton: Princeton University Press, 1972), pp. 3–4, 6–7, 491–2.

185 Gregory J. Massell, *The Surrogate Proletariat: Moslem Women and Revolutionary Strategies in Soviet Central Asia, 1919–1929* (Princeton: Princeton University Press, 1974).

186 Ronald Grigor Suny, *The Revenge of the Past: Nationalism, Revolution, and the Collapse of the Soviet Union* (Stanford: Stanford University Press, 1993); Yuri Slezkine, "The USSR as a Communal Apartment, or How a Socialist State Promoted Ethnic Particularism," *Slavic Review* LIII, 2 (Summer 1994), pp. 414–52; *Arctic Mirrors: Russia and the Small Peoples of the North* (Ithaca, NY: Cornell University Press, 1994); Terry Martin, *The Affirmative Action Empire: Nations and Nationalism in the Soviet Union, 1923–1939* (Ithaca, NY: Cornell University Press, 2001); and Francine Hirsch, *Empire of Nations: Ethnographic Knowledge and the Making of the Soviet Union* (Ithaca: Cornell University Press, 2005).

Soviet Studies in the Post-Soviet World

By the 1990s, the former Soviet Union became an historical object, an imperial relic to be studied in the archives, rather than an actual enemy standing defiantly against the West. At the same time, the dominance of social history gave way to greater acceptance of new cultural approaches. Instead of British Marxists or the Italian Communist Antonio Gramsci, the principal influences now came from French social and cultural theorists, like Michel Foucault and Pierre Bourdieu; the German political theorist, Jürgen Habermas; the American cultural anthropologist, Clifford Geertz; and the Russian literary theorist, Mikhail Bakhtin. Scholars gravitated to investigating cultural phenomena such as rituals and festivals, popular and ethnic culture, and the daily life of ordinary people, topics that increasingly became possible to investigate with the opening of Soviet archives at the end of the 1980s. Fitzpatrick's own work turned in an ethnographic direction, as she scoured the archives to reconstruct the lost lives of ordinary workers and peasants.[187] Historians moved on from the 1930s to "late" Stalinism and into the post-Stalin period. The "cultural turn" led to an interest in the mentalities and subjectivities of ordinary Soviet citizens.

As a popular consensus developed that nothing less than history itself had decisively proven the Soviet experience a dismal failure, historians of Communist *anciens régimes* turned to summing up the history of the recent past.[188] Among the more inspired post-mortems was Martin Malia's *The Soviet Tragedy*, that turned the positive progress of modernization into a darker view of modernity. Launching a sustained, ferocious attack on Western Sovietology, which, in his

187 Sheila Fitzpatrick, *Stalin's Peasants: Resistance and Survival in the Russian Village After Collectivization* (New York and Oxford: Oxford University Press, 1994); *Everyday Stalinism: Ordinary Life in Extraordinary Times: Soviet Russia in the 1930s* (New York and Oxford: Oxford University Press, 1999).

188 Martin Malia, *The Soviet Tragedy: A History of Socialism in Russia, 1917–1991* (New York: The Free Press, 1994); François Furet, *The Passing of an Illusion: The Idea of Communism in the Twentieth Century*, trans. Deborah Furet (Chicago: University of Chicago Press, 1999); Stéphane Courtois, Nicolas Werth, Jean-Louis Panné, Andrzej Paczkowski, Karel Bartošek, Jean-Louis Margolin, *The Black Book of Communism: Crimes, Terror, Repression*, trans. Jonathan Murphy and Mark Kramer (Cambridge, MA: Harvard University Press, 1999); and John Earl Haynes and Harvey Klehr, *In Denial: Historians, Communism, and Espionage* (San Francisco: Encounter Books, 2003).

view, contributed to a fundamental misconception and misunderstanding of the Soviet system by consistently elevating the centrality of society and reducing ideology and politics to reflections of the socio-economic base, Malia put ideology back at the center of causation with the claim that the Soviet leadership worked consistently to implement integral socialism, that is, full non-capitalism. In one of his most redolent phrases, he concluded: "In sum, there is no such thing as socialism, and the Soviet Union built it."[189] Because the moral idea of socialism is utopian and unrealizable, the only way it could be "realized" on the ground was through the terroristic means that Lenin and Stalin used. The collapse of the Soviet system was inevitable; the regime was illegitimate and doomed from the beginning; its end was inscribed in its "genetic code."

Malia placed the Soviet project in the larger problematic of modernity from the Enlightenment on. Socialism, the logical extension of the idea of democracy, was the highest form of this modernist illusion. In a similar vein, Stephen Kotkin offered a seminal study of the building of the industrial monument, Magnitogorsk, in which he borrowed insights from Foucault to show how Stalin's subjects learned to "speak Bolshevik" as they built "a new civilization."[190] Kotkin dismissed the idea of "the Russian Revolution as the embodiment of a lost social democracy, or, conversely, as a legitimation of Western society through negative example." Instead, he likened "the Russian Revolution to a mirror in which various elements of the modernity found outside the USSR are displayed in alternately undeveloped, exaggerated, and familiar forms."[191] Like Malia, Kotkin saw ideology as having "a structure derived from the bedrock proposition that, whatever socialism might be, it could not be capitalism. The use of capitalism as an anti-world helps explain why, despite the near total improvisation, the socialism built under Stalin coalesced into a 'system' that could be readily explained within the framework of October."[192] Positioning himself apart from both Fitzpatrick, who argued that Stalinism was the conservative triumph of a new post-revolutionary elite, and Lewin, who saw that triumph as a

---

189   Ibid., p. 496.

190   Stephen Kotkin, *Magnetic Mountain: Stalinism as a Civilization* (Berkeley and Los Angeles: University of California Press, 1995).

191   Ibid., p. 387.

192   Ibid., p. 400.

betrayal of the initial promise of the revolution (preserved by Lenin) and a backward form of modernization, Kotkin argued that what Stalin built was socialism, the only real fully non-capitalist socialism the world has ever seen.[193]

If a political dedication to socialism was rendered "academic" for most Western scholars after 1991, particularly in the United States, interest in the internal workings of the Soviet system, the USSR as a distinct culture, the construction of subjects and subjectivity, and the officially ascribed and self-generated identifications of Soviet citizens remained high. Neither the notion of atomized, cowed "little screws" or crypto-liberals acting as if they were believers adequately captured the full, complex range of Soviet subjectivity. Different people, and sometimes the same individual, could both resist and genuinely conform, support the regime performatively or with real enthusiasm. Even dissent was most often articulated within "the larger frame of the Soviet Revolution," appropriating the language of the regime itself.[194] That frame was extraordinarily powerful, as are hegemonic discursive formations in any society, but it also was never without contradictions, anomalies, or imprecise meanings that allowed for different readings and spaces for action. Soviet power, Foucault would have told us, had its creative side as well as its repressive aspects and constituted a landscape of categories and identifications that may have precluded "any broad, organized resistance challenging the Soviet state," but also permitted much small-scale subversion of the system, from evasion of duties, slowdowns at the workplace, and indifference to orders from above.[195] As historians as different as Lewin, Fitzpatrick, and Malia have contended, ordinary citizens agreed with the regime that together they were building socialism, even as they incessantly complained about the failure of the authorities "to deliver the goods."

While post-Soviet scholars rejected the concept of modernization, with its optimism about the universality and beneficence of that process, a darker, more critical view of modernity became the talisman for a distinct group of younger historians who wished to contest the idea of

193 Ibid., pp. 5, 379, fn. 21.
194 Jochen Hellbeck, "Speaking Out: Languages of Affirmation and Dissent in Stalinist Russia," *Kritika* I, 1 (Winter 2000), p. 74.
195 Ibid., p. 80.

Soviet exceptionalism.[196] An unusually protean term, modernity was used to explain everything from human rights to the Holocaust. Following the lead of theorists like Zygmunt Bauman and James C. Scott, the "modernity school" noted how Bolsheviks, like other modernizers, attempted to create a modern world by scientific study of society, careful enumeration and categorization of the population, and the application of planning and administration.[197] For Russianists, the frame of "modernity" presented an all-encompassing comparative syndrome in which the Soviet experiment appeared to be a particularly misguided effort that led to unprecedented violence and state-initiated bloodshed.[198]

In reaction to the "modernity school," some historians and political scientists, attentive to the insights of Max Weber, considered the neo-traditionalist aspects of the Soviet experience that denied or contradicted the move to a generalized modernity.[199] Simply put, the modernity school emphasized what was similar between the West and the Soviet Union, and the

196 See, for example, David L. Hoffman and Yanni Kotsonis (eds.), *Russian Modernity: Politics, Knowledge, Practices* (New York: St. Martin's, 2000); Amir Weiner, *Making Sense of War: The Second World War and the Fate of the Bolshevik Revolution* (Princeton: Princeton University Press, 2001); Peter Holquist, "'Information is the Alpha and Omega of Our Work': Bolshevik Surveillance in its Pan-European Context," *Journal of Modern History* LXIX, 3 (September 1997), pp. 415–50. While eclectic and inclusive in its selection of articles, the journal *Kritika: Explorations in Russian and Eurasian History*, which began publication in the winter of 2000, has established itself as the mouthpiece of what its editors conceive of as "post-revisionist" scholarship, attempting to move beyond the debates of the Cold War years. See, particularly, the editorial introduction, "Really-existing Revisionism?" in *Kritika* II, 4 (Fall 2001), pp. 707–11.

197 Bauman wrote, "In my view, the communist system was the extremely spectacular dramatization of the Enlightenment message . . . I think that people who celebrate the collapse of communism, as I do, celebrate more than that without always knowing it. They celebrate the end of modernity actually, because what collapsed was the most decisive attempt to make modernity work; and it failed. It failed as blatantly as the attempt was blatant." *Intimations of Postmodernity*, pp. 221–2.

198 For a spirited defense of the modernity paradigm, see Michael David-Fox, *Crossing Borders*, pp. 1–71.

199 Terry Martin, "Modernization or Neo-Traditionalism? Ascribed Nationality and Soviet Primordialism," in Sheila Fitzpatrick (ed.), *Stalinism, New Directions* (New York and London: Routledge, 2000), pp. 348–67; Kenneth Jowitt, "Neo-Traditionalism" (1983), reprinted in his *New World Disorder: The Leninist Extinction* (Berkeley: University of California Press, 1992), pp. 121–58; Victor Zaslavsky, *The Neo-Stalinist State: Class, Ethnicity, and Consensus in Soviet Society* (Armonk, NY: M. E. Sharpe, 1982).

neo-traditionalists were fascinated by what made the USSR distinct. Modernity was concerned with the discursive universe in which ideas of progress and subjugation of nature led to state policies that promoted the internalization and naturalization of Enlightenment values. Neo-traditionalism was more interested in social practices, down to the everyday behaviors of ordinary people. Whereas modernity talked about the "disenchantment of the world," in Weber's characterization of secularization, neo-traditionalists were impressed by the persistence of religion, superstition, and traditional beliefs, habits, and customs. Their attention was turned to status and rank consciousness, personalities and personal ties (in Russia phenomena such as *blat* [pull, personal connections], family circles, or *tolkachy* [facilitators]), patron-client networks, petitioning, and deference patterns. Kenneth Jowitt saw neo-traditionalism as a corruption of the modernist ideals of the revolutionary project, while sociologist Andrew Walder, in an influential study of Chinese neo-traditionalism, argued that the more the Communist regime tried to implement its core principles, the more neo-traditional elements came forth.[200] Abolishing the market and attempting to plan production and distribution led to soft budgeting, shortages, distribution systems based on rationing or privileged access. Petitioning was an effective substitute for recourse to the law or the possibility of public action. The end of a free press elevated the importance of gossip and rumor, and the efforts of a modernizing state to construct nationality eventually led to embedding peoples in a story of primordialist ethnogenesis. The reintroduction of ascribed identities, resurrecting the idea if not the actual categories of *soslovnost* (legally ascribed categories), was characteristic of the interwar period in the way the Soviets dealt with both class and nationality.[201]

After 1991, Sovietological political scientists had lost their subject and turned to a cluster of new questions: How did a great state self-destruct; why did the Cold War end; will the "transition" from command to market economy, from dictatorship to democracy, be successful; are post-Soviet transitions comparable to democratization in capitalist states?[202] Several

---

200   Andrew G. Walder, *Neo-traditionalism: Work and Authority in Chinese Industry* (Berkeley: University of California Press, 1986).

201   Sheila Fitzpatrick, "Ascribing Class: The Construction of Social Identity in Soviet Russia," in Fitzpatrick (ed.), *Stalinism, New Directions*, pp. 20–46; Martin, *The Affirmative Action Empire*.

202   For an analytical and critical review of Post-Sovietology, see David D. Laitin, "Post-Soviet Politics," *Annual Review of Political Science* III (2000), pp. 117–48.

explained the Gorbachev "revolution" as largely emanating from the very top of the Soviet political structure and underlined the agency of the General Secretary, his chief opponent, Boris Yeltsin, and other actors over structural factors. Others focused on institutions, the actual "Soviet constitution" of power, and the loss of confidence and eventual defection of Soviet *apparatchiki* to the side of the marketers and self-styled democrats. Still others argued that Leninist nationality policies had created a structure of national polities within the USSR that fostered potent nationalist constituencies, and proved to be a "time bomb" that with the weakening of central power tore the union apart. Rather than nationalism as the chief catalyst of state collapse, they found that state weakness and disintegration precipitated nationalist movements.[203]

"Transitologists" who had studied the fall of Latin American and Iberian dictatorships had developed a model of democratization that largely eschewed the cultural, social, and economic prerequisites for successful democratization that modernization theorists had proposed. Instead, they argued that getting the process right—namely negotiating a "pact" between the old rulers and the emerging opposition—was the best guarantee for effective democratic transition.[204] Post-Sovietologists disputed the universal applicability of the transitological model by specifying the differences between non-market economies and capitalist societies and authoritarian dictatorships in the West, and "totalitarian" states in the East.[205] Michael

---

203 Suny, *The Revenge of the Past*; Rogers Brubaker, *Nationalism Reframed* (Cambridge, MA: Cambridge University Press, 1996).

204 Guillermo O'Donnell and Philippe C. Schmitter, *Transitions from Authoritarian Rule: Tentative Conclusions about Uncertain Democracies* (Baltimore: Johns Hopkins University, 1986); Adam Przeworski, *Democracy and the Market: Political and Economic Reforms in Eastern Europe and Latin America* (Cambridge: Cambridge University Press, 1991); and Przeworski, et al., *Sustainable Democracy* (Cambridge: Cambridge University Press, 1995).

205 Valerie Bunce, *Subversive Institutions: The Design and the Destruction of Socialism and the State* (Cambridge: Cambridge University Press, 1999); Michael McFaul, *Russia's Unfinished Revolution: Political Change From Gorbachev to Putin* (Ithaca, NY: Cornell University Press, 2001); Philippe C. Schmitter with Terry Lynn Karl, "The Conceptual Travels of Transitologists and Consolidologists: How Far to the East Should They Attempt to Go?" *Slavic Review* LIII, 1 (Spring 1994), pp. 173–85; Valerie Bunce, "Should Transitologists Be Grounded?" *Slavic Review* LIV, 1 (Spring 1995), pp. 111–27; Terry Lynn Karl and Philippe C. Schmitter, "From an Iron Curtain to a Paper Curtain: Grounding Transitologists or Students of Postcommunism?" *Slavic Review* LIV, 4 (Winter 1995), pp. 965–78; and Valerie Bunce, "Paper Curtains and Paper Tigers," ibid., pp. 979–87.

McFaul showed how the transition in Russia was revolutionary, occurred without pacting, and involved mass participation—all of which were excluded from the original model.[206] But, as the new century began and Vladimir Putin solidified his power in the Kremlin, the jury remained out on how consolidated, liberal, or effectively representative Russian (or, for that matter, Ukrainian, Armenian, or any other post-Soviet) democracy was.

Even as it claimed to break with the old Sovietology, Western scholarship reproduced many of its older concerns a decade and a half after the dissolution of the Soviet Union and remained true to fundamental assumptions deriving from Western liberalism. The T-model had counterposed the indoctrinated, believing "Soviet Man" against an imagined free and liberal individual in the West, a person self-directed and capable of independent thought.[207] Cold War scholars were dismayed by the destruction of the individual in Sovietized societies and the inability of citizens to effectively resist the regime. They found it hard to believe in the authentic commitment of people to such an illiberal project as Stalinism, or to accept the legitimacy of such political deviance from a Whig trajectory. Images of Koestler's Rubashov confessing to crimes he had not committed, or Orwell's Winston Smith capitulating to Big Brother, powerfully conveyed Soviet socialism's threat to liberal individuality. Yet, as social historians had demonstrated, Soviet subjects were neither atomized, nor completely terrorized and propagandized victims of the system; they managed to adapt to and even shape the contours imposed from above.

When post-Soviet scholars or journalists looked back at the seventy-four years of the Soviet experience, they most often turned to the Stalinist horrors as the emblem of Leninist hubris. In 1999, a team of scholars produced a massive catalogue of crimes, terror, and repression by Soviet-style communisms. *The Black Book of Communism* contended that "Communist regimes did not just commit criminal acts (all states do so on occasion); they were criminal enterprises in their very essence: on principle, so to speak, they all ruled lawlessly, by violence and without regard for human life."[208] Given this foundational claim, it followed that

---

206 McFaul, *Russia's Unfinished Revolution*.

207 For development of this theme, to which this paragraph is indebted, see the insightful discussion in Anna Krylova, "The Tenacious Liberal Subject in Soviet Studies," *Kritika* I, 1 (Winter 2000), pp. 119–46.

208 Courtois, et al., *The Black Book of Communism*, p. xvii.

"there never was a benign, initial phase of communism before some mythical 'wrong turn' threw it off track."[209] Its violence was a deliberative, not a reactive, policy of the revolutionary regimes, and was based in a Marxist "science" that elevated the class struggle to the central driving force of history. The aim of *The Black Book* was not only to show that the very essence of communism was terror as a form of rule, but even more ambitiously to demonstrate that communism was not just comparable to fascism but ultimately worse than Nazism. *The Black Book* laid the burden of guilt on intellectuals, those who thought up, spread, and justified the idea that liberation and secular salvation ought to be purchased at any price.

Yet in its attempt to judge Soviet killing by the standard of Nazi crimes, *The Black Book* actually dehistoricizes Soviet violence. Context and causation are less important than the equation with the colossal, seemingly inexplicable evil that led to the Holocaust. These claims led to an intense international debate around *The Black Book*, recapitulating arguments that had divided historians of the Soviet Union for decades: Is explanation to be sought in the social or the ideological? Is there an essential connection between all communist movements that stems from their roots in Leninism, to produce the violence that has accompanied them in all parts of the world? Or are these movements, while related, more particularly the products of their own social, political, and cultural environments?

For all the claims that the old controversies of the Cold War had ended with the end of the Soviet Union, the problematical meaning of the Soviet Union remains an open question among scholars and in the public sphere. While some continue to look for some deep essence that determined the nature of the USSR, others search for the contradictions and anomalies that disrupt any facile model. Neutrality remains a worthy if elusive stance, complete objectivity an unobtainable ideal. While conservative scholars celebrate what they see as the victory of their views over "left-wing" Sovietology, and the pursuit of modernity appears dubious to many scholars, Russian and Soviet studies, ironically, hold firm to the broad liberal values that marked Western attitudes toward the East a century ago. Without a "socialist" alternative with which to contend,

---

209 Ibid., p. xviii.

pundits proclaim that the expectations of the modernizationists have been realized—a single world gravitating toward capitalist democracy. The West continues to regard itself as superior in what is now called the globalizing world, and its most zealous advocates are prepared to export its political and economic forms, even if this requires military force, against the resistance of those who reject Western modernity and its liberal values. The states of the former Soviet Union exist in the twilight of a failed socialism, but without the full light of the anticipated democratic-capitalist dawn. Well into the third decade after the formal fall of the USSR, the Soviet Union continues to unravel, with wars on Russia's peripheries—in Chechnya, Georgia, Armenia, Azerbaijan, and Ukraine—desperately determining the boundaries of legitimate authority. As those who had insisted that capitalist economics and democratic politics would wipe away the East's deviant past confront the persistence of Soviet institutions, practices, and attitudes long after the collapse, they must humbly reconsider the power of that past. You can take Russia and Ukraine out of the Soviet Union, but you cannot take the Soviet Union out of Russia and the Ukraine. Whether one thinks of this as the "Leninist legacy," or Soviet path dependency, or the continuities of a relatively fixed Russian (or Georgian or Uzbek) political culture, looking backwards in order to understand the present and future has become ever more imperative for social scientists and historians.

CHAPTER THREE

The Empire Strikes Out: Imperial Russia, "National" Identity, and Theories of Empire

At a time when Russian politicians have re-employed the term *derzhava* (Great Power) to provide a vision of a future Russia, Western writers have resurrected the metaphor of "empire" to describe the former Soviet Union, and even post-Soviet Russia.[1] Earlier "empire" either referred to the external relationship between the USSR and its East European dependencies or, if used for the internal relations between Moscow and the non-Russian peoples, it usually had a highly partisan valence and signaled to the reader a conservative, anti-Soviet interpretation of nationality policy.[2] Consistent with Ronald Reagan's sense of the USSR as the

---

1 During the Yeltsin years *Derzhava* was the name of General Aleksandr Rutskoi's political organization and the title of a book by Gennadii Zyuganov, head of the Communist Party of the Russian Federation. General Aleksandr Lebed, a presidential candidate of one of the nationalist parties, has written a book entitled *Za derzhavu obidna* (Shameful for a Great Power). This chapter was originally given as a talk in a seminar at the Center for International Security and Arms Control at Stanford University, where I was an associate in 1995–96 and originally published in Ronald Grigor Suny and Terry Martin (eds.), *A State of Nations: Empire and Nation-Making in the Age of Lenin and Stalin* (New York: Oxford University Press, 2001). I extend gratitude to my colleagues at the Center, its co-director David Holloway, along with special thanks for comments and/or careful reading of various drafts to Lowell Barrington, Rogers Brubaker, Valerie Bunce, Prasenjit Duara, Lynn Eden, Barbara Engel, Matthew Evangelista, Ted Hopf, Michel Khodarkovsky, Jeremy King, Valerie Kivelson, David Laitin, Gail Lapidus, Stephen Pincus, Norman Naimark, Lewis Siegelbaum, and Katherine Verdery.
2 See, for example, G. P. Fedotov, "Sud'ba imperii," in *Novyi grad: Sbornik statei* (New York: Izdatel'stvo imeni Chekhova, 1952) ; Olaf Caroe, *Soviet Empire* (London: Macmillan, 1953, 1967); Albert Herling, *The Soviet Slave Empire* (New York: W. Funk, 1951); U S Library of Congress Legislative Reference Service, *The Soviet Empire: Prison House of Nations and Races* (Washington: US Government Printing Office, 1958); Walter Kolarz, *Russia and Her Colonies* (London: George Philip and Son, 1952); George Gretton (ed.), *Communism and Colonialism: Essays by Walter Kolarz* (London: Macmillan, 1964); Hélène Carrière d'Encausse, *Decline of an Empire* (New York: Newsweek Books, 1979); and Robert Conquest (ed.), *The Last Empire: Nationality and the Soviet Future* (Stanford, CA: Hoover Institution Press, 1986).

"Evil Empire," empire applied to states that were considered internally repressive and externally expansionist. But in the late 1980s, with the rise of nationalist and separatist movements within the Soviet Union, the term was used more widely as a seemingly transparent empirical description of a particular form of multinational state.[3] As Mark R. Beissinger noted, "What once was routinely referred to as a state suddenly came to be universally condemned as an empire."[4] Though free of any theorization at first, the concept of a "Soviet Empire" implied immediately a state that had lost its legitimacy and was destined to collapse. Rather than expansion, implosion was heightened. Beissinger continued: "The general consensus now appears to be that the Soviet Union was an empire and therefore it broke up. However, it is also routinely referred to as an empire precisely because it did break up."[5] This sense of the lack of legitimacy and disposition to disintegration continues to be part of the imperial metaphor, but those examining the policies of Yeltsin and Putin's Russia toward the so-called "Near Abroad" have once again employed "empire" in its original expansionist meaning.

Whatever its power of explanation or prediction (or as they say in social science, robustness), the concept of empire was the organizing metaphor for a series of conferences, projected volumes and on-going debate in the journals during the first years after the Soviet

---

3 A partial list would include: David Pryce-Jones, *The Strange Death of the Soviet Empire* (New York: Metropolitan Books, 1995); Kristian Gerner, *The Baltic States and the End of the Soviet Empire* (London: Routledge, 1993); David Remnick, *Lenin's Tomb: The Last Days of the Soviet Empire* (New York: Random House, 1993); Sanford R. Lieberman (ed.), *The Soviet Empire Reconsidered: Essays in Honor of Adam B. Ulam* (Boulder: Westview Press, 1994); Jack F. Matlock, *Autopsy on an Empire: The American Ambassador's Account of the Collapse of the Soviet Union* (New York: Random House, 1995); Robert Cullen, *Twilight of Empire: Inside the Crumbling Soviet Union* (New York: Atlantic Monthly Press, 1991); John B. Dunlop, *The Rise of Russia and the Fall of the Soviet Empire* (Princeton: Princeton University Press, 1993); Neil Felshman, *Gorbachev, Yeltsin and the Last Days of the Soviet Empire* (New York: St. Martin's Press, 1992); Marco Buttino (ed.), *In a Collapsing Empire: Underdevelopment, Ethnic Conflicts and Nationalisms in the Soviet Union* (Milano: Felltrinelli, 1993); G. R. Urban, *End of Empire: The Demise of the Soviet Union* (Washington: American University Press, 1993); Richard L. Rudolph and David F. Good (eds.), *Nationalism and Empire: The Habsburg Empire and the Soviet Union* (New York: St. Martin's Press, 1992); and Ryszard Kapuscinski, *Imperium* (New York: Alfred A. Knopf, 1994).

4 Mark R. Beissinger, "The Persisting Ambiguity of Empire," in *Post-Soviet Affairs* XI, 2 (April–June 1995), p. 155.

5 Ibid.

disintegration.[6] At the same moment that scholars confidently predicted the end of the age of empires, they found a new growth industry in the comparative study of that extinct species. This chapter investigates empire as a problem in the internal construction of states, as in contiguous state empires—a set of states that has been far less discussed in the comparative and theoretical literature than have overseas colonial empires. Looking at problems of state maintenance, decay, and collapse, through the interplay of nations and empires, I argue that understanding empire requires historical contextualization, since its viability is related to the operative discourses of legitimation and the international environment in which empires are located. In this chapter I, first, elaborate theories of imperial survival, decay, and collapse that I hope will give us some purchase on understanding the dynamics and the collapse of the Russian and Soviet empires. And then, I employ ideal types of empire and nation to help understand the structure, evolution, and failure of the tsarist empire to construct a viable "national" identity. I begin with some definitions.

Empire, State, Nation

Among the various kinds of political communities and units that have existed historically, empires have been among the most ubiquitous, in many ways the precursors of the modern bureaucratic state. Anthony Pagden has traced the various meanings attached to empire in European discourses. In its original meaning in classical times, *imperium* described the executive authority of Roman magistrates and eventually came to

---

6 Among them were: "Great Power Ethnic Politics: The Habsburg Empire and the Soviet Union," held at the Center for Austrian Studies, University of Minnesota, April 26–28, 1990, which led to the Rudolph and Good volume cited on the previous page; an SSRC workshop, "The End of Empire: Causes and Consequences," at the Harriman Institute, Columbia University, November 20–21, 1994, and the subsequent publication of Karen Barkey and Mark von Hagen (eds.), *After Empire: Multinational Societies and Nation-Building: The Soviet Union and the Russian, Ottoman, and Habsburg Empires* (Boulder, CO: Westview Press, 1997); and a conference on "The Disintegration and Reconstitution of Empires: The USSR and Russia in Comparative Perspective," at the University of California, San Diego, January 10–12, 1996, which has appeared as Karen Dawisha and Bruce Parrott (eds.), *The End of Empire? The Transformation of the USSR in Comparative Perspective* (Armonk, NY and London: M. E. Sharpe, 1997). For debate, see Mark R. Beissinger, "The Persisting Ambiguity of Empire"; and the reply by Ronald Grigor Suny, "Ambiguous Categories: States, Empire and Nations," *Post-Soviet Affairs* XI, 2 (April-June 1995), pp. 185–96.

refer to "non-subordinate power." Such a usage can be found in the first line of Machiavelli's *The Prince*: "All the states and dominions which have had and have empire over men ..."[7] By the sixteenth century, empire took on the meaning of *status*, state, the political relationships that held groups of people together in an extended system, but from Roman times on it already possessed one of the modern senses of empire as an immense state, an "extended territorial dominion."[8] Finally, "to claim to be an *imperator* [from Augustus's time] was to claim a degree, and eventually a kind of power, denied to mere kings."[9] Absolute or autocratic rule was then identified with empire, along with the idea that an empire referred to "a diversity of territories under a single authority."[10] Pagden emphasizes the durability of these discursive traditions:

> All these three senses of the term *imperium*—as limited and independent or "perfect" rule, as a territory embracing more than one political community, and as the absolute sovereignty of a single individual—survive into the late eighteenth century and sometimes well beyond. All three derived from the discursive practices of the Roman empire, and to a lesser extent the Athenian and Macedonian empires.[11]

Moreover, empire was connected with "the notion of a single exclusive world domain," both in Roman times and later, and the great European overseas empires, especially that of Spain, never quite abandoned "this legacy of universalism, developed over centuries and reinforced by a powerfully articulate learned elite."[12]

Though sensitive to the variety of historical meanings attached to empire, social scientists have attempted a more limited understanding of empire as a political relationship. Michael W. Doyle's definition— "Empire ... is a relationship, formal or informal, in which one state controls the effective political sovereignty of another political

---

7 Anthony Pagden, *Lords of All the World: Ideologies of Empire in Spain, Britain, and France, c. 1500–c. 1800* (New Haven and London: Yale University Press, 1995), p. 12.

8 Ibid., p. 15.

9 Ibid.

10 Ibid., p. 16.

11 Ibid., p. 17.

12 Ibid., pp. 27–8.

society"—is extremely useful, even though he is concerned almost exclusively with non-contiguous empires.[13] Elaborating further he argues that empire is "a system of interaction between two political entities, one of which, the dominant metropole, exerts political control over the internal and external policy—the effective sovereignty—of the other, the subordinate periphery."[14] John A. Armstrong, as well, speaks of empire as "a compound polity that has incorporated lesser ones."[15] For my purposes, looking at contiguous empire-states that do not necessarily have states within them, political society must be defined more loosely than as state.[16]

Borrowing from Armstrong and Doyle, I define empire as a particular form of domination or control, between two units set apart in a hierarchical, inequitable relationship, more precisely a composite state in which a metropole dominates a periphery to the disadvantage of the periphery. Rather than limit empires and imperialism (the building and maintaining of empires) to relations between polities, I extend the definition of imperialism to any deliberate act or policy that furthers a state's extension or maintenance, for the purpose of aggrandizement of that kind of (direct or indirect) political or economic control over any other inhabited territory, in a way which involves the inequitable treatment of those inhabitants in comparison with its own citizens or subjects. Like Doyle, I emphasize that an imperial state differs from the broader category of multinational states, confederations, or federations in that it "is not organized on the basis of political equality among societies or individuals. The domain of empire is a people subject to unequal rule."[17] Not all multinational, multicultural, or multireligious states are necessarily empires, but where distinctions remain and treatment is unequal, as in areas that remain ethnically distinct, then the relationship continues to be imperial. Inequitable treatment might involve forms of cultural or linguistic discrimination or disadvantageous redistributive practices from the periphery to the metropole (but not necessarily, as, for example, in the Soviet empire). This ideal type of empire, then, is fundamentally different

---

13   Michael W. Doyle, *Empires* (Ithaca: Cornell University Press, 1986), p. 45.

14   Ibid., p. 12.

15   John A. Armstrong, *Nations Before Nationalism* (Chapel Hill: University of North Carolina Press, 1982), p. 131.

16   Doyle, *Empires*, p. 45.

17   Ibid., p. 36.

from the ideal type of the nation-state. While empire means inequitable rule over something different, nation-state rule is, at least in theory if not always in practice, the same for all members of the nation. Citizens of the nation have a different relationship with their state than do the subjects of empire.

Besides inequality and subordination, the relationship of the metropole to the periphery is marked by difference—by ethnicity, geographic separation, administrative distinction.[18] If peripheries are fully integrated into the metropole, as various appanage principalities were into Muscovy, and treated as well or badly as the metropolitan provinces, then the relationship is not imperial. Very importantly, the metropole need not be defined ethnically or geographically. It is the ruling institution. In several empires, rather than a geographic or ethnic distinction from the periphery, the ruling institution had a status or class character, a specially endowed nobility or political class, like the *Osmanlı* in the Ottoman Empire, or the imperial family and upper layers of the landed gentry and bureaucracy in the Russian Empire, or, analogously, the Communist *nomenklatura* in the Soviet Union. In my understanding, neither tsarist Russia nor the Soviet Union was an ethnically "Russian Empire" with the metropole completely identified with a ruling Russian nationality. Rather, the ruling institution—nobility in one case, the Communist Party elite in the other—was multinational, though primarily Russian and ruled imperially over Russian and non-Russian subjects alike. In empire, unlike nations, the distance and difference of the rulers is part of the ideological justification for the superordination of the ruling institution. The right to rule in empire resides with the ruling institution, not in the consent of the governed.

All states have centers, capital cities and central elites, which in some ways are superior to the other parts of the state, but in empires the metropole is uniquely sovereign, able to override routinely the desires and decisions of peripheral units.[19] The flow of goods, information, and power

---

18 As Alexander J. Motyl argues, the peripheries must be distinct by population—class, ethnicity, religion, or something else—have a distinct territory, and be either a distinct polity or a distinct society. "From Imperial Decay to Imperial Collapse: The Fall of the Soviet Empire in Comparative Perspective," in Rudolph and Good (eds.), *Nationalism and Empire*, p. 18.

19 Of course, as an imperial metropole grows weaker and peripheries stronger, as in the Habsburg Empire after 1848, it is forced to negotiate with powerful peripheries, as Vienna did with Budapest, and in time the empire may become a hybrid empire with

runs from periphery to metropole and back to periphery, but seldom from periphery to periphery. The degree of dependence of periphery on metropole is far greater and more encompassing than in other kinds of states. Roads and railroads run to the capital; elaborate architectural and monumental displays mark the imperial center off from other centers; and the central imperial elite distinguishes itself in a variety of ways from both peripheral elites, often their servants and agents, and the ruled population.[20] The metropole benefits from the periphery in an inequitable way; there is "exploitation," or at least the perception of exploitation. That, indeed, is the essence of what being colonized means.

While subordination, inequitable treatment, and exploitation might be measured in a variety of ways, they are always inflected subjectively and normatively. As Beissinger has suggested:

Any attempt to define empire in "objective" terms—as a system of stratification, as a policy based on force, as a system of exploitation— fails in the end to capture what is undoubtedly the most important dimension of any imperial situation: perception . . . Empires and states are set apart not primarily by exploitation, nor even by the use of force, but essentially by whether politics and policies are accepted as "ours" or are rejected as "theirs."[21]

To this should be added that the perception of empire is not only about the attitude of peripheries but of metropoles as well. Empire exists even if peripheral populations are convinced that the result of their association with the empire is beneficial rather than exploitative, as long as the two conditions of distinction and subordination obtain. Indeed, much of the "post-colonialism" literature has dealt precisely with the ways in which hegemonic cultures of difference and development have sanctioned imperial relations and mediated resistance.

---

various autonomous "kingdoms" and "principalities" that no longer respect the authority of the center as it had in the past.

20 Fatma Müge Göçek, "The Social Construction of an Empire: Ottoman State Under Suleiman the Magnificent," in Halil Inalcik and Cemal Kafadar (eds.), *Suleiman II and His Time* (Istanbul: Isis Press, 1993), pp. 93–108.

21 Mark R. Beissinger, "Demise of an Empire-State: Identity, Legitimacy, and the Deconstruction of Soviet Politics," in Crawford Young (ed.), *The Rising Tide of Cultural Pluralism: The Nation-State at Bay?* (Madison: University of Wisconsin Press, 1993), pp. 98, 99.

To sum up, empire is a composite state structure in which the metropole is distinct in some way from the periphery, and the relationship between the two is conceived or perceived by metropolitan or peripheral actors as one of justifiable or unjustifiable inequity, subordination, and/or exploitation. "Empire" is not merely a form of polity but also a value-laden appellation that as late as the nineteenth century (and even, in some usages, well into our own) was thought of as the sublime form of political existence (think of New York as the "empire state"), but which in the late twentieth century cast doubts about the legitimacy of a polity and even predicted its eventual, indeed inevitable, demise.[22] Thus, the Soviet Union, which a quarter of a century ago would have been described by most social scientists as a state and only occasionally, and usually by quite conservative analysts, as an empire, is almost universally described after its demise as an empire, since it now appears to have been an illegitimate, composite polity unable to contain the rising nations within it.

Recognizing that forms of the state as well as concepts of the state have changed over time, I adopt a fairly basic definition of "state" as a set of common political institutions capable of monopolizing legitimate violence and distributing some goods and services within a demarcated territory. As Rogers Brubaker has noted, the generation of modern statehood meant a movement from what was essentially "a network of persons" in the medieval sense to "territorialization of rule," as the world was transformed into a set of bounded and mutually exclusive citizenries.[23] The modern "state" (basically post fifteenth century) is characterized by relatively fixed territorial boundaries, a single sovereignty over its territory, and a permanent bureaucratic and military apparatus. As states homogenized their territories in the late medieval and early modern periods, eliminating competing sovereignties and standardizing administration, a number of states that at first looked a lot like the empires described above consolidated a relatively coherent internal community, either on linguistic, ethnocultural, or religious lines, that made an idea of "nation" conceivable with the coming of the late eighteenth-century revolutions and the subsequent "age of nationalism."[24] At the same time less

---

22 A point made eloquently by Mark Beissinger.

23 Rogers Brubaker, *Citizenship and Nationhood in France and Germany* (Cambridge, MA: Harvard University Press, 1992), p. 22.

24 This process of internal political and cultural integration, developing urban centers, and consolidation of state forms has usually been limited by analysts to Western

homogeneous states, those that emerged into the modern period as contiguous empires, tightened their internal interconnections in order to be competitive in the new international environment, but without achieving the degree of internal homogeneity of proto-nation-states such as Portugal or France.

In his study of "internal colonialism," Michael Hechter argues that it is only after the fact that one can determine whether (nation)-state-building or empire-building has occurred. If the core has been successful in persuading the population of its expanding territory into accepting the legitimacy of the central authority, then (nation)-state-building has occurred, but if the population rejects or resists that authority, then the center has only succeeded in creating an empire.[25] Many, if not most, of the oldest nation-states of our own time began their historic evolution as heterogeneous dynastic conglomerates with the characteristics of imperial relationships between metropole and periphery, and only after the hard work of nationalizing homogenization by state authorities were hierarchical empires transformed into relatively egalitarian nation-states based on a horizontal notion of equal citizenship. Yet in the dubiously named "age of nationalism," that very process of nationalization stimulated the ethnonational consciousness of some populations able to distinguish themselves (or having been distinguished by others), who then resisted assimilation into the ruling nationality, became defined as a "minority," and ended up in a colonial relationship with the metropolitan nation. In these cases, "nation-making" laid bare the underlying imperialism of the state.

Following the lead of constructivist theorists of the nation, I define a nation as a group of people who imagines itself to be a political community that is distinct from the rest of humankind, believes that it shares characteristics, perhaps origins, values, historical experiences, language, territory, or any of many other elements, and on the basis of their defined culture

Europe, the traditional site of the first national states; but Victor Lieberman has convincingly argued that the whole of Eurasia, from Britain to Japan, underwent similar and connected processes in the early modern period, from roughly 1450 to 1830. See his "Introduction" and "Transcending East–West Dichotomies: State and Culture Formation in Six Ostensibly Disparate Areas," *Modern Asian Studies* XXXI, 3 (1997), pp. 449–61, 463–546.

25 Michael Hechter, *Internal Colonialism: The Celtic Fringe in British National Development, 1536–1966* (Berkeley: University of California Press, 1975), pp. 60–4.

deserves self-determination, which usually entails control of its own territory (the "homeland") and a state of its own.[26] Neither natural nor primordial but the result of hard constitutive intellectual and political work of elites and masses, nations exist in particular understandings of history, stories in which the nation is seen as the subject moving continuously through time, coming to self-awareness over many centuries.[27] Though there may be examples of political communities in the distant past that approach our notions of modern nations, in the modern era political communities exist within a discourse that came together in the late eighteenth and early nineteenth centuries around the notion of bounded territorial sovereignties in which the "people," constituted as a nation, provide legitimacy to the political order. From roughly the late eighteenth century to the present the state merged with the "nation," and almost all modern states claimed to be nation-states, either in an ethnic or civic sense, with governments deriving power from and exercising it in the interest of the nation. Modern states legitimized themselves in reference to the nation and the claims to popular sovereignty implicit in the discourse of the nation.[28]

Although the discourse of the nation began as an expression of state patriotism, through the nineteenth century it increasingly became ethnicized until the "national community" was understood to be a cultural community of shared language, religion, and/or other characteristics, with a durable, antique past, shared kinship, common origins and narratives of progress through time. Lost to time was the ways in which notions of shared pasts and common origins were constructed and reimagined,

---

26 The distinction between ethnic group and nationality/nation need not be territory but rather the discourse in which they operate. The discourse of ethnicity is primarily about kinship, culture, cultural rights, and some limited political recognition, while the discourse of the nation is more often about popular sovereignty, state power, and control of a territorial homeland. But this is not necessarily or exclusively so, for one can conceive of non-territorial nationalisms, like those of the Jews before Zionism, the Armenians in the nineteenth century, and the Roma. For another view on the problems of definitions, see Lowell W. Barrington, "'Nation' and 'Nationalism': The Misuse of Key Concepts in Political Science," *PS: Political Science & Politics* XXX, 4 (December 1977), pp. 712–16.

27 See, for example, Etienne Balibar, "The Nation Form: History and Ideology," from Etienne Balibar and Immanuel Wallerstein, *Race, Nation, Class: Ambiguous Identities* (London: Verso, 1991), pp. 86–106; Benedict Anderson, *Imagined Communities: Reflections on the Origin and Spread of Nationalism* (London: Verso, 1983).

28 Brubaker, *Citizenship and Nationhood in France and Germany*, pp. 22, 27.

how primary languages were selected from dialects and elevated to dominance through print and schooling, and how history itself was employed
to justify claims to the world's real estate. Nationalists strove to make the
nation and the state congruent, an almost utopian goal, and it is not a
great stretch to argue that much of modern history has been about
making nations and states fit together in a world where the two almost
never match.

By the twentieth century such imagined communities were the most
legitimate basis for the constitution of states, displacing dynastic, religious, and class discourses—and coincidentally challenging alternative
formulas for legitimation, like those underpinning empires. Once-viable
imperial states became increasingly vulnerable to nationalist movements
that in turn gained strength from the new understanding that states ought
to represent, if not coincide with, nations. The simultaneous rise of
notions of democratic representation of subaltern interests accentuated
the fundamental tension between inequitable imperial relationships and
horizontal conceptions of national citizenship. Though liberal states
with representative institutions, styling themselves as democracies, could
be (and were) effective imperial powers in the overseas empires of Great
Britain, France, Belgium, and the Netherlands, the great contiguous
empires resisted a democratization that would have undermined the right
to rule of the dominant imperial elite and the very hierarchical, inequitable relationship between metropole and periphery in the empire. While
empires were among the most ubiquitous and long-lived polities in
premodern history, they were progressively subverted in modern times by
the powerful combination of nationalism and democracy.[29]

---

29 Nation-states and empires can be seen as two poles in a continuum, but rather
than fixed and stable, they may flow into one another, transforming over time into the
other. A nation-state may appear stable, homogeneous, coherent, and yet with the rise
of ethnic, sub-ethnic, or regionalist movements be perceived by subaltern populations as
imperial. For those identifying with the dominant population in Belgium, it is a nation-
state, perhaps a multinational state, but for a Flemish militant who feels the oppression
of the Walloon majority, Belgium is a kind of mini-empire. The term empire has been
used polemically for small states like Belgium, Georgia, and Estonia, and it may seem
anomalous to refer to such nationalizing states as empires. But it is precisely with the
assimilating, homogenizing, or discriminating practices of the nationalizing state that
relationships of difference and subordination—here considered the ingredients of an
imperial relationship—are exposed. Coercive assimilation can be at one and the same
time a nationalizing and an imperializing process.

Modernizing Empires

Some macrohistorical accounts of state and nation development argue that there has been a universal process of territorial consolidation, homogenization of population and institutions, and concentration of power and sovereignty that laid the groundwork for the modern nation-state. While such accounts certainly capture a principal pattern of state formation in the early modern period, that powerful metanarrative neglects the persistence and durability under certain conditions of less "modern" political forms such as empires. The question arises, why did the last empires of Europe not evolve into nation-states by the nineteenth and twentieth centuries? How did the practices and preferences of imperial elites prevent nation-making, even when becoming a nation might have made their state more competitive in the international arena? In several contiguous empires, state authorities in fact attempted to homogenize the differences within the state in order to achieve the kinds of efficiencies that accompanied the more homogeneous nation-states, but for a variety of reasons they ultimately failed. What was possible in medieval and early modern times when quite heterogeneous populations assimilated into relatively homogeneous proto-nations, perhaps around common religious or dynastic loyalties, became in the "age of nationalism" far more difficult, for now the available discourse of the nation—with all its attendant attractions of progress, representation, and statehood—became available for anyone to claim. At the same time the appeals of popular sovereignty and democracy implied in the nation-form challenged the inequity, hierarchy, and discrimination inherent in empire, undermining its very raison d'être. Modern empires were caught between maintaining the privileges and distinctions that kept the traditional elites in power or considering reforms along liberal lines that would have undermined the old ruling classes. While the great "bourgeois" overseas empires of the nineteenth century were able to liberalize, even democratize in the metropoles, at the same time maintaining harsh repressive regimes in the colonies, pursuing different policies in core and periphery was far more difficult in contiguous empires than in non-contiguous ones. While it was possible to have a democratic metropole and colonized peripheries in overseas empires, as the examples of Britain, France, and Belgium show, it was potentially destabilizing to implant constitutionalism or liberal democracy in only part of a contiguous empire. In Russia the privileges enjoyed by the Grand Duchy of Finland, or even the constitution granted to Bulgaria, an independent state outside the empire, were constant reminders to the tsar's educated subjects of his refusal to allow them similar institutions. Here is a major tension of contiguous empires. Some kind of separation, apartheid, is essential to maintain a democratic and non-democratic political order in a single state. But this is a highly unstable compromise, as the governments of South Africa and Israel discovered in the twentieth century.

In contiguous empires, where the distinction between the nation and the empire is more easily muddled than in overseas empires, ruling elites may attempt to construct hybrid notions of an empire-nation, as in tsarist Russia or the Ottoman Empire in the nineteenth century.[30] Responding to the challenges presented by the efficiencies of the new national states, imperial elites promoted a transition from "ancien régime" empires to "modern" empires, from a more polycentric and differentiated polity in which regions maintained quite different legal, economic, and even political structures, to a more centralized, bureaucratized state in which laws, economic practices, even customs and dialects, were homogenized by state elites. The more modern empires adopted a number of strategies to restabilize their rule. In Russia the monarchy became more "national" in its self-image and public representation, drawing it closer to the people it ruled. In Austro-Hungary the central state devolved power to several of the non-ruling peoples, moving the empire toward becoming a more egalitarian multinational state. In the Ottoman Empire, modernizing bureaucrats abandoned certain traditional hierarchical practices that privileged Muslims over non-Muslims, and in the reforming era known as *Tanzimat* they attempted to create a civic state of all the peoples (*milletler*) of the empire, an Ottomanist idea of a new imperial community. In the last two decades of the nineteenth century the tsarist government attempted yet another strategy, a policy of administrative and cultural Russification that privileged a single nationality. The Young Turks after 1908 experimented with everything from an Ottomanist liberalism to Pan-Islamic, Pan-Turkic, and increasingly nationalist reconfigurations of their empire.[31] But

---

30 See Benedict Anderson's chapter on "Official Nationalism and Imperialism" in *Imagined Communities*, pp. 83–112; and Jane Burbank's unpublished essay, "The Imperial Construction of Nationality."

31 On the Ottoman case, see Ronald Grigor Suny, *"They Can Live in the Desert But Nowhere Else": A History of the Armenian Genocide* (Princeton: Princeton University Press, 2015); on the Russian case, see Valerie A. Kivelson and Ronald Grigor Suny, *Russia's Empires* (New York: Oxford University Press, 2017).

modernizing imperialists were caught between these new projects of homogenization and rationalization, and policies and structures that maintained distance and difference from their subjects as well as differentiations and disadvantages among the peoples of the empire. Modernizing empires searched for new legitimation formulae that softened rhetorics of conquest and divine sanction and emphasized the civilizing mission of the imperial metropole, its essential competence in a new project of development.

Given the unevenness of the economic transformations of the nineteenth and twentieth centuries, all within a highly competitive international environment, most states, even quite conservative imperial states like the Ottoman and Romanov empires, undertook state programs of economic and social "modernization." Developmentalism was soon deeply embedded both in national and imperial state policies. Needing to justify the rule of foreigners over peoples who were constituting themselves as nations, the idea of "developing" inferior or uncivilized peoples became a dominant source of imperial legitimation and continued well into the twentieth century.[32]

There is a subversive dialectic in developmentalism, however. Its successes create the conditions for imperial failure. If the developmentalist program succeeds among the colonized people, realizing material well-being and intellectual sophistication, urbanism and industrialism, social mobility and knowledge of the world, the justification for foreign imperial rule over a "backward" people evaporates. Indeed, rather than suppressing nation-making and nationalism, imperialism far more often provides conditions and stimulation for the construction of new nations. Populations are ethnographically described, statistically enumerated, ascribed characteristics and functions, and as a result they are more easily able to reconceive themselves in ways that qualify them as "nations." Not accidentally the map of the world at the end of the twentieth century is marked by dozens of states with boundaries drawn by imperialism. And if clearly defined and articulated nations do not exist within these states by the moment of independence, then elites busily set

32 See Frederick Cooper and Randall Packard, "Introduction," in Cooper and Packard (eds.), *International Development and the Social Sciences: Essays on the History and Politics of Knowledge* (Berkeley, Los Angeles, and London: University of California Press, 1997), pp. 1–41.

about creating national political communities to fill out the fledgling state.

Developmentalism, of course, was not the project of "bourgeois" nation-states and empires alone, but of self-styled socialist ones as well. The problem grew when empires which justified their rule as agents of modernity and modernization, instruments of development and progress, achieved their stated task too well—supplying their subordinated populations with languages of aspiration and resistance (as Cooper and Packard put it, "What at one level appears like a discourse of control is at another a discourse of entitlement"[33]), and indeed creating subjects that no longer required empire in the way the colonizers claimed. This dialectical reversal of the justification for empire, embedded in the theory and practice of modernization, was, in my view, also at the very core of the progressive decay of the Soviet Empire. The Communist Party effectively made itself irrelevant. Who needed a "vanguard" when you now had an urban, educated, mobile, self-motivated society? Who needed imperial control from Moscow when national elites and their constituents were able to articulate their own interests, in terms sanctioned by Marxism-Leninism in the idea of national self-determination?

Maintaining Empires

Earlier in this century, when the problem of imperialism gripped scholars and theorists as well as politicians, their attention focused on the causes and dynamics of empire-making—expansion and conquest, incorporation and annexation.[34] More recently, theorists have elaborated the conditions under which empires successfully maintain themselves. Following a suggestion by the classical historian M. I. Finley, Michael Doyle looks at a series of premodern empires—Athens, Rome, Spain, England, and the Ottoman—and argues that among the factors that

---

33 Ibid., p. 3.

34 Among the most familiar were Vladimir Lenin's theory that the falling rate of profit in developed capitalist states propelled European states to build empires to absorb their surplus capital, and J. A. Hobson's, on which Lenin built, that the imbalanced distribution of wealth within capitalist societies leads to underconsumption by the masses, oversaving by the wealthy, and a need to find new markets in underdeveloped countries. Historians critical of economic explanations, like Carlton J. H. Hayes, countered that rather than the imperatives of capitalism, the metropole's national interests or nationalism drove states toward colonization of the non-European world.

make empire possible, sustainable, and, more dynamically, expansionist are: a differential of power, greater in the metropole, less in the peripheries; political unity of the imperial or hegemonic metropole, which involves not only a strong, united central government but a broader sense of legitimacy and community among the imperial elite; and some form of transnational connection—forces or actors, religion, ideology, economy, a form of society based in the metropole and capable of extending itself to subject societies. Athens had such a transnational society and became imperial, while Sparta did not have one and could exercise only hegemony over other states.[35]

The greater "power" of the unified metropole over the peripheries ought to be understood not merely as greater coercive power but discursive power as well. Following the lead of Edward Said, scholars have moved beyond material and structural analyses to investigate how empires maintained themselves, not only by the obvious means of physical force, but also through a kind of manufactured consent. "Colonial" and "postcolonial" scholars have explored the ways in which coercive power was supplemented and sanctioned by discursive power. "Colonialism," one influential collection asserts, "(like its counterpart, racism), then, is an operation of discourse, and as an operation of discourse it interpellates colonial subjects by incorporating them in a system of representation. They are always already written by that system of representation."[36] Whether it was the story of *The Water Babies*, the adventure stories of Robert Dixon or Rudyard Kipling, or the tales of Babar the Elephant, the fantasies elaborated contained naturalized images of superior and inferior races and nations. One of the most telling sets of arguments from colonial studies has been the way in which colonialism and its attendant racism not only inscribed the position of the colonized but also fundamentally shaped the self-representation of the colonizer. The problem for imperialism was creating and maintaining difference and distance between ruler and ruled. In a discussion that began with Said's seminal work, *Orientalism*, and continued with his later *Culture and Imperialism*, scholars have investigated the ways in which Europe understood itself in

35 Doyle, *Empires*, pp. 71–2.
36 Chris Tiffin and Alan Lawson (eds.), *De-scribing Empire: Post-Colonialism and Textuality* (London and New York: Routledge, 1994), p. 3.

terms of what it was not, the colonized world.[37] In their collection of essays on *Tensions of Empire*, Ann Laura Stoler and Frederick Cooper reverse the usual way of looking at influences: "Europe was made by its imperial projects, as much as colonial encounters were shaped by conflicts within Europe itself."[38]

Yet at the base of European self-understandings lay the underlying problem of constructing and reproducing the categories of the colonized and the colonizer, keeping them distinct, one inferior to the other. The great nineteenth-century European overseas empires were "bourgeois" empires in which "ruling elites trying to claim power on the basis of generalized citizenship and inclusive social rights were forced to confront a basic question: whether those principles were applicable—and to whom—in old overseas empires and in newly conquered territories that were now becoming the dependencies of nation-states."[39] European ideas of citizenship were about membership in the nation, but that membership implied culture and learning. Attitudes toward both domestic lower classes and subject peoples in the colonies were bound up in serious questions of the boundaries of the nation—who should be included, and on what basis, and who should be excluded. European notions of egalitarianism clashed with imposed hierarchies; notions of democratic participation with authoritarian exclusion from decision-making; and ideas of universal reason with "native" understanding. To reinforce European authority, power, and privilege, difference between ruler and ruled had to be maintained, protected, and policed. Race was the most powerful inscription of difference, related to the language of class within Europe, which already "drew on a range of images and metaphors that were racialized to the core."[40] Ruling classes had to reaffirm their difference from the ruled, which became ever more difficult as the extension of democracy opened the way for the popular classes to enter politics. In the nineteenth century discourses of civility and respectability distinguished those with the cultural competence to govern from those

---

37 Edward W. Said, *Orientalism* (New York: Pantheon Books, 1978); *Culture and Imperialism* (New York: Alfred A. Knopf, 1993).

38 Frederick Cooper and Ann Laura Stoler, "Between Metropole and Colony: Rethinking a Research Agenda," in their *Tensions of Empire: Colonial Cultures in a Bourgeois World* (Berkeley and Los Angeles: University of California Press, 1997), p. 1.

39 Ibid.

40 Ibid., p. 9.

who merely needed to be represented. As Cooper and Stoler point out, "the most basic tension of empire" lies in the fact that "the otherness of colonized persons was neither inherent nor stable; his or her difference had to be defined and maintained . . . Social boundaries that were at one point clear would not necessarily remain so."[41]

No polity exists forever, and many historians and social scientists have been most interested in why empires decline and collapse. Several have concluded that crisis and collapse of empires is written into their very nature.[42] Alexander J. Motyl writes that "imperial decay appears to be inevitable . . . Empires, in a word, are inherently contradictory political relationships; they self-destruct, and they do so in a very particular, by no means accidental and distinctly political, manner." Collapse stems "from the policies that the imperial elites adopt in order to halt state decline." Whether it was war, as in the case of the Habsburgs, the Romanovs, and the Ottomans, that crushed the central state, or the revolution from above, as in the case of Gorbachev's Soviet Union, the implosion of the center allowed the subordinate peripheries to "search for independent solutions to their problems."[43] Yet unless one sees an inevitable tendency in empires to enter losing wars, something that can happen to any state, or one believes that events like the selection of Gorbachev as party leader or the adoption of his particular form of reform was unavoidable rather than contingent, then there is no inevitability in the collapse of empires based on policy choices. Rather the likelihood of collapse stems, as I have tried to suggest, from two factors: the delegitimizing power of discourses

41 Ibid., p. 7.

42 One of these "inevitablists," Alexander J. Motyl, makes a useful distinction between imperial decay and imperial collapse and highlights the place of crisis in the final collapse. Decay occurs "when the absolute power of the center over the periphery can no longer be effectively maintained and the periphery can, and does, act contrary to the will of the center." A second form of decay, according to Motyl, involves the loss of the absolute quality of the emperor's rule. But rather than accept Motyl's notion that "the power of emperors must be relatively absolute for their decision-making capacity to be considered imperial," which runs counter to the experience of those nineteenth-century empires that were parliamentary monarchies or republics, it is enough to follow Doyle's formulation: that in order to remain effective the metropole must maintain internal political unity able to overcome the actual or potential resistance of the periphery. Shifts in metropolitan polities from absolutism to shared power arrangements do not necessarily lead to imperial decay, as long as elites remain united in their imperial policies.

43 Ibid., pp. 40, 36–7.

of the nation and democracy that severely undermine imperial justifications; and the subversive effect of other legitimizing formulae, like developmentalism, that produce precisely the conditions under which imperial hierarchies and discriminations are no longer required.

Decolonization is far more difficult for a contiguous empire than for an overseas empire, for it changes the very shape of the state itself. Downsizing the state means abandoning certain ideas of the very enterprise that had maintained that state and searching for new sources of legitimation. Contiguous empires, like the Habsburg, Ottoman, tsarist Russian, and Soviet, did not have hard borders within the empire, and therefore migration created a mixed population, a highly integrated economy, and shared historical experiences and cultural features—all of which make extrication of the core or any of the peripheries from the empire extremely difficult without complete state collapse. Understandably in three of the four cases at hand—the Habsburg, Ottoman and tsarist— defeat in war preceded the end of the empire. And while secession of peripheries weakened these empires, in two of the four cases—the Ottoman and the Soviet—it was the secession of the core from the empire—Kemal's nationalist Turkey in Anatolia and Yeltsin's Russia— that dealt the final blow to the old imperial state.[44]

To conclude this theoretical discussion, I am arguing that the collapse of empires in our own times can only be understood in the context of the institutional and discursive shifts that have taken place with the rise of the nation-state. Historically many of the most successful states began as empires, with dynastic cores extending outward by marriage or conquest to incorporate peripheries that over time were gradually assimilated into a single, relatively homogeneous polity. By the late nineteenth century, empires were those polities that were either uninterested or had failed in the project of creating a nation-state. The efforts of Romanov and Ottoman rulers were directed at modernizing their empires, maintaining imperial hierarchies and distinctions rather than creating homogeneous, egalitarian nation-states, a haphazard process that produced sporadic moments of Russification in one case and genocide in the other. The

---

44 Jeremy King suggested to me that a similar process occurred in the Austro-Hungarian Empire where the German, Czech, and Hungarian urban bourgeoisies had withdrawn their support from the monarchy at the end of the nineteenth and beginning of the twentieth centuries.

fragility of twentieth-century empires was related to the extraordinary power of the discourse of the nation as it became the dominant universe of political legitimation. Its claims of popular sovereignty, together with its inherently democratic thrust and its call for a cultural rootedness alien to the transnational cosmopolitanism practiced earlier by European aristocracies, acted like a "time bomb" placed at the feet of empire.

As it spread from France, the discourse of the nation carried with it the claim that a cultural community possessed political rights over a specific territory that justified independence from alien rulers. Whether a monarch or a nobility was of the same nationality or not as the people, they could be defined as part of the nation or alien to it. As nationalisms shifted from state patriotism to identification with ethnic communities, themselves the product of long historical and cultural evolutions, the seeming longevity, indeed, antiquity of ethnicity provided an argument for the naturalness, the primordiality, of the nation, against which the artificial claims of dynasties or religious institutions paled. Over time any state that wished to survive had to become a nationalizing state, to link itself with a nation in order to acquire legitimacy in the new universal discourse of the nation. In the age of nationalism, certainly by World War I, the term empire had in many cases (though hardly all; think of where the sun never set) gained the opprobrium of which Beissinger speaks. The Wilsonian and Leninist promotion of national self-determination powerfully subverted the legitimacy of empires, even as each of the states which Wilson and Lenin headed managed empires of one kind or another through another half century.[45]

This leads us, finally, to consider the ways in which the international context contributes to the stability and fragility of empires, not only in the sense that a highly competitive international environment presents empires with difficult challenges economically and militarily but also at the level of dominant understandings of what constitutes legitimacy for states. In our century when the nation gives legitimacy to states, international law and international organizations, such as the United Nations, have established new norms that have sanctioned national self-determination, non-intervention into the affairs of other states, and the

---

45   Erez Manela, *The Wilsonian Moment: Self-Determination and the International Origins of Anti-Colonial Nationalism* (New York and Oxford: Oxford University Press, 2007).

sovereign equality of states. After both world wars new states and former colonies quickly were accepted as fully independent actors in the international arena. This acceptance set the stage for 1991, when the former Soviet republics—but no political units below them—were quickly recognized as independent states with all the rights and privileges appertaining. In the post-1945 period particularly, the wave of decolonizations constructed empires as antiquated forms of government, justifiable only as transitory arrangements that might aid in the development of full nation-states. This justification of empires was read back into the retrospective histories of empires. As Miles Kahler puts it, "The empire-dominated system of the early twentieth century swiftly tipped toward a nation-state-dominated system after World War II; in dramatic contrast to the 1920s and 1930s empires were quickly defined as beleaguered and outdated institutional forms."[46] Kahler notes that the two dominant powers of the post-World War II period, the USA and USSR, were both "rhetorically anti-colonial, despite their own imperial legacies," and American economic dominance, with its liberal, free trade approach, "reduced the advantages of empires as large-scale economic units."[47] Thus, both on the level of discourse and on the level of international politics and economics, the late twentieth century appeared to be a most inhospitable time both for formal external empires and contiguous empire-states.

Russia, Empire and Identity

Until quite recently historians of imperial Russia concentrated much of their attention on Russian state-building, either eliding altogether the question of nation or collapsing it into a concept of state. Neither much empirical nor theoretical work was done on the nature of tsarism as empire or of Russia as a nation. This may in part have been the consequence of the early identification of Russia more as a dynastic realm than as an ethnonational or religious community. As Paul Bushkovitch points out, the earliest Russian histories are tales of the deeds of ruling

---

46   Miles Kahler, "Empires, Neo-Empires, and Political Change: The British and French Experience," in Dawisha and Parrott (eds.), *The End of Empire?*, p. 288. This delegitimatizing of empires seems to have occurred at several historical conjunctures, not only after the two world wars but, for example, in the second half of the eighteenth century as the French, Spanish, and British empires in the Americas began to break down. See Pagden, *Lords of All the World*.

47   Kahler, "Empires," p. 288.

princes, and the foundation legends are about the dynasty. Russia was understood, from the end of the fifteenth century until the reign of Aleksei Mikhailovich in the mid-seventeenth century, to be the territories controlled by the Riurikid and later Romanov dynasties.[48] In his study of the rites, rituals, and myths generated by and about the Russian monarchy, Richard S. Wortman argues that the image of the monarchy from the fifteenth to the late nineteenth century was of foreignness, a separation of the ruler and the elite from the common people.[49] The origin of the rulers was said to be foreign (the Varangians were from beyond the Baltic Sea), and they were likened to foreign rulers of the West. "In expressing the political and cultural preeminence of the ruler, foreign traits carried a positive valuation, native traits a neutral or negative one."[50] Even the models of rulership were foreign—Byzantium and the Mongol khans—and foreignness conveyed superiority. As intriguing and suggestive as Wortman's concept is, difference and superiority, rather than foreignness, was the constant in images of the rulers. In the eighteenth and nineteenth centuries, the myth of the ruler as conqueror was used to express the monarchy's bringing to Russia the benefits of civilization and progress, and the ruler was portrayed as a selfless hero who saved Russia from despotism and ruin. As distinct and Western as the ruling elite fashioned itself from the reign of Peter the Great on, Russian monarchs from Catherine the Great through the following century supplemented their self-representations with ethnic and national Russian elements.

What kind of early identity, or identities, formed among "Russians"? From the earliest records the peoples of what became Russia were culturally and linguistically diverse.[51] The Primary Chronicle notes that Slavs,

---

48 Paul Bushkovitch, "What Is Russia? Russian National Consciousness and the State, 1500–1917," unpublished paper, p. 3.

49 Richard Wortman, *Scenarios of Power: Myth and Ceremony in Russian Monarchy, Vol. I, From Peter the Great to the Death of Nicholas I* (Princeton: Princeton University Press, 1995).

50 Ibid., p. 6.

51 This is a point well made by Andreas Kappeler, *Russland als Vielvolkerreich: Entstehung, Geschichte, Zerfall* (Munich: C. H. Beck'sche Verlagsbuchhandlung, 1992). In the original version of this chapter I used the French translation by Guy Imart: *La Russie, Empire multiethnique* (Paris: Institut d'Etudes Slaves, 1994), pp. 25–30. See also *The Russian Empire*, trans. Alfred Clayton (Harlow: Pearson Education, 2001), pp. 14–20.

Balts, Turkic and Finnic peoples lived in the region and that the Slavs were divided into distinct groups. As the Chronicle tells the tale, the various Eastern Slavic peoples drew together only after the Varangians, called Rus', came to "Russia."[52] Those few scholars who have asked this question generally agree that from the adoption and spread of Orthodox Christianity in 988 (traditional date) through the next few centuries, Russians constituted a community that fused the notions of Orthodoxy and Russianness and saw themselves as distinct from both the Catholics of Poland and Lithuania and the non-Christian nomadic peoples of the Volga region and Siberia.[53] Affiliation with a dynastic lord was important, but this should not be confused with loyalty to a state. Indeed, the word "realm" might be preferred instead of "state," for in these early times the people as community was not conceived of separately from political authority. As Valerie Kivelson notes,

> The grand princes of Kiev appear to have had little or no conception of a state as a bounded territorial unit governed by a single sovereign entity, aspiring to administer, tax and control its people. Rather, the territory of the Kievan polity remained amorphous and fluid. The concept and title of "grand prince" of a unitary Kievan realm entered Kievan vocabulary and political consciousness slowly, as an import from Byzantium. The polity itself (if there was one) was constituted imprecisely around a loosely defined people ("the Rus") and was ruled piecemeal by interconnected competing and conflicting branches of the princely line. Grand princely deathbed testaments demonstrate that the goal of princely politics remained personal, familial, rather than encompassing any broader aspirations toward unified sovereignty or territorial rule.[54]

---

52 For an extended discussion of the historiographical disputes over the nature of Rus' identity and its ties to the modern nations of Belarus, Russia, and Ukraine, see Serhii Plokhy, *The Origins of the Slavic Nations: Premodern Identities in Russia, Ukraine, and Belarus* (Cambridge: Cambridge University Press, 2006), pp. 10–48.

53 Nicholas V. Riasanovsky, "Historical Consciousness and National Identity: Some Considerations on the History of Russian Nationalism" (New Orleans: The Graduate School of Tulane University, 1991), pp. 2–3; Omeljan Pritsak, "The Origin of Rus'", *Russian Review* XXXVI, 3 (July 1977), pp. 249–73.

54 Valerie Kivelson, "Merciful Father, Impersonal State: Russian Autocracy in Comparative Perspective," *Modern Asian Studies* XXXI, 3 (1997), pp. 637–8.

Identity was formed both internally by the consolidation of religion in the Orthodox Church, and eventually by a single Muscovite state (from roughly the fifteenth century), and externally at the frontiers in the struggles with peoples seen to be different. From its beginning, then, Russian identity was bound up with the supranational world of belief, the political world loosely defined by the ruling dynasty, and was contrasted to "others" at the periphery.[55] Religion served in those pre- and early-modern times much as ethnicity does today, as the available vocabulary of identity. It was within the realm of religion and the polity that contestations over what constituted membership and what behavior was proper or improper took place.[56] As Richard Hellie put it, "The Muscovites defined themselves as *pravoslavnye* (Orthodox) more frequently than as *russkie*, which of course many of them were not."[57] Even as the realm became increasingly heterogeneous ethnically and religiously, the "test" for belonging in Muscovy was profession of Orthodoxy. Yet for all its isolation and oft-touted xenophobia, Russia was surprisingly ecumenical in its attitudes toward foreigners. "The conversion to Orthodoxy by any foreigner automatically made him a Muscovite, fully accepted by the central authorities and seemingly the native populace as well."[58]

If not from the very beginning, then in the next few centuries Russian identity became closely tied with religion, a shifting, expanding territory, and the state. When Ivan III the Great took on the titles *tsar* and *samoderzhets* (autocrat) in the mid-fifteenth century, he was making a claim to be the sovereign ruler of Russia. Moscow, which had often been favored among Russian principalities, even promoted, by the Mongols in the previous century, now "replaced the Golden Horde as the sovereign power within the Rus' lands" and adopted the "mantle of Chingisid imperial legitimacy."[59] "Imperial sovereignty," writes Wortman, "was the

---

55 Michael Cherniavsky, "Russia," in Orest Ranum (ed.), *National Consciousness, History, and Political Culture in Early-Modern Europe* (Baltimore and London: The Johns Hopkins University Press, 1975), pp. 119–21.

56 Gregory Guroff and Alexander Guroff, "The Paradox of Russian National Identity," a paper presented at the Russian Littoral Project Conference, "The Influence of Ethnicity on Russian Foreign Policy," May 1993, no. 16, pp. 7–9.

57 Richard Hellie, *Slavery in Russia* (Chicago: University of Chicago Press,1982), p. 392.

58 Ibid.

59 Kivelson, "Merciful Father, Impersonal State," p. 643.

only true sovereignty" in Russian understanding.[60] At the same time, appropriating and modifying the double-headed eagle of Byzantium and the Holy Roman Empire, Ivan claimed parity with the monarchs of the West. Tracing their ancestry back to the ninth-century Scandinavian chieftain Riurik, the Muscovite princes allied with the Orthodox clergy, who collaborated in the construction of an imperial myth elaborately visualized in the coronation rites: "Ceremony turned the fiction of imperial succession into sacred truth."[61] Michael Cherniavsky saw this ideological amalgam of khan and basileus as a playful, somewhat inconsistent synthesizing of various traditions. "Hence, the Russian grand prince as khan, as Roman emperor, as *the* Orthodox sovereign, and as descendant of the dynasty of Ivan I (a loyal subject of the khan) were concepts that existed simultaneously, not contradicting but reinforcing each other."[62]

With Ivan IV's conquests of Kazan and Astrakhan in the mid-sixteenth century, the Muscovite state incorporated ethnically compact non-Russian territories, indeed an alien polity, and transformed a relatively homogenized Russia into a multinational empire. The tsars adopted the designation *Rossiia* for their realm instead of *Rus'*, which referred to the core Russian areas. But unlike the Byzantine emperor or the Mongol khan, the Russian tsar was not ruler of the whole universe but only the absolute and sovereign ruler of all of Russia (*tsar' vseia Rusi*).[63] Yet as conqueror of Kazan and Astrakhan, the Muscovite tsars acquired some of the prestige of the Mongol khans, and as Ivan pushed further south and east he sought the allegiance and subordination of the lesser rulers of Siberia and the North Caucasus. As Michael Khodarkovsky has shown, when the Shamkhal of Daghestan or the Kabardinian princes made an agreement with the tsar, they believed they had concluded a treaty between equals, but the Russians invariably

60 Wortman, *Scenarios of Power*, p. 25.

61 Ibid., p. 28.

62 Cherniavsky, "Russia," p. 123; see also his "Khan or Basileus: An Aspect of Russian Medieval Political Theory," *Journal of the History of Ideas* XX (October–December 1959), pp. 459–76; reprinted in Cherniavsky (ed.), *The Structure of Russian History: Interpretive Essays* (New York: Random House, 1970), pp. 65–79; and *Tsar and People: Studies in Russian Myths* (New Haven: Yale University Press, 1961).

63 Paul Bushkovitch, "The Formation of a National Consciousness in Early Modern Russia," *Harvard Ukrainian Studies* X, 3/4 (December 1986), p. 363.

mistranslated the agreement as one of an inferior's supplication to the Russian sovereign.[64]

Russian imperial power went into the frontier world as a sovereign, superior to whatever lesser lords and peoples it encountered. Conquest and annexation of the frontier lands meant an extension of the tsar's sovereignty, exercised through his household or the court and conceived as another stage in the "gathering of the Russian lands." The non-Russian elites were generally co-opted into the Russian nobility, as were the Kazan and Astrakhan notables, but part of the obligations of the peasantry were now diverted to Moscow. Once a region had been brought into the empire, the tsarist state was prepared to use brutal force to prevent its loss. Rebellion was suppressed mercilessly. But when the problem of security was settled, Moscow allowed local elites, though no longer sovereign, to rule, and traditional customs and laws to continue in force. As these frontier regions became integrated in some ways into the empire as borderlands, many of them remained administratively distinct, though always subordinate to the center.[65]

Russian expansion was overdetermined, driven by economic, ideological, and security interests. The lure of furs in Siberia and mineral wealth in the Urals, the threats from nomadic incursions along the Volga or the southern steppe, the peasants' hunger for agricultural land, and the pull of freedom in the frontier regions stimulated appetites for expansion. Missionary zeal was not a primary motivation, though after conquest missionaries followed. When in the east and south Russians engaged in trade that brought them into contact with the myriad peoples of Siberia, the Kalmyks of the southern steppe, and the Caucasians of the mountains, differences of religion, custom, food, smell were duly noted. Though some, like the Cossack traders on the eastern frontier, were largely indifferent to what was foreign, others, particularly clerics, sought

---

64 Michael Khodarkovsky, "From Frontier to Empire: The Concept of the Frontier in Russia, Sixteenth-Eighteenth Centuries," *Russian History* XIX, 1–4 (1992), pp. 115–28; *Where Two Worlds Met: The Russian State and the Kalmyk Nomads, 1600–1771* (Ithaca: Cornell University Press, 1992); and his "Of Christianity, Enlightenment and Colonialism: Russia in the North Caucasus, 1550–1900," *Journal of Modern History* LXXI, 2 (June 1999), pp. 394–430.

65 Marc Raeff, "Patterns of Russian Imperial Policy Toward the Nationalities," in Edward Allworth (ed.), *Soviet Nationality Problems* (New York: Columbia University Press, 1971), pp. 22–42.

to spread Orthodoxy among the heathen.[66] Once converted, foreigners were easily assimilated into the Russian community. "Slaves, wives, or state servitors, the new Christians seem to have been accepted as Christians and Russians ... Thus, the tribute-paying foreigners who wished to remain foreigners were welcome to stay in the woods and pay tribute, whereas those who were convinced or compelled to become Russian could do so if they played by the rules."[67]

At the same time that peoples with different religions and ways of life remained distinct from and subordinate to the imperial power, the tsar's ruling institution also distinguished itself from the people (*narod*) of the empire. With the internal collapse of Russia in the Time of Troubles of the early seventeenth century, some people reconceived of Russia not simply as the possession of the Muscovite tsar but as a state, ruled by the tsar and including the people. But the newly-chosen Romanov dynasty did not adopt this new conception after 1613, and rather than emphasizing election by a popular assembly, the new rulers depicted the election as divinely inspired.[68] Again, the dynasty distanced itself from the people, claiming descent from Riurik and St. Vladimir, prince of Kievan Rus'.[69]

With the annexation of Ukraine (1654) and Vilnius (1656), the imperial claims were bolstered, and the monarch was proclaimed "tsar of all Great, Little, and White Russia."[70] The state seal of Aleksei Mikhailovich,

---

66 Yuri Slezkine, *Arctic Mirrors: Russia and the Small Peoples of the North* (Ithaca and London: Cornell University Press, 1994), pp. 41–5.

67 Ibid., pp. 44–5.

68 The themes of authority from above rather than popular sanction from below, as well as the reciprocity between rulers and ruled, are explored much more extensively in Valerie Kivelson and Ronald Grigor Suny, *Russia's Empires* (New York: Oxford University Press, 2016).

69 Bushkovitch notes a little-recognized development in the seventeenth century, the arrival of what he calls "Renaissance Slavism": the idea developed in Poland, Croatia, and elsewhere that the Slavs in general have an ancient and distinguished origin. Polish writers linked them back to the ancient Sarmatians, and scholars like Simeon Polotskii brought the idea that Russians were a Sarmatian tribe into Russian circles. In the eighteenth century the idea found its way into the writings of Tatishchev and Lomonosov, who attached it to their state-centered histories. But it died out with the elevation of a more imperial ideology following the importation of Enlightenment ideas, and is not found in Karamzin's early nineteenth-century history. [Bushkovitch, "What is Russia?" pp. 4–7]

70 James Cracraft, "Empire Versus Nation: Russian Political Theory Under Peter I," *Harvard Ukrainian Studies* X, 3/4 (December 1986), pp. 524–40; reprinted in Cracraft (ed.), *Major Problems in the History of Imperial Russia* (Lexington and Toronto: D. C. Heath, 1994), pp. 224–34. Citations hereafter are from the latter publication.

adopted in 1667, depicted an eagle with raised wings, topped with three crowns symbolizing Kazan, Astrakhan, and Siberia, and bordered by three sets of columns, representing Great, Little, and White Russia. The tsar, now also called *sviatoi* (holy), further distanced himself from his subjects "by appearing as the supreme worshipper of the realm, whose piety exceeded theirs."[71] Finally, toward the end of the century, Tsar Fedor referred to the "Great Russian Tsardom" (*Velikorossiiskoe tsarst-vie*), "a term denoting an imperial, absolutist state, subordinating Russian as well as non-Russian territories."[72] In this late seventeenth-century vision of empire, Great Russia, the tsar and state were all merged in a single conception of sovereignty and absolutism. State, empire, and autocratic tsar were combined in an elaborate system of reinforcing legitimations. In Russia, according to Wortman,

> The word *empire* carried several interrelated though distinct meanings. First, it meant imperial dominion or supreme power unencumbered by other authority. Second, it implied imperial expansion, extensive conquests, encompassing non-Russian lands. Third, it referred to the Christian Empire, the heritage of the Byzantine emperor as the defender of Orthodoxy. These meanings were conflated and served to reinforce one another.[73]

Not only was the tsar the holy ruler, a Christian monarch, the most pious head of the Church, he was also a powerful secular ruler of a burgeoning bureaucratic state, a conqueror, and the commander of nobles and armies. With Peter the Great, the Christian Emperor and Christian Empire gave way to a much more secular "Western myth of conquest and power."[74] "Peter's advents gave notice that the Russian tsar owed his power to his exploits on the battlefield, not to divinely ordained traditions of succession ... The image of conqueror disposed of the old fictions of descent."[75] Peter carried the image of foreignness to new extremes, imposing on Russia his preference for beardlessness, foreign dress, Baroque architecture, Dutch, German, and English technology, a

---

71 Wortman, *Scenarios of Power*, p. 33.
72 Ibid., p. 38.
73 Ibid., p. 6.
74 Ibid., p. 41.
75 Ibid., p. 44.

new capital as a "window on the West." He created a new polite society
for Russia, bringing women out of seclusion into public life, culminating
in the coronation of his second wife, the commoner Marta Skavronskaia,
as Empress Ekaterina I (Catherine) of Russia. He took on the title *imperator* in 1721 and made Russia an *imperiia*. "Peter's ideology was very
much of the age of rationalism, his contribution to the 'general welfare'
of Russia legitimating his rule."[76] The emperor was "father of the fatherland" (*Otets otechestva*), and "now the relationship between sovereign
and subjects was to be based not on hereditary right and personal obligation, but on the obligation to serve the state."[77]

Some historians have read national consciousness back into the
Russian seventeenth century or at least to the time of Peter. Michael
Cherniavsky, for example, argued that a dual consciousness emerged with
the Church schism of the late seventeenth century and the reforms of
Peter I: that of the Europeanizing gentry, who identified themselves with
"Russia" and considered what they were doing as "by definition, Russian;"
and the consciousness of the Old Believers and peasants in general who
"began to insist on beards, traditional clothes, and old rituals—creating,
in reaction, their own Russian identity."[78] In this view, "national
consciousness emerged as a popular reaction to the self-identity of the
absolutist state, with the threat that those things which challenged it—
the absolutist consciousness of tsar, empire, and Orthodoxy—could be
excluded from Russian self-identity."[79] But in a useful corrective James
Cracraft points out that much of the reaction to the Nikonian and Petrine
reforms, rather than constituting xenophobia or national consciousness,
was in large part "an anguished opposition to a pattern of behavior which
did great violence to a world view that was still essentially religious."[80]
Undoubtedly, ideas about what constituted Russia and Russians existed,
and identities competed between and within social groups in a confused,
shifting, unsystematized discursive space in which religious and ethnocultural distinctions overlapped and reinforced one another. Being Russian
was closely identified with being Orthodox Christian, but also with living
in the tsar's realm, and as the state moved away from the more traditional

---

76   Ibid., p. 61.
77   Ibid., p. 64.
78   Cherniavsky, "Russia," p. 141.
79   Ibid., p. 140.
80   Cracraft, "Empire Versus Nation," p. 225.

ethnoreligious sense of community toward a non-ethnic, cosmopolitan, European sense of political civilization, people were torn between these two understandings of the "Russian" community.

Cracraft argues that an imperial nationalism—pride in empire, sovereign, and state—developed under Peter I. Absolutist theory, which he calls "Petrine hegemony theory," celebrated the absolute, unlimited power of the emperor, who received his legitimacy from an originary consent of the people and from God. Once that power had been granted to the tsar, all had to obey him. Cracraft conflates Petrine hegemony theory and "Russian national consciousness in the Petrine period," but his evidence and examples appear to attest more to a respect for state authority than any sense of community. A strong sense of "national pride," meaning pride in the achievements of the state and the empire, imperial dignity and glory, existed in the Russian elite, while the people were almost completely left out.[81]

Though a number of other specialists, most notably Hans Rogger, have written about national consciousness later in eighteenth-century Russia, identification with Russia, at least among nobles and the educated population, continued to be largely contained in a sense of state patriotism—that is, identification with the state and its ruler rather than with the nation as a broader political community conceived separately from the state.[82] As Cynthia Hyla Whittaker demonstrates, the forty-five amateur historians of eighteenth-century Russia were principally concerned with replacing religious with new secular justifications for autocracy, on the basis of dynastic continuity, dynamism of the ruler, his or her concern for the welfare of the people, or the superiority of autocracy over alternative forms of government.[83] And though some historians, such as Vasilii Tatishchev (1686–1750), argued that an originary contract had been forged between people and tsar, even they believed that once that agreement had been made it could "be destroyed by no one."[84] Historians were commissioned by the rulers to counteract the "lies" and "falsehoods"

---

81   Ibid., p. 540.

82   Hans Rogger, *National Consciousness in Eighteenth Century Russia* (Cambridge, MA: Harvard University Press, 1960).

83   Cynthia Hyla Whittaker, "The Idea of Autocracy among Eighteenth-Century Russian Historians," in Jane Burbank and David Ransel (eds), *Imperial Russia: New Histories for the Empire* (Bloomington: Indiana University Press, 1998), pp. 32–59.

84   Ibid., p.41.

spread by foreigners. Russians of every social level probably had a sense of identity that either positively or negatively contrasted things Russian with those German or Polish or French. Russian writers shared in the general European practice of remarking on national distinctions, or what would be called "national character," something in which Enlightenment figures from Voltaire and Montesquieu to Johann Gottfried Von Herder and Johann Blumenbach engaged. This sensitivity to difference was evidenced by the resistance and resentment of "Russian" nobles to "foreigners" who advanced too high in state service. When this principle was breached during the reign of Anna, Russian nobles protested the visibility of the German barons surrounding the empress. Here patriotism was a way not only of protecting privilege and discouraging competition for power but also, more positively, of nurturing solidarities within one group against another. In conscious reaction against the Germanophilia of Anna or Peter III, the coronations of Elizabeth and Catherine II were conceived as acts of restoration, bringing back the glories of Peter the Great. In the view of these monarchs, Peter now represented the authentic Russia, and Elizabeth made the most of being the daughter of Peter and Catherine I. The German princess who became Catherine II may have been a usurper with no legitimate right to rule, yet her seizure of power was sanctioned as an act of deliverance from a tyrant with foreign airs. Besides being portrayed as Minerva, the embodiment of enlightenment, she was seen as one who loved Russia and respected its Orthodox religion. Although enveloped in a cosmopolitan culture that preferred speaking French to Russian, the noble elite was not above sentimental attachments to elements of Russian ethnic culture: "Imperial patriotism with a Great Russian coloration was a theme of late-eighteenth-century history and literature."[85] At Catherine's court, nobles of various ethnic backgrounds wore the same dress, and the empress introduced a "Russian dress" with native features for the women.

By the eighteenth century Russia was an empire in the multiple senses of a great state whose ruler exercised full, absolute sovereign power over its diverse territory and subjects. Its theorists consciously identified this polity with the language and imagery of past empires. Peter the Great established an image of emperor as hero and god, someone who stood

---

85 Wortman, *Scenarios of Power*, p. 136.

above other men and worked for the general welfare of his subjects.[86] His successors, four of whom were women, were backed by guards' regiments who decided struggles for the throne. "The guards' regiments and the court elite advanced the interests of the entire nobility in defending an alliance with the crown that lasted until the accession of Paul I in 1796."[87] Despite several attempted and successful coups, tsar and nobility assisted each other in a symbiotic arrangement in which the interests of the imperial court and the nobility were configured as the general welfare of the country.[88] The eighteenth-century monarchs combined aspects of the conqueror and renovator "while they maintained and reinforced the stability that would preserve the predominance of the serf-holding nobility. The conqueror was also the conserver, who helped defend and extend the elite's authority."[89]

Russia followed a particular logic of empire-building. After acquiring territory, usually by conquest, often by expanding settlement, the agents of the tsar co-opted local elites into the service of the empire.[90] But in many peripheries, like the Volga, Siberia, Transcaucasia and Central Asia, integration of the elites was only partial, and it did not include the basic peasant or nomadic populations, which retained their tribal, ethnic, and religious identities. Some elites, like the Tatar and Ukrainian nobles, dissolved into the Russian nobility (*dvoriantsvo*), but others, like the German barons of the Baltic or the Swedish aristocrats of Finland, retained privileges and separate identities. "Nationalizing," homogenizing policies, integrating disparate peoples into a common "Russian" community (particularly among the nobles) coexisted with policies of discrimination and distinction. After subduing their khanate, Russia gave the Bashkirs rights as a military host in the Volga region. Some peoples, like the Georgians, were allowed to keep their customary laws; Greek and

---

86   Wortman, *Scenarios of Power*, p. 81.

87   Ibid.

88   Ibid., p. 82; for a discussion of the state as defender of noble interests, see Ronald Grigor Suny, "Rehabilitating Tsarism: The Imperial State and its Historians," *Comparative Studies in Society and History*, XXXI 1 (January 1989), pp. 168–79.

89   Wortman, *Scenarios of Power*, pp. 82–3.

90   Marc Raeff, "Patterns of Russian Imperial Policy Toward the Nationalities"; "In the Imperial Manner," in Marc Raeff (ed.), *Catherine the Great: A Profile* (New York: Hill & Wang, 1972), pp. 197–246; S. Frederick Starr, "Tsarist Government: The Imperial Dimension," in Jeremy Azrael (ed.), *Soviet Nationality Policies and Practices* (New York: Praeger, 1978), pp. 3–38.

Armenian merchants enjoyed economic and legal benefits, while Jews were restricted from migrating out of the Pale of Settlement. Tolerant of its Muslim subjects, the state nevertheless regulated their religious and social life.

Religion remained the principal marker of difference between Russians and non-Russians, and religious identity was believed to reveal essential qualities that helped to predict behavior. Orthodox Christians were expected to be more loyal than the duplicitous Muslims. Not infrequently, "enlightened" state officials argued that conversion to Orthodox Christianity would strengthen the empire as well as help civilize the borderlands.[91] Though efforts at such religious "Russification" were haphazard, beginning with Peter's efforts to modernize Russia, the state and church intensified the previously sporadic attempts to bring the benefits of Orthodoxy and Western learning to the benighted non-Russians of the east and south.[92]

As Europe went through the fallout from 1789, Russia represented "the most imperial of nations, comprising more peoples than any other." The academician Heinrich Storch boasted of the ethnographic variety of Russia in 1797, commenting that "no other state on earth has such a mixed and diverse population . . . as citizens of a single state, joined together by their political order."[93] In its own imagery Russia was the Roman Empire reborn. As the discourse of the nation took shape in and after the French Revolution and the Napoleonic wars, as concepts of "the people" and popular sovereignty spread through Europe, the traditional monarchical concepts of rulership sanctioned by God, conquest, and superiority of origins held at bay any concession to the new national populism. Russian resistance to Napoleon, as well as the expansion of the empire into the Caucasus and Finland, only accentuated the imperial image of irresistible power, displayed physically on both battlefield and parade ground by the martinet tsars of the early nineteenth century.[94] At the moment of the French invasion of Russia in 1812, Alexander I issued a rescript that concluded: "I will not lay down arms while the last enemy soldier remains

91 Michael Khodarkovsky, "'Not by Word Alone': Missionary Policies and Religious Conversion in Early Modern Russia," *Comparative Study of Society and History* XXXVIII, 2 (April 1996), pp. 267–93.
92 Slezkine, *Arctic Mirrors*, pp. 47–71; Kappeler, *La Russie*, p. 47.
93 Quoted in Kappeler, *The Russian Empire*, p. 141.
94 Wortman, *Scenarios of Power*, p. 170.

in my empire."[95] No mention was made of the Russian people, and the empire was presented as a possession of the emperor. Even as the French moved toward Moscow, Alexander had to be convinced by advisors to go to Moscow and take on the role of national leader. His manifestos, written by the conservative poet Admiral A. S. Shishkov, "appealed to the people's patriotic and religious feelings."[96] The tsar was depicted by writers of the time as the "Angel of God," "Our Father," loved by his subject people whom he in turn loves, and after the French had retreated from Russia, the "powerful valor of the people entrusted to Us by God" and Divine Providence were seen as jointly responsible for ridding Russia of its enemies.[97] Russian authorities resisted portraying the great victory as a popular triumph, instead projecting it as a divinely-ordained triumph of autocracy supported by a devoted people. As Wortman puts it,

> The people's involvement in the imperial scenario threatened the tsar's image as a superordinate force, whose title came from outside or from above, from divine mandate, or the emanations of reason. In social terms it was impossible to present the people as a historical agent in a scenario that glorified the monarch's authority as the idealization of the ruling elite.[98]

Russia emerged from the Napoleonic wars even more imperial than it had been in the eighteenth century. Now the possessor of the Grand Duchy of Finland, the emperor served there as a constitutional monarch subject to the public law of the Grand Duchy, and in the Kingdom of Poland (1815–32), he served as *Tsar' Polskii*, the constitutional king of Poland. According to the Fundamental Laws codified in 1832, "the Emperor of Russia is an autocratic (*samoderzhavnyi*) and unlimited (*neogranichennyi*) monarch," but his realm was governed by laws, a *Rechtsstaat*, and was distinct from the despotisms of the East.[99] Victorious Russia, the conservative bulwark

---

95 Ibid., p. 217.
96 Ibid., p. 218.
97 Ibid., p. 221.
98 Ibid., p. 222.
99 Marc Szeftel, "The Form of Government of the Russian Empire Prior to the Constitutional Reforms of 1905–06," in John Shelton Curtiss (ed.), *Essays in Russian and Soviet History in Honor of Geroid Tanquary Robinson* (New York: Columbia University Press, 1962), pp. 105–19.

against the principles of the French Revolution, was in many ways the antithesis of nationalism. Alexander I expressed this personally in his scheme for a Holy Alliance in which various states would consider themselves members "of a single Christian nation" ruled over by the "Autocrat of the Christian People," Jesus Christ.[100]

Four reasons for the failure to create a Russian "nation" in the nineteenth century might be suggested. The first is deeply rooted in tsarist Russia's vast geography, limited resources, and lack of population and communications density.[101] There was no thickening web of economic, legal, and cultural links on the scale of those, say, in early modern France, which Jonathan Dewald credits with having "involved an enlargement of social space and a quickening of exchanges within that space."[102] Russia was so large, its road system so poor, its urban settlements so few and far between that it was extraordinarily difficult for the state either to impose its will on its subjects very frequently or even to make its presence known. Peasants largely ran their own affairs, dealt with local lords or their stewards instead of state authorities, and felt the state's weight only when the military recruiter appeared, or they failed to pay taxes or dues. Indirect rule over non-Russians was often the norm, and little effort was made until very late in the nineteenth century to interfere with their culture.

This leads to the second reason for the failure to form a nation in the empire—the misfortune of timing. By the early nineteenth century, with the emergence of the discourse of the nation, subaltern elites could conceptualize of their peoples as "nations," with all the attendant claims to cultural recognition, political rights, territory, and even statehood. With the legitimation of nationalism, the process of assimilating other peoples into the dominant nationality became progressively more difficult than it had been in early modern times.

The third reason was that imperial state structures and practices, from the autocratic concentration of power to the state hierarchy and built-in ideas of social and ethnic superiority and inferiority stood in the way of horizontal, egalitarian nation-making. As much of the literature on nation-formation and nationalism suggests, the making of nations is the

---

100 Ibid., p. 230.

101 Victor Lieberman, "Transcending East–West Dichotomies."

102 Jonathan Dewald, *Pont-St-Pierre, 1398–1789: Lordship, Community, and Capitalism in Early Modern France* (Berkeley, Los Angeles, and London: University of California Press, 1987), p. 284.

social and cultural construction of a new kind of space. Not only are nations usually spatially and conceptually different from the fractured and particularized spaces of *ancien régime* polities or from the vastness and diverse geographies of empires, but they are consciously and deliberately emptied of particularization, traditional or customary divisions, certain older forms of hierarchy and vested privilege, and turned into what William H. Sewell, Jr. calls "homogeneous empty space," paraphrasing Benedict Anderson's use of Walter Benjamin's notion of "homogeneous empty time."[103] What the French Revolution did for *ancien régime* France, ridding it of provincial and local privileges, abolishing internal duties and tariffs, standardizing weights and measures over a broader space, was only in part accomplished under tsarism.

The "modernizing" practices of eighteenth- and nineteenth-century Russian emperors and bureaucrats that homogenized disparate economic and legal practices were certainly significant, but they must be placed against programs and policies that moved in another direction, creating new or reinforcing old differences, distinctions, privileges, disadvantages based on social class, region, ethnicity, or religion. Among Russians the literary elite developed a sense of national distinction in the eighteenth century, but through the first half of the next century there was very little sense of "nation," in the developing Western conception of a political community in which the people were the source of legitimacy and even sovereignty. Russia was a state and an empire whose population was divided horizontally among dozens of ethnicities and religions, and vertically between ruling and privileged estates and the great mass of the peasantry. These divisions were formalized in the law and fixed most people and peoples in positions of discrimination and disadvantage. Such hierarchies and separations inhibited the development of the kinds of horizontal bonds of fraternity and solidarity that already marked the rhetoric of the nation in the West. To the very last days of the empire the Romanov regime remained imperial in this sense, a complex, differentiated, hierarchical, traditional Old Regime, with structures and laws that restricted efforts at equalization and homogenization. The very lack of vertical

---

103 William H. Sewell, Jr., "The French Revolution and the Emergence of the Nation Form," in Michael Morrison and Melinda Zook (eds.), *Revolutionary Currents: Transatlantic Ideology and Nation-building, 1688–1821* (Lanham, MD: Rowman and Littlefield, 2004), pp. 91–125.

integration along the lines of a homogeneous nation facilitated the emergence of horizontal strong class identities that combined social and ethnic characteristics.[104]

And finally, the fourth reason was the failure of Russian elites to articulate a clear idea of the Russian nation, to elaborate an identity distinct from a religious (Orthodox), imperial, state, or narrowly ethnic identity. Russia was never equated with ethnic Russia; almost from the beginning it was something larger, a multinational "Russian" state with vaguely conceived commonalities—religion, perhaps, or loyalty to the tsar—but the debate among intellectuals and state actors failed to develop a convincing, attractive notion of Russianness separate from the ethnic, on the one hand, and the imperial state, on the other. Notions of nation dissolved into religion and the state, and did not take on a powerful presence as a community separate from these.

Imagining the Russian "Nation"
The sources for discerning popular identities are elusive indeed, but looking at what ordinary Russians read confirms many of the points made about Russian identities. As Jeffrey Brooks points out, "We know little about the popular conception of what it meant to be Russian in premodern Russia, but," he goes on,

> the early lubok tales suggest that the Orthodox Church, and, to a lesser extent, the tsar were the foremost emblems of Russianness throughout the nineteenth century. These two symbols of nationality recur in the early stories and their treatment by the authors implies that to be Russian was to be loyal to the tsar and faithful to the Orthodox Church.[105]

Brooks's reading of popular literature like the pictorial narratives in the *lubok* prints, confirms that "the concept of a nation of peoples with shared loyalties was not well developed."[106] Yet there were several hints to

---

104   This is a theme developed in Ronald Grigor Suny, *The Revenge of the Past: Nationalism, Revolution, and the Collapse of the Soviet Union* (Stanford: Stanford University Press, 1993).

105   Jeffrey Brooks, *When Russia Learned to Read: Literacy and Popular Literature, 1861–1917* (Princeton: Princeton University Press, 1985), p. 214.

106   Ibid., p. 215.

"national" identity indicated in the *lubok* tales. Conversion to Orthodoxy and allegiance to the tsar signaled inclusion within the Russian community and permitted intermarriage. At the same time there was a sense of the empire as a vast geographical space of diverse landscapes and peoples, in which Russians were contrasted with the other peoples. Difference from and fear of the "other," particularly the Islamic other, was emphasized in portrayals of Turks and Tatars and in popular captivity tales.[107]

With the emergence of an autonomous intelligentsia in the second third of the nineteenth century an intense discussion developed on the nature of Russia, its relationship with the West and with Asia, as well as with its internal "others," the non-ethnic Russians within the empire. As with other peoples and states of Europe in the post-revolutionary period, intellectuals, particularly historians, were in a sense thinking nations into existence or at least elaborating and propagating the contours, characteristics, symbols and signs that would make the nation familiar to a broader public. From Nikolai Karamzin's *Istoriia gosudarstva rossiiskogo* (1816–26) through the great synthetic works of Sergei Solov'ev and Vasilii Kliuchevskii, historians treated Russia as something like a nation-state, in many ways reflecting in the West European models but uniquely multiethnic in its composition. Karamzin's contribution was particularly significant, for his work was extremely popular among educated readers, and it provided a colorful, patriotic narrative of Russia's past up to the Time of Troubles. As he also emphasized in his secret memorandum to Alexander I, *Memoir on Ancient and Modern Russia* (1811), Karamzin believed that autocracy and a powerful state were responsible for Russia's greatness.[108] Though an adequate discussion of Russian historiography's contribution to the national imaginary cannot be elaborated at length in this essay, one

---

107 To my mind there is a serious methodological problem in regarding popular literature as a window into the peasant mind, as if the willingness to buy a book implies agreement or identity with the views in that book. Representations in print may not even reflect the views of the authors but idealizations of what they conceived to be the desires of peasant readers. Artistry and skill in presentation, appeals to emotion, not to mention the constraints of form, genre, literary convention, and the censorship must be considered. The market should not be seen as a perfect medium through which sovereign consumers express their desires in an unmediated way by freely choosing among available choices.

108 Richard Pipes, *Karamzin's Memoir on Ancient and Modern Russia: A Translation and Analysis* (Cambridge, MA: Harvard University Press, 1959; Ann Arbor: University of Michigan Press, 2005).

should note that it coincided with the development of an ideology of imperialism and the emergence of a Russian school of ethnography and geography in journals like *Vestnik Evropy* (Bulletin of Europe) and *Russkii vestnik* (Russian Bulletin), and was refracted through poetry, novels and short stories, music, and the visual arts.[109] Convinced of their cultural, not to mention material, superiority over the southern and eastern peoples of their empire, Russian intellectuals and statesmen evolved a modernist program of developing, civilizing, categorizing, and rationalizing the non-Russian peoples of the borderlands by means of regulations, laws, statistical surveys and censuses. Whatever sense of inferiority Russians might have felt toward Europeans, particularly the Germans and the English, they more than made up for in their condescension toward their own colonized peoples. And Russians frequently mentioned that they were much better imperialists than the British or the French.[110] Occasionally, however, the immensity of the civilizing mission daunted even the most enthusiastic advocates of expansion. Mikhail Orlov, for example, wearily (and prophetically) remarked, "It is just as hard to subjugate the Chechens and other peoples of this region as to level the Caucasian range. This is something to achieve not with bayonets but with time and enlightenment, in such short supply in our country."[111]

The early nineteenth century was a moment of imperial expansion to the south, into Caucasia. As Russian soldiers moved over the mountains into the Georgian principalities, the Muslim khanates, and Armenia, Russian writers created their own "literary Caucasus," contributing to the Russian discourses of empire and national identity that shaped perceptions and self-understandings of the Russian nineteenth-century elite. Pushkin's evocative poem, "The Prisoner of the Caucasus," was at one and the same time travelogue, ethnography, geography, and even war correspondence. In Pushkin's imaginative geography the communion with nature "averted the eye from military conquest" and largely

---

109 See, for example, Susan Layton, *Russian Literature and Empire: Conquest of the Caucasus from Pushkin to Tolstoy* (Cambridge: Cambridge University Press, 1994); and Austin Jersild, *Orientalism and Empire: North Caucasus Mountain Peoples and the Georgian Frontier, 1845–1917* (Montreal: McGill-Queen's University Press, 2003).

110 A point made to me by Kenneth Church and illustrated in his work on Russian rule in Western Georgia. See his unpublished paper, "Production of Culture in Georgia for a Culture of Production" (1996).

111 Quoted in Layton, *Russian Literature and Empire*, p. 108.

disregarded the native peoples of the Caucasus, who represented a vague menace to the Russian's lyrical relationship with the wilderness. His epilogue to the poem celebrated the military conquest of the Caucasus and introduced a dissonant note into his celebration of the purity, generosity, and liberty of the mountaineers. To paraphrase Petr Viazemskii's telling rebuke, here poetry became an ally of butchers.[112]

The Russian colonial encounter with the Caucasus coincided with an intense phase of the intelligentsia's discussion of Russia's place between Europe and Asia. In the first decades of the nineteenth century scholars laid the foundations of Russian orientalism, and through their perception of the Asian "other" Russians conceptualized ideas of themselves. Russian "civilization," usually taken to be inferior to the West's, was at least superior to the "savagery" of Caucasian mountaineers or Central Asian nomads. A compensatory pride marked the complex and contradictory attitudes toward, and images of, the Caucasian Orient. Emotional intensity and primitive poetry mixed with macho violence. For some the "civilizing mission" of Russia in the south and east was paramount; for others, like military volunteers, adventure and a "license to kill" was the main attraction. In the young Mikhail Lermontov's "Izmail-Bey" and Elizaveta Gan's oriental tales, the mountaineers also become sexual aggressors, "real men" both terrifying and seductive, a threat to the wounded masculine pride of the more restrained Russian. For literary and social critic Vissarion Belinskii, "a woman is created by nature for love" but the Caucasians go too far, making them exclusively objects of passion. Russian writers treated Georgia as a dangerous woman, capable of murder, who had to be dominated for her own good.[113] While Muslim tribesmen were featured as heroes, Christian Georgian men played no

---

112   Ibid., p. 53.

113   Kenneth Church suggests that while Susan Layton is certainly correct that the Russian image of the Georgian woman as a dangerous virago is suggested by the literary texts she explores, a wider acquaintance with travel literature reveals a counter-image of the Georgian woman, not only as the quintessence of feminine beauty, but also as "attractive victims in the history of Islamic conquests" and "victims to the categorically deceitful, lazy, and impotent Georgian male characters of these works" (p. 4). Rather than just being depicted as Oriental others, they were often seen "as fallen Christians, debauched and uncultivated to be sure, but redeemable" (p. 5): "Conjuring 'the Most Beautiful Women in the World' in Nineteenth-Century Descriptions of Georgian Women," paper delivered at the AAASS annual convention, Boca Raton, Florida, September 26, 1998.

role in Russian literature except as the impotent or absent opposites of virile Russian empire-builders. History seemed to reinforce the vulnerability felt by Russian men. When the historic leader of the mountain people's war against Russia, Shamil, married an Armenian captive, she converted to Islam and stayed with him in a loving relationship for life. The eroticism that accompanied imperialism was contained in the Russian fear of the physical prowess of the Caucasians that extended from the battlefield to the bedroom.

In more popular hack literature of the 1830s, the ambiguities of Russia's colonial encounters were lost, and an unabashedly celebratory account of imperialism contended with earlier visions until the young Lev Tolstoy challenged the dominant literary tradition of romanticizing and sentimentalizing the Russian–Caucasian encounter. Yet his stories of the 1850s–1870s—"The Raid," "The Wood-felling," "The Cossacks," and his own "Prisoner of the Caucasus"—along with the developing Caucasian scholarship of regional specialists that criticized the "romance of noble primitivity" did not have the impact of the still-popular Romantic writers.[114] The public feted the defeated Shamil, who made a triumphal tour of Russia and was treated nostalgically as a noble warrior.

While expanding in territory and upholding the traditional principles of autocracy and Orthodoxy, the Russian monarchy, at least up to the time of Nicholas I, imagined Russia as a modern Western state. But the "West" had changed since Peter's time. No longer embracing the ideal of absolutism, Europe increasingly embodied the principles of nationality and popular sovereignty, industrialism and free labor, constitutionalism and representative government. The task for the ideologists of empire in mid-century was to reconceive Russia as "modern" and rethink its relationship to its own imagined "West." Setting out the terms of what would become an interminable debate, the conservative Moscow university professor, Stepan Shevyrev, wrote in 1841, "The West and Russia, Russia and the West—here is the result that follows from the entire past; here is the last word of history; here are the two facts for the future."[115] As attractive at times as European ideas and practices were for reforming monarchs

114 Layton, *Russian Literature and Empire*, p. 254.

115 S. Shevyrev, "Vzglad russkogo na sovremennoe obrazovanie Evropy," *Moskvitianin*, no. 1, p. 219; cited in Nicholas Riasanovsky, *Nicholas I and Official Nationality in Russia, 1825–1855* (Berkeley and Los Angeles: University of California Press, 1967), p. 134.

and intellectuals, in the last years of Catherine II's reign and again in the period after 1815 the emperors and their advisers saw foreign influences as alien, dangerous, and subversive. The threat presented by innovative ideas to absolutism became palpable with the Decembrist rebellion of 1825, and state officials themselves attempted to construct their own Russian idea of nation, one that differed from the dominant discourse of the nation in the West.

Nicholas's ideological formulation, known as "Official Nationality," was summed up in the official slogan "Orthodoxy, Autocracy, Nationality [*narodnost'*]." Elaborated by the conservative minister of education, Sergei Uvarov, Official Nationality emphasized the close ties between the tsar and the people, a bond said to date back to Muscovy. Russians, it was claimed, had chosen their foreign rulers, the Varangians, and worshipped their successors. Russia was distinct in the love of the people for the Westernized autocracy and their devotion to the Church. The link of autocracy, Orthodoxy, and the people was present at Russia's creation, claimed the journalist Fedor Bulgarin:

> Faith and autocracy created the Russian state and the one common fatherland for the Russian Slavs … This immense colossus, Russia, almost a separate continent, which contains within itself all the climates and all the tribes of mankind, can be held in balance only by faith and autocracy. That is why in Russia there could never and cannot exist any other nationality, except the nationality founded on Orthodoxy and on autocracy.[116]

At the heart of Official Nationality lay the image of Russia as "a single family in which the ruler is the father and the subjects the children. The father retains complete authority over the children while he allows them to have full freedom. Between the father and the children there can be no suspicion, no treason; their fate, their happiness and their peace they share in common."[117] "Nationality," the most obscure and contested of the official trinity, was intimately linked with ideas of obedience, submission, and loyalty. As an authentically Christian people, Russians were said to be marked by renunciation and sacrifice, calm and contemplation, a

---

116 Cited in Riasanovsky, *Nicholas I and Official Nationality*, p. 77.
117 Mikhail Pogodin, cited in ibid., pp. 118–19.

deep affection for their sovereign, and dedicated resistance to revolution. At his coronation, which was delayed because of the Decembrist mutiny of progressive nobles, Nicholas bowed three times to the people, inventing a new tradition that continued until the dynasty's fall. At the same time he nationalized the monarchy more intensively. At the ball that followed the coronation, nobles danced in national costumes surrounded by Muscovite decor. Russian was to be used at court; Russian language and history became required subjects at university; churches were built in a Russo-Byzantine style; a national anthem, "God Save the Tsar," was composed under the emperor's supervision. A national opera, *A Life for the Tsar*, by Mikhail Glinka, incorporated folk music to tell the tale of a patriotic peasant, Ivan Susanin, who leads a band of Poles astray rather than reveal the hiding place of the future tsar.[118]

"Official Nationality" was an attempt to make an end run around the Western discourse of the nation and to resuture nation to state, to the monarch and the state religion at the moment when in Western Europe the political community known as nation was becoming separable from the state, at least conceptually, and was fast gaining an independent potency as the source of legitimacy.[119] In contrast, tsarist ideology resisted any such challenge to the *ancien régime* sense of political community (and sovereignty) being identified with the ruler or contained within the state. Generalizing from the Russian case, Benedict Anderson sees "official nationalisms" as a category of nationalisms that appears after popular linguistic-nationalisms, "*responses* by power-groups—primarily, but

---

118   In Western Europe after the French Revolution a new image of monarchy, one in which the ruler was less like a god and more like a human with conventional family values, developed. Monarchs "became exemplars of human conduct, of modest virtue, to be admired by their subjects." The idealization of the monarch's family elevated the ruling dynasty as the historical embodiment of the nation. The move toward family lessened the distance between monarch and his people, as now all were part of a common nation. This ideal of bourgeois monarchy took on a distinctive shape in tsarist Russia. Nicholas I identified his dynasty with the historical destinies of the Russian state and people. "His scenario ... portrayed the emperor as exemplifying the attributes of Western monarchy, but now as a member of his family, as a human being elevated by heredity and his belonging to a ruling family that embodied the highest values of humanity ... The private life of the tsar was lavishly staged to portray a Western ideal before the Russian public." Wortman, *Scenarios of Power*, p. 402; see also George Mosse, *Nationalism and Sexuality: Middle-Class Morality and Sexual Norms in Modern Europe* (Madison: University of Wisconsin Press, 1985), passim.

119   Anderson, *Imagined Communities*, pp. 86–7, 110.

not exclusively, dynastic and aristocratic—threatened with exclusion from, or marginalization in, popular imagined communities." Official nationalism "concealed a discrepancy between nation and dynastic realm" and was connected to the efforts of aristocracies and monarchies to maintain their empires.[120] Certainly the official tsarist view of what was national was deeply conservative, in the sense of preserving a given state form that was being questioned by rival conceptions in the West. Looking back to an idealized past of harmony between people and ruler, Nicholas's notion of Holy Rus' was contrasted to godless, revolutionary Europe. At the same time the monarchy, which was uneasily both Russian and European, resisted those domestic nationalists, like the Slavophile Konstantin Aksakov, who identified with the simple people (*narod*) by wearing a beard and Russian national dress. "In Nicholas's Western frame of mind, beards signified not Russians but Jews and radicals. The official view identified the nation with the ruling Western elite," and not with the mass of the people.[121] In the official scenario the people adored the tsar but did not sanction or legitimize his right to rule, which was conferred by God, by conquest, by hereditary right, the inherent superiority of the hereditary elite, and the natural affection of the Russian people for the autocrat whose rule benefited them.

In many ways the appearance of the intelligentsia in the 1830s spurred a social dialogue about what constituted "the nation." Made up of members from various classes, the intelligentsia lived apart from society and the people, isolated from and alien to official Russia, questioning fundamentals about the political order and religion, yet deeply desirous of becoming close to the people and serving it. As Alan Pollard suggests, "Herein lay the intelligentsia's dilemma. The elements which created consciousness tended to be products of the West, so that the very qualities which endowed the intelligentsia with understanding, and thus with its very essence, also alienated it from national life, to represent which was its vital function. Therefore, the intelligentsia's central problem was to establish a liaison with the people."[122] Between the 1830s and the 1860s, young Russian intellectuals moved from contemplating the world to

---

120   Ibid., pp. 109–10.
121   Wortman, *Scenarios of Power*, p. 402.
122   Alan P. Pollard, "The Russian Intelligentsia: The Mind of Russia," *California Slavic Studies* III (1964), p. 15.

attempting to transform it through action. The opening event in the intel-ligentsia dialogue was the 1836 "Philosophical Letter" by Petr Chaadaev that Aleksandr Herzen reported had the effect of "a pistol shot in the dark night." Radically anti-nationalist, the Letter proclaimed that Russia was unique in that it had no history or traditions, a *tabula rasa* on which new ideas and forms could be written. This extreme Westernizer position was diametrically opposed to Official Nationality, that contrasted Russia's healthy wholeness to the rottenness of the West. After he was condemned as insane and placed under house arrest, Chaadaev published his *Apology of a Madman*, in which he argued that Russia's backwardness presented a unique opportunity for his country "to resolve the greater part of the social problems, to perfect the greater part of the ideas which have arisen in older societies."[123]

The ensuing discussion divided the intelligentsia into those who subscribed to a more rationalist, Enlightenment agenda for Russia— reform in a generally modernist European direction—and those inclined to a more conservative reconstruction of what made up the Russian or Slavic tradition. While some liberals appeared to be indifferent or even hostile to issues of national identity, Ivan Kireevskii, Aleksei Khomiakov, and other Slavophiles followed the European Romantics and looked to the *narod*, which was largely identified with the peasantry, and for *narod-nost'*, the essential character of the Russian or Slav. National character was for Khomiakov contained in religion or a certain form of religiosity.[124] Slavs were the most highly spiritual, artistic, and talented of the peoples of the Earth. Peace-loving and fraternal, spontaneous, loving, and valu-ing freedom, they realized their fullness in an organic unity of all in love and freedom which he called *sobornost'*. Russians were the greatest of the Slavs and possessed an abundance of vital, organic energy, humility and brotherly love. In the pre-Petrine past they had lived freely and harmoni-ously, until Peter the Great introduced alien Western notions of rational-ism, legalism, and formalism and destroyed the organic harmony of the nation. For Konstantin Aksakov and other Slavophiles, not only was

---

123   P. Chaadaev, *Philosophical Letters and Apology of a Madman*, trans. and introduced by Mary-Barbara Zeldin (Knoxville, TN: University of Tennessee Press, 1969), p. 174.

124   See Austin Jersild's unpublished paper, "Khomiakov and Empire: Faith and Custom in the Borderlands," presented at the AAASS annual convention, Boca Raton, Florida, September 26, 1998.

Orthodox Christianity the essential heart of Slavic nature, but the peasant commune was envisioned as "a union of the people who have renounced their egoism, their individuality, and who express their common accord." Critical of the newly triumphant capitalism of the West, they feared the depersonalization of human relations, the dominance of things over men, that came with private property. In Andrzej Walicki's telling analysis, Slavophilism was a "conservative utopianism" that defended community against the fragmenting effects of society.[125]

Both the state authorities and the Westernizer intellectuals rejected the Slavophile vision. For the autocracy the repudiation of the Petrine reforms was an unacceptable challenge, while for the Westernizers the Slavophile reading of the Russian past was a narcissistic fiction. Though Slavophilism was in its origins chiefly "a cultivation of the native and primarily Slavic elements in the social life and culture of ancient Russia," this "conservative nationalism" later blended into a larger concern with the whole of Slavdom (Pan-Slavism), rather than a focused development of Russian national character.[126] In both official and unofficial presentations Russia was submerged either into an identification with the state, the monarchy, and the empire or with Orthodoxy and Slavdom. "The Slavophiles," writes Bushkovitch, "though they moved in that direction, failed to fully establish a tradition of ethnic, rather than statist, identity for Russia."[127] Yet their contribution to Russian political and social thought was profound. From Herzen's "Russian socialism" and the celebration of the peasant commune to the revolutionary populism of the 1870s, ideas of Russian exceptionalism, of overcoming the burdens of Western capitalism and moving straight on to a new communitarianism, dominated the left wing of the Russian intelligentsia. Likewise, their influence was felt on more conservative figures like Dostoevsky and Solov'ev.

The Westernizer Belinskii was critical both of the Slavophiles' celebration of folk culture and the views of "humanist cosmopolitans," like Valerian Maikov, who believed that modernity would eliminate the

125   Andrzej Walicki, *The Slavophile Controversy: History of a Conservative Utopia in Nineteenth-Century Russian Thought*, trans. Hilda Andrews-Rusiecka (Oxford: Oxford University Press, 1975).

126   Andrzej Walicki, *A History of Russian Thought From the Enlightenment to Marxism*, trans. by Hilda Andrews-Rusiecka (Stanford: Stanford University Press, 1979), p. 92.

127   Bushkovitch, "What Is Russia?" p. 12.

specificities of nationality. Belinskii argued, instead, that nation must not be confused with ethnicity but was the result of a progressive civilizing development that came about when the people were raised to the level of society and not, as the Slavophiles suggested, when society was lowered to the level of the people.[128] Rather than condemn Peter's reforms for dividing people from society, Belinskii praised the tsar for turning Russians from a *narod* into a *natsiia* by breaking with instinctive nationality and allowing national consciousness to arise. Turning to literature, the critic claimed that national art was not to be confused with folk production but must refer to the new social and cultural amalgam that came through contact with universal values. For Russia's "truly national works should undoubtedly be sought among those depicting the social groups that emerged after the reforms of Peter the Great and adopted a civilized way of life."[129] Reflecting the early nineteenth-century discussions in Europe about nationality, Belinskii agreed that "nationalities are the individualities of mankind. Without nations mankind would be a lifeless abstraction, a word without content, a meaningless sound."[130]

If nation existed in any sense in mid-nineteenth century Russia, it existed in the fierce discussion over what constituted the *narod* and the *natsiia*. Historians entered the debate over the nature of the Russian nation and the effects of Peter the Great's intervention, usually in opposition to the Slavophile interpretation. In a series of lectures in 1843–44, the liberal Westernizer Timofei Granovskii attacked the Slavophile idealization of the people. But more long-lasting was the work of the so-called "statist" school of Russian historians—Konstantin Kavelin, Boris Chicherin, and Sergei Solov'ev—who by proposing that the Russian state was the principal agent of progress in Russia's history assured that state rather than nation would dominate the subsequent historical discussion. Russian "nationalist" thought, such as it was, usually centered either on the state or on a religious conception of identity and community, and in the minds of its more conservative representatives included in that community all Slavs. The "nation," while always present as a palimpsest, was overlaid by other more pressing social and political themes, and

---

128   Walicki, *A History of Russian Thought*, p. 137.

129   V. G. Belinskii, *Polnoe sobranie sochineniia* (Moscow, 1953–59), VII, p. 435; Walicki, *A History of Russian Thought*, p. 140.

130   Belinskii, *Polnoe sobranie sochineniia*, X, p. 29; Walicki, *A History of Russian Thought*, p. 143.

occupation with problems of the simple people (the more widespread meaning of *narod*) and its relationship to *obshchestvo* (society) indicates the conceptual difficulties of imagining a nation that cut across estate boundaries and included the whole of the "national" community.

The tsarist empire tried to extend official nationalism, first bureaucratic then cultural Russification, to suppress non-Russian nationalisms and separatisms, and to identify the dynasty and the monarchy with a Russian "nation." But all of these various and often contradictory attempts foundered before opposing tendencies, most significantly the powerful countervailing pull of supranational identifications of Russia with empire, Orthodoxy, and Slavdom. Even the conservative nationalist Mikhail Katkov (1818–1887) conceived of Russian identity as basically state-centered. Since the state was not ethnically homogeneous, that condition had to be changed. Russification would provide the state with the ethnic nation below. Although his newspaper, *Moskovskie Vedomosti* (Moscow News), was the most popular on the political Right, Katkov's nationalist views had only limited appeal to the broader population. The idea of a Pan-Slavic unity, perhaps headed by "the tsar of all the Slavs" and not just Russia (an idea expressed by the poet Fedor Tiuchev among others), was continually undermined by the resistance of other Slavic peoples, most importantly the Poles, who not only did not share Orthodoxy with the Russians but whose whole self-identity was bound up in resistance to Russian domination. Closer to home both Pan-Slavism and the more modest concept of the Russian people including both "Little Russians" (Ukrainians) and "White Russians" (Belarusians), as well as "Great Russians," was dealt a severe blow by an emerging separate national identity among Ukrainians. After the government suppressed the Ukrainian Brotherhood of Cyril and Methodius, a radical Pan-Slavic group, in 1847, it not only reversed its Ukrainophilic policy (directed against Polish influences) but officially condemned Pan-Slavism as a dangerous and subversive doctrine.[131]

Expansion and Collapse

The articulation by intellectuals and government officials of the Russian people's special character, different from and inherently superior to the

---

131 P. A. Zionchkovskii, *Kirilo-Mefodievskoe obshchestvo (1846–1847)* (Moscow: Izdatel'stvo Moskovskogo universiteta, 1959).

chaotic amoralism of the West, provided Russian policymakers with motivation and justification for imperial expansion to the east and colonization of the "empty spaces" of Siberia and Central Asia. The voluminous writings of a conservative nationalist like Mikhail Pogodin (1800–1875), a historian who worshipped Karamzin and held the first chair in Russian history at Moscow University, contained all of these themes—Russian exceptionalism, Pan-Slavism, and a civilizing mission in the east.[132] Whereas in the west Russia met resistance to its expansion—the Crimean War (1853–56), the Treaty of Berlin (1878)—and rebellion (the Polish insurrections of 1831 and 1863), the east offered opportunities. With the defeat of Imam Shamil, battle-hardened troops were available to be deployed further east. While Russia's cautious foreign minister, Prince Aleksandr Gorchakov, opposed annexing the khanate of Kokand, even after General Mikhail Cherniaev had seized Tashkent in 1865, the energetic general's policy of abolishing the khanate's autonomy eventually gained powerful supporters in the government. Russia's principal concern in Central Asia was neither economic nor religious, but was largely strategic at first—directed against the expansion of Bukhara and later of the British—and only later preoccupied with trade and settlement. After General Konstantin von Kaufman defeated Bukhara and Khiva, they were made dependencies of the Russian tsar but allowed to keep their autonomy. Where Russians ruled directly, the military remained in charge, with all of its rigidity and authoritarianism. Even after civilians became more influential after 1886, the administration, manned by petty and ill-educated officials, was marked by pervasive corruption and callous and arbitrary treatment of the local peoples. In Central Asia a cultural and class chasm separated Russian administrators and settlers from the Muslim peoples. Educated Muslims either entered the Islamic clergy or accepted the benefits of European knowledge, mediated through Russian. Muslim reformers known as Jadidists (followers of the "new method") attempted to bring Western learning to Central Asia, but found themselves caught between suspicious Russians on one side and hostile Muslim clerics on the other.

---

132 Pogodin's writings are scattered but can be sampled in N. Barsukov, *Zhizn' I trudy M. P. Pogodina*, 22 vols. (St. Petersburg, 1888–1910); *Bor'ba ne na zhivot, a na smert s novymi istoricheskimi eresiami* (Moscow, 1874); *Sobranie statei, pisem i rechei po povodu slavianskogo voprosa* (Moscow, 1978). Riasanovsky, *Nicholas I and Official Nationality*, passim., discusses Pogodin at length.

Though tsarist Russia was not a "bourgeois" empire (in the sense used by Cooper and Stoler) and did not have an inherent conflict between universal rights and liberties and the forms of its imperial rule, it nevertheless existed within a bourgeois European world and adopted a modernizing agenda in the late nineteenth century that undermined some of the earlier stabilities in the relationship of colonizer to colonized. Russian colonizers adopted the notion of "civility" (*grazhdanstvennost'*) as a way of expressing both the civilizing mission of the empire and a sense of the civic virtues that would bring "the other" into a multinational Russian world.[133] But even as they acculturated to imperial society, many educated, upwardly mobile, Russian-speaking non-Russian subjects found their access to the civil service and upper ranks of society blocked to a degree. One of the most telling arguments for the growth of nationalism among peripheral elites is precisely this frustrated mobility—what Benedict Anderson refers to as "cramped" or "vertically barred" "pilgrimages of Creole functionaries"[134]—that encourages them to consider reshaping the political and economic arena in which they can operate. In conditions of multinationality, nationalism often becomes an argument for privileged access, both on the part of majority peoples and minorities, to state positions.

As an imperial polity, engaged in discriminatory as well as nationalizing policies in the nineteenth century, the Russian state maintained vital distinctions between Russians and non-Russians, in their differential treatment of various non-Russian and non-Orthodox peoples, as well as between social estates. Whole peoples, designated *inorodtsy*, continued to be subject to special laws, among them Jews, peoples of the North Caucasus, Kalmyks, nomads, Samoeds and other peoples of Siberia. The Great Reforms of the 1860s did not extend *zemstva* (local assemblies) to non-Russian areas. While distinctions and discriminations were maintained between parts of the empire and the constituent peoples, more concerted efforts were made to Russify some parts of the population. The government considered all Slavs potential or actual Russians, and officials

---

133   On *grazhdanstvennost'*, see the essays by Dov Yaroshevski and Austin Lee Jersild, in Daniel R. Brower and Edward J. Lazzerini (eds.), *Russia's Orient: Imperial Borderlands and Peoples, 1700–1917* (Bloomington: Indiana University Press, 1997), pp. 58–79, 101–14.

134   Anderson, *Imagined Communities*, p. 57.

restricted Polish higher education and the use of Ukrainian.[135] The Polish university in Vilno was closed after the rebellion of 1830–31, only to be reopened later in Kiev as a Russian university. Alexander III's advisors, Dmitrii Tolstoi and Konstantin Pobedonostev, equated Russianness and Orthodoxy and were particularly hostile to Catholics and Jews. All Orthodox students were to be educated in Russian, even if they considered themselves Ukrainian, Belarusian, Georgian, or Bessarabian. At the same time, however, the government was concerned that people have access to religious instruction in their own faith. Therefore, it permitted the establishment of Catholic, Protestant, Armenian, Muslim, and Jewish schools, and occasionally allowed non-Orthodox education in languages other than Russian. Non-Christian confessional schools were also allowed to impart instruction in other languages, while non-Christian state schools had to use Russian. The Church's own educational reformer, N. I. Il'minskii, argued persuasively that the heathen had to hear the Gospel in their own language, and in 1870 the so-called "Il'minskii system" establishing a network of missionary schools in local languages became official policy.[136]

The most conventional image of late tsarism's "nationality policy" is that it was dedicated to Russification. But this image, in which every action from administrative systematization to repression of national movements is homogenized into a seemingly consistent program, is sorely deficient. In Russia, Russification had at least three distinct meanings. For Catherine the Great and Nicholas I, *obruset'* or *obrusevanie* was a state policy of unifying and making uniform the administrative practices of the empire. Second, there was a spontaneous process of self-adaptation of people to the norms of life and language in the Russian empire, an unplanned *obrusenie* (again the verb *obruset'* was employed) that was quite successful among the peoples of the Volga region and the western Slavic peoples, and continued to be particularly powerful in the middle decades of the nineteenth century when the empire was inclusive, relatively tolerant (except toward Poles and Ukrainians), and appealed to non-Russians as an available path to European enlightenment and

135   Theodore R. Weeks, *Nation and State in Late Imperial Russia: Nationalism and Russification on the Western Frontier, 1863-1914* (DeKalb, IL: Northern Illinois University Press, 1996), pp. 70-91.

136   Isabelle Kreindler, "A Neglected Source of Lenin's Nationality Policy," *Slavic Review*, XXXVI, 1 (March 1977), pp. 86-100.

progress. The third form of Russification is the one conventionally referred to, the effort to *obrusit'*, to make Russian in a cultural sense. Cultural Russification, a latecomer to the arsenal of tsarist state-building, was a reaction to the nationalisms of non-Russians that the governments of Alexander III and Nicholas II, in their panic, exaggerated beyond their actual strength.[137]

One of the fields where nationality began to emerge as a significant marker of difference in Russia was in education, where the state's religious policy had the unintended consequence of raising the relevance of nationality. As John Slocum suggests, "a state policy aimed at language rationalization, when pursued simultaneously with the implementation of a system of public education, induces a politics of nationality when the state encounters entrenched societal actors (in this case, non-Orthodox religious hierarchies) with a vested interest in upholding alternative world-views."[138] As elementary school enrollment in Russia increased fivefold from 1856 to 1885 and again fourfold by 1914, the issue of language of instruction became a major concern of the government. Non-Russianness was associated more and more with language, and the government intervened more frequently in favor of Russian education. In 1887, for example, elementary schools in the Baltic region, allowed to teach in Russian, Estonian, or Latvian for the first two years, were required to teach exclusively in Russian in the last year, except for religion and church singing. "By about 1910," Slocum argues, "'nationality' had become a politically salient category within imperial Russia . . . Language-based nationality achieved the status of the primary criterion for distinguishing Russians from non-Russians (and one group of non-Russians from another) by overturning an earlier official definition of the situation, according to which religion was the primary criterion for determining Russianness and non-Russianness."[139] From a politics of difference based primarily, but not entirely, on religion Russia passed to a politics in which nationality counted as never before.

---

137 For a fascinating treatment of the varieties of Russification, see Edward C. Thaden (ed.), *Russification in the Baltic Provinces and Finland, 1855–1914* (Princeton: Princeton University Press, 1981), pp. 7–9, passim.

138 John Willard Slocum, "The Boundaries of National Identity: Religion, Language, and Nationality Politics in Late Imperial Russia" (Ph.D. diss., University of Chicago, 1993), p. 10.

139 Ibid., pp. 4–5.

In the more open political arena in the period between the two revolutions, from 1905 to 1917, the "nationality question" became an issue of extraordinary interest both to the government and the opposition. Very often those Russians living in ethnically non-Russian areas, like the western provinces, Ukraine, or Transcaucasia, were ferociously nationalist. They were represented in the Nationalist Party, which flourished in the western provinces, and chauvinist publicists like Vasilii Velichko, with his anti-Armenian diatribes, became influential in Transcaucasia.[140] A widely read debate in the press between the "conservative liberal" Petr Stuve and the Ukrainian activist Bohdan Kistiakivskyi exposed the statism and assimilationist nationalism that lay below much Russian political thinking, even among the opposition to autocracy.[141] While Russian nationalists insisted that Ukrainians and Belarusians were lesser branches of a single Russian people, nationalists among Ukrainians claimed a nationhood based on a distinct culture. As a variety of ethnic nationalisms developed, both among conservative Russians and non-Russian peoples, the government held a series of conferences on nationality matters: one on Pan-Turkism, another interdepartmental conference on the education of *inorodtsy*. The organizers of the latter conference hoped to attract *inorodtsy* into the general educational system of the Russian-language state schools, to develop the use of Russian "as the state language," though forcible Russification was to be avoided. This was clearly an abandonment of the "Il'minskii system," for now instruction, except in the first and possibly the second year of primary school, was ultimately to be in Russian. The goal no longer was the development of backward peoples within their own culture along with the Orthodox religion, but assimilation of non-Russians to the greatest extent possible. The conference opposed "artificial awakening of self-consciousness among separate *narodnosti* [peoples], which, according to their cultural development and

---

140 Robert Edelman, *Gentry Politics on the Eve of the Russian Revolution: The Nationalist Party* (New Brunswick: Rutgers University Press, 1980); Ronald Grigor Suny, *The Making of the Georgian Nation* (Bloomington, IN and Stanford, CA: Indiana University Press in association with the Hoover Institution Press, 1988; second edition: Bloomington, IN: Indiana University Press, 1994), p. 142.

141 Susan Heuman, *Kistiakovsky: The Struggle for National and Constitutional Rights in the Last Years of Tsarism* (Cambridge, MA: Harvard Ukrainian Research Institute, 1998), pp. 130–46.

numerical size, cannot create an independent culture."[142] As the conference report concluded,

> The ideal school from the point of view of state unity would be a unified school for all the *narodnosti* of the Empire, with the state language of instruction, not striving for the repression of individual nationalities [*natsional'nosti*], but cultivating in them, as in native Russians, love of Russia and consciousness of her unity, wholeness [*tselost'*], and indivisibility.[143]

The state was prepared to use its resources to gain converts to Orthodoxy and the Russian language, but also seemed to realize that "the majority of the empire's population was not and never would be truly Russian."[144] Religious boundaries were real and were to be enforced, while nationalism and separatism were to be repressed. While religion continued to be the primary distinction between Russians and non-Russians, language and nationality had become highly relevant markers of difference in the last years of tsarism, and the shift from a distinctiveness based on religion to one based on language, though never complete, was, in Slocum's words, "a transformation in the discursive regime, a revolutionary break in the political conversations between Russians and non-Russians."[145]

In empire's last years the tsarist upper classes and state authorities were divided between those who no longer were willing to tamper with the traditional institutions of autocracy and nobility and those who sought to reform the state to represent the unrepresented, reduce or eliminate social and ethnic discriminations, and move toward forming a nation.[146] But the resistance to social egalitarianism or ethnic neutrality overwhelmed nation-making processes. An attempt to establish elective *zemstva* in the western provinces precipitated a political crisis. If the usual principle of representation by estate were observed, local power

---

142   Slocum, "The Boundaries of National Identity," p. 214.

143   Ibid., p. 216.

144   Ibid., p. 256.

145   Ibid., p. 258.

146   This conflict between rival views of how to construct a modern Russian political community is worked out in Joshua A. Sanborn, *"Drafting the Nation": Military Conscription, Total War, and Mass Politics, 1905–1925* (DeKalb: Northern Illinois University Press, 2003).

would pass into the hands of Polish landlords, but when a system of representation by ethnic curiae favoring Russians was proposed, the law was defeated in the conservative upper house of the duma because it compromised representation by estate. A law on municipal councils in Poland's cities collapsed before the resistance by anti-Semitic Poles, who feared Jewish domination of the municipal legislatures. Russian nationalists triumphed briefly in 1912 when the region of Kholm (Chelm), largely Ukrainian and Catholic in population, was removed from the historic Kingdom of Poland and made into a separate province.[147] In each of these three cases particularistic distinctions about nationality and class dominated the discussion and divided the participants. Universalist principles about allegiance to a common nation were largely absent.

In his forced retirement, the former prime minister, Sergei Witte, an extraordinarily thoughtful analyst of the autocracy, perceptively charted the principal difficulties faced by traditional empires as they entered the twentieth century. In his *Zapiski* (Memoirs), Witte noted:

> To preserve Autocracy when the unrestricted autocrat for years shatters the State with actions not only inappropriate but fatally flawed, and when his subjects do not see any relatively realistic hopes for the future, is especially difficult [to do] in the 20th century when the self-consciousness of the popular masses has grown significantly and is nurtured, in our country, by what is called a "liberation movement."[148]

To these failures of the center and the mobilization of the masses, Witte added the threat presented by nationalism:

> The borderlands . . . began to avenge very real discrimination that had gone on for years, as well as measures which were entirely justified but unreconciled with the national feelings (*natsional'noe chuvstvo*) of conquered ethnic groups (*inorodtsy*) . . . The big mistake of our decades-long policy is that we still today do not understand that there hasn't been a Russia from the time of Peter the Great and Catherine the Great. There has been a Russian Empire. When over 35 per cent of the

---

147 Weeks, *Nation and State*, pp. 131–92.
148 Francis C. Wcislo, "Witte, Memory, and the 1905 Revolution: A Reinterpretation of the Witte Memoirs," *Revolutionary Russia* VIII, 2 (December 1995), p. 175.

population are ethnics, and Russians are divided among Great Russians, Little Russians, and White Russians, it is impossible, in the 19th and 20th centuries, to conduct a policy that ignores . . . the national tendencies (*natsional'nye svoistva*) of other nationalities who have entered the Russian Empire, their religion(s), their languages, and so on. The motto of such an empire cannot be "I will make them all true Russians"—this is not an ideal that will inspire all subjects of the Russian Emperor, unify the population, create one political spirit.[149]

Tsarism never created a nation within the whole empire nor even a sense of nation among the core Russian population, even though what looked to others like imperialism was for the country's rulers "part of larger state-building and nation-building projects."[150] Tsarist Russia managed only too well in building a state and creating an empire; it failed, however, to construct a multiethnic "Russian nation" within that empire. The history of tsarism is of an empire that at times engaged in nation-making, often through religious conversion and occasionally through forced Russification, but such state practices were always in tension with the structures and discourses of empire. The imperial tended to thwart if not subvert the national, just as the national worked to erode the stability and legitimacy of the state. While Muscovy and imperial Russia were successful in integrating the core regions of its empire, often referred to as the *vnutrennie guberniia*, into a single nationality, diverse administrative practices, as well as the compactness of the local ethnicities and the effects of settlement policies, maintained and intensified differences between the Russian core and the non-Russian peripheries. After relatively successfully conquering and assimilating the Orthodox Slavic population of central Russia (Vladimir, Novgorod, other appanage states), Muscovy set out to "recover" lands with non-Slavic, non-Orthodox populations, like Kazan. In some areas the tsarist regime managed to create loyal subjects through the transformation of cultural identities, but its policies were inconsistent and varied enormously. It neither created an effective civic national identity nor succeeded (or even tried very hard) forging an ethnic nation, even among Russians. Localism, religious identity, and a pervasive concept of Russia as tied up with tsar

---

149   Ibid., p. 176.
150   Beissinger, "The Persisting Ambiguity," p. 2.

and state, rather than with the people as a whole, hindered the imagining of a cross-class, cross-cultural nation within the empire. The tsarist government, it might be said, even failed to turn peasants into Russians.[151] There was no program, as in France, to educate and affiliate millions of people around an idea of the nation. Tsarist Russia's experience was one of incomplete nation-making. Here the parallels between England's success in integrating Britain but failing in Ireland, and France's success in nationalizing the "hexagon" but failing in Algeria (as discussed by Ian Lustick), are suggestive in the Russian case.[152]

Russia was a composite state with unequal relations between a "Russian" metropole, which itself was a multiethnic though culturally Russified ruling elite, and non-Russian populations. For all the haphazard nationalizing efforts of the ruling institution, both the programs of discrimination and inequity between metropole and periphery, and the resistant cultures and counter-discourses of nationalism of non-Russians, prevented the homogenization and incorporation of the population into a single "imagined community" of a Russian nation. Though tsarist Russia's collapse did not occur because of nationalisms from the peripheries but because of the progressive weakening and disunity of the center, much of the legitimacy of the imperial enterprise had withered away by 1917. Elites withdrew support from the monarchy, and more broadly the regime was alienated from the intelligentsia and workers, strategically located in the largest cities. Policies of industrialization and the limited reforms after 1905 had created new constituencies in tsarist society that demanded representation in the political order that the tsar refused to grant. In the new world in which discourses of civilization centered on the nation, constitutionalism, economic development (which tsarism was seen to be hindering), and (in some quarters) socialism and revolution, tsarism's political structure—autocracy—was increasingly understood to be a fetter on further advances.

In its last years the dynasty appeared increasingly to be incompetent and even treacherous. As Russians suffered defeats and colossal losses in World War I, the fragile aura of legitimacy was stripped from the emperor and his wife, who were widely regarded as distant from, even foreign to,

---

151   An idea suggested to me by Roman Szporluk.

152   Ian Lustick, *State-Building Failure in British Ireland and French Algeria* (Berkeley: Institute of International Studies, University of California, Berkeley, 1985).

Russia. What the dynasty in the distant past had imagined was empowering, their difference from the people, now became a fatal liability. Elite patriotism, frustrated non-Russian nationalisms, and peasant weariness at intolerable sacrifices for a cause with which they did not identify combined lethally to undermine the monarchy. The principles of empire, of differentiation and hierarchy, were incompatible with the modern ideas of democratic representation and egalitarian citizenship that gripped much of the intelligentsia and urban society. When the monarchy failed the test of war, its last sources of popular affection and legitimacy fell away, and in the crucial test of the February Days of 1917, Nicholas II was unable to find the military support to suppress the popular resistance to its rule in a single city.

PART II

Russia's Revolutions

CHAPTER FOUR

Toward a Social History of the October Revolution

For the first sixty-five years after the October Revolution, Western scholars had been unable to formulate a consensus on the reasons for the Bolsheviks' rapid rise to power between February and October 1917.[1] Deep divisions existed among academic historians in Europe and America on fundamental questions of value, causation, and methodology, while a more frigid scholarly Cold War separated Western historians from their Soviet counterparts. Carried on in the polite and moderate language appropriate to "scientific" prose, the debate over 1917 was, despite all intentions, implicitly politicized and involved an attempt to explain not only the progress of a major revolution but also the roots of a new type of social and political order, one that some praised as socialism and others condemned as Stalinism or totalitarianism. Because possible justifications of the "legitimacy" of the Soviet system seemed to be implied in certain explanations of how the Bolsheviks came to power, much of the literature emphasized the artificiality, the accidental or manipulated quality, of the October Revolution and concomitantly de-emphasized the deep and long-term social developments that provided both the context and the momentum in which Lenin's party was able to emerge victorious. That impasse in scholarship began to be breached most effectively when, in the 1970s, an engaged group of social historians tackled the thorny questions of the revolutionary year.

Historians have understandably had difficulty separating their political preferences for or abhorrence of the Soviet Union from their treatment of the complexities of the revolutionary years. Frequently, history has been written backwards, beginning with the knowledge of the single-party dictatorship, Stalin, collectivization, and the Great Purges and retreating in

---

1   This chapter first appeared in *The American Historical Review* LXXXVIII, 1 (February 1983), pp. 31–52. This version owes much to critical readings by Geoff Eley and William G. Rosenberg of the University of Michigan, Alexander Rabinowitch of Indiana University, Bloomington, and Allan K. Wildman of Ohio State University. All dates are Old Style.

time toward the heady days of 1917 to find what went wrong. Western interpretations of the Russian Revolution are arrayed all along the political spectrum, from nostalgic reactionary views regretting the passage of the tsarist regime to radical apologia for the necessity of violence and terror. But none are free, or ultimately can be free, from explicit or unconscious value judgments about the benefits or costs of this revolution.

Although history is never entirely devoid of ideological preconditioning and cannot be completely "objective," historians are still obligated to be clear about their values and preferences and their politics, and to attempt, within these limits, to be as sensitive and fair to the evidence as possible. Not surprisingly, most Western historians of the Russian Revolution come to the study of 1917 committed to an evolutionary, democratic political and social system and are highly suspicious of the possibility of creating a non-capitalist, socialist economic order—particularly out of whole cloth as the Bolsheviks attempted to do. Despite frequent claims of detachment and objectivity, scholars often make their judgments about the revolution and the Soviet Union against the standard of quite different European and American experiences. It is helpful, therefore, to explore the connection between conscious or unconscious ideological intrusions and the approach to a historical problem, for a particular angle of vision may illuminate some aspects while obscuring others.

Not unconnected to political values brought to the study of the revolution are the kinds of analyses preferred by most Western historians. Up until the 1970s, Western historiography of 1917 had been concerned primarily with political explanations, emphasizing the importance of governmental forms and ideas but underestimating the more fundamental social and economic structures and conflicts in Russian society. Approaching the revolution from the top down, these writers were concerned with the politics of the tsarist and provisional governments, with parties and revolutionary organizations, and with the dynamic personalities of Lenin, Trotsky, and Kerensky as well as with ideological questions.[2] This tendency

2 See, for example, George Katkov, *Russia 1917: The February Revolution* (New York: Longmans, 1967); Rex A. Wade, *The Russian Search for Peace: February to October 1917* (Stanford: Stanford University Press, 1969); Adam B. Ulam, *The Bolsheviks: The Intellectual and Political History of the Triumph of Communism in Russia* (New York: Macmillan, 1965); John Shelton Curtiss, *The Russian Revolutions of 1917* (Princeton: Van Nostrand, 1957); and John M. Thompson, *Revolutionary Russia, 1917* (New York: Charles Scribners's, 1981).

to stay with the most articulate political actors has always been popular and remains influential to the present, although studies of political parties have incorporated socio-historical material.[3]

Russian history in general and the study of the revolution in particular were latecomers to social history. This might seem anomalous to people outside the field, given that scholars in the Soviet Union wrote exclusively in a Marxist tradition. But during the Stalinist years Soviet Marxist historiography of the revolution was limited to explorations of the role of the party and key party leaders, and only in the post-Stalin years were there more broadly gauged investigations of workers, peasants, the soviets, and other mass organizations and movements.[4] In the West the socio-historical approach has also long been hindered by the inaccessibility of Soviet archives, but after 1991 the picture changed dramatically. Scholars turned away from the most visible participants in the revolution to look at the rest of Russian society and

---

3   See Oliver Radkey, *The Agrarian Foes of Bolshevism: Promise and Default of the Russian Socialist Revolutionaries, February to October 1917* (New York: Columbia University Press, 1958), and *The Sickle under the Hammer: The Russian Socialist Revolutionaries in the Early Months of Soviet Rule* (New York: Columbia University Press, 1963). On the Mensheviks, see Leopold H. Haimson (ed.), *The Mensheviks: From the Revolution of 1917 to the Second World War* (Chicago: University of Chicago Press, 1974); on the Kadets, see William G. Rosenberg, *Liberals in the Russian Revolution: The Constitutional Democratic Party, 1917–1921* (Princeton: Princeton University Press, 1974); on the Bolsheviks, see Alexander Rabinowitch, *Prelude to Revolution: The Petrograd Bolsheviks and the July 1917 Uprising* (Bloomington, IN: Indiana University Press, 1968), and *The Bolsheviks Come to Power: The Revolution of 1917 in Petrograd* (New York: W. W. Norton, 1976); and, on the anarchists, see Paul H. Avrich, *The Russian Anarchists* (Princeton, Princeton University Press, 1967).

4   Among Soviet works dealing with the social history of the revolution, see E. N. Burdzhalov, *Vtoraia russkaia revoliutsiia*, 2 vols. (Moscow,: Nauka 1967–71); A. M. Andreev, *Sovety rabochikh i soldatskikh deputatov nakanune Oktiabria* (Moscow: Nauka, 1970); L. S. Gaponenko, *Rabochii klass Rossii v 1917 godu* (Moscow, 1970); G. L. Sobolev, *Revoliutsionnoe soznanie rabochikh i soldat Petrograda v 1917 godu* (Leningrad: Nauka, 1973); V. I. Miller, *Soldatskie komitety russkoi armii v 1917 g.: Vozniknovenie i nachal'nyi period deiatel'nosti* (Moscow: Nauka, 1974); P. N. Pershin, *Agrarnaia revoliutsiia v Rossii*, 2 vols. (Moscow: Nauka, 1966); and P. V. Volobuev, *Proletariat i burzhuaziia v Rossii v 1917 godu* (Moscow: Nysl', 1964). For discussions of Soviet historiography, see David A. Longley, "Some Historiographical Problems of Bolshevik Party History (The Kronstadt Bolsheviks in March 1917)," *Jahrbücher fur Geschichte Osteuropas* 22 (1975), pp. 494–514; and John L. H. Keep, "The Great October Socialist Revolution," in Samuel H. Baron and Nancy W. Heer (eds.), *Windows on the Russian Past* (Columbus, Ohio: American Association for the Advancement of Slavic Studies, 1977), pp. 139–56.

to outlying regions, and produced a number of socio-historical studies of workers (by Mark David Mandel, Robert Devlin, William G. Rosenberg, Diane Koenker, Stephen A. Smith, and Ziva Galili, of revolution in the provinces (by Donald J. Raleigh, Roger Pethybridge, Ronald Grigor Suny, and Andrew Ezergailis), of the soldiers (by Allan K. Wildman), of the sailors (by Norman E. Saul and Evan Mawdsley), and the whole array of spontaneous mass organizations (by Marc Ferro, Oskar Anweiler, Rex A. Wade, John L. H. Keep, and Tsuyoshi Hasegawa). The Russian peasantry, hitherto largely neglected in the revolutionary period, was the subject of monographs by Graeme J. Gill and later by Orlando Figes.[5]

---

5 On workers, see Mandel, *The Petrograd Workers and the Fall of the Old Regime* (New York, 1983); and his *The Petrograd Workers and the Soviet Seizure of Power* (New York: Macmillan, 1984); Devlin, "Petrograd Workers and Workers' Factory Committees in 1917: An Aspect of the Social History of the Russian Revolution" (Ph.D. dissertation. State University of New York, Binghamton, 1976); Rosenberg, "Workers' Control on the Railroads and Some Suggestions Concerning Social Aspects of Labor Politics in the Russian Revolution," *Journal of Modern History* XLIX (1977), pp. 1181–219, and "The Democratization of Russia's Railroads in 1917," *American Historical Review* LXXXVI (1981), pp. 983–1008; Koenker, *Moscow Workers and the 1917 Revolution* (Princeton: Princeton University Press, 1981); Smith, *Red Petrograd: Revolution in the Factories, 1917–1918* (Cambridge: Cambridge University Press, 1983); and "Craft Consciousness, Class Consciousness: Petrograd 1917," *History Workshop* II (1981), pp. 33–56; and Galili, *The Menshevik Leaders in the Russian Revolution: Social Realities and Political Strategies* (Princeton; Princeton University Press, 1989). On the provinces, see Raleigh, *Revolution on the Volga: 1917 in Saratov* (Ithaca: Cornell University Press, NY, 1986); and "Revolutionary Politics in Provincial Russia: The Tsaritsyn 'Republic' in 1917," *Slavic Review* XL (1981), pp. 194–209; Pethybridge, *The Spread of the Russian Revolution: Essays on 1917* (London: Palgrave Macmillan, 1972); Suny, *The Baku Commune, 1917–1918: Class and Nationality in the Russian Revolution* (Princeton: Princeton University Press, 1972); and Ezergailis, *The 1917 Revolution in Latvia* (Boulder: East European Quartery CO, 1974). On the soldiers, see Wildman, *The End of the Russian Imperial Army*, 2 vols. (Princeton: Princeton University Press, 1983, 1987). On the sailors, see Saul, *Sailors in Revolt: The Russian Baltic Fleet in 1917* (Lawrence, KS: University Kansas Press, 1978); and Mawdsley, *The Russian Revolution and the Baltic Fleet: War and Politics, February 1917–April 1918* (London: Macmillan, 1978). And, on mass organizations, see Ferro, *The Russian Revolution of February 1917*: Prentice-Hall, (London, 1972), and *October 1917: A Social History of the Russian Revolution* (London: Routledge & Kegan Paul, 1980); Anweiler, *The Soviets: The Russian Workers', Peasants', and Soldiers' Councils* (New York, 1974); Wade, "Spontaneity in the Formation of the Workers' Militia and Red Guards, 1917," in Ralph Carter Elwood (ed.), *Reconsiderations on the Russian Revolution* (Cambridge, 1976), pp. 20–41, and *Red Guard and Workers' Militias: Spontaneity and Leadership in the Russian Revolution* (Stanford: Standford University Press, 1983); Keep, *The Russian Revolution: A Study in Mass Mobilization* (New York: W. W. Norton, 1976); and Hasegawa, *The February Revolution: Petrograd, 1917* (Seattle: University of

The debate about social and political history has been both fruitful and divisive within the profession—fruitful in that it has forced more conscious appreciation by all historians of the tasks in which they are engaged, but divisive in that it has hardened positions and distorted the dialogue between Marxist and non-Marxist social historians.[6] The study of the Russian Revolution has been spared the sparring that has divided European social historians, in part because Russian scholars have neglected or consciously avoided theoretical and methodological issues and in part because they have not written much non-narrative, quantitative, apolitical social history of the sort done by some family historians.[7] Russian social history has been more concerned with the movement and movements of social groups and classes than with patterns of fertility or mortality, and has emphasized those moments of intense conflict, such as 1905 and 1917. That focus has always demanded some attention to politics. An appreciation of the estate (*soslovie*) structure of Russian society and the emergence of classes has long been a part of this tradition of historical writing. Yet there have been influential examples of histories written without much concern for the underlying social context, as well as studies that have dealt almost exclusively with social movements without adequate consideration of political issues. And, perhaps most surprisingly, the October Revolution has often been studied without taking into account the socio-political developments of the late tsarist period, particularly the crucial last years of constitutional impasse and rising urban unrest.

The overthrow of the tsar, accomplished by workers and soldiers in Petrograd, was the product of largely spontaneous action by thousands of

---

Washington Press, 1980); Gill, *Peasants and Government in the Russian Revolution* (London: Palgrave Macmillan, 1979); and Figes, *Peasant Russia, Civil War: The Volga Countryside in Revolution, 1917–1921* (Oxford: Oxford University Press, 1989).

6 For the debate, see Gareth Stedman Jones, "From Historical Sociology to Theoretical History," *British Journal of Sociology* 27 (1976), pp. 295–305; Tony Judt, "A Clown in Regal Purple: Social History and the Historians," *History Workshop Journal* 7 (1979), pp. 66–94; Elizabeth Fox Genovese and Eugene D. Genovese, "The Political Crisis of Social History: A Marxist Perspective," *Journal of Social History* 10 (1976), pp. 205–20; and Louise Tilly et al., "Problems in Social History: A Symposium," *Theory and Society* 9 (1980), pp. 667–81.

7 For a statement of this view, see Edward Shorter's belligerent contribution to the symposium "Problems in Social History" in *Theory and Society* IX (1980), pp. 670–4. For a plea for the reconciliation of the various forms of social history, see Charles Tilly's contribution, ibid., pp. 679–81.

hungry, angry, and war-weary women and men who had lost all confidence in the government of Nicholas II. But, along with the political revolution aimed at autocracy, a deeply rooted social antagonism, particularly on the part of certain groups of workers, against the propertied classes (the so-called *tsenzovoe obshchestvo*) was evident. This social cleavage was not simply a product of the war years but antedated that conflict, as Leopold H. Haimson showed in his seminal two-part article published half a century ago.[8] Haimson argued that a dual polarization had been taking place in urban Russia in the last years before the war. As all but the most conservative strata of society moved away from the bureaucratic absolutist regime, the working class or, more precisely, workers in large firms, such as the metallurgical plants, were pulling away from the liberal intelligentsia, from moderates in the Social Democratic party, and from Duma politicians. By 1914, Haimson stated, "a dangerous process of polarization appeared to be taking place in Russia's major urban centers between an *obshchestvo* [society] that had now reabsorbed the vast majority of the once-alienated elements of its intelligentsia (and which was beginning to draw to itself many of the workers' own intelligentsia) and a growing discontented and disaffected mass of industrial workers, now left largely exposed to the pleas of an embittered revolutionary minority."[9]

In contrast to the usual picture of the Bolsheviks as an isolated clique among a working class generally concerned with economic issues, the workers became steadily and increasingly radicalized in the metal industry and in St. Petersburg particularly, such that Bolshevik influence grew at the expense of the Mensheviks and Socialist Revolutionaries (SRs). Haimson's work of the early 1960s and later demonstrated that workers had an increasing sense of class unity and separation from the rest of society as well as an awareness that they could solve their own problems. Ever more militant and far-reaching demands were put forth, most notably by St. Petersburg metalworkers, and the high incidence of defeat in their economic strikes only propelled them further toward a revolutionary opposition to the regime and the industrialists. "Given this correspondence of mood, given the even more precise correspondence between the image of the state and society that the Bolsheviks advanced and the

---

8   Leopold H. Haimson, "The Problem of Social Stability in Urban Russia, 1905–1917," *Slavic Review* XXIII, 4 (1964), pp. 619–42; XXIV, 1 (1965), pp. 1–22.

9   Ibid., XXIII, p. 689.

instinctive outlook of the laboring masses, the Bolshevik party cadres were now able to play a significant catalytic role. They succeeded ... in chasing the Menshevik 'Liquidators' out of the existing open labor organizations."[10] By 1914 the key labor unions were in the hands of the Bolsheviks, and working-class discontent exploded in a sharp increase in the number and duration of strikes and political protests.

While the war years demonstrated the fragility of the Bolsheviks' newly conquered positions within the working class and arrests and patriotism ate into their influence, the potential for a renewal of militancy remained intact. Much more visible than the exiled Bolshevik leaders were those more moderate socialists who remained in the capital and worked in the legal and semi-legal institutions permitted by the autocracy. With the collapse of tsarism, timing and geography promoted even the less-prominent Mensheviks and SRs into positions of enormous power and influence. Although in the first month of revolution workers were neither unified around any one program nor tightly tied to any one party, there was a striking consensus among most Petrograd workers on the question of power in both the state and the economy.[11] Except for the most militant, the metalworkers of the Vyborg district, the workers were not yet anxious either to take state power or to run the factories themselves. Thus, there was a strategic parallel between their conditional support of the Provisional Government—*poskol'ko, postol'ko* (insofar as) their policies corresponded to the interests of the Soviet—and the notion of *rabochii kontrol'* (workers' control), which at this time meant merely the supervision of the owners' operations by representatives of the workers, not the organization of production directly by the workers.[12] Both the political and economic policies

---

10 Ibid., XXIII, p. 638.

11 For a detailed treatment of the revolutionary days of February-March, see Hasegawa, *The February Revolution: Petrograd, 1917*, pp. 215–409; and, on the question of party consciousness outside the capital, see Diane Koenker, "The Evolution of Party Consciousness in 1917: The Case of the Moscow Workers," *Soviet Studies* XXX (1978), pp. 38–62.

12 There has been some debate on the exact meaning and dimensions of workers' control in 1917–18. See Chris Goodey, "Factory Committees and the Dictatorship of the Proletariat (1918)," *Critique* 3 (1974), pp. 27–47; M. Brinton, "Factory Committees and the Dictatorship of the Proletariat," ibid., IV (1975), pp. 78–86; and William G. Rosenberg, "Workers and Workers' Control in the Russian Revolution," *History Workshop Journal* V (1978), pp. 89–97.

favored by active workers in the first months of revolution entailed watching over and checking institutions that continued to be run by members of propertied society.

Yet the social polarization that Haimson noted was already evident even in the euphoria of February and early March, as the workers and soldiers set up their own class organizations—factory committees, soldiers' committees, militia, and, most importantly, the soviets—to articulate and defend their interests.[13] From the beginning of the revolution they registered a degree of suspicion toward the Duma Committee and the Provisional Government, even though significant concessions were made to the representatives of educated society. Among the rank-and-file soldiers the sense of distance and distrust toward their officers led them to form their own committees and draft the famous Order Number One, which both legitimized the committees and placed the Petrograd garrison under the political authority of the Soviet. Among the sailors of the Baltic Fleet, a force in which workers were much more heavily represented than in the peasant-based army, the hatred of the crewmen toward the officer elite resulted in an explosion of summary "executions."[14] The genuine suspicions of the *demokratiia* (lower classes) were reflected by their leaders, who rejected any notion of a coalition government with the bourgeoisie and maintained that the Soviet should remain a separate locus of power critical of but not actively opposing the government. Thus, *dvoevlastie* (dual power) was an accurate mirror of the real balance of forces in the city and the mutual suspicion that kept them from full cooperation.

---

13 Tsuyoshi Hasegawa, "The Formation of the Militia in the February Revolution: An Aspect of the Origins of Dual Power," *Slavic Review* XXXII (1973), pp. 303–22; "The Problem of Power in the February Revolution of 1917 in Russia," *Canadian Slavonic Papers* XIV (1972), pp. 611–32, and "The Bolsheviks and the Formation of the Petrograd Soviet in the February Revolution," *Soviet Studies* XXXIX (1977), pp. 86–106.

14 Saul, *Sailors in Revolt*, pp. 15–16. Saul denied that the executions of officers provide evidence of "class warfare" in the navy, but after eliminating other reasons for the violence he left the reader without any convincing explanation: ibid., pp. 77–80. Mawdsley has portrayed the mutiny in February as the result of accumulated grievances—involuntary service, low pay, inactivity, harsh discipline, and the poor treatment of sailors by officers. But what made these problems so much more explosive in the navy than in the army was that sailors were recruited from the working class, were relatively well educated, and were quite young. They were highly susceptible to socialist propaganda and responded to developments among the urban workers. Mawdsley, *The Russian Revolution and the Baltic Fleet*, pp. 2–10.

The irony of the February Revolution was that the workers and soldiers had effectively overthrown the old government, but neither they nor their leaders were yet confident enough of their abilities to form their own government or to prevent a counterrevolutionary challenge if the propertied classes were excluded. At the same time that soldiers and workers were reluctant to be ruled by their old class enemies, they realized that without agreement with the Temporary Duma Committee the loyalty of the army at the front was problematic.[15] The Duma leadership, for its part, understood that real power—the power to call people into the streets, defend the city, make things work or fall apart—was in the hands of the Soviet, not the government. Moderate leaders in both the government and the Soviet were willing to play down the conflict within society in the face of a possible reaction from the right. Realism and caution through March and early April allowed a brief period of cooperation and conciliation, that at first convinced many of the possibility of collaboration between the top and bottom of society, but that ultimately created, when collaboration failed, a bitter and divisive aftermath.

As early as March 10, the Soviet and the Petrograd Society of Industrialists agreed to introduce an eight-hour working day in the factories. This victory for the workers on an issue that had caused deep hostility in the prewar period was achieved with surprising ease, and the conciliatory attitude of industrialists like Konovalov seemed to herald further concessions. Demands for higher wages were met with sympathy, and during the first three months of the revolution nominal wages rose on the average of 50 percent in Russia. Although there was greater resistance to the idea of a minimum wage, it too was finally approved by the industrialists on April 24. In a sense workers were trespassing on prerogatives traditionally held by capitalists when they demanded the removal of unpopular administrative personnel, but early in the revolution even such desires as these were satisfied.

As Ziva Galili has convincingly shown, workers' expressions of suspicion toward the "bourgeoisie" declined substantially in March, but significant groups within the industrial class began to express their opposition to the "excessive demands" of the workers.[16] Even Konovalov, an advocate of cooperation with the workers, held that the overthrow of tsarism

---

15 Wildman, *The End of the Russian Imperial Army*, p. 172.
16 Galili, *The Menshevik Leaders in the Russian Revolution*, pp. 69–114.

should rightly result in the establishment of the commercial-industrial bourgeoisie as the dominant force in Russia's social and economic life. Although this notion seems to coincide with the Menshevik conception of the revolution as "bourgeois-democratic," serious tactical differences emerged between the Progressist leaders, representing powerful industrialists, and the Revolutionary Defensists, who led the Soviet. Whereas the First Congress of Trade and Industry called for restoration of "free trade" and the placing of food supply in the hands of the "experienced commercial-industrial class," the Menshevik economists favored price regulation and state control of the economy. But the issue that brought the fragile dual power arrangement down was not the emerging economic issue but the conflict between the upper and lower classes over the war. Initially, the soldiers were suspicious of dual power and even of the Soviet to some extent, but Allan K. Wildman has demonstrated that, as a result of a campaign by the "bourgeois" press to turn the army against workers struggling for the eight-hour day and of a successful propaganda effort by Soviet agitators directed at the lower ranks, soldiers began to perceive the Provisional Government as a "class" instead of a "national" institution.[17] One by one, the soldiers' congresses held at the various fronts came out in support of Soviet control over the government and a "democratic peace without annexations or contributions"—the positions taken by the Revolutionary Defensists. The April Crisis marked the end of the futile attempt by Foreign Minister Pavl Miliukov and his closest associates to maintain a foreign policy independent of the Soviet. The cleavage that was visible in Petrograd between the *demokratiia* and the *tsenzovoe obshchestvo* on the questions of power, the economy, and the war was also reflected within the army between the soldiers and their officers.

The dependence of the Provisional Government on the Soviet, clear from the first days of their coexistence, required in the view of the members of the government the formation of a coalition. At first resistant to joining a government of the bourgeoisie, the Mensheviks reluctantly agreed in order to bolster the government's authority. For the Revolutionary Defensist leader Iraklii Tsereteli, coalition meant the unification of the workers with other "vital forces of the nation" in an effort to end the war and fight social disintegration. The successful collaboration of the bourgeoisie and the Soviet in the first months of the revolution

---

17   Wildman, *The End of the Russian Imperial Army*, p. 320.

had lulled the Mensheviks into a belief that class hostility could be overcome, but almost simultaneously with the formation of the coalition the
economic situation grew worse. Inflation forced more demands for wage
increases, but industrialists who had recently been so generous were now
resistant to further raises. In May and June workers began to suspect that
factory shutdowns were deliberate attempts at sabotage by the owners.
Economic difficulties, so intimately tied to the war, turned workers
against the industrialists and the government.[18] Although some workers
supported coalition, the great bulk of Petrograd's factory workers grew
increasingly suspicious, both of the government and of those socialists
who collaborated with the bourgeoisie. The beneficiaries of this suspicion and distrust were those parties that opposed the coalition and advocated a government composed of the representatives of the working
people—that is, the Bolsheviks.[19]

The association of the Menshevik and SR leaders of the Soviet with
the coalition government—and, consequently, with the renewed war
effort in June—placed a stark choice before the workers and soldiers:
either cooperation and collaboration with the upper classes, who were
increasingly perceived as enemies of the revolution, or going it alone in an
all-socialist soviet government. The first efforts of the *demokratiia* were
directed at convincing the Soviet leaders of the necessity of taking power
in their own hands. The erosion of lower-class support for the government was already quite clear on May 31, when the workers' section of the
Petrograd Soviet voted for the Bolshevik resolution calling for "All Power
to the Soviets!" Even more dramatic was the demonstration of June 18, in
which hundreds of thousands of workers marched carrying slogans such
as "Down with the Ten Capitalist Ministers!" By early July, with the
distressing news of the failure of the June offensive filtering into the city,
the more militant soldiers, sailors, and workers attempted through an

---

18   Galili, *The Menshevik Leaders in the Russian Revolution*, pp. 203–15.

19   The predominant Western image of the Bolshevik party as a party of *intelligenty* (intellectuals) divorced from the working class has been challenged in quantitative studies by William Chase and J. Arch Getty on the Moscow Bolsheviks. They
have concluded that the party, while "primarily composed of and dominated by"
intelligenty up to 1905, "so radically altered its social composition [after 1905]
that, by 1917, the Bolsheviks could honestly claim to represent a large section of
the working population." Chase and Getty, "The Moscow Bolshevik Cadres of
1917: A Prosopographical Analysis," *Russian History* V (1978), pp. 95, 84–105.

armed rising to force the Soviet to take power. Emblematic of the paradox of the situation is that famous scene when sailors surrounded the SR leader Chernov and yelled at him, "Take power, you son-of-abitch, when it is given to you."[20]

But, as is well known, the Soviet did not take power, and a series of weak coalition governments followed the July crisis until their forcible overthrow in October. The brief eclipse of the Bolsheviks in July and their rapid rise from isolation and persecution through the summer to state power in October have been the object of an enormous amount of historical study, but in their search for explanations historians have tended to overemphasize the role of political actors, like Lenin and Trotsky, and to underestimate the independent activity of workers and soldiers. Before setting out a socio-political interpretation of the Bolshevik victory based on the social historical research of a generation of historians, I shall consider the limitations exhibited by several influential works that focus too exclusively on either the political or the social aspects of the revolution.

A half-century ago, one of the most stimulating views of the October Revolution was what might be called the "conservative-accidentalist" interpretation shared by Sergei Petrovich Melgunov and Robert V. Daniels.[21] Melgunov, who was a minor participant in the events he described, revealed his approach in his opening quotation from Kerensky: "By the will of men, not by the force of the elements, did October become inevitable." To Melgunov, the October Revolution was in no sense inevitable; indeed, he made clear from the beginning his disagreement with those historians for whom "social processes almost fatalistically predetermined the course of events . . . 'October' was not the realization of 'February'."[22] Melgunov deliberately distinguished his approach from his notion of the Marxist approach to history—inevitability, social

20 Rabinowitch, *Prelude to Revolution*, p. 188. The source for this scene is P. N. Miliukov, *Istoriia vtoroi russkoi revoliutsii* I (Sofia, 1921), p. 244. Leon Trotsky called Miliukov's account "nothing more than anecdote," but one that "expresses with crude accuracy the essence of the July situation." Trotsky, *The History of the Russian Revolution*, trans. Max Eastman, vol. 2 (Ann Arbor: University of Michigan Press, 1957), p. 40.

21 Sergei Melgunov, *Kak Bol'sheviki zakhvatili vlast': Oktiabr'skii perevorot 1917 goda* (Paris, 1953), translated, abridged, and edited by Sergei G. Pushkarev as *The Bolshevik Seizure of Power* (Santa Barbara: ABC-Clio, 1972); and Robert Daniels, *Red October: The Bolshevik Revolution of 1917* (New York: Scribner, 1967).

22 Melgunov, *The Bolshevik Seizure of Power*, pp. 2, 3.

determinism, and the idea that revolutions, like societies, march lockstep through a series of succeeding stages.

Melgunov emphasized instead the power and persuasiveness of Lenin, who singlehandedly was able to turn the central committee of the Bolshevik party from moderation to the radical alternative of seizing power by force. Melgunov treated Lenin as if he had been mad: "With the stubbornness of a maniac under self-hypnosis, he insisted now or never . . . The uprising had become an obsession with Lenin."[23] Lenin was "still raving" on page 7, made "hysterical demands" on page 9, and fell "into a complete fit of rage" on page 16. Moreover, the government was lulled to sleep. With the exception of the energetic prime minister, Kerensky, the cabinet had, in Melgunov's terminology, become "spineless." No adequate measures were taken to stop the Bolsheviks until it was too late. There was a false sense of confidence that the government with the support of the garrison could put down a Bolshevik uprising.[24] Thus, in Melgunov's treatment the Bolshevik seizure of power appears to have been a matter of competing wills—the determined will of Lenin to take power by any means before the Second Congress of Soviets, the misguided will of Kerensky to allow the Bolsheviks to make a move so that they could be exposed and crushed, and the vacillating wills of cabinet officers and the military who did not take resolute action in time. Once the Bolsheviks began their occupation of government buildings, the Kerensky government found no one in Petrograd willing to defend the Winter Palace, except some military cadets and the famous Women's Battalion of Death.

The Kerensky government's inability to mobilize military and popular support in the moment of crisis is well known and indisputable, but Melgunov argued further that the Bolsheviks, too, lacked mass support in the October Days. The garrison, on the whole, remained neutral; "only individual soldiers or sub-regimental units—at best" came out into the streets at the call of the Military Revolutionary Committee. Workers and their Red Guard units participated in the uprising only sporadically. The decisive force on the Bolshevik side were the sailors of Kronstadt and Helsinki, who arrived in Petrograd on the afternoon of October 25. Here, then, was the extent of mass backing for the Bolsheviks: a few

---

23 Ibid., p. 5.
24 Ibid., pp. 29–33.

strategically placed armed units of soldiers, sailors, and workers. "The Russian public was almost completely absent on that tragic day."[25]

Melgunov conceded that the Bolsheviks did manage to have enough force at the right place to win the day in October, and he quoted Lenin in seeming agreement: "To have an overwhelming superiority of forces at the decisive moment at the decisive point—this law of military success is also a law of political success." With their "powerful backing in the capital cities," the Bolsheviks were able to take over the rest of the country.[26] Melgunov did not explain how the Bolsheviks received the backing that they managed to mobilize in October, nor did he explain why the "revolutionary democracy proved impotent," except to note that the forces in the center had no unity of will.[27] This, of course, begs the question why there was no unity of will among the moderates in the face of their impending loss of power. Why were the Bolsheviks capable of the necessary will and determination, and not Kerensky or the moderate socialists? Indeed, the moderates had leaders of determination and will, most notably the Menshevik Tsereteli and the conservative General Lavr Kornilov. Yet their attempted political solutions failed. Ultimately, the momentous events in October require more than explanations based on such accidental qualities as personality and mood.

In his *Red October*, published to mark the fiftieth anniversary of Lenin's seizure of power, Robert Daniels portrayed the revolution as a "veritable orgy of democracy," "galloping chaos," and "violent political struggle." Although Daniels acknowledged early in his book that the workers of Petrograd "played a decisive role in the flow of events because they were the strongest social force in the deciding center of the country, the capital city," he did not provide much in the way of an explanation for their leftward shift; indeed, the body of his book essentially ignores the role of the workers.[28] Daniels's view echoes that of Melgunov: the people in power were indecisive, and one party—the Bolsheviks—was able and willing to take decisive action. The October insurrection, largely the product of Lenin's determination, "succeeded against incredible odds" and was a "wild gamble, with little chance that the Bolsheviks'

---

25 Ibid., pp. 63, 75.
26 Ibid., p. 193. Melgunov went on to say, "There is no question that capitals decide the political fate of nations to a considerable degree."
27 Melgunov, *The Bolshevik Seizure of Power*, p. 193.
28 Daniels, *Red October*, p. 11.

ill-prepared followers could prevail against all the military force that the government seemed to have . . . To Lenin, however, it was a gamble that entailed little risk, because he sensed that in no other way and at no other time could he have any chance at all of coming to power."[29]

Daniels's idea that Lenin produced the October crisis, that he "single-handedly polarized Russian political life in the fall of 1917," is crucial to what followed:

> If the revolution had not occurred as it did, the basic political cleavage of Bolsheviks and anti Bolsheviks would not have been so sharp, and it is difficult to imagine what other events might have established a similar opportunity for one-party Bolshevik rule. Given the fact of the party's forcible seizure of power, civil violence and a militarized dictatorship of revolutionary extremism followed with remorseless logic.[30]

But Lenin's victory was neither inevitable nor necessitated by social causes. Lenin was personally responsible for and indispensable to the Bolshevik victory; if he had been kept out of Russia in 1917, or had been "recognized by the cadet patrol" that stopped him on the way to Smolny on the very eve of the October Revolution, "his followers could not have found a substitute."[31] Thus, for Daniels, October is a historical accident contingent upon just the right, somewhat arbitrary elements, present at just the right moment. There is no sense here, except for a few sentences in the first pages, of the great social and economic forces at play in 1917, the movements of workers and soldiers, that made Lenin's success possible and Kerensky's defeat a near certainty. Such a sense, of course, cannot be gained from a largely biographical or political approach to the revolutionary events of 1917.[32]

---

29 Ibid., pp. 215–16.

30 Ibid., pp. 81, 218.

31 Ibid., p. 225.

32 Another result of the focus on personalities and parties has been a sense of the mass activity of the lower classes being without form or meaning. Activity of workers and soldiers is equivalent to anarchy for many historians. This theme of the revolution as anarchy is central to the interpretation of Adam B. Ulam, who wrote, "The Bolsheviks did not seize power in this year of revolutions. They picked it up. First, autocracy, then democracy capitulated to the forces of anarchy. Any group of determined men could have done what the Bolsheviks did in Petrograd in October 1917: seize the few key points of the city and proclaim themselves the government." *The Bolsheviks*, p. 314.

Useful as a corrective to the approach of Melgunov and Daniels is the work of Alexander Rabinowitch, a meticulous student of the Bolshevik party in 1917, who has attacked the cliché that the key element in Bolshevik success was the party's superior leadership and organization. This stereotype of Bolshevism stems from a reading of Lenin's 1902 tract, *Chto delat'?* ("What Is to Be Done?"), in which Lenin put forth an image of a centralized, disciplined party of underground, professional revolutionaries. Such a party was the crucial instrument, it is often argued, that brought off the coup d'état of October and established order in the midst of anarchy. Rabinowitch has argued instead that this stereotype is overdrawn, that "the party's internally relatively democratic, tolerant, and decentralized structure and method of operation, as well as its open and mass character," made possible a flexible, dynamic relationship between the party hierarchy and its potential supporters.[33]

On the question of mass backing for the Leninists, Rabinowitch has convincingly established that in the aftermath of the July Days the Bolsheviks did not lose as much support, particularly among workers, as many contemporaries and later historians believed. Their recovery was swift, thanks to "worsening economic conditions and the unpopular policies of the government and the majority of socialists."[34] The shift to the right by the Soviet was unpopular in many workers' districts, and the re-establishment of the death penalty at the front alienated the soldiers of the Petrograd garrison. The attempt by Kornilov to establish a military dictatorship raised industrial workers and soldiers from their summer lethargy to come out against the "counterrevolution." Kerensky was discredited in the eyes of the left and the masses for his involvement with Kornilov.

Even workers in industrial plants that heretofore had been Menshevik and Socialist Revolutionary strongholds, as well as soldiers in some of

---

33   "For all the lively debate and spirited give-and-take that I find to have existed within the Bolshevik organization in 1917, the Bolsheviks were doubtless more unified than any of their major rivals for power. Certainly this was a key factor in their effectiveness. Nonetheless, my research suggests that the relative flexibility of the party, as well as its responsiveness to the prevailing mass mood, had at least as much to do with the ultimate Bolshevik victory as did revolutionary discipline, organizational unity, or obedience to Lenin." Rabinowitch, *The Bolsheviks Come to Power*, p. xxi.

34   Ibid., pp. 90, 311.

the politically restrained regiments of the garrison ... now turned against the government ... [Some of] the political resolutions passed at this time ... called for the creation of a government representing workers, soldiers, and peasants; others, perhaps a majority, insisted on transfer of power to the soviets or creation of a revolutionary government responsible to the Soviet ... Common to virtually all were concern that Kornilov and his supporters be dealt with harshly so as to avoid further attacks by the "counter-revolution," aversion to political collaboration with the propertied classes in any form, and attraction for the immediate creation of some kind of exclusively socialist government which would bring an end to the war.[35]

After the Kornilov Affair, the possibility of collaboration with the liberals and upper classes, especially with the compromised Kadet party, had become anathema to the lower strata of the Petrograd population.

Rabinowitch's treatment of 1917 is still primarily political history, though not of the state but of an intermediate political organization with effective links to the lower classes. He has clearly demonstrated that the Bolshevik-Left SR positions on the war, opposition to the coalition government, and advocacy of a government by soviets were consonant with the aspirations of the lower classes in Petrograd. Most interestingly of all, he emphasized that the actual conquest of power in Petrograd by the Military Revolutionary Committee occurred a week before the fall of the Winter Palace. The question of who ruled in Petrograd was resolved by answering who had real control over the army in the city, and the decisive moment arrived when the Petrograd Soviet, in Bolshevik hands from early September, challenged the government's authority over the garrison. In the week before the Bolshevik insurrection, "the Military-Revolutionary Committee of the Petrograd Soviet took control of most Petrograd-based military units, in effect disarming the Provisional Government without a shot."[36] Once again, as in the first months of the revolution, the Soviet made it clear to the government that real power, the power to call troops into the streets and implement decisions, belonged to the Soviet. Formal power fell to the Soviet with the capture of the Winter Palace and the ratification by the Second Congress of Soviets.

---

35   Ibid., pp. 158–9.
36   Ibid., pp. 313–14.

Rabinowitch also took issue with the exaggeration of Lenin's role, so dominant a theme in the work of Melgunov and Daniels:

> early on the morning of October 24, Kerensky initiated steps to suppress the Left. Only at this point, just hours before the scheduled opening of the Congress of Soviets and in part under the continuous prodding by Lenin, did the armed uprising that Lenin had been advocating for well over a month actually begin . . . Only in the wake of the government's direct attack on the Left was an armed uprising of the kind envisioned by Lenin feasible. For . . . the Petrograd masses, to the extent that they supported the Bolsheviks in the overthrow of the Provisional Government, did so not out of any sympathy for strictly Bolshevik rule but because they believed the revolution and the congress to be in imminent danger.[37]

Thus, although Lenin was instrumental in preparing the armed uprising, the actual social and political constellation of forces on October 24—most importantly the provocation by Kerensky—was responsible for the move into the streets.

Clearly, to isolate Lenin or his party from this rich and contradictory social context in which they operated not only distorts an understanding of the events of 1917, but may lead to unwarranted conclusions about the artificial, unorganic, manipulated nature of October and to the more general view that great revolutions, like more modest acts of political protest, are the creations of outside agitators. Although Rabinowitch has left many questions unanswered, including the critical one of the sources of the Bolsheviks' mass support, he has provided a persuasive reassessment of the personal and political factors that led to the October Revolution.

At the other pole of historical writing on October is *The Russian Revolution* (1976), the massive work of John Keep, a well-known specialist on Russian social democracy. Keep has focused on the mass organizations of the Russian people—the soviets, factory committees, trade unions, peasant committees, Red Guard units, and so forth—rather than on political parties or the government. Indeed, the book is quite difficult to follow if the reader does not have a firm grasp of the basic historical

---

37   Ibid., p. 314.

events of the period. There is, for example, no discussion whatsoever of the "April crisis" or the "July Days," and only the most cursory allusions to the *Kornilovshchina*. His approach seems, at first, to be diametrically opposed to the personality-dominated views of Melgunov and Daniels and also to the close political analysis of Rabinowitch. Yet the hundreds of pages spent on looking at the bottom of society reflect a peculiarly condescending view of the lower classes and reinforce the more traditional interpretations of the revolution.

Like so many other works on the Russian Revolution, Keep's book is history written backwards, from the results to their causes. He states, "Any evaluation of this revolution's place in history must proceed from an awareness of the consequences to which it led: namely, the world's first experiment in totalitarian rule." And he seeks material for this type of evaluation not so much in Leninist ideology or Bolshevik organization, though both clearly play a role, but in the methods and effects of mass mobilization. Keep claims that revolutions begin as anarchistic movements against the bureaucratic state but end up by installing new bureaucratic organizations. "Chaos and anarchy . . . best describe the state of Russia during 1917."[38] Categories such as class interests or ideologies are not helpful, in Keep's view, in understanding the complexity of these events. More important is "instinct"! Of the crowds of workers in October Keep notes, "the mob followed its instincts" in destroying things of value that it did not understand, or, later on, "the crowds followed a logic all their own, in which instinct was more important than reason."[39] The subrational, spontaneously generated political behavior of the workers is even more typical of the peasantry. "The agrarian movement," for Keep, "was neither a product of external agitation nor a manifestation of class struggle. It was a phenomenon sui generis—plebian, anarchic and anti-centralist." At times Keep shows little regard for the capacity of peasants and workers to understand the events and programs of 1917, as, for example, in his discussion of a gathering of trade unionists, where he states, "Such intellectual subtleties were beyond the grasp of many delegates to the conference, let alone to their rank-and-file supporters." Or: "it is scarcely surprising that to the politically untutored Russian masses this propaganda [of the

---

38 Keep, *The Russian Revolution*, pp. x–xi, 468.
39 Ibid., pp. 214–56.

Bolsheviks] had a strong appeal." Yet, despite their lack of comprehension, workers in Keep's portrait were able, without intellectual leadership, to acquire some political consciousness, to arrive eventually at "a new awareness of their dignity as human beings, their rights as citizens and consumers." Indeed, "a class-oriented viewpoint came naturally to Russia's industrial workers," though Keep never explains why such a class outlook "came naturally."[40]

Underlying and informing all of Keep's preferences and conclusions is a bedrock belief that ideological solutions to social and political problems are utopian, dangerous, and doomed to failure; that moderation and a spirit of compromise are the desired and most pragmatic political postures; and that checks and balances are needed in government just as conciliation and cooperation are required in the economic conflicts between employers and employees. His great regret is that political democracy could not weather the storms of 1917, and his sympathies clearly lie with the right wing of the Soviet leadership, with men like Avram Gots, Iraklii Tsereteli, and Alexander Kerensky, rather than with Viktor Chernov, Iulii Martov, or Vladimir Lenin. Yet in passages that echo Oliver Radkey, Keep castigates even these Russian socialist intellectuals, who were "brought up in a tradition that was ideological rather than pragmatic . . . By instinct they were hostile to governmental authority even if the regime in question was one with which they themselves were associated."[41] And, by their own manipulation of the working masses, Soviet moderates prepared the ground for the cruder direction of workers' affairs by the Bolsheviks.

Keep's explanation of the demise of soviet democracy is subtle and intriguing. The seizure of power was only one moment in a long process that began earlier in the revolution, as real power shifted within the soviets from the plenary assemblies to cadre elements in executive positions. Autonomous soviets representing workers, soldiers, and peasants merged and were increasingly subjected to control from above. These tendencies "were in part spontaneous in origin and in part the deliberate outcome of official Bolshevik policy."[42] As early as the end of September the several hundred delegates attending meetings of the plenum could feel that they

---

40 Ibid., 213–14, 108, 114, 27, 26.
41 Ibid., p. 140.
42 Ibid., p. 340.

were shaping the country's destiny. Their aspirations seemed to accord so closely with the directives they received that they were scarcely conscious of being guided at all. The plenum of the Petrograd soviet became a genuine revolutionary assembly, a resonator automatically echoing the signals emitted from above.[43]

Keep explains "this state of affairs . . . in terms not merely of crowd psychology but also of institutional mechanics." By the end of his analysis, the Soviet plenum becomes the chorus in a Greek tragedy: "blind instruments of fate, [the members] could scarcely follow the intricate maneuvers of their leaders upon which they were called to pronounce." The Military Revolutionary Committee of the Petrograd Soviet was "in essence a junta whose powers were defined solely by the ambitions of its leaders."[44]

Three factors doomed the moderate socialists. First, the radicalism of many workers, especially metalworkers, which Keep has explained as the product of "their eagerness to renounce their close involvement in what seemed to them a disastrous and senseless war," played into the hands of the Leninists. Second, "the weakness of the Provisional Government obliged [the moderate socialists] to assume joint responsibility for direction of the nation's affairs, yet by doing so they inevitably became ever more isolated from their popular following." And, third, the skills of the Bolsheviks in conquering the working class and the soldiers through the soviets: "the soviets had never been conceived as organs reflecting the full range of their members' opinions; they were cadre organizations, whose purpose was to mobilize support for their leaders' policies. The Bolsheviks were simply more ruthless and systematic than their rivals in eliminating dissent by their long-familiar manipulative techniques."[45] Thus, radicalism from below, the class-oriented views of workers and others, and Bolshevik manipulation combined to turn the soviets into directors of popular affairs rather than reflectors of popular interests.

John Keep's "study in mass mobilization" is, in actuality, a study of mass manipulation by the radical intelligentsia. Evidently the Leninists,

---

43 Ibid., p. 348. On this theme, also see Marc Ferro, "The Birth of the Soviet Bureaucratic System," in Elwood (ed.), *Reconsiderations of the Russian Revolution*, pp. 100–32.

44 Keep, *The Russian Revolution*, pp. 348–9.

45 Ibid., pp. 68–9, 140, 335–6.

who "sought a complete monopoly of power for their own party," were the best of the manipulators. And this study of history at the bottom returns us full circle to the Melgunov–Daniels perspective. The mass organizations were simply the means through which the Bolsheviks worked to secure power; as "the soviets were converted from means of mass mobilization into instruments of party dictatorship," the masses of revolutionary Russia were shown to be the first dupes of the communists.[46]

In describing at a distance the shift to the left of Petrograd's masses, Keep does not provide much of an explanation for their radicalization, except—as did Melgunov and Daniels—through an appreciation of the superiority of Bolshevik will and skill. What seems at first to be a "social history with the politics left out" might be characterized more accurately as "political history disguised as social history," for there is no feel in *The Russian Revolution* for the coincidence of workers' aspirations and Bolshevik ideals in the context of deepening social polarization. For this aspect of the picture we must turn to those historians who have studied the working class, the army, and the navy. Although the works under review do not individually present a complete synthesis of social dynamics and political developments, through such works Western historians are providing the raw material for a new paradigm to explain the "deepening of the revolution" and the victory of the Bolsheviks in October.

Several Western historians have made much of the workers' instinctive rebelliousness or propensity for anarchy; but the real and incipient violence in the revolution does not necessitate concluding, as John Keep has argued, that workers were instinctively distrustful of

---

46 Ibid., pp. 447, 358. In Keep's explanation, both spontaneity and political action by the Bolsheviks contributed to their victory. The Bolsheviks were "being carried along on the tide of 'revolutionary spontaneity'"; this "'bolshevization of the masses' to some extent came spontaneously," but "it was also to some extent the product of conscious political action by a segment of the intelligentsia." Ibid., pp. 350, 478. Keep does not deny the importance of Bolshevik ideas and their resonance in the populace, but he argues that "the organization devices they employed" were essential: "On the Russian Left the Bolsheviks alone—or to be more precise, those identified with the 'hard' Leninist positions—possessed the will and experience to turn vague and transient mass attitudes into firm political commitments." Ibid., pp. 380–8.

authority in any form.[47] Given their long and painful experience with arbitrary authority under the Romanovs, workers were understandably concerned about the proper exercise of power, and they searched for forms of self-organization and demanded authorities responsive to their needs. The growing feeling that the Provisional Government, even in its coalition variant, was not a responsive authority made workers gravitate toward soviet power. This sense among workers of their own interests being frustrated by hostile middle and upper classes can be seen both as a revival of prewar attitudes of the most militant workers and as a reaction to perceived counterrevolutionary attitudes and actions by industrialists, intellectuals (both liberal and socialist), and, in time, the government. Among historians who have looked most closely at workers' activities, the superficial impression of chaos has been superseded by the realization that workers' actions in 1917 demonstrate a "cautious and painful development of consciousness" that was "an essentially rational process." After distinguishing three principal strata of workers—the politically aware skilled workers (primarily the metalworkers of the Vyborg district), the unskilled workers (largely women textile workers), and the "worker aristocracy" (best characterized by the pro-Menshevik printers)—David Mandel has shown that the metalworkers were most radical in the political sphere, calling for the early establishment of soviet power, while the unskilled workers, who tended to be more moderate on political issues, showed the greatest militancy in the struggle for higher wages.[48] The contours of worker activity are complex but not chaotic. Stephen Smith has broken down the metalworkers into shops and carefully delineated between "hot" shops, such as foundries, where most newly arrived peasant–workers were located, and "cold" shops, such as machine shops, where highly skilled and literate workers were most receptive to social democratic activists. In examining the Putilov Works, Smith found that workers there moved more slowly toward Bolshevism than in other metalworking plants, and that "shopism" and "conciliationism" remained

---

47 Keep, *The Russian Revolution,* p. 77.
48 Mandel, *The Petrograd Workers and the Fall of the Old Regime; The Petrograd Workers and the Soviet Seizure of Power.*

stronger there than elsewhere.[49] Both Smith and Mandel have presented pictures of growing worker suspicion of the upper levels of society, especially after the formation of the coalition government—a suspicion that translated into struggles for control in the factories and increased opposition to those moderate socialists who were backing the government.[50]

Although the rapidity of labor radicalization in Petrograd is certainly distinctive, similar processes, marked by growing class cohesion and consciousness, were evident in other parts of the country, as my own work on Baku and Donald Raleigh's study of Saratov demonstrate.[51] By engaging in a detailed quantitative analysis of the dynamics of labor activity in Moscow, Diane P. Koenker has also reached a similar conclusion:

> One must . . . reject the image of the Russian working class as uniformly irrational, poorly educated, and incapable of independent participation in the political process. One must reject in particular the myth that the revolution in the cities was carried out by dark semi-peasant masses "who did not understand the real meaning of the slogans they loudly repeated." Yes, of course, many Moscow workers were more rural than urban; but when one looks at the participation levels of different segments of the urban labor force, the fact that

---

49   Smith, "Craft Consciousness, Class Consciousness," pp. 36–7. The central argument of Smith's article coincides with Mandel's view of growing worker militancy and class consciousness. Smith has pointed out that "shopism" and "factory patriotism" did not preclude labor militancy, or inhibit "the development of a broader sense of belonging to a class of working people whose interests were antagonistic to those of the employers." Ibid., p. 51.

50   For similar findings, see the later work of Diane P. Koenker and William G. Rosenberg, *Strikes and Revolution in Russia, 1917* (Princeton: Princeton University Press, 1989), which I discuss at length in Chapter 5.

51   Suny, *The Baku Commune, 1917–1918*; and Raleigh, *Revolution on the Volga*. In Baku, economic collapse and food shortages stimulated workers to rely less on their soviet leaders and to take actions into their own hands. Particularly important in their growing impatience was their sense that both industry and government were unnecessarily delaying the signing of a labor contract for the oil workers. The general strike of September 1917 was initiated by workers in factory committees against the advice of the socialist parties, including the Bolsheviks. See "From Economics to Politics," Chapter 4 of Suny, *The Baku Commune, 1917–1918*, pp. 102–46.

skilled urban cadres, not the unskilled peasant mass, were the leading political actors can be seen over and over again. These workers possessed experience, political connections, and the degree of economic security which enabled them to function freely and easily in the political life of 1917.[52]

To Koenker, the radicalization of workers in the first year of the revolution was an "incremental process, which took place in response to specific economic and political pressures." Her conclusion is supported in other studies as well. Galili, for example, noted the delayed radicalization of the less politically conscious, unskilled workers in the second quarter of 1917, observing that these less well-organized workers had not benefited from the initial round of wage raises in March and April. By the time they made their bid for higher pay, the industrialists had adopted a more intransigent attitude.[53] By mid-May there were already 40,000 unemployed workers in Petrograd, and as real wages began to plummet and mass dismissals accelerated, more and more less-skilled workers joined the "proletarians" in a commitment to soviet power. By June–July a majority of Petrograd workers were already opposed to the coalition government, and shared a sense of separate and antagonistic interests between workers and the propertied classes. A greatly heightened sense of class was apparent among the mass of workers by the summer.

The studies of Galili, Koenker, Mandel, Rosenberg, and others provide the specifics of the economic and political stimuli that led to radicalization, and for the first time it has become possible to understand how individual grievances within the larger context of social polarization combined to create class antagonisms. Given that Russia's workers had long been closely involved with a radical, socialist intelligentsia anxious to forge a Marxist political culture within the urban labor force, it is hardly surprising that workers in 1917 should "naturally" come to a "class-oriented viewpoint." Koenker summed up this development in her conclusion, which gives us social history with the politics left in:

52 Koenker, *Moscow Workers and the 1917 Revolution*, p. 360.
53 Ibid., pp. 363–4; and Galili, *The Menshevik Leaders in the Russian Revolution*, pp. 203–31.

That the revolutionary unity of March fell apart along class lines can be attributed to economic conditions in Russia but also to the fact that the class framework was after all implicit in socialist consciousness. Capitalists began to behave as Marx said they would: no concessions to the workers, no compromise on the rights of factory owners. Mensheviks and SRs tried to straddle both sides of the class split; this appeal can be seen in the mixed social composition of their supporters. The Bolsheviks, however, had offered the most consistent class interpretation of the revolution, and by late summer their interpretation appeared more and more to correspond to reality . . . By October, the soviets of workers' deputies, as the workers' only class organ, seemed to class-conscious workers to be the only government they could trust to represent their interests.[54]

The perception by workers of common interests with fellow workers and of shared antagonisms toward the rest of society was complemented by the growing hostility from the upper levels of society toward the lower classes. William G. Rosenberg has illustrated this shift to the right by the Constitutional Democrats (Kadets), the leading liberal party, as their growing identification with commercial and industrial circles changed them from a party of liberal professionals and intellectuals into Russia's party of the bourgeoisie.[55] Even as they persisted in maintaining their "non-class" ideology, the Kadets emerged as the de facto defenders of a capitalist order and the determined opponents of the approaching social revolution desired by the more militant of the *nizy* (lower classes). Their isolation from the socialist workers and soldiers led the liberals to turn to the military as a source of order and power. Rosenberg has argued, as had the Left Kadets in 1917, that the only hope for a democratic political outcome in Russia was lost when the Kadets failed to work effectively with the moderate socialists in the coalition government and to make significant concessions to the lower classes. "The very coalition with moderate socialists that Miliukov and the new tacticians strove for so persistently in emigration [after the Civil War] was possible in the summer of 1917."[56] The failure to form such a liberal–socialist

54 Koenker, *Moscow Workers and the 1917 Revolution*, p. 364.
55 Rosenberg, *Liberals in the Russian Revolution*, pp. 31, 154–5.
56 Ibid., p. 469.

alternative to Bolshevism might be seen as the consequence of the Kadets' lack of "true liberal statesmanship," but Rosenberg's analysis permits an alternative explanation.[57] As the Kadet party evolved into the principal spokesman for propertied Russia, it was increasingly unlikely to compromise the interests of the privileged classes that backed the party in order to form a dubious alliance with the *demokratiia*, whose ever more radical demands threatened the very existence of privilege and property. *Nadklassnost'* (the Kadet notion of standing above class considerations) was a merely utopian stance in a Russia that was pulling apart along class lines.

Against this background of deepening social cleavage with all its inherent fear and suspicion, hope and despair, the question of power was posed in the summer and fall of 1917. Underestimating the extent of social polarization, the growing intensity of class hostility, and the perceived irreconcilability of the interests of the *demokratiia* and the *tsenzovoe obshchestvo* within the constraints of the February regime leads historians away from any satisfactory explanation of the failure of the moderates and the victory of the Bolsheviks, forcing them to rely on accidental factors of will and personality. Only through a synthesis of political and social history in which the activity and developing political consciousness of workers, soldiers, and sailors is taken seriously can the Bolsheviks' success be adequately explained.

By the summer of 1917, there were four possible solutions to the problem of who would rule Russia. The first solution was that advocated by Tsereteli and Kerensky, by the Menshevik Revolutionary Defensists and the Right Socialist Revolutionaries: a continuation of the coalition government, pursuing a policy of social unity and class collaboration to defend Russia against her enemies and prevent civil war. But such a solution was doomed in the face of the deepening social crisis and political paralysis. Given the hostility between classes and their mutually antagonistic aspirations and interests, a coalition government could move neither to the left nor to the right without stirring up opposition. It could neither satisfy the demands of the peasants for land, nor attempt to

---

57 For a fuller exposition of my pessimism concerning a liberal-moderate socialist coalition in 1917, see "Some Thoughts on 1917: In Lieu of a Review of William Rosenberg's *Liberals in the Russian Revolution*," in *Sbornik: Papers of the First Conference of the Study Group on the Russian Revolution* (Leeds: Study Group on the Russian Revolution, 1975), pp24–7.

protect the landlords' rights to private property. Paralyzed between competing constituencies, all movement looked like vacillation, the product of a lack of will or determination, but was in fact the result of the real political bind faced by a government stretched between the extremes of a splintering society.

A second solution was a government made up of the upper classes alone—that is, a dictatorship of the center and the Right. The Kadet leader Miliukov had desired such a government at the beginning of the revolution, but, without a base of support in the population, that hope collapsed finally in the April crisis. Real power was in the hands of the Soviet; as the moderate socialist Vladimir Stankevich quipped, "The soviet could make the Provisional Government resign with a telephone call."[58] The only possible way for the upper classes to rule—and the liberals as well as the Right came to this conclusion by mid-summer— was to establish a military dictatorship. Kerensky and Kornilov worked toward that goal in August, but it ended in Kornilov's ill-fated grasp for power, thwarted not just by his disagreement with Kerensky over the final disposition of power but by the actions of workers, soldiers, and soviets. With the failure of the military coup d'état, the only possibilities remaining were for a government by one or several of the Soviet parties.

The third solution—and probably the one most desired by the lower classes in urban Russia—was an all-socialist regime (*odnorodnoe sotsialisticheskoe pravitel'stvo*), a government representing the workers, soldiers, and peasants of Russia but excluding the *tsenzovoe obshchestvo*. A broader variant of this solution, the *odnorodnoe demokraticheskoe pravitel'stvo* (homogeneous democratic government), would have included non-soviet "democratic" elements such as municipal and government workers, people from cooperatives, and small shopkeepers. Historians seem to agree that, when workers and soldiers voted for soviet power, they were in fact opting for a multiparty government of the leftist parties. This solution was never really implemented because of the serious divisions between the moderate socialists and the Bolsheviks, and

---

58 Stankevich, as quoted in David S. Anin, "The February Revolution: Was the Collapse Inevitable?" *Soviet Studies* XVIII (1967), p. 448. For Stankevich's original statement, see I. G. Tsereteli, *Vospominaniia o fevral'skoi revoliutsii*, vol. 1 (Paris-la-Haye, 1963), p. 97.

there is legitimate doubt that the former defenders of coalition and the advocates of working-class rule could have lasted long in an all-socialist coalition.

In October 1917 the Bolsheviks came to power in the name of the soviets. The coalition government had been completely discredited, and almost no one would defend it in its last hours. The Military Revolutionary Committee merely completed the process of political conquest of the population of Petrograd that the Bolsheviks had begun months earlier.[59] Bolshevik policy, alone among the political programs, corresponded to and reflected the aspirations and perceived interests of workers, soldiers, and sailors in Petrograd. Even without much direct participation in the October Days, the workers acquiesced in and backed the seizure of power by the soviets. Lenin and a few others had seen the potential in 1917 for a government of the lower classes. Earlier than almost all the political leaders, he had understood that in this revolution—marked by deep, long-standing social tensions and stoked by a seemingly endless war— unification of "all the vital forces of the nation" had become increasingly unlikely. By late spring, an all-class or non-class government was no longer possible, and by linking his party's fortunes with the real social movement in Petrograd he was able to destroy the flimsy coalition of liberals and moderate socialists and to facilitate a seizure of power in the name of the soviets.

Instead of soviet power or socialist democracy, however, the Russian people eventually received a dictatorship of the Bolshevik party. This was the fourth possible solution to the question of power. Why it prevailed over the more democratic third solution is a question that goes beyond the limits of this essay, for the answer in this instance lies not so much in the events of 1917 as in the long years of the Civil War. But again, the answer cannot be provided by resorting to personal and ideological

---

59 Soviet historians estimate that the actual balance of forces in Petrograd on the eve of the insurrection involved about 300,000 armed supporters of the Bolsheviks and only about 25,000 ready to fight for the Provisional Government. At the storming of the Winter Palace, the Bolshevik Red Guards, soldiers, and sailors numbered approximately 20,000, with defenders of the palace estimated at about 3,000. In the fighting from October 24 to 26, fewer than fifteen people were killed and less than sixty wounded. Roy A. Medvedev, *The October Revolution*, trans. George Saunders (New York: Columbia University Press, 1979). Medvedev based his figures on E. F. Erykalov, *Oktiabr'skoe vooruzhenoe vosstanie v Petrograde* (Leningrad, 1966), pp. 303–4, 434–5, 461, 462.

influences or by extending the analysis based on politics alone; rather, it lies in an examination of the intense class struggle that was carried beyond the limits of the city of Petrograd into the countryside and all the provinces of Russia.[60]

As historians shifted their attention away from the political elites that formerly dominated explanations of the Russian Revolution and to the people in the streets, the victorious Bolsheviks have appeared less like Machiavellian manipulators or willful conspirators and more like alert politicians, with an acute sensitivity to popular moods and desires. Without forgetting the authoritarian traits in Lenin, Trotsky, and other Bolshevik leaders, or the power of the image of the party outlined in *Chto delat'?*, we can move on to a new paradigm for understanding 1917 that reduces the reliance on party organization or personal political skills so central to older explanations. The key to this new paradigm is an appreciation of the deepening social polarization that drew the upper and middle classes together and away from the workers, soldiers, and peasants. The *tsenzovoe obshchestvo*, after an initial period of compromise in the early spring of 1917, began to resist encroachments on its prerogatives in the economy and in foreign policy and, faced by growing militancy among workers and soldiers, developed a clearer and more coherent sense of its own political interests. Likewise, the workers and soldiers, confronted by lockouts, falling wages, a renewal of the war effort, and perceived sabotage of the revolution as they hoped it to be, evolved their own sense of class interests. In time, both parts of Russian society found their interests to be incompatible, and those parties that tried to stand "above class" or to unite "all the vital forces of the nation" were either compelled to take sides with one major force or abandoned by their former supporters.

For Russians in 1917, the revolution was a struggle between classes in the inclusive sense of the *verkhi* (upper classes) versus the *nizy* (lower classes). Those broad, antagonistic "classes" coalesced in the course of 1917. This heightened feeling of class, forged in the actual experience of 1917, contained both social hostilities bred over many years and

---

60 For my attempt at an answer to the question of why dictatorship followed the euphoria of grassroots democracy in 1917, see Ronald Grigor Suny, *The Soviet Experiment: Russia, the Soviet Union, and the Successor States*, 2nd ed. (New York: Oxford University Press, 2011), Chapter 5, "The Evolution of a Dictatorship," pp. 139–56.

intensified under wartime and revolutionary conditions, and a new political understanding that perceived government by soviets as a preferable alternative to sharing power with the discredited upper classes. The Bolsheviks had since April been advocating such a government by the lower classes. With the failure of the coalition and its socialist supporters to deliver on the promise of the revolution, the party of Lenin and Trotsky took power with little resistance and with the acquiescence of the majority of the people of Petrograd. The Bolsheviks prevailed not because they were superior manipulators or cynical opportunists, but because their policies as formulated by Lenin in April and shaped by the events of the following months placed them at the head of a genuinely popular movement. Sadly for those who had overthrown autocracy and turned to the Bolsheviks to end the war and alleviate hunger, that solution based on a government by soviets evolved inexorably through a ferocious civil war into a new and unforeseen authoritarianism.

CHAPTER FIVE

Revision and Retreat in the Historiography of 1917: Social History and Its Critics

I

One of the most intriguing ironies of the studies of the great European revolutions in the late twentieth century was that the dominant interpretations of the French and Russian revolutions moved in precisely opposite directions.[1] While the "revisionists" of the French Revolution were dismantling a Marxist orthodoxy—what was called in a pioneering attack, the "social interpretation"—and proposing a renewed emphasis on ideas and cultural representations, their counterparts in the Russian field steadily eroded an anti-Marxist orthodoxy that largely focused on ideology and personality and rejected social or class analysis. In its place, they constructed a social historical interpretation that re-evaluated and considerably modified the concept of class.[2]

The French revisionists, led by François Furet, had set out to make the French Revolution "more opaque" than it appeared in the Lefebvrean synthesis.[3] Expanding their explanatory repertoire beyond demography, economics, social structures, most importantly class, so central to Albert Mathiez, Ernest Labrousse, and Georges Lefebvre and his

---

1 This chapter has benefitted from critical readings and suggestions from Geoff Eley, Valerie Kivelson, Lewis Siegelbaum, Andrew Verner, Allan K. Wildman, and other colleagues. A modified version of this chapter was published in *Russian Review* LIII, 2 (April 1994), pp. 165–82.

2 For historiographical discussion of the French Revolution, see the introduction to Lynn Hunt, *Politics, Culture, and Class in the French Revolution* (Berkeley and Los Angeles: University of California Press, 1984), pp. 1–16; Benjamin R. Barber, "The Most Sublime Event," *The Nation*, March 12, 1990, pp. 351–60. On the Russian Revolution, see Ronald Grigor Suny, "Toward a Social History of the October Revolution," *American Historical Review* LXXXVIII, 1 (February 1983), pp. 31–52, updated as Chapter 4 in this volume.

3 Furet used these words in conversation with the author. François Furet, *Interpreting the French Revolution*, trans. Elborg Forster (Cambridge: Cambridge University Press, 1981).

followers, Furet and others used the insights from Saussurian structural linguistics and semiotics to investigate the role of ideas, belief systems, "political languages," and modes of speech.[4] Politics were no longer to be derived from social environment or structures. As Lynn Hunt summarized Furet, "The new political culture is driven only by its own internal logic of democracy."[5] The struggle was seen as more a match between traditional liberals and Rousseauian egalitarians than between the classical bourgeoisie and working people. Now a much more problematic event than the *locus classicus* of the "bourgeois revolution," and certainly not the heroic drama of Lefebvre and Albert Soboul, the French Revolution appeared to revisionist historians as a great event that had gone astray, and the *ancien régime* was to some extent rehabilitated.

This more negative assessment of the revolution can also be culled from the work of revisionists who differed from Furet on both methodological and interpretative grounds. In William Doyle's work, class is largely dismissed as a causal factor, and ideas and politics play dominant determinant roles.[6] The English revisionists tended to be more committed to an empiricist approach that reveled in the complexities of the revolution, and were less concerned with theory and more suspect of overarching interpretations of the Furet variety. But revisionists on both sides of the Channel, and indeed across the Atlantic, mounted a concerted attack on structural analyses, raised the challenge of a cultural and linguistic interpretation, and returned politics to the center of attention. Studies of symbols and ceremonies by Maurice Agulhon and Mona Ozouf, of political culture by Lynn Hunt, and of the power of cultural representations to disempower women by Joan B. Landes, dissolved the boundaries between politics

---

4   This body of work is enormous. For a representative sample, see Albert Mathiez, *The French Revolution* (New York: Knopf, 1929); Ernest Labrousse, *Esquisse du mouvement des prix et des revenus en France au XVIIIe siècle* (Paris: Librairie Dalloz, 1933); Georges Lefebvre, *The French Revolution*, 2 vols. (New York: Columbia University Press, 1962, 1964), and his classic *The Coming of the French Revolution, 1789* (Princeton: Princeton University Press, 1947); Albert Soboul, *The French Revolution, 1787–1799: From the Storming of the Bastille to Napoleon*, trans. Alan Forrest and Colin Jones (New York: Random House, 1974).

5   Hunt, *Politics, Culture, and Class in the French Revolution*, p. 11.

6   William Doyle, *Origins of the French Revolution* (Oxford: Oxford University Press, 1980).

and culture and reduced the causal power of the unmediated social world.[7]

In a famous polemic, "The Revolution is Over," Furet quite explicitly linked French historiography on the French Revolution to "a confused encounter between Bolshevism and Jacobinism."[8] He saw much of the writing on the French Revolution as committed to the dual promises of liberation of 1789 and 1917, and the turn to social history did not change the dominant interpretation that the revolution had been a radical break with the past. Calling for greater attention to continuity and to critique of the conceptualizations of the revolutionary actors themselves, Furet laid down a radical challenge to historians of revolution who, he believed, "have taken the revolutionary discourse at face value because they themselves have remained locked into that discourse."[9]

In contrast, a new generation of historians of Russia, primarily in the United States, began in the 1960s to dismantle the dominant liberal or orthodox interpretation of the revolution and, with the help of social historical approaches, to reconceptualize 1917 as a struggle between social classes. The orthodox interpretation, which one might call the "political/personality" view of the revolution, had argued that the Russian Revolution was an unfortunate intervention that ended a potentially liberalizing political evolution of tsarism, from autocracy through constitutional reforms to a Western-style parliamentary system. Weakened by World War I, the tsarist government collapsed before the impatience of the lower classes and liberal and radical intellectuals. The democratic institutions created in February 1917 failed to withstand the dual onslaught from the Germans and the Leninists and fell in a conspiratorial coup organized by a party that was not genuinely popular, indeed a minority movement that could maintain itself in power only through

---

7 Maurice Agulhon, *Marianne into Battle: Republican Imagery and Symbolism in France, 1789–1880*, trans. Janet Lloyd (Cambridge: Cambridge University Press, 1981); Mona Ozouf, *La Fête révolutionnaire, 1789–1799* (Paris: Gallimard, 1976); Joan B. Landes, *Women and the Public Sphere in the Age of the French Revolution* (Ithaca and London: Cornell University Press, 1988). For an anti-revisionist defense of the structural and Marxist interpretations of the revolution, see E. J. Hobsbawm, *Echoes of the Marseillaise: Two Centuries Look Back on the French Revolution* (London and New York: Verso, 1990).

8 Furet, *Interpreting the French Revolution*, p. 13.

9 Ibid., p. 16.

repression and terror. Informed by memoirs by participants, a visceral anti-Leninism, and a steady focus on political maneuvering and personalities, this orthodox paradigm dealt with the Bolsheviks as rootless conspirators representing no authentic interests of those who foolishly followed them.

Though no consensus united the entire scholarly community and there were major historiographical fractures between the older generations and the new revisionist scholarship, the emerging trend that poured forth in a series of monographs in the 1970s and 1980s was a more structuralist appreciation of the movements of social groups and a displacement of the former emphasis on leaders and high politics. By looking below the political surface at the actions and aspirations of workers and soldiers, the revisionist historiography argued that a deep and deepening social polarization between the top and bottom of Russian society prevented the consolidation of a political consensus, so desired by moderate socialists and liberals, and thus undermined the Provisional Government. Rather than being dupes of radical intellectuals, workers articulated their own concept of autonomy and lawfulness at the factory level, while peasant soldiers developed a keen sense of what kind of war (and for what regime) they were willing to fight. More convincingly than any of their political opponents, the Bolsheviks pushed for a government of the lower classes institutionalized in the soviets, advocated workers' control over industry and an end to the war. By the fall of 1917, a coincidence of lower-class aspirations and the Bolshevik program resulted in elected Leninist majorities in the soviets of both Petrograd and Moscow, and the strategic support of soldiers on the northern and western fronts. But, after a relatively easy accession to power in Petrograd, Moscow, Baku, and a few other cities, the Bolsheviks faced armed challenges from conservative White forces and newly-mobilized nationalists, peasant resistance to their policies of forced grain requisitions, and foreign interventionists, as well as the general dissolution of political authority and economic collapse. As Russia slid into civil war, the Bolsheviks ruthlessly rebuilt state power through economic centralization and the wanton use of violence and terror against their opponents.

The historiographical debates were deeply embedded, not only in the politics of different generations of academic historians, but also in wider discussions of the appropriate attitudes toward the Soviet

Union.[10] The orthodox interpretation, dominant in the West for the first fifty years of Soviet Power (*Sovetskaia vlast'*), contained within it a powerful argument for political opposition to the Soviet regime, for the illegitimacy of the Communist government, that took on a new relevance with the introduction of *perestroika* and *glasnost'* by Mikhail Gorbachev in the 1980s. The stakes were high, as Martin Malia indicated:

> For if the Soviet regime originated in a genuinely popular revolution, then Stalin is an "aberration" from the Leninist norm, and the system has the capacity, despite a temporary detour into horror, to return to a democratic and humane socialism. But if the system was born in a conspiratorial coup, then Stalin is Lenin writ large, and there is no democratic source to return to: Communism therefore cannot be reformed, but must be abolished. Recent Anglo-American historiography has almost uniformly adopted the first, "optimistic" perspective, and has consequently been organized around the questions: What went wrong? When did it go wrong? How can it be set right? But this historiography ignores the possibility that these might be false questions: that nothing went wrong with the Revolution, but that the whole enterprise, quite simply, was wrong from its inception.[11]

Twenty years earlier, Richard Pipes had made a similar argument:

> The elite that rules Soviet Russia lacks a legitimate claim to authority . . . Lenin, Trotsky, and their associates seized power by force, overthrowing an ineffective but democratic government. The government

---

10   Here too there is an interesting parallel and interfiliation with the historiography of the French Revolution. The French Revolution, writes Furet, is "an unlimited promise of equality and a special form of change. One only has to see in it not a national institution but a matrix of universal history, in order to recapture its dynamic force and its fascinating appeal. The nineteenth century believed in the Republic. The twentieth century believes in the Revolution . . . At the very moment when Russia—for better or worse—took the place of France as the nation in the vanguard of history, because it had inherited from France and from nineteenth-century thought the idea that a nation is chosen for revolution, the historiographical discourses about the two revolutions became fused and infected each other." *Interpreting the French Revolution*, p. 6.

11   Martin Malia, "The Hunt for the True October," *Commentary* XCII, 4 (October 1991), pp. 21–2.

they founded, in other words, derives from a violent act carried out by a tiny minority.[12]

While somewhat extreme in its formulation, the point made by Malia and Pipes was not only shared by a broad spectrum of Western liberals and conservatives, it also resonated among late Soviet and post-Soviet intellectuals disillusioned by the economic and moral failures of the Soviet system. When the rereading of Soviet history proposed in the first phases of the Gorbachev reforms tried to limit the critique to Stalinism, it was overwhelmed (after 1987) by more fundamental attacks on the legacy of the revolution. Interpretations of the October seizure of power as either a coup d'état without popular support or the result of a fortuitous series of accidents amid the "galloping chaos" of the revolution (the view of Robert V. Daniels) re-emerged, first among Soviet activists and politicians, journalists and publicists and later in the West in the discussion around the publication of Pipes's own two-volume study of the revolutions of 1917.[13]

Along with the normative reassessments of Bolshevik practices and ideas, the anti-revisionists have revived older approaches and methodologies, once again bringing politics back to center stage, focusing on Lenin himself, and subjecting social history to a savage critique. In a long review of the revisionist challenge to the orthodox interpretation of the Russian Revolution, Walter Laqueur asserts:

> While the analysis of revolution can never be based on politics alone, the political factors are the decisive ones; attempts to downplay or even ignore them are bound to lead to misleading conclusions . . .
>
> The problem for which Marxist scholars have not found a satisfactory answer is the fact that the revolution was, in the final analysis, the work of one man. Without him the revolution would not have happened, and there is no Soviet history book which has not stressed this many times over . . . It can be said about Lenin, as about Hitler, that the fate of the world depended on one man . . . For this reason, the attempt to

12   Richard Pipes, "Why Russian Act Like Russians," *Air Force Magazine* (June 1970), pp. 51–5; cited in Louis Menasche, "Demystifying the Russian Revolution," *Radical History Review*, no. 18 (Fall 1978), p. 153.

13   Richard Pipes, *The Russian Revolution* (New York: Alfred A. Knopf, 1990).

look for social explanations and class analyses is not very helpful. It can show us whether the preconditions for a revolution existed, but not why it took place.[14]

Affiliated as it was with a Left politics, social history was attacked by academic conservatives, most notably Gertrude Himmelfarb, as fundamentally biased in its anti-elitism, self-proclaimed populism, and Marxist ideology.[15] At the same time, the critics defending political history contended that social historians had fostered an artificial separation of political and social elements and reduced the former to the latter. In a review of the work of a group of social historians studying the Russian Revolution, David Longley argued that their "passionate objectivity" was misplaced, for it is impossible to deduce political events from social conditions. "Radical politics cannot be deduced simply from bad conditions, even from very bad conditions," and therefore Russian social historians have had to make "in effect a political argument in the disguise of social analysis."[16] Besides their reductionism, he maintained, the social historians used terms inaccurately and inconsistently, most importantly ideas of class and legitimacy. This same cudgel was taken up in a later review by political scientist Richard Sakwa of a collection of essays on the Civil War, where he applauded "the quality of the detailed research" but derided "the claims of the methodology, which are flawed, contradictory, and exaggerated." While "the exploration of the social elements of political power is a great achievement," Sakwa argued that this was again "history with the politics left out."[17] In his generally positive review of Richard Pipes's history of the revolution ("a magisterial and original synthesis"), Marc Raeff accused the revisionists of both political bias and

14 Walter Laqueur, *The Fate of the Revolution: Interpretations of Soviet History from 1917 to the Present* (Revised edition: New York: Macmillan, 1987), p. 220.

15 See, for example, Gertrude Himmelfarb, "A History of the New History," a review of Lawrence Stone's *The Past and the Present* (Boston: Routledge & Kegan Paul, 1981), in the *New York Times Book Review,* January 10, 1982, pp. 9, 24–5.

16 D. A. Longley, "Passionate Objectivity," a review of Daniel H. Kaiser (ed.), *The Workers' Revolution in Russia, 1917: The View from Below* (Cambridge: Cambridge University Press, 1987), in *Revolutionary Russia* II, 1 (June 1989), p. 160.

17 Richard Sakwa, review of Diane P. Koenker, William G. Rosenberg and Ronald Grigor Suny (eds.), *Party, State and Society in the Russian Civil War: Explorations in Social History* (Bloomington, IN: Indiana University Press, 1989), in *Revolutionary Russia* III, 2 (December 1990), pp. 257–9.

determinism, but tweaked Pipes for his unwillingness to take on his opponents openly.

> In the 1960s there arose a "revisionist" historiography rooted in the methodology and presuppositions of avant-garde, Marxist-colored, social history. These young historians were the first foreigners to gain access to some of the archival sources in the USSR, in order to work on topics approved by Soviet authorities. Unfortunately, although these works put into circulation an appreciable amount of new factual information, they are often marred by a "philosophy" of history that assumes the inevitability of revolution and justifies the Bolshevik coup for allegedly reflecting the dynamics of the proletariat's class consciousness and values. By ignoring this literature (with some merited exceptions), Professor Pipes implies its irrelevance for a genuine understanding of the events. I would agree; but he commits the rhetorical (and professional) mistake of not stating clearly and forcefully his reasons for ignoring it.[18]

The study of the Russian Revolution, it was argued, demonstrates how the angle of historical vision conspires with political bias to produce a justification of the radicalization of the revolution, and a legitimation of the October events. Once the Soviet Union was relegated to the "trash bin of history," there was a triumphal assertion that "the self-designated revisionist vanguard risks finding itself well in the rear."[19] The revisionists rejected the accusation that they were "legitimizing" the revolution by elaborating on its popular base. As William G. Rosenberg wrote, "To explore social contexts and their relation to the contours of change is hardly to exculpate human behavior but to situate it in its broader and conditioning context and thus make it more comprehensible."[20]

Social history was given a bum rap. While some Russian historians defiantly called for a non-political social history, most social historians

---

18 Marc Raeff, "In the Grand Manner," *The National Interest*, Summer 1991, pp. 86–7.

19 Richard Pipes, "Seventy-Five Years On: The Great October Revolution as a Clandestine Coup d'Etat," *Times Literary Supplement*, no. 4675, November 6, 1992, p. 3.

20 William G. Rosenberg, "Who Is to Be Blamed?" *The Nation*, February 18, 1991, p. 202.

working on 1917 were negotiating the difficult relationship between ideas and circumstances, social and political determinants, without necessarily justifying the excesses of revolutions. Revolutions, by their very nature, are illegitimate, extra-legal actions overthrowing constituted political regimes, and do not require the sanction of academic historians. Moreover, the first forays against the seemingly invulnerable orthodox reading of the revolution were launched even before social history was widely practiced by historians of Russia. Alexander Rabinowitch's early study of the July Days, which largely concentrated on internal party politics and the actions of key leaders, undermined one of the most persistent clichés of Russian historiography by questioning the notion of the superior organization and single-mindedness of the Bolshevik party. Directed against the Soviet assertion of a monolithic party subordinated to the will of Lenin, Rabinowitch's analysis showed that the party was deeply divided and that the attempt by some Bolsheviks and workers to seize power in July occurred against Lenin's wishes. Already in this work the unruly forces of workers and soldiers were shouldering their way onto the historical scene, and though they were not yet center stage the inadequacy of explanations dependent on the demiurge Lenin and a Stalinist reading of the party had become apparent.[21]

II

For all his unwillingness to engage directly with the works that constituted the dominant interpretation of the revolution through the 1970s and 1980s, Richard Pipes spearheaded the assault on the social historical interpretation and made a self-conscious retreat to the terrain of high politics, personalities, and ideology, as if the intervening historiography of the last several decades had never been written. In a sweeping narrative full of mostly weak-willed politicians and intellectuals obsessed with power and reshaping human beings, Pipes develops his own concept, if not full-blown theory, of revolution, which manages at one and the same time to be highly deterministic and highly voluntarist. Though he does not explore deeply the rhetoric and cultural codes of the revolutionary actors, as do the French revisionists, Pipes emphasizes the extent to which attitudes, rather than "institutions or 'objective' economic and social

---

21   Alexander Rabinowitch, *Prelude to Revolution: The Petrograd Bolsheviks and the July 1917 Uprising* (Bloomington: Indiana University Press, 1968).

realities determine the course of politics."[22] For Pipes, "the Revolution was the result not of insufferable conditions but of irreconcilable attitudes."[23] He lays out his credo in the introduction: "The Russian Revolution was made neither by the forces of nature nor by anonymous masses but by identifiable men pursuing their own advantages. As such it is very properly subject to value judgment."[24]

Beginning with a view of human beings, or at least those in Russia, as irrational creatures driven by "anger, envy, resentments of every imaginable kind," that eventually blew off the "lid of awe and fear" that contained them, the masses (a term he favors) are not the agents of their own fate.[25] Their inchoate grievances are mobilized (manipulated might be a better word) by revolutionary intellectuals, who are the real makers of revolution. The two conditions for revolution involve the lack of "democratic institutions able to redress grievances through legislation," and "the ability of intellectuals to fan the flames of social discontent for the purpose of gaining power. For it is the intellectuals who transmute specific, and therefore remediable, grievances into a wholesale rejection of the status quo. Rebellions happen; revolutions are made."[26]

While he admires pragmatic politicians and businessmen, Pipes despises intellectuals, who, he argues, envy the wealth, authority, and prestige of business and political elites. In contrast to his own view of human nature and the requirements of gradual, organic social and political development, radical intellectuals possess a rationalist, environmentalist view that sees humans as infinitely malleable. "A life ruled by 'reason' is a life ruled by intellectuals: it is not surprising, therefore, that intellectuals want to change the world in accord with the requirements of

---

22 Pipes, *The Russian Revolution*, p. 51.

23 Ibid., p. 7.

24 Ibid., p. xxiv. Later Pipes writes: "To the historian [of the prewar years], the most striking—and most ominous—impression is the prevalence and intensity of hatred: ideological, ethnic, social . . . All these passions were held in check only by the forces of order—the army, the gendarmerie, the police—who themselves were under constant assault from the left. Since political institutions and processes capable of peacefully resolving these conflicts failed to emerge, the chances were that sooner or later resort would again be had to violence, to the physical extermination of those who happened to stand in the way of each of the contending groups." Ibid., p. 194.

25 Ibid., p. 26.

26 Ibid., p. 121.

'rationality'."[27] But the intelligentsia, in fact, deliberately detaches itself from reality, invents its own idea of "the people" on whose behalf they speak and act, and aims to make people virtuous through politics by creating a rational order called socialism. Socialist doctrines provide the intelligentsia with both a means to power and a justification for imposing their particular rationality. When it finds itself in power the intelligentsia creates its own preferred reality through censorship.[28]

As elaborated in this earlier study, *Russia Under the Old Regime* and sketched in here, Pipes's *ancien régime* was a patriarchal or patrimonial despotism, the appropriate government for Russia's peasants, who did not crave civil or political rights. Since "private property is arguably the single most important institution of social and political integration" and "ownership of property creates a commitment to the political and legal order," Pipes concludes that the mass of Russians, with scant experience of property or natural law, had a weakly-developed respect for law and little interest in the preservation of the status quo.[29] The paternalism of the autocratic state, dependent on its landed nobility and bureaucracy, had a baneful effect on social and political developments as tsarism both initiated and restrained the capitalist development that proved subversive to it. Had the state opened up to society, revolution might have been avoided, but because of the social threats to unity and stability the monarchy failed to reform.

> Russia could have averted a revolutionary upheaval only on one condition: if the unpopular, but experienced bureaucracy, with its administrative and police apparatus, made common cause with the popular but inexperienced liberal and liberal-conservative intelligentsia. In late 1915 neither of these groups was capable of governing Russia on its own. By preventing such an alliance when it was still possible [in August 1915], Nicholas ensured that sooner or later both would be swept away and he along with them, plunging Russia into anarchy.[30]

For Pipes, Russia was an artificial construct, made by the state, with neither a shared civil sense nor patriotism. Disloyal intellectuals were

---

27 Ibid., p. 127.
28 Ibid., p. 131.
29 Ibid., p. 112.
30 Ibid., p. 228.

matched by unpatriotic peasants who tended toward primitive anarchism, until by the second decade of the century the tsar had lost all support from society. Soldiers were little more than peasants, and the "muzhik had little sense of 'Russianness.' He thought of himself, not as a 'Russkii,' but as a 'Viatskii' or 'Tulskii'—that is, a native of Viatka or Tula province—and as long as the enemy did not threaten his home territory, he had no quarrel with him."[31] The Revolution was "due, first and foremost to political causes—namely, the unwillingness of government and opposition to bury their differences in face of a foreign enemy. The absence in Russia of an overriding sense of national unity was never more painfully in evidence."[32]

Pipes dismisses the arguments of Leopold H. Haimson—the Western historian of prerevolutionary Russia who set much of the agenda that social historians pursued—that worker unrest, and growing polarization both between workers and the moderate intelligentsia and between the autocracy and the bulk of educated society, were leading toward a revolutionary crisis on the eve of World War I. Rather he holds that Russia was still stable, dependent as it was on the peasant masses, and indeed moving toward greater conservatism and patriotism. The constitutional experiment after 1905 failed because the autocrat tried to restrict political activity within an order in which the Emperor, bureaucracy, and gentry retained enormous powers. Stolypin's heroic efforts to reform rural Russia could not have worked without the backing of the Crown. Yet for all its serious flaws, tsarism was a complex set of institutions built up through trial and error over many centuries, and Pipes follows Edmund Burke in holding that such structures ought not be destroyed in the futile hope that an ideal system might be constructed. The particular delusion of intellectuals that they could bring a rational order out of the chaos of human experience eventually brought disaster on Russia.

Only the February overthrow of the tsar was a genuine revolution, according to Pipes. October was a classic coup d'état engineered cynically by power-hungry conspirators, led by the cowardly, cruel, unscrupulous Lenin. To understand Lenin, a figure he has written about over much of his career, Pipes suggests a peculiar methodological innovation. Since Lenin's writings, all fifty-five volumes of them, "are

---

31 Ibid., p. 203.
32 Ibid., p. 209.

overwhelmingly propaganda and agitation, meant to persuade potential followers and destroy known opponents rather than reveal his thoughts," and because Lenin "rarely disclosed what was on his mind, even to close associates," Pipes reconstructs his thinking by proceeding "retroactively, from known deeds to concealed intentions." This fierce antipathy prevents Pipes from engaging in a balanced and nuanced treatment of the very figure he sees as central to the narrative of 1917—even when Lenin "inadvertently revealed what had been on his mind," as, for example, in his self-justification after the April Days.[33]

Pipes is nearly alone among Russian historians to interpret the April protests against Foreign Minister Pavl Miliukov's declaration that Russia would carry the war "to a victorious conclusion" as the first bid for power by the Bolsheviks. He quotes Lenin as saying: "This was an attempt to resort to violent means. We did not know whether at that anxious moment the mass had strongly shifted to our side . . . We merely wanted to carry out a peaceful reconnaissance of the enemy's strength, not to give battle."[34] Pipes is simply misusing his sources here to prove the unprovable—that Lenin encouraged violence as early as April. In fact, Lenin was speaking critically of the Petersburg Committee of the party, as the full quotation shows:

> What did our adventurism consist of? This was an attempt to resort to violent means. We did not know whether at that anxious moment the mass had strongly shifted to our side, and the question would have been another had they shifted strongly. We gave the slogan of peaceful demonstrations, but some comrades from the Petersburg Committee gave another slogan, which we annulled, but we did not manage to hold back the mass who followed that slogan. We say, that the slogan "Down with the Provisional Government" is adventurist, that to overthrow the government now is impossible, and because of this we gave the slogan of peaceful demonstrations. We merely wanted to carry out a peaceful reconnaissance of the enemy's strength, not to give battle.[35]

---

33 Ibid., p. 404.

34 Ibid.

35 V. I. Lenin, *Polnoe sobranie sochinenii*, 55 vols. (Moscow, 1958–65), XXXI, p. 361.

Pipes, who has just distorted Lenin's meaning by omitting passages from his speech, audaciously accuses in a footnote Alexander Rabinowitch of adopting "the Bolshevik thesis that the April demonstrations were a peaceful demonstration," and omitting in his citation Lenin's reference to "violent means."[36] Rabinowitch, in fact, does begin his citation just after that phrase, which is discussing the Petrograd Committee's position, not his own, but shows correctly that Lenin opposed the use of violence at this time.[37] What Pipes does here is hardly exemplary scholarship, but what is known in boxing and basketball as a cheap shot.

The question that has agitated historians ever since 1917 has been how did the Bolsheviks, an insignificant minority in the February Days, win power eight months later. Aligned with this query is the story of the shift of the urban lower classes from support of the moderate socialists in the soviets, the liberal-socialist government, and a foreign policy of "revolutionary defensism" to the idea of lower-class government embodied in Soviet Power, radical opposition to the "bourgeoisie," the liberals, and their sympathizers, and a desperate desire to withdraw from the war. The political/personality approach that Pipes elaborates describes in faint outlines the social radicalization but offers no explanation of the growing gulf between the propertied classes and the *demokratiia* (as the socialists styled their constituents), except the disgust of the workers, soldiers, and sailors with the vacillations of the moderate socialists and the effectiveness of Bolshevik propaganda. Absent here are the complex and subtle discussions by labor historians (William G. Rosenberg, Diane Koenker, Ziva Galili, David Mandel, S. A. Smith) of the growing desperation of workers facing the inflationary erosion of their wage gains of the early months of the revolution, lockouts and factory closures. The parallel radicalization of soldiers, detailed by Allan K. Wildman in two volumes,[38]

36 Pipes, *The Russian Revolution*, p. 404n.
37 Rabinowitch, *Prelude to Revolution*, p. 45.
38 Ziva Galili, *The Menshevik Leaders in the Russian Revolution: Social Realities and Political Strategies* (Princeton: Princeton University Press, 1989); Diane Koenker, *Moscow Workers and the 1917 Revolution* (Princeton: Princeton University Press, 1981); Diane P. Koenker and William G. Rosenberg, *Strikes and Revolution in Russia, 1917* (Princeton: Princeton University Press, 1989); David Mandel, *The Petrograd Workers and the Fall of the Old Regime: From the February Revolution to the July Days, 1917* (New York: St. Martin's Press, 1983); *The Petrograd Workers and the Soviet Seizure of Power: From the July Days 1917 to July 1918* (New York: St. Martin's Press, 1984); S. A. Smith, *Red Petrograd: Revolution in the Factories, 1917–1918* (Cambridge: Cambridge University Press, 1983).

that turned the ranks against officers as the government and the moderate leadership of the soviets failed to end the war, is left out of Pipes's account.[39] The growing hostility of *tsensovoe obshchestvo* (propertied society) and the liberal intelligentsia toward the lower classes and the plethora of committees and councils that undermined what they considered legitimately constituted authority has been eloquently analyzed by Rosenberg in his study of the Kadet party, but finds no resonance here.[40] Taken together these works have shown that the Bolsheviks came to power in 1917 with considerable popular support in the largest cities of the empire—a case, as Terence Emmons puts it, that is "incontrovertible."[41] What might still be disputed is the degree, consistency, durability, and meaning of that support.

For Pipes, the twelve-year constitutional and revolutionary interlude (1905–17) ended within two weeks of the "October coup" when the Bolsheviks began setting up a system of government that "marked a reversion to the autocratic regime that had ruled Russia before 1905."[42] But it was both something like and something more than the "totalitarian" police regime of the late nineteenth and early twentieth century. For Lenin's political practices were, in Pipes's view, precursors of the most vicious forms of totalitarianism, not only domestic Stalinism, but Nazism as well. This intemperate claim, which outraged the scholar-participants when he made it at a January 1988 conference on 1917 held in Jerusalem, is sprinkled through the text: "Like his pupils and emulators, Mussolini

---

39   Allan K. Wildman, *The End of the Russian Imperial Army: Vol. I: The Old Army and the Soldiers' Revolt (March–April 1917)*; *Vol. II: The Road to Soviet Power and Peace* (Princeton: Princeton University Press, 1980, 1987).

40   William G. Rosenberg, *Liberals in the Russian Revolution: The Constitutional Democratic Party, 1917–1921* (Princeton: Princeton University Press, 1974). The revolution outside of Petrograd, the subject of several monographs (Orlando Figes, Donald Raleigh, Ronald Grigor Suny), was treated by Pipes thirty years ago in his very first book (*The Formation of the Soviet Union: Communism and Nationalism, 1917–1923* [Cambridge, MA: Harvard University Press, 1954]), but is omitted almost entirely here. See, for example, Figes, *Peasant Russia, Civil War: The Volga Countryside in Revolution, 1917–1921* (Oxford: Oxford University Press, 1989); Raleigh, *Revolution on the Volga: 1917 in Saratov* (Ithaca, NY: Cornell University Press, 1986); and Suny, *The Baku Commune, 1917–1918: Class and Nationality in the Russian Revolution* (Princeton: Princeton University Press, 1972).

41   Terence Emmons, "Unsacred History," *The New Republic*, November 5, 1990, p. 36.

42   Pipes, *The Russian Revolution*, p. 525.

and Hitler, Lenin won power by first breaking the spirit of those who stood in his way, persuading them that they were doomed." The July Days were "the equivalent of Hitler's 1923 beer-hall putsch," he claims, despite the evidence that the Bolsheviks were only reluctantly dragged into supporting the street demonstrations of radical soldiers, sailors, and workers. "Lenin hated what he perceived to be the 'bourgeoisie' with a destructive passion that fully equaled Hitler's hatred of the Jews: nothing short of its physical annihilation would satisfy him." How, one wonders, are we to square this "holocaust" against the middle classes with Lenin's policy of employing "bourgeois specialists"? And finally: "The Stalinist and Nazi holocausts were carried out with much greater decorum [than the Red Terror of the Russian Civil War]."[43] For Pipes, not only totalitarianism, but Nazism and the Holocaust has a Russian and a Leninist pedigree.[44]

Rather than providing a synthesis of what we know about the revolutionary processes of 1917–18 or a reinterpretation that contends with the major contributions of recent historiography (almost none of which is even referred to in notes or bibliography), Pipes has offered a personal political vision, an indictment, highly selective, and uneven in its treatment of significant events and processes. By setting out such a strong version of the view that the Bolshevik regime was unpopular and illegitimate, his account prevents an understanding of the complex relationship between the lower classes, which favored Soviet power and a broadly democratic political order, and the Bolsheviks, who eventually turned that order into a one-party dictatorship. An entire range of questions stemming from the motives of the actors and the imperatives of the

43   Ibid., pp. 399, 419, 728, 820. I am indebted to my colleague Lewis H. Siegelbaum for emphasizing this theme in Pipes's work. One might compare Pipes's views on the Russian-Nazi connection with the so-called *Historikerstreit* (historians' conflict) among German historians. See, for example, Geoff Eley, "Viewpoint: Nazism, Politics and Public Memory: Thoughts on the West German *Historikerstreit* 1986–1987," *Past and Present*, no. 121 (November 1988), pp. 171–208; Charles S. Maier, *The Unmasterable Past: History, Holocaust, and German National Identity* (Cambridge, MA and London: Harvard University Press, 1988).

44   In Jerusalem it was pointed out that Lenin had a variety of attitudes and policies toward the Russian "bourgeois," among which was working together with them in a state capitalist arrangement to revive the Russian economy in 1917–18, employing "bourgeois specialists" in the NEP period; but in no sense did he argue for the wholesale physical annihilation of this social group.

economic and social context are neglected by such a concentrated focus on personalities.

For a time, Pipes's compelling narrative found a ready audience, both among those in the West celebrating the demise of what they understand to have been socialism, and among those in the Soviet Union who believe that their recent past could be completely expunged. In the 1990s when Russia and what was once the Soviet Union were materially and spiritually vulnerable, when explanations of the past were sought as a guide to possible futures, works of history briefly took on an enviable power in the struggle over the political choices in the post-Soviet states. Just as he was an important voice in the renewed Cold War of the Reagan years, so Pipes proved to be an influential player in this volatile arena—for a time.[45] Yet, Russian (and Western) attitudes toward the Russian Revolution, as Furet reminds us in his reading of the French Revolution, continued to be part of a larger discourse about identity, and a foundational moment in the development of a political culture, such as the 1917 Revolution, could not easily be remolded into an alien, artificial, anomalous occurrence.

III

If Pipes's work is in many ways a throwback to an earlier historiography, the end of the era of Soviet-style Communism, at least in Europe, forced many social historians also to rethink much of twentieth-century Russian and Soviet history. Not only had formerly forbidden archives become available in ways undreamt of before 1991, but new approaches from other historiographies destabilized many of the old clarities about the Russian/Soviet past. Though the insights from literary theory and the fallout from the Foucauldian revolution were latecomers to historical writing on Russia (and confined for decades to Western historians), it eventually became apparent that neither the older political history, nor the social determinism of many Soviet and social historians, had proven adequate in dealing with central issues of social categories and transformations.

Social history has always been a diverse practice not only in its methodologies and interests, but also in its range of approaches, from social

---

45 A flurry of conservative evaluations of the revolution (by Robert Conquest, Malia, Pipes, and Adam Ulam) appeared after the disintegration of the USSR in *Times Literary Supplement*, November 6, 1992, pp. 3–9.

"scientific" quantification to cultural anthropologies. Its fundamental concern has been the expansion of the field of historical inquiry. Though some investigators launched studies of "society" with little explicit discussion of politics, the major effect of the turn to the social was to open up the very conception of the political in two important ways. First, borrowing from the insights of feminism and the legacy of the New Left that the "personal is political," politics has been seen as deeply embedded in the social realm, in aspects of everyday life far beyond the state and political institutions.[46] Second, the realm of politics has been recontextualized within society, so that the state and political actors are seen as constrained by social possibilities and influenced by actors and processes outside political institutions.[47] Not surprisingly, this rethinking of power relations has involved consideration of cultural and discursive hegemony and exploration of "the images of power and authority, the popular mentalities of subordination."[48]

While a variety of works—among them, those by Galili, Mandel, Rabinowitch, Rosenberg, Smith, Suny, and Wildman—attempted to marry social history with political history, that vital synthesis had not been influenced by the kinds of investigations of language and culture in which the historians of 1789 had long been engaged.[49] Such an integration of social, political, and discursive histories both demonstrated the limits of the social history as practiced in the 1970s and 1980s, and promised to provide new understandings of the way in which antagonistic "classes" formed in 1917 and how the Bolsheviks succeeded in their bid for power.

One the most suggestive works dealing with class in 1917 has looked at one dimension of the revolution, strike activity, to show how it intersected with other dimensions to contribute to social polarization and class

---

46 Geoff Eley, "Edward Thompson, Social History and Political Culture: The Making of a Working-class Public, 1780–1850," in Harvey J. Kaye and Keith McClelland (eds.), *E. P. Thompson: Critical Perspectives* (Philadelphia: Temple University Press, 1990), p. 13.

47 Here the work of Moshe Lewin has been particularly influential, integrating political history with his own brand of historical sociology.

48 The phrase is E. P. Thompson's, quoted in Eley, "Edward Thompson, Social History and Political Culture," p. 16.

49 Besides the works mentioned earlier, one should note Alexander Rabinowitch, *The Bolsheviks Come to Power: The Revolution of 1917 in Petrograd* (New York: W. W. Norton, 1976).

antagonism. While Diane P. Koenker and William G. Rosenberg integrate other articulations into their account, structural, indeed what they call "ecological" factors, dominate in their explanations. Using quantitative methodology, Koenker and Rosenberg correlate objective elements, such as plant size, industrial concentration, the level of organization of industrialists, changing work environments, and declining real wages, to strike propensity. On plant concentration, for example:

> Concentration of industrial plants in Russia's major administrative centers, and within these cities in particular industrial districts like Vyborg, virtually invited industrial conflict to spread from plant to plant. News of unrest travelled almost at once through factory districts even without newspaper reports. Such concentration fostered a network of communication among workers, itself contributing to the process of class formation and a growing sense of class identity.[50]

Throughout their dense discussion more subjective factors, such as rising expectations, notions of personal dignity, perceptions and attitudes are woven into a complex explanation. "What shaped the limits of activism after February, as before," they contend, "were economic circumstances, organization, tradition, and what might roughly be called a 'sense of the possible.'"[51] But, here, workers' feelings and ideas arise primarily from material and structural sources, from their position of disadvantage in existing relations of power. For example, during World War I Russian workers were subjected to the arbitrary power of industrialists who could fire them and condemn them to frontline service.

> As economic strains increased, loyalties to the government obviously weakened along with patriotic feelings and the power of common national or civic identities. The importance of changing work environments during these months was thus not simply that new circumstances created new grounds for protest, but also that they kindled or strengthened class identities, and tied a sense of well-being directly to workplace conditions. One's role in production in wartime Russia, one's source of income, access to essential goods and services, and

---

50 Koenker and Rosenberg, *Strikes and Revolution in Russia, 1917*, p. 42.
51 Ibid. p. 62.

dependency on employment all reinforced one's sense of what it meant to be a "worker," and hence strengthened the basis for new collective action.[52]

During the revolutionary year as well, strikers' activities are seen as reactions to

initial successes [that] may have engendered in workers generally a somewhat grandiose sense of what it was possible to achieve by various forms of direct collective action, strengthening, in effect, the powerful residues of February. Petrograd workers *had*, after all, overthrown one of Europe's oldest and most entrenched regimes, and the very experience of success in February must have left many in the factories feeling confident that if they wanted to, they could overthrow the new government as well.[53]

Koenker and Rosenberg convincingly show that strikes were key to the formation of working-class solidarity.

They brought together in collective actions workers who knew each other well, who shared everyday work experience, who worked for the same foremen and owners . . . In important if less tangible ways, strikes were also "schools for collective organization," as Social Democrats had long understood. They provided object lessons in politics and class relations. They tied workers to Russia's revolutionary past, evoking memories in particular of 1905 and 1912, as well as more recent wartime protests.[54]

Strikes, the argument goes, arose from material difficulties and the belief in the possibility to improve one's life. They mobilized labor and developed

components of proletarian identity and class consciousness . . . Support from outsiders bolstered morale and helped workers overcome their

---

52 Ibid., pp. 56–7.
53 Ibid., pp. 145–6.
54 Ibid., p. 98.

initial fears and inhibitions, but it also communicated clearly the importance of "proletarian solidarity," a phrase that was often used by labor activists in Petrograd and elsewhere but that sounded slightly foreign to many. Strike experience could not be taught. For women laundry workers and others long on the periphery of Russia's labor movement, strikes brought dignity and a sense of social identity.[55]

Though explanation of worker activity stems from material conditions and social experience, this account is by no means a social history with the politics left out. Labor activism mobilized management, and two "contending power blocs" emerged with different mentalities, "competing and incompatible sets of values," and "broadly different conceptions about fundamental elements of social order." Conflict revolved around what was "appropriate" and "legitimate" protest.[56] The moderate socialist leaders of the soviets and the members of the Provisional Government shared a view of "bourgeois democracy" that dominated the political discourse in Petrograd in the first months of the revolution. The minister of trade and industry, Aleksandr Konovalov, best represented this idea of a legal, conciliatory approach to labor-management conflicts. Yet from the very beginning of the revolution many workers took matters into their own hands, attacking foremen and managers, often carting them out in wheelbarrows, to settle their grievances with their own ideas of rough justice. After nearly two months of conciliation and relative harmony, the deep differences between the government and the soviet over war policy exploded in the April demonstrations against Foreign Minister Pavl Miliukov's note to the Allies. The first Provisional Government fell, to be replaced by a Coalition Government that included socialists and Russia's first Ministry of Labor. But with their own representatives in government, "a second round of workers' expectations" emerged.[57] Strikes now became the tactic of choice to gain better wages and working conditions, and the number of strikes escalated, not only in the capitals but in the provinces as well. Workers who had won wage hikes in the first months of the revolution had fallen behind as inflation ate away at their gains. Managers were now less able and willing to grant further increases,

---

55 Ibid., pp. 117–18.
56 Ibid., pp. 129–30.
57 Ibid., p. 154.

and the conciliationism associated with Konovalov eroded rapidly. In the spring of 1917, particularistic worker interests were subordinated to larger class solidarities.

> The overall pattern of strikes involving concerns about other workers in the spring suggests a process of proletarian cohesion, not conflict. In all likelihood, strengthening class identities were therefore reinforcing the strong undercurrent of protest . . . challenging traditional forms of managerial authority, just as the clear resistance to these challenges on the part of employers, especially those in smaller enterprises, suggests an increasing coalescence of both industrial and non-industrial employers, at least in their common concern about eroding enterprise power.[58]

The degree of polarization in Russian society became dramatically clear in the so-called July Days, when workers went into the streets in massive political demonstrations and strikes. Koenker and Rosenberg emphasize how such activities helped forge stronger, broader social identities, overcoming sectional divisions both at the top and bottom of society:

> In the summer of 1917, strikes were thus clearly educating working men and women on an increasingly national scale and in the process integrating workers into a class with important shared experiences. As strikes spread, the patterns of protest they reflected also seemed to be shifting away from more routine elements of labor-management interaction to confrontation increasingly over broader matters of industrial organization and authority. Political conflicts were becoming more bitter, more intense, inside the workplace and out.[59]

After the failure of the conservative forces of order to take power in the Kornilov movement and to discipline the soviets, the industrialists and the liberal Kadet party became even more antagonistic to the lower classes and their representatives. A third cluster of strikes reflected the widespread militancy of workers, now prepared to change relations in the workplace radically, no matter how this might affect the economy and the regime. With prices rising rapidly, wage demands continued to

---

58 Ibid., p. 212.
59 Ibid., pp. 252–3.

predominate, but, Koenker and Rosenberg argue, this should not be read as "a purely economic phenomenon, as a manifestation of the paradigm of routine labor-management relations."[60] Alongside wage demands were much higher frequencies of demands for improved conditions, dignity, and workplace control, though not of specifically political issues. Workers were once again, as in the early days of the revolution, resorting to more direct, violent treatment of managerial personnel. "By early October, the boundaries of legitimate labor protest were as insecure as the legal barriers around gentry property or the no-man's-lands at the front."[61] Strikes by October "symbolized the rejection of bourgeois values (and the processes for resolving labor-management conflicts in Western bourgeois societies). For both management and labor, they had largely come instead to reflect the developing tensions, mentalities, and violence of civil war."[62]

In their concluding chapter, Koenker and Rosenberg investigate a number of chronic historiographical issues—the vanguard hypothesis, the social composition of strikers, the role of skill, plant size, urban concentration, and gender—and correct many prevalent notions about Russian strikes. Plant size, for example, cannot be correlated very satisfactorily with strike propensity in 1917. Petrograd was not as prominent in strikes during the revolution as in the years preceding. Moscow, Kazan, Saratov, the provinces of Vladimir and Kostroma, and Baku rivaled the capital in the number of strikers. They show that "an advanced guard of politically conscious, experienced, militant worker activists clearly existed in 1917."[63] Although metal and textile workers have often been said to have constituted the vanguard of strike activists, they actually "remained in the forefront of strike activism only until approximately the first week of July."[64] Semi-skilled workers predominated both numerically and proportionately among strikers. Women were disproportionately active in strikes. "Workers historically less favored in Russia's economy were now able to use this powerful weapon routinely against their employers, a weapon placed

---

60   Ibid., p. 273.
61   Ibid., p. 286.
62   Ibid., p. 324.
63   Ibid., p. 302.
64   Ibid., pp. 321–2.

at their disposal by new conditions of political freedom."[65] And finally
the authors argue

> for the formation in the course of 1917 of a working class largely
> conscious of its identity, a class formed in the process of these struggles
> in the workplace . . . We embrace the notion of class and the role of
> strikes in class formation . . . Workers possessed regional, shop, and
> trade loyalties that often produced stronger ties than classwide identi-
> ties; economic divisions between workers in favored well-paying indus-
> tries and workers in unfavored sectors of the economy also loomed
> large during the war. But in the economic conditions of 1917, with a
> massive decline in productivity and utter uncertainty about Russia's
> economic future, distinctions between favored and unfavored sectors
> tended to disappear. All workers, however privileged or unprivileged,
> began to see themselves as common partners in the struggle against
> this collapse.[66]

In their repertoire of explanations, Koenker and Rosenberg include both
"the material component of a developing class identity" and the "subjective experience of strikes and labor relations in 1917." Patterns of mobilization, the use of the language of class, representations in the socialist
and bourgeois press—all shaped and reinforced perceptions of class identity. But even as they represent both the material and the non-material
sides of the process of class formation, Koenker and Rosenberg have
located class formation squarely in the real economic and social world,
the world of deprivations and disadvantages that gave rise to perceptions
of differences, and the experience of strikes that both created and reinforced identities. Though they also make important gestures to "the
subjective experience of strikes and labor relations in 1917" and the press,
they locate the sources of consciousness in the social position and experience of workers. The generation of worker and class solidarity largely
arises from within the sphere of the workers, and the authors do not treat
systematically the ways in which a sense of class was shaped by discourses
outside the workers' milieu. They acknowledge, for example, that
"Bolshevik programs and politics have been largely absent from this

---

65 Ibid., p. 309.
66 Ibid., pp. 327–8.

discussion."[67] As stunning as their achievement is, as powerful and subtle their arguments, I believe that Koenker and Rosenberg have taken us as far as the usual practice of a political social history can take us.

IV

While it is not difficult to cite instances of social reductionism or inadequate attention to the political in works of social historians, what is most striking with social historians of Russia such as Koenker and Rosenberg is how their repertoire of explanations includes both "material," environmental elements and more subjective experiences of discrimination, humiliation, and a sense of social justice. Yet even though the social as well as the discursive sides coexist in their discussions of identities or class formation, the importance of structural factors is paramount. In my own study of the revolution in Baku, for example, in a chapter entitled "From Economics to Politics," I argued that the "tremendous pressures on the masses, caused by the war and its stepchild, hunger, drove [the masses] to more radical alternatives." Without denying that social structures and economic problems have determining effects, inattention to cultural and discursive elements can lead to reductionist (and condescending) conclusions, like "Nationalism was the form that the expression of ill-understood economic and social problems took." Both nationality and class are treated in my text as objective categories at various stages of realization, and while Social Democratic and nationalist articulations are discussed, the thrust of the narrative is toward "material" explanations.[68] Whether it was within the factories themselves or while participating in strikes and demonstrations, workers' experience, primarily at the level of economic conflict, was seen as both creating and reinforcing identities.

Though social history has often been uncomfortable with its pedigree in Marxism, central to much of its agenda has been the concept of class and the exploration of the social and political processes that have validated (or undermined) that particular identity. Following the pioneering work in other historiographies by E. P. Thompson, William H. Sewell, Jr., Gareth Stedman Jones, Joan Scott, and others, Russian historians have begun to pay growing attention to language, culture, and the available repertoire of

---

67 Ibid., pp. 56–7, 117–18, 130–2, 212, 252–3, 327–8.
68 Suny, *The Baku Commune, 1917–1918*, pp. 102, 115.

ideas.[69] Investigating class formation in the post-Thompsonian period has involved exploring not only the structures of the capitalist mode of production or the behavior of workers during protests and strikes—all of which remain important sites for investigation—but also the available discourses in which workers expressed their sense of self, defined their "interests," and articulated their sense of power or, more likely, powerlessness. Representations in the socialist and bourgeois press, which shaped and reinforced social identities and the sense of social distance, were extraordinarily influential in forming the workers' (and others') understanding of the way the world worked. Whatever the experience of workers might have been, the availability of an intense conversation about class among the intellectuals closest to them provided images and language with which to articulate and reconceive their position.

The interesting problem for historians is neither the wholesale rejection of categories like class, particularly in a context like 1917 where the discourse of class was so insistently present, nor the taking of the categories for granted, but rather the demonstration of how they were conceived, perceived and constructed. The story of class formation of workers is appropriately told against the narrative of the class formation of the "bourgeoisie" and social "others." Workers' activities, if taken by themselves, by definition leave out other social groups, most importantly the soldiers and certain lower-middle-class groups that moved toward the workers by late summer and early fall 1917. Since the politics of forming class is always a matter of inclusions and exclusions, of politically eliminating some distinctions between "us" and "them" and constructing others, the working class cannot be treated in isolation from its allies and its enemies. Classes are political coalitions of diverse elements, and in 1917 the formation of class in Russia occurred on the basis of a broad conception of the *demokratiia* that included workers, soldiers, peasants and others. Through 1917 myriad groups began to believe and articulate that they shared a cluster of "interests" and that those "interests" could not be reconciled with the existing political and social order. Among

69 E. P. Thompson, *The Making of the English Working Class* (London: Victor Gollancz, 1963); Gareth Stedman Jones, *Languages of Class: Studies in English Working Class History, 1832–1982* (Cambridge: Cambridge University Press, 1983); William H. Sewell, Jr., *Work and Revolution in France: The Language of Labor from the Old Regime to 1848* (Cambridge: Cambridge University Press, 1980); Joan Wallach Scott, *Gender and the Politics of History* (New York: Columbia University Press, 1988).

wage-earning workers all kinds of distinctions and antagonisms between women and men, younger and older workers, skilled and unskilled, those in "hot" shops and "cold," had to be overcome until a new community was imagined and created through political understanding and activities. How the boundaries of the lower classes were negotiated between soldiers, artisans, the petite bourgeois and white-collar population, as the concept of *demokratiia* evolved, can be inferred from the works of the social historians of the 1970s and 1980s, though we still lack a full discussion of these processes.

Second, a sense of "class" solidarity was not created simply out of shared experiences, however intensely felt, or the elimination of internal differences, but only in the process of giving meaning to activities in which one was engaged. Here the approaches associated with discursive analyses, with concepts of political culture, and with ideas of cultural hegemony and cultures of resistance provide the necessary links to bring structure, experience, and the generation of meaning together. In that way we may better see the ways in which languages of class constituted a world of classes. Historians of Russian labor might begin by reintegrating the older, often too narrowly political and institutional histories of Social Democracy that proliferated in the 1950s and 1960s. The languages of class and the variety of ways in which class was conceived by radical intellectuals were an intimate part of the moral and cultural universe in which workers, particularly the so-called "advanced," lived and worked. The workers of 1917 cannot be surgically separated out from the larger intellectual and cultural experiences over many decades, which involved their self-styled Marxist and populist leaders from beyond the working class.

Whether marching in a demonstration, participating in a strike, or voting for a deputy to the soviet or a factory committee, the choice for a worker to participate or not did not arise simply from his or her social position but was already embedded in all kinds of understandings about the nature of society, who one was, who the enemy was, what would result from such action. Attitudes and ideas of interest were fragmented and melded together in imperfect fits. Creating class or political solidarities was a matter of reconciling seemingly irreconcilable positions. Consider two conclusions from monographic social historical studies that grapple with attitudes of revolutionary actors and the contradictory elements within their positions. As he sums up the major themes in his two-volume treatment of the soldiers, Allan K. Wildman struggles with the complex interplay of social and political factors.

> The overriding theme has been the soldiers' longing for peace, which conditioned all other aspects of their behavior. But it is hoped that it has been sufficiently stressed that the peace aspirations were but a part of the way the soldiers looked at the world in general, as scions of a peasant culture with its indigenous parochial concerns. The war was simply one more intrusion into this private world of the demands of the holders of political and social power, robbing them of their lives and substance. The social concerns may have been at times obscured by the striving for peace, but they were ever present in the soldiers' thinking, as evidence in their favorite retort: "What good is land and freedom to me if I am dead?"[70]

Similarly, in a close reading of the worker press, David Mandel finds that:

> The workers—and Bolshevik workers were scarcely an exception—started out with an essentially bourgeois-democratic or liberal conception of the revolution and clung to it long after they had begun to surpass it in their practice. As late as the Kornilov affair, even the most militant workers summoned their comrades to the "defence of freedom," without mentioning socialism as an immediate prospect for Russia ... The workers' massive participation in the Constituent Assembly elections, tactical considerations aside, also represented a belated attempt to reconcile October with February, a working-class-led soviet revolution with an all-national democratic one.[71]

In other words, for workers and soldiers in 1917, taking to the street already presupposed certain identities and meanings that existed prior to activity but which were then amplified, shaped, reconstructed by participation. The discursive construction of the world of the workers, as well as that of peasants, soldiers, or the "bourgeoisie," has often been implied, sometimes more explicitly elaborated, but, I would argue, still needs to be foregrounded in our histories. The focus on strikes illuminates much about the formative experience of workers in the revolution, but becoming a

---

70 Wildman, *The End of the Russian Imperial Army*, p. 404.
71 Mandel, *The Petrograd Workers and the Soviet Seizure of Power*, p. 414.

striker already presupposed certain identities and meanings that existed prior to the strike. Beginning with structure rather than meaning may be fine, but it is also necessary to explore how meaning determines one's place. Structures and social positions, or even "experience," in and of themselves do not lead in an unmediated way to meaning or action. The discursive universe in which experience occurs must also be explored. The arrow of determination does not fly in only one direction.

Arguing with great power and usually after prodigious research, social history may have taken us as far as it can, at least when it privileges "material" explanations. We can imagine a scene where workers toiled side by side in a mill in early 1917, each consuming roughly the same inadequate number of calories day after day. These rough-and-ready men and women might have thought of their miserable lot as something ordained by nature or birth and accepted it with little resistance; or they might have conceived instead with pride that they were duty-bound to sacrifice, to tighten their belts for the fatherland; or they might have thought—as they would increasingly as the year progressed—that they were the undeserving victims of ruthless capitalists who had only their own "bourgeois" interests at heart. The material conditions of these workers could "objectively" have been calculated in hours or wages or even in calories, but their self-representation as loyal subjects or as militant proletarians cannot be deduced from these "material" conditions: they must be referred to the larger, competitive discursive universes in which these workers found themselves. To understand why Social Democratic rather than monarchist or liberal rhetoric resonated among widening circles of workers and soldiers in 1917 requires pushing out the bounds of social history.

In the same way, to explain the shift among workers and soldiers from a "class collaborationist" (Menshevik/SR) position in the first three or four months of the revolution to a "class conflict" (Bolshevik) position by the late summer, early fall of 1917, it is not enough simply to speak of "deepening economic crisis" or "social polarization." Both of these seemingly objective, impersonal processes existed as much in perceptions as in the "real" world and were inextricably bound up with political issues, such as the Provisional Government's failure to take Russia out of the war, the moderate socialists' identification with the "bourgeois" government, and the conviction that liberals and the middle class had moved toward counterrevolution.

Against what he calls the "complacent materialism" that has dominated labor history, William H. Sewell, Jr. has advocated a post-materialist approach. Even the "economy," which is the bedrock on which the "material" explanation stands, is shown by Sewell to be symbolic (consider, for example, money and advertising), and he concludes that historians

> must imagine a world in which every social relationship is simultaneously constituted by meaning, by scarcity, and by power. This would imply, for example, that all social relations are discursive, but that social relations are never exhausted by their discursivity. It also implies something much more radical: that the discursive features of the social relationship are themselves always constitutively shaped by power relations and by conditions of choice under scarcity. It further implies that this constitutive shaping is reciprocal—just as meanings are always shaped by scarcity and power, so scarcity is always shaped by power and meaning, and power is always shaped by meaning and scarcity.[72]

Just as in its "deconstructive" phase social history undermined and expanded the old political history, so it is itself now challenged by the discursive investigations of meanings and the rejection of simple referential recordings of "realities." No longer can social categories or identities be taken as given, as fairly stable, or as expressing clear and objective interests emanating from their essential nature. Though historians of Russia and the Soviet Union have long been suspicious of the available social categories, only recently have they questioned their objectivity and essentialism and highlighted the provisional, subjective, and representational character of estate, class, nationality, generation, and gender.[73]

---

72   William H. Sewell, Jr., "A Post-Materialist Rhetoric for Labor History," in Lenard Berlanstein (ed.), *Rethinking Labor History: Essays on Class and Discourse Analysis* (Urbana-Champaign: University of Illinois Press, 1993), pp. 15–38.

73   See, for example, Gregory L. Freeze, "The Soslovie (Estate) Paradigm and Russian Social History," *American Historical Review* XCI, 1 (February 1986), pp. 11–36; Leopold H. Haimson, "The Problem of Social Identities in Early Twentieth Century Russia," *Slavic Review* XLVII, 1 (Spring 1988), pp. 1–20, and the discussion that follows with William G. Rosenberg and Alfred J. Rieber, pp. 21–38; Sheila Fitzpatrick, "L'usage bolchévique de la 'classe': Marxisme et construction de l'identité individuelle," in *Actes de la recherche en sciences sociales*, no. 85 (November 1990), pp. 70–80; Ronald Grigor Suny, "Nationality and Class in the Revolutions of 1917: A Re-examination of Categories," in Nick Lampert and Gabor T. Rittersporn (eds.), *Stalinism: Its Nature and Aftermath. Essays in Honour of Moshe Lewin* (London: Macmillan, 1992), pp. 211–42.

In the last several decades, historians more allied to literary studies and cultural anthropology than to older practices of sociology have conceived of culture as an autonomous symbolic system, irreducible to the social system. The post-Marxist historians of the French Revolution, most notably François Furet, Lynn Hunt, William H. Sewell, Jr., and Keith Baker, see social practices as themselves cultural systems, derived from internal codes and discourses. To leave behind what Margaret Somers calls the "tyranny of structure," many culturally oriented historians have reversed the old hierarchy: from structure determining culture, to culture determining everything.[74] That is not what is being suggested here. Structures exist, apparent in social positions and relations of power, and they have an ability both to determine and restrain—as Koenker and Rosenberg well demonstrate—but only within universes of specific meanings.

In the current practice of Russian revolutionary studies, ideology and circumstances—to use the vocabulary most often invoked in that literature—have most often been treated in hierarchical configurations, though some authors have been attempting to approach them as complexly interrelated, equivalent, and irreducible to one another. Social historians convincingly demonstrated decades ago that personality/political explanations leave too much out and explain too little. Their critics, in turn, countered that social history was frequently insufficiently attentive to politics and ideology. In my "radical middle position" suggested here, one way to bring politics and society back together is to discover the hidden ways in which people understand what they are doing and who they are. Culture, political and ethnographic, language, identities and representations must be respected as irreducible variables. Rather than concentration on—or the psychoanalysis of—great figures in history, or the search for objective social and political interests, the "cultural" or "discursive turn" has redirected us to the deep investigation of the construction of meanings and identities.

---

74 See Margaret R. Somers, *Genealogies of Citizenship: Markets, Statelessness, and the Right to Have Rights* (Cambridge: Cambridge University Press, 2008), pp. 171–210, 254–88, for her discussion of the political culture concept.

CHAPTER SIX

Breaking Eggs, Making Omelets: Violence and Terror in Russia's Civil Wars, 1918–1922

The civil wars in Russia were, in their fundamental aspects, a continuation of the long crisis that divided imperial and revolutionary Russia in the first two decades of the twentieth century.[1] The structures and discourses of empire combined with the destabilizing effects of what has been characterized in an older literature as "modernization" (capitalist industrialization, movement from town to city, the breakdown of traditional norms, secularization, etc.) to produce, already in the 1890s, an accelerating social polarization in which the mass of peasants and the small but increasingly concentrated industrial working class pulled away and grew antagonistic to the middle and upper classes of imperial society. Just after the turn of the century, in 1902–03, more violently in the revolutionary upheavals of 1905–07, and again in the last years before the outbreak of World War I, that polarization and social hostility exploded in a cascade of demonstrations, strikes, acts of individual terrorism, mutinies, rebellions, official retaliation, repression, punitive expeditions, and mass killing by the police and army. In 1917 the distancing of the lower classes—now workers, peasants, and soldiers—pulling away from the upper classes—the "bourgeoisie," as it was frequently referred to in Russia, encompassing the nobility, clergy, army officers, and the liberal intelligentsia—was reflected in the curious emergence of "dual power" (*dvoevlastie*) in the February Revolution, when socialist activists and their supporters (self-styled as the *demokratiia*) formed soviets of workers', peasants', and soldiers' deputies to confront and restrain the official and formal authority, the Provisional Government, and the political institutions (the dumas and executive committees of social organizations) in which "propertied society" (*tsenzovoe obshchestvo*) was represented. The seven-month struggle between soviets and government ended in

---

1   This essay has benefitted from critical readings by Yusuf Has, Joshua A. Sanborn and S. A. Smith.

October 1917 with the victory of the Bolsheviks, the most radical mass political party in Russia. By seizing power, and later by dissolving the widely elected Constituent Assembly in January 1918, the Bolsheviks, in a sense, declared war on that part of the country that refused to recognize *sovetskaia vlast'* (Soviet Power). Russia's civil wars, in their most immediate and violent sense, can be said to have begun in late 1917–early 1918 and to have continued until the Communists put down the massive peasant and nationalist movements in 1921–22.

Civil wars were probably unavoidable, given the extreme polarization of politics in Russia even before the revolution. In this chapter, I am writing about "Russian" civil wars in the plural, rather than as a single conflict, for these wars were part of the dissolution of an empire, in the context of diverse efforts at state-building and the ultimate integration of parts of the old empire into a new state structure. By the fall of 1917 and into 1918 the country was split four or five ways: between those liberals, conservatives, and some socialists who hoped to preserve the gains of the anti-monarchist February Revolution and establish a Western-style parliamentary regime based on individual rights, private property, and a unitary Russian empire; holdouts from the *ancien régime* who longed for either restoration of the autocracy or a conservative constitutional monarchy; moderate socialists who favored a multi-party socialist coalition without people of property; Leninists who staunchly defended a socialist revolution and a war on the bourgeoisie; and masses of peasants who more than anything else wanted to be left alone to run their own affairs and enjoy their newly seized lands. To these centrifugal forces might be added the variety of nationalists, separatists, and anarchists who over time moved away from notions of remaining within a democratic Russia toward national or local independence.

The employing of revolutionary and state terror under Lenin and Stalin is a topic that not only cuts to the heart of the Soviet political project but unavoidably involves empirical, interpretive, and normative questions intricately intertwined one with another. As a first step toward working through my own answers to why terror and can it be justified, I want to review how others within the profession and outside have wrestled with this issue, and then go on to suggest another angle from which the origins and expansion of intentional violence and terror might be explained.

From Edmund Burke on, conservatives have emphasized the willfulness of revolutionaries, their decision or at least willingness if not enthusiasm for violence, bloodshed, and terror. Personal character or an ideology of total transformation is seen as the precondition from which violence is likely to be employed. Among the Left, violence and terror have often been excused as unavoidable, a corollary of the chaos accompanying social change. Eggs must be broken. No white gloves or polished floors. Defenses of state terror have ranged from the conviction that such instrumental violence was unavoidable, albeit undesirable—revolutionaries reluctant to use it were forced to do so by their enemies—to a more rationalist (rationalizing?) argument, that terror was the most efficient means to the desired end. Oppositions to revolutionary and state terror begin with the view that it is immoral, and specifically to be condemned in the Bolshevik case, where judicious violence that might be deemed necessary quickly became surplus violence. Further, it is argued that such means taint the ends. You cannot build socialism, or for that matter democracy, with bayonets, torture, and executions. Opponents of the Bolsheviks argued from the earliest days that terror was a choice of the Bolsheviks, not something imposed on them: a conscious policy to suppress all actual and perceived enemies, so as to maintain the Leninists in power. The inevitable result was the end of any democratic alternative to one-party dictatorship.

Sensationalist accounts of Red terror accompanied the first news of the revolution, while scholarly interest in the question of violence and terror developed more slowly. Terror was a topic related to the central tenets of the totalitarian model dominant during the Cold War years, but declined somewhat in the heyday of social history and later with the cultural turn. As a subject of academic study, violence and terror re-emerged after the fall of the Soviet Union when the archives of party and even police became available. The conservative journalist Anne Applebaum's synthetic work won the Pulitzer Prize.[2] The Russian publisher Rosspen and Yale University Press have issued weighty volumes of archival documents on terror, with commentary by historians, and a new generation of graduate students and younger scholars has established a new subfield of scholarly investigation. Here the market has played a role as well, for general readership books on the Gulag or the Great Purges sell well.

---

2 Anne Applebaum, *Gulag: A History* (New York: Doubleday, 2003).

First, some definitions are in order. The words of Hannah Arendt written down some forty years ago still have resonance: "It is, I think, a rather sad reflection on the present state of political science that our language does not distinguish between such key terms as power, strength, force, might, authority, and finally, violence—all of which refer to distinct phenomena."[3] Without taking on the vast intervening literature, a few necessary distinctions should be made. *Force* usually refers to natural movements outside human control that have physical effects, as in forces of nature, but also to instruments of compulsion, such as armed forces. Force is legitimized by its association with the state, unless it is excessive or arbitrary. In ordinary language, force is usually thought to be organized, controlled, and limited, the work of police or, on occasion, soldiers. *Violence* occurs when a physical force causes harm. A storm or volcanic eruption may stand as a metaphor for violence, but here we are concerned with political violence, that perpetrated by actors, more specifically political actors, or what Stathis Kalyvas defines as "the deliberate infliction of harm on people."[4] *Power* is about command and obedience, getting others to do what you want them to do. As Robert Dahl famously explained his "intuitive idea of power," "A has power over B to the extent that he can get B to do something that B would not otherwise do."[5] Power is a capacity, an ability to do something, which can be extended politically to become power over something or someone. Power is relational; it is about domination and subordination. Therefore, for many theorists, violence appears to be built into power, a necessary ingredient in maintaining the relationship of superiority and inferiority.

Yet Arendt importantly constructs an opposition between an expanded sense of power and violence. Rather than power growing out of the barrel of a gun, as in Mao's notorious "non-Marxian conviction," power is not simple obedience to command but arises from the capacity of people acting in concert.[6] Here she appears to be referring to legitimate political power, power consented to by the government, which she sharply

---

3   Hannah Arendt, "Reflections on Violence," *New York Review of Books* XII, 4 (February 27, 1969), accessible at nybooks.com/articles/11395.

4   Stathis Kalyvas, *The Logic of Violence in Civil War* (Cambridge: Cambridge University Press, 2006), p. 19.

5   Robert Dahl, "The Concept of Power," *Behavioral Science* II, 3 (July 1957), pp. 202–3.

6   Arendt, "Reflections on Violence."

distinguishes from the violence of rebels or of a government based on terror. "Rule by sheer violence comes into play where power is lost." "Politically, loss of power tempts men to substitute violence for power."[7] Arendt's power is connected to authority, the agreement of others to give recognition, respect, and legitimacy to a constituted source of power. She did not agree with either Marx or Weber that all governments ultimately rest on the threat of violence, but she conceded that political order begins with violence, with what Paul Ricœur calls the "founding crime" that eventually will gain the legitimacy that absolves it. Violence recedes when power grows. Finally, Arendt provides important guidance on the normative question: "Violence can be justifiable, but it never will be legitimate . . . Its justification loses in plausibility the farther its intended end recedes into the future. No one questions the use of violence in self-defense, because the danger is not only clear but also present, and the end justifying the means is immediate."[8]

Arendt's notion of power is useful for the early Soviet case, for the revolution and subsequent civil war were contests over the reconstitution of state sovereignty, over which side had the ability to win an armed contest and rule. In my own view, which is in tension with Arendt's insight, power is neither merely about consent nor about violence. Whatever the "founding crime," state power uses coercion to secure obedience and acquiescence in its right to rule. Power has both coercive and discursive aspects. The move from overt violence to acceptance by the ruled of the right of the rulers to rule is at the same time a move from greater coercion to the diffusion of discourses of legitimacy and lawfulness. Historically, many governments have moved from coercion and enforced obedience to persuasion through discursive, cultural, and symbolic—not to mention political and institutional—practices.

Violence is often something that is chosen by political actors—to express grievances, to destabilize social order, to overthrow the government, or to put down opponents or insurgents. These overt acts of violence, the willed and intentional actions that cause harm to others, are the broad subject of this chapter.[9] More specifically, I am concerned

---

7 Ibid.

8 Ibid.

9 I am not concerned here with the notion of "structural violence," the idea that violence lies in the domination of some over others, a "violence" embedded in social and political relations to the degree that those systems of dominance are not consensual.

with the deployment of *terror*, that particularly vicious form of violence that is employed by state actors or insurgents to instill fear in populations and enforce obedience through violence, and which often targets specified groups of people—the bourgeoisie, the Jews, the Reds. Terror is not the same as *terrorism*, which, in my view, involves individual or group violence deliberately employed to further the opposition against state authority or to bring a revolutionary movement to power. The aim of terrorism is to disrupt the existing power structure, to demonstrate the vulnerability and perversity of the present order, and by the "propaganda of the deed" to illustrate the possibility of change. *Revolutionary terror* is a policy of intimidation through violence as well as the systematic physical elimination of actual, perceived, or potential enemies at the moment of contest over state sovereignty. *State terror* is government-initiated violence by an established sovereign state to maintain its authority, repress its actual or imagined enemies, or frighten its own population into obedience. Both terror and terrorism involve aspects of psychological warfare: terror as persuasion to join, to obey, to desist, to defect or not to defect.

Historians Look at Civil War Violence and Terror

In some ways, the debate about the use of violence by the revolutionary state began in the first days after October, among participants, supporters, and opponents of the Bolsheviks themselves. Perhaps most famously, half a year after the October Revolution, a bitter dialogue began between the patriarch of German Social Democracy, Karl Kautsky, who blasted the Bolsheviks' use of terror in his *The Dictatorship of the Proletariat* (1918); Lenin, who answered him with *The Proletarian Revolution and the Renegade Kautsky* (1918); and Trotsky, who answered Kautsky's *Terrorism and Communism* (1919) with a pamphlet of the same name (1920). Trotsky's maxims in *Terrorism and Communism* illustrate the thinking of the Bolsheviks: "Who aims at the end cannot reject the means." "The bourgeoisie, hurled from power, must be forced to obey." "The man who repudiates terror in principle, i.e., repudiates measures of suppression and intimidation towards determined and armed counter-revolution, must reject all idea of the political supremacy of the working class and its revolutionary dictatorship. The man who repudiates the dictatorship of the proletariat repudiates the socialist revolution and digs the grave of socialism." While Kautsky wanted to move toward socialism *only* through democracy, not dictatorship—as he put it, "There exist only two possibilities, either democracy, or civil war"—Trotsky argued that given that the bourgeoisie has all the weapons in its hands—factories, banks, newspapers, universities, schools, the army, the police—democracy works for them. "There is only one way: to seize power, taking away from the bourgeoisie the material apparatus of government." He then went on to justify the dissolution of the Constituent Assembly and censorship of the opposition press, which was a weapon in the hands of enemies. "The White Terror is the weapon of the historically reactionary class . . . The Red Terror is a weapon utilized against a class, doomed to destruction, which does not wish to perish. If the White Terror can only retard the historical rise of the proletariat, the Red Terror hastens the destruction of the bourgeoisie."[10]

Among historians and social scientists, approaches to Russian civil war violence and terror have clustered around two poles: agent-centered analyses, with emphasis on personality and ideological commitment; and structural-circumstantialist explanations, focusing on resistance to the revolution and the dynamics and imperatives of civil war. One of the most ubiquitous explanations of terror holds that violence was endemic to Marxism, Leninism, or Bolshevism, an essential quality of the revolutionary movement—not so much because of its strategic needs, but rather because of the personal predilections of its participants or the ideological influences of the doctrine. Violence is a political pathology that originates in personality and ideology, argues Anna Geifman in her book *Thou Shalt Kill*. Geifman sets up her work as deliberately revisionist of what she takes to be an overly romantic view of the Russian revolutionary movement, one that accepts "at face value what its members chose to reveal about themselves" and sees Marxism as relatively benign, opposed to terrorism, and guided more by rational strategic calculations than deep-seated resentments, envy, anger, and hatred.[11] In "addition to the criminal elements attracted to the radical camp," she writes, "an unusually large number of individuals with clearly pathological disturbances also joined the revolutionary ranks."[12] Social dislocation stemming from the lethal mix of

10 Leon Trotsky, *Terrorism and Communism: A Reply to Karl Kautsky* [1920] (Ann Arbor: University of Michigan Press, 1961), pp. 63–4.

11 Anna Geifman, *Thou Shalt Kill: Revolutionary Terrorism in Russia, 1894–1917* (Princeton: Princeton University Press, 1993), p. 7.

12 Ibid., p. 8.

modernization and backwardness "created irreconcilable tensions among and within newly emerging social groups, whose members suddenly found themselves out of place in the traditionally static structure of the autocratic system. It was among these superfluous people, who quickly became alienated and frustrated, that most potential terrorists originated."[13] In the Russian Empire, a disproportionate number of terrorists were from the ethnic borderlands or minorities like the Jews, Poles, Baltic peoples, and Caucasians. Women participated in such activities, and though their numbers were few, their extraordinary boldness and commitment impressed the public and the press. Workers carried out almost half the political assassinations by members of the leading terrorist party, the Socialist Revolutionaries.[14] In the revolutionary years 1905–07, thousands of government officials were murdered, and the tsarist authorities answered with military campaigns, massive arrests, and summary executions, most brutally in the non-Russian frontier regions.

As compelling as are the stories she tells, Geifman's account biases her argument by inadequately dealing with the countervailing violence of state authorities. Further, there is almost no discussion of terrorism or violence from the political Right. All references to the Black Hundreds, who carried out assassinations and instigated pogroms, portray them as victims or targets of retaliation by the Left.[15] By either failing to mention tsarist repressions or excusing them as necessary responses to revolutionary violence, she presents the violence of the revolutionaries as gratuitous, stemming from personal preferences rather than political imperatives. Leaving out other forms of mass resistance such as strikes and protests, she turns terrorism, which for most Russian revolutionary parties was a minor part of their oppositional arsenal, into the most distinctive mark of the radicals.

Where Soviet terror is concerned, one of the most widely read works is the famous (or infamous) *Black Book of Communism*, edited by Stéphane Courtois and introduced by Martin Malia.[16] A massive volume that has

---

13   Ibid., p. 11.

14   Ibid.

15   Ibid., pp. 93, 100, 110, 126, 187, 196, 217–18.

16   Stéphane Courtois, Nicolas Werth, Jean-Louis Panné, Andrzej Paczkowski, Karel Bartošek, Jean-Louis Margolin, *The Black Book of Communism: Crimes, Terror, Repression*, trans. Jonathan Murphy and Mark Kramer, with a foreword by Martin Malia (Cambridge, MA: Harvard University Press, 1999).

been translated into many languages, *The Black Book* may be the single most influential text on the Soviet Union and other state socialist regimes and movements published since Alexander Solzhenitsyn's *The Gulag Archipelago*. A painful record of crimes, terror, and repression by Soviet-style communism, its story is of colossal horror, of mass killing by states and revolutionary movements of their own citizens in the name of emancipation and human perfection, but often in the service of more mundane aims such as political advantage or personal vengeance. The principal arguments of the book are retreads that had thrived during the Cold War, been marginalized during the heyday of social history, and revived with the collapse of the Soviet Union and the emergence of a neo-totalitarianist approach to Soviet history. As Malia puts it in his foreword, "Communist regimes did not just commit criminal acts (all states do so on occasion); they were criminal enterprises in their very essence: on principle, so to speak, they all ruled lawlessly, by violence and without regard for human life."[17] Given this foundational claim, it follows that "there never was a benign, initial phase of communism before some mythical 'wrong turn' threw it off track."[18] Communist violence was a deliberative, not a reactive, policy of the revolutionary regimes, and was based in a Marxist "science" that elevated the class struggle to the central driving force of history.

Piling explanation upon explanation, as if the very weight of numbers will solve the problem of causation, Courtois explains communist atrocities sometimes by ideology and context, other times by personality, and still other times simply by the strategic requirements of holding power. "Having gone beyond individual crimes and small-scale ad-hoc massacres," he writes in the introduction, "the Communist regimes, in order to consolidate their grip on power, turned mass crime into a full-blown system of government."[19] But the variety of explanations tends to carry us away from the essentialist approach, back to contextualization and specification, which would undermine the principal purpose of such a global treatment of communism. In his concluding chapter Courtois proposes a more systematic answer to his "fundamental question," which

---

17 Martin Malia, "Foreword," *The Black Book of Communism*, p. xvii.

18 Ibid., p. xviii.

19 Stéphane Courtois, "Introduction: The Crimes of Communism," *The Black Book of Communism*, p. 2.

is: "Why did modern Communism, when it appeared in 1917, almost immediately turn into a system of bloody dictatorship and into a criminal regime?" He begins by following François Furet (originally slated to write the introduction to the original French edition before his untimely death) in tracing a revolutionary ideology and practice back to the Jacobins, although he recognizes that more pacific and democratic tendencies dominated much of the later Marx and the second socialist international.[20] The infamous nihilist Sergei Nechaev becomes emblematic of the revolutionary movement, rather than a pathological offspring.[21] And Lenin, through his older brother Aleksandr, is linked back to Nechaev, a genealogy that most historians would reject. Moreover, Courtois claims that a culture of violence is endemic to Russian life. Consider Ivan IV and Peter the Great, both of whom in their rage murdered their own sons, or the savagery of peasant revolts. As Maxim Gorky put it, "Russians have a unique sense of particular cruelty in the same way the English have a unique sense of humor."[22] Added to this was the mass violence of World War I, which a whole generation of historians now sees as central to the escalating violence of the twentieth century.

Ultimately, Bolshevik violence "was imposed on the Party by Lenin himself as soon as it seized power."[23] "Lenin's primary objective was to maintain his hold on power" in order "to put his ideas into practice and 'build socialism.'"[24] Context and culture contribute, but here we have reached the basic cause of communist violence: "Leninist ideology and the utopian will to apply to society a doctrine totally out of step with reality."[25]

The *Black Book*'s Soviet chapter by Nicolas Werth is, in the view of one favorable reviewer, the "rock on which the rest of the book stands."[26] Werth's central argument is that the Bolshevik use of violence was instrumental, driven by its need "to consolidate its hold on the institutions of power."[27] A minority government faced by hostility from the great

20 Courtois, "Conclusion: Why?" ibid., p. 727.
21 Ibid., pp. 730–1.
22 Ibid., p. 732.
23 Ibid., p. 735.
24 Ibid., p. 737.
25 Ibid.
26 Michael Scammell, "The Price of an Idea," *The New Republic*, December 20, 1999.
27 Ibid., p. 52.

peasant mass of the population, as well as significant parts of the intelligentsia and working class, Soviet power used the instruments of state violence and terror against its own people from the very beginning, throughout the 1920s, reaching a climax in the 1930s and 1940s.

The Bolshevik state is seen as a relatively unitary actor, determined to establish itself in power and willing to use violence to subdue the population, which Werth treats as a largely undifferentiated aggregate that did not share the values and ambitions of the Soviet regime. His focus is primarily, indeed almost entirely, on the perpetrators of violence, the state and party, rather than on the diverse groups and individuals that were the victims of violence or on defectors and supporters. Non-combatants are seen exclusively as objects, rather than agents in their own right.[28]

Werth's own discussion centers not so much on ideology as on the circumstances in which the Bolsheviks, weak and threatened, found themselves after having seized power. While there were a number of instances of violence against opponents in the first months of the new regime, terror did not follow the October Revolution immediately but was initiated on a wide scale only in the fall of 1918. The "Red Terror," during which somewhere between ten and fifteen thousand people were slaughtered, "marked the definitive beginning of the Bolshevik practice of treating any form of real or potential opposition as an act of civil war."[29] But rather than this practice being inherent in Bolshevism, Werth notes the doubts that many Bolsheviks had about employing terror. A commission led by Lev Kamenev even proposed the abolition of the Soviet political police agency, the Cheka. Key Bolsheviks, however, among them Lenin, Trotsky, Stalin, Sverdlov, and Dzerzhinskii, defended the Cheka and insisted that terror was necessary and justified. They easily won the day. Will the end, will the means, to paraphrase Trotsky. "The absence of any juridical or moral norm often resulted in complete autonomy for local Chekas," writes Werth. "No longer answerable for their actions to any higher authority, they became bloodthirsty and tyrannical regimes,

---

28 This point is made by Kalyvas, *The Logic of Violence in Civil War*, pp. 36–7, who notes a "partisan bias" in much of the literature on civil wars that finds it hard not to take sides in such conflicts and to sympathize with non-combatants. One side is treated as inherently moral, the other as inherently immoral.

29 Nicolas Werth, "A State Against Its People: Violence, Repression, and Terror in the Soviet Union," *The Black Book of Communism*, p. 78.

uncontrolled and uncontrollable."[30] Habits of violence formed that were difficult to change, and ideology made certain things possible or likely though often in ways unintended. When Marxists originally spoke of the liquidation of classes, it referred primarily to the elimination of the relations of production that made possible the existence of a given class, not to the physical liquidation of the individuals who made up that class. The problem, of course, was that the former meaning was easily abandoned in favor of the latter, for Marxism believed that violence underlay the dominance of one class over another.[31]

Even though he includes all forms of violence and official repression, as well as deaths from famines, in his calculations, Werth's figures for the victims of the various forms of repression, based as they are on the archives opened in the 1990s, are significantly lower than those of Courtois or Robert Conquest and other historians who did not have the benefit of the archives. Werth's answer to the twofold question of cause and effect of Soviet violence is judicious, if not definitive. Leninist violence was connected to civil war and "intended to be of short duration." The "short truce" of the NEP years indicated the possibility of more tranquil relations between state and society. But Stalin's war on the peasants, coming in peacetime and institutionalizing terror as a means of government, launched violence as a way of life for a quarter of a century.[32] Though not unconnected with practices of the civil war, Stalinist terror was something very different from what had gone before. Werth is unwilling to go further and identify some essential characteristic of Bolshevism that made these episodes, rather than the more peaceful periods, the norm for Soviet socialism.

In a mammoth comparative history of the French and Russian revolutions, Arno Mayer lays out a circumstantialist theory of violence.[33] "The Furies of revolution are fueled primarily," he writes, "by the inevitable

---

30 Ibid., p. 103.

31 Werth tells the story of a certain Smirnov who reported to Dzerzhinskii that he had discovered instances of torture and summary execution by Cheka units, and when challenged the local leader explained to him: "We didn't have time to write the reports at the time. What does it matter anyway, when we are trying to wipe out the bourgeoisie and the kulaks as a class?" Ibid.

32 Ibid., p. 263.

33 Arno J. Mayer, *The Furies: Violence and Terror in the French and Russian Revolutions* (Princeton: Princeton University Press, 2000).

and unexceptional resistance of the forces and ideas opposed to it, at home and abroad. This polarization becomes singularly fierce once revolution, confronted by this resistance, promises as well as threatens a radical refoundation of both polity and society."[34] War, of course, is the other great instance of collective violence, but "the violence accompanying revolution runs to extremes, or appears to do so, precisely because revolution entails *both* foreign and civil war."[35] *C'est la guerre* excuses, naturalizes, even glorifies, foreign wars, while revolutionary violence is seen as reprehensible, avoidable, often more a matter of choice than of necessity. Mayer rejects the primacy of personal pathology or ideology as explanations. When the state's undivided sovereignty collapses, and several centers compete for a monopoly of the legitimate use of coercion, he argues, violence ensues.[36] Revolution and counterrevolution tango together. One has to win, the other to lose. "Counter-revolution is essentially a vocation of the upper ten thousand determined not to yield their privileged positions in civil and political society."[37] There is no pact here of the kind that democratic theorists of the transition from authoritarian to liberal regimes have applauded as the most favorable means to a democratic conclusion. And, problematically, in revolution, the masses also come onto the stage of history! Besides counterrevolution there is also the "spontaneous and irregular *anti*-revolution" from below—peasant resistance to the urban revolution and counterrevolution.[38] "Evidently, counter-revolution, not unlike revolution, can be made only *with* the masses, which is not to say either the one or the other is made *for* them."[39] When counterrevolution cannot find support from below, it imports it; that is, it depends on foreign intervention. Three sources of resistance to revolution—from above, from below, and from abroad—compel the revolutionaries to defend their transformative social project with violence and terror.

In his treatment of Russian revolutionary violence, Mayer is careful to distinguish the "first terror of 1917–22" from the "second terror of the 1930s": the one inseparable from the civil war with the Whites, European

---

34 Ibid., p. 4.
35 Ibid., p. 5.
36 Ibid., p. 6.
37 Ibid., p. 57.
38 Ibid., p. 7.
39 Ibid., p. 57.

intervention, and peasant jacqueries, the other a "domestic and fratri-cidal" war of the regime on itself and its citizens.[40] The operative motive in revolutionary and counterrevolutionary violence is—in Mayer's model—vengeance, which in turn is driven by various emotions, includ-ing anger, resentment, envy, hatred, spite, malice, and pent-up rage.[41] The White Terror, he points out, was more cold-blooded and calculated than the earlier Red Terror.[42] Like Werth, he notes that the Bolsheviks were initially reluctant to turn to terror. The Whites fired the first shots of the Civil War, and their resistance led to the Red violence. With no coher-ent ideology, the Whites "were driven by a common sensibility, temper, and prepossession."[43] The diversity and lack of organization of the opponents of the Soviets were matched by the laxity and disorganization of the resistance to the Whites. All this changed with the assassination of the Petrograd Cheka chief, Moisei Uritskii, and the attempted killing of Lenin. Systematic terror was henceforth justified as necessary to maintain Soviet Power, but also as vengeance. Both sides employed terror to win the civil war, and more people were killed by the White than the Red Terror. But the two terrors were related to one another, an attribute of civil war that did not require, though was aided by, ideology.[44] For Mayer, the Russian civil wars look more like the Vendée or the Paris Commune than 1789 or 1917—spirals of distrust and hatred in a struggle over sovereignty in the state.[45] Having prevailed against all their enemies, "a certain hubris" marked the Bolshevik leaders. Their projects and methods seemed legitimated.[46] The Civil War "invited and justified recourse to violence and terror, summary justice, and iron governance . . . At the end of the civil war and the beginning of NEP, the Bolsheviks were an embattled vanguard with a siege mentality, in both national and international

40 Hannah Arendt also distinguished Leninist terror during the Civil War from Stalinist "totalitarian terror" aimed not at specific enemies but at fulfilling ideological goals, most importantly solving the problem of inequality and poverty. "Every attempt to solve the social question with political means leads into terror, and . . . it is terror which sends revolutions to their doom." *On Revolution*, p. 108.
41 Mayer, *The Furies*, pp. 172–3, 177.
42 Ibid., pp. 209–20.
43 Ibid., p. 269.
44 Ibid., p. 312.
45 Ibid., p. 348.
46 Ibid., p. 405.

terms."[47] While Mayer is certainly correct to point out that revolutionary violence is often a response to counterrevolutionary violence, the reverse is equally true. Actors in revolution and civil war, however, may also calculate that they cannot win without violence, no matter what the other side does, and choose to act violently to secure an advantage. Historians need to look beyond action and reaction to find explanation.

Responding in part to Mayer, as well as to other earlier historiography, Peter Holquist has argued for a synthetic integration of ideology and context, with particular attention to the specific conjuncture of Russia in the years 1905–21. Borrowing from Hannah Arendt, he emphasizes the practices of empire that treated the peripheries of the tsarist realm differently, far more cruelly and arbitrarily, than metropolitan Russia. Punitive expeditions in 1905 and afterwards, population removals planned or executed, and summary executions eroded the "boundary between a colonial realm of militarized 'extraordinary rule' and a domestic civil realm. This boundary was to collapse entirely with World War I and the Russian Revolution."[48] The Great War was experienced in Russia as a "long war" extending into 1921, in which "methods forged . . . for external war were turned [after 1918] inward, to domestic conflicts."[49] Civil war was the extension of the world war and the general East and Central European civil war. Holquist echoes the liberal leader Pavl Miliukov's own insight that "many, many of the developments which are commonly considered specific to the revolution actually preceded the revolution and were brought about by the conditions of wartime."[50] "Russia moved from total war to total revolution."[51]

Holquist gives us a kind of continuity model: "the violence of the Russian Civil War appears not as something perversely Russian or uniquely Bolshevik but as the most intense case of a more extended European civil war, extending through the Great War and stretching several years after its formal conclusion."[52] This conception, which reminds one of the early work of Arno Mayer, provides essential

---

47 Ibid., p. 406.
48 Peter Holquist, "Violent Russia, Deadly Marxism? Russia in the Epoch of Violence, 1905–21," *Kritika* IV, 3 (Summer 2003), p. 636.
49 Ibid., p. 637.
50 Ibid., p. 638; Pavl Miliukov, *Istoriia vtoroi russkoi revoliutsii* (Sofia, 1921), p. 25.
51 Holquist, "Violent Russia," p. 641.
52 Ibid., p. 645.

contextualization (the conjuncture of the war and revolution), but does not elaborate the causal mechanisms whereby the violence of external war becomes the violence of internal war. Implied is a simple socialization to violence—but that would be true of most of Europe, not just Russia. Here Holquist adds the dynamic that drove the story farther: "It was not 'circumstances' of war and revolution that forced the Bolsheviks into civil war, thereby derailing an otherwise popular and legitimate revolution. Civil war was what the Bolsheviks *sought*."[53] Ideology for Holquist is not a set of disembodied ideas but a program embraced as a "compelling interpretation" of people's "lived experience."[54] "The desire to remake Russian society provided the urge; the tools of wartime mobilization, the means." Practices "originally devised in colonial contexts and massively expanded during the Great War" were now employed in a domestic civil war."[55] The Soviets, the Whites, and Green insurgents all drew on "a common repertoire of measures," what Holquist calls "a common unspoken set of regularities in political practice," that were imported from the war fronts. In his major book on the civil wars, Holquist asserts more starkly: "The ideology propounded by the Bolsheviks was explicitly antagonistic, envisioning constant class war until the achievement of communism."[56] Although he locates the principal cause in political goals, nevertheless he gravitates quite close to an argument that the structure or logic of civil war may best explain its attendant violence.

In Russia, "the practices of the governing and the governed crystallized in a concrete experience of civil war."[57] Bolshevik violence, however, is different, writes Holquist. It was "not a temporary and extraordinary tool intended only for the period of civil conflict. Rather, the Soviet state would wield state violence throughout the following decades as part of its open-ended project to shape a new, revolutionary society."[58] Here his continuity model takes us through the 1920s into Stalinism and, presumably, beyond. What had been learned in war became "a permanent feature

---

53 Ibid.
54 Ibid.
55 Ibid.
56 Peter Holquist, *Making War, Forging Revolution: Russia's Continuum of Crisis, 1914–1921* (Cambridge, MA: Harvard University Press, 2002), p. 166.
57 Holquist, "Violent Russia," p. 650.
58 Ibid., p. 651.

of the Soviet state," but refracted through and amplified by Bolshevik ideology, which, "sustained by resentments fostered in the late imperial period and exacerbated by the course of 1917, came to structure Soviet state violence."[59]

In his work on the civil war in the Don region, Holquist explains the "merciless mass terror" aimed at decossackization in 1919 as the product of a pan-European modernist episteme in which population manipulation—including deportations, ethnic cleansing, and even genocide—are legitimized by the goal of creating (what Zygmunt Bauman has referred to as) a "gardening state."[60] Yet in his narrative he carefully distinguishes between the brief period (January 24 to March 16, 1919) when physical extermination of the Cossack elite and active rebels was permitted and promoted by the Bolshevik center and local zealots, like Sergei Syrtsov, and the prior and succeeding policies of more restrained repression, relocation, and re-education. Marxism, a modernist ideology, would seem to favor changing mentalities and allegiances through social and economic reform, rather than taking the biological view of Cossacks as an ethnicity essentialized as irreparably anti-Soviet and therefore requiring extirpation. Yet thousands were killed, not by vindictive peasants or even by order of militant local officials: for an infamous month and a half, they were executed at the express instruction of a central party organ, the Orgburo (Organizational Bureau). After mid-March, this elimination of a class reverted to a policy of ending the Cossacks' special status, abolishing their privileges and ownership of land and their special administration. Cossacks were no longer treated monolithically but, like other groups, as differentiated by class.

The origins of Soviet "state" terror are explored in the third volume of what will turn out to be a quartet on the revolution in the Russian capital, Petrograd, by Alexander Rabinowitch. His detailed exploration of post-October builds on his earlier work to ask what is certainly the central question of the post-October period: Why did a democratic revolution based on grassroots councils and committees turn into a dictatorship that employed state terror against its opponents, real and imagined, within

---

59   Ibid., p. 652.
60   Peter Holquist, "'Conduct Merciless Mass Terror': Decossackization on the Don, 1919," *Cahiers du Monde Russe* XXXVIII, 1-2 (January–June 1999), p. 152. See also Holquist, *Making War, Forging Revolution,* pp. 166–7.

months of its coming to power? Especially consequential was the decision of leading Bolsheviks in January 1918 to dissolve the Constituent Assembly, a grand constitutional convention that had been elected relatively democratically, rather than let it continue to meet and present an alternative sovereign authority to the Soviet government. By using armed force, first against demonstrators and then in preventing the delegates from reassembling, the Soviets declared civil war on all those in propertied society, on the non-Russian peripheries, and among moderate socialists who were unprepared to accept the Leninist conceptualization of socialist revolution. October drove many important political groups into opposition, and January drove many more to armed rebellion. Transcaucasia, for example, began its drift, first toward autonomy, then an independent federation, and eventually to three separate republics.[61]

Lenin was unafraid of civil war; indeed, he may have welcomed it. For him and his comrades, the lessons of history, as interpreted by Marx, came from France in 1792 and 1871. Lenin was convinced that the liberal Kadet party and their military supporters had already started the civil war.

> *When a revolutionary class is waging war against the possessing classes that resist it, then it must suppress this resistance; and we shall suppress the suppressors' resistance by all the methods they used to suppress the proletariat; other methods have not yet been invented . . .*
>
> *It is ridiculous to stop at measures of isolation. The bourgeoisie is using its capital to organize counterrevolution, and to this there can be but one reply: prison! That is how [the Jacobins] acted in the great French revolution; they declared the bourgeois parties outside the law.*[62]

Indeed, the Kadets abandoned their strategy of working legally once the Constituent Assembly was dissolved on January 5 (18), 1918. A secret

---

61 See Ronald Grigor Suny, *The Making of the Georgian Nation*, 2nd ed. (Bloomington and Indianapolis, IN: Indiana University Press, 1994), pp. 185–208.

62 Lenin's speech at the seventeenth session of the Central Executive Committee of the Soviets, December 1, 1917, in John L. H. Keep (trans. and ed.), *The Debate on Soviet Power: Minutes of the All-Russian Central Executive Committee of Soviets, Second Convocation, October 1917–January 1918* (Oxford: Clarendon Press, 1979), pp. 175–6.

meeting of their Central Committee in Moscow resolved to "unite all available forces around the authority of a single person, and establish a temporary military dictatorship." The Constituent Assembly, they believed, was inadequate to the task of establishing "authority" and "order."[63]

What is most striking about the first months, even the greater part of the first year, of Bolshevik rule is that mass terror was not employed; that the use of violence was restrained, arose sporadically, tactically, and was reactive, usually prompted by armed challenges from opponents. Moreover, even these piecemeal measures, along with censorship, the closing of rival party organizations and the municipal Dumas, were condemned as "terror," an indication that in the early revolutionary environment many expected a far more benign transition to socialism than did the Bolsheviks. For Rabinowitch, terror was "the price of survival."

> Contrary to conventional wisdom, the Red Terror that exploded in Petrograd on 30 August was not the consequence of a nationwide political crackdown inspired by Lenin and orchestrated by the Cheka, nor was it a spontaneous, popular response to the assassination [of Uritskii] on 30 August and the failed attempt on Lenin's life that evening. The burden of available evidence indicates that these events can best be understood as the culmination of a gradual process during which the moderating influence of such key individuals as Uritskii, Krestinskii, and Proshian was replaced by pressure for systematic Red Terror, in part "from below."[64]

Rabinowitch provides a description of the process rather than a causal analysis, but his narrative can be read to argue that three factors led to the terror:

- The propensity of some leaders like Lenin, Trotsky, and Zinoviev to favor the use of terror silenced more moderate voices.
- Mass unrest and resistance to the Bolsheviks provided positive incentives to the use of terror.

---

63   William G. Rosenberg, *Liberals in the Russian Revolution: The Constitutional Democratic Party, 1917–1921* (Princeton: Princeton University Press, 1974), p. 285.
64   Ibid., p. 398.

- A fatal combination of resistant reality and the Bolsheviks' ideological framing, their understanding of the nature of their revolution and their enemies, led them to believe that terror was essential for the survival of the socialist struggle.

By contextualizing Lenin's choices, Rabinowitch distances himself from those historians who believe in essential characteristics of Russia or Russians that inevitably lead to authoritarianism and violence. Rather than arising from national character or a fatalistic political culture, terror was inscribed in civil war, which in turn was unavoidable once the Leninists had made certain strategic choices. Contingency and human agency are central to his arguments, though the devastation of the world war, the chaos of the revolution, and the weakened fabric of Russian society tightly constrained what any leader could have done.

Civil War as Explanation

Power is war, the continuation of war by other means. At this point, we can invert Clausewitz's proposition and say that politics is the continuation of war by other means. This would imply three things. First, that power relations, as they function in society like ours, are essentially anchored in a certain relationship of force that was established in and through war at a given historical moment that can be historically specified. And while it is true that political power puts an end to war and establishes or attempts to establish the reign of peace in civil society, it certainly does not do so in order to suspend the effects of power or to neutralize the disequilibrium revealed by the last battle of a war. According to this hypothesis, the role of political power is perpetually to use a sort of silent war to reinscribe that relationship of force, and to reinscribe it in institutions, economic inequalities, language, and even the bodies of individuals.

Michel Foucault[65]

War was a central metaphor for Marxists—class war, civil war—and particularly for more radical Marxists such as Lenin. General William E. Odom goes so far as to claim that "Lenin had not missed the key feature

---

65   Michel Foucault, *"Society Must Be Defended": Lectures at the Collège du France, 1975–1976*, trans. David Macey (New York: Picador, 2003), pp. 16–17.

of Marxism: it was, at root, a theory of war."[66] And revolution was, for Lenin, not an election campaign with rules of engagement that included gracious retreat from the contest, but warfare, in which the consequence of losing could easily be death. Elections are about garnering majority support; war and revolution are about having sufficient forces, almost invariably armed men, at the right place at the right time This was a concept equally well understood by Lenin's principal enemies, the White generals. For them, the Civil War was simply war, a matter of overwhelming the opposition militarily and subduing the population that supported the enemies of the old order. Both sides understood that support can more easily be a product of revolutionary or military victory than a precondition, that hearts and minds could be conquered more easily by victors than by embattled contestants.

Intrigued with insurrection and concerned with its proper preparation, Lenin read Clausewitz's *On War* early in 1915 in exile in Switzerland. He wrote that "With reference to wars the main thesis of dialectics is that *'war is simply the continuation of politics by other* (namely violent) *means.'*"[67] In his view, Clausewitz was perfectly consistent with Marx and Engels. He would also have agreed with Kalyvas that most revolutions, along with sustained peasant insurrections, revolutionary or ethnic insurgencies, anti-colonial uprisings, and resistance wars against foreign occupiers should all be considered civil wars.[68]

Civil war has best been defined as "armed combat within the boundaries of a recognized sovereign entity between parties subject to a common authority at the outset of the hostilities." It is an "internal war," "the violent physical division of the sovereign entity into rival armed camps" that occurs when there is an "effective breakdown of the monopoly of violence by way of armed internal challenge."[69] Civil war, then, is an armed struggle over sovereignty between people or groups with rival, exclusive claims to supreme authority. In 1917 the concept and practice of *dvoevlastie* (dual power), the division of power between the soviets and the Provisional Government, already contained the seeds of civil war

---

66 William E. Odom, *The Collapse of the Soviet Military* (New Haven and London: Yale University Press, 1998), p. 5.

67 Jacob W. Kipp, "Lenin and Clausewitz: The Militarization of Marxism, 1914–1921," *Military Affairs* XLIX, 4 (October 1985), p. 186.

68 Kalyvas, *The Logic of Violence in Civil War*, p. 19.

69 Ibid., pp. 17–18.

once either side no longer recognized the right of the other to share in power. Already in mid-1917, society was divided between the *demokratiia* (revolutionary democracy, the lower classes) and *tsenzovoe obshchestvo* (propertied society and the liberal intelligentsia), with the lower classes overwhelmingly voting socialist and supporting the soviets. In July 1917, for example, in the Volga region of Saratov, 82.3 percent voted for social-ist parties in the municipal duma elections, about the same percentage that would vote for the Constituent Assembly in November in that prov-ince.[70] Soviets were the popular expression of working people, institu-tions that represented only the lower classes and opposed the privileges of the middle and upper classes. Those seeds of civil war came to fruition with the October Revolution, when the Bolsheviks constituted a govern-ment, but not yet a state. They held power but hardly a monopoly of legitimate violence, could not control vast areas in the country they claimed to rule, and were faced by numerous rival governments each claiming their own sovereign authority, either over Russia as a whole or over national regions. For Reds as well as Whites, the Civil War was both a contest over supreme power and a process of trying to build a state. Over the next four years the Soviets managed that successfully, but the Whites failed to restore or build anew a counterrevolutionary state.[71]

Revolution, like war, plays by different rules from normal, institution-alized politics, whether democratic or authoritarian. Kalyvas notes that "War structures choices and selects actors in radically different ways from peace—even violent peace."[72] "Civil war induces polarization, intro-duces uncertainty, alters expectations."[73] As international relations scholars have noted in their turn toward explaining civil and ethnic wars, the weakening or breakdown of an effective unified sovereign authority creates a condition like that of interstate anarchy, in which rival groups cannot expect a credible commitment from others to protect them. As they seek pre-emptively to defend themselves or destroy the enemy, these

70 Donald Raleigh, *Experiencing Civil War: Politics, Society, and Revolutionary Culture in Saratov, 1917–1922* (Princeton and Oxford: Princeton University Press, 2002), p. 27.

71 In the national borderlands there were several examples of relatively successful state-making, e.g., Poland, Finland, Latvia, Lithuania, Estonia, and Menshevik Georgia, though the latter was cut short by the invasion of the Red Army.

72 Ibid., p. 22.

73 Ibid., p. 38.

groups create a security dilemma that in turn incites its rivals to arm and act. A spiral of violence follows.[74]

But this cool rationalist and structuralist analysis must be supplemented by consideration of why the various actors, individuals and groups, perceive that they face dangers or even existential threats, and why they desire exclusive state power. Here the mediations of what might be called ideological framings, political cultures or affective dispositions related to collective identifications come into play. The Bolsheviks were not Buddhists. As politicians and revolutionaries, they believed in acquiring, even seizing, state power as a necessary condition of achieving the socialist transformation domestically and, more importantly, internationally. When in June 1917 the moderate Menshevik Iraklii Tsereteli asked his rhetorical question, is there a party ready to take power, Lenin shouted out without hesitating, *Est!* (There is). Once in power, the Bolsheviks, eventually even the moderates, were willing to accept the consequences of that choice to take power. They were never prepared to give it up, however, convinced that history had moved beyond the bourgeois democratic stage and that they were not bound by the results of elections that went against them. It goes without saying that if, in a political contest, possessors of power are unwilling to step down when a majority or winning plurality decides they should, there can be no talk of democracy. The Bolsheviks were certain that their struggle was about destroying or being destroyed, dedicating all efforts toward the preservation of Soviet power in Russia and working toward the international socialist revolution then on the horizon. As the Bolshevik defender of Cheka terror Martyn Latsis put it, "one must not only destroy the forces of the enemy, but also demonstrate that whoever raises the sword against the existing order of class, will perish by the sword."[75]

Besides strategic choices and ideology, emotions are ubiquitous in wars, revolutions, and civil wars; they motivate actors and mobilize groups, guide preferences and choices, heighten commitment, and provide heuristics for discriminating friend from foe, danger from security. Yet it would be a mistake to make the easy Hobbesian deduction that violent

---

74 David Lake and Donald Rothchild (eds.), *The International Spread of Ethnic Conflict: Fear, Diffusion, and Escalation* (Princeton: Princeton University Press, 1998), p. 4.

75 Martyn Latsis [Jānis Sudrabs], *Izvestiia*, August 1918; cited in Courtois (ed.), *The Black Book of Communism*, p. 74.

emotions are so fundamental to universal human nature that the simple removal of restraints is sufficient explanation for violence in these anarchic conditions. More specificity regarding which emotions are involved, their etiology and progress, is required. Rather than bubbling up from below and being primarily identified with the primitive urges of the masses, emotions are very often aimed toward a specific action and a particular goal. Revenge, for example, an emotion often rooted in a sense of justice—the *lex talionis* of the Bible, "an eye for an eye"—aims at re-establishing a lost equilibrium, setting things right; but civil war vengeance can produce not an equitable balance but an escalation of exactions and an uncontrolled spiral of violence. In conditions of great uncertainty and unpredictability, emotions like anxiety—fear without a clear and present object—may be prevalent. When horrors befall loved ones, unfocused rage may explode. But more directed emotions, such as anger at what someone has done to you or yours, or hatred of a person or group that poses by their very presence an existential threat to you, or resentment at unfair distributions of wealth, power, or privilege, are also loose in the revolutionary land. Violence can be both the product of emotions and the cause of emotions.

Violence preceded the revolution, for the revolution broke out in the midst of the most ferocious war in which humankind had engaged up to that time. The use of arms to get one's way and to survive was a daily occurrence, and ordinary people could make the simple equation between physical force and political power. In February 1917, the mystique of state power evaporated when the counterforce of the crowds in the streets of Petrograd overwhelmed the government's forces within a few days. The unwillingness of the tsar's troops, even Cossacks and guards regiments, to fire on the demonstrators made it impossible for the monarchy to remain. Witnesses described a kind of euphoria, a new open horizon of possibility. But fear and resentment were also present. The struggle in Petrograd then became a contest for sovereign power in Russia, for possession of the state authority. The internationally recognized legitimate authority, the Provisional Government, did not however possess a monopoly (or even a preponderance) of legitimate violence. While officers and some soldiers were prepared to defend the regime, real influence over the bulk of the rank and file, both in the army and more so in the navy, was in the hands of the Petrograd Soviet. Governments were shaken or fell when armed people in the street (in April and July) demanded it, and in

August only the resistance of armed workers prevented a rightist military coup (by Kornilov). When the Bolsheviks made their bid for power in October, they already controlled the Petrograd garrison and had the loyalty of most of the army in the region. Their "coup" was relatively bloodless, though to the opponents of Soviet Power it signaled the beginning of civil war.[76]

Rabinowitch's research shows how fragile the Soviet government was in its early months. Not only did the bulk of the intelligentsia and professionals refuse to cooperate with the Bolsheviks, armed resistance to their government broke out immediately. Civil servants of the tsarist and the Provisional Government, who went on strike for months, were the initial targets of repression. "In the course of its struggle with the civil servants," a Menshevik report stated, "the Soviet government departed from democratic principles for the first time. It resorted to the arrest of strike leaders, depriving them of their rights, dissolving their organizations and trade unions, and forbidding them to assemble and convene congresses."[77] An even more immediate danger came from anti-Bolshevik military leaders. After he escaped from the Winter Palace, Alexander Kerensky tried to retake Petrograd with the aid of the Cossack General Petr Krasnov. A revolt of cadets was organized in the capital but quickly suppressed. Right SRs plotted the assassination of Lenin and other top Bolsheviks, and a group of army officers actually fired on his car on New Year's Eve. The Cossack government in the south invited the Provisional Government to their region where they could together organize the anti-Bolshevik struggle. Generals Mikhail Alekseev, Aleksei Kaledin, Anton Denikin, and Lavr Kornilov organized the Volunteer Army in southern Russia, attracting tsarist officers, disaffected university students, and liberal and conservative politicians to their cause. In January 1918, Bolshevik headquarters in the Smolny Institute was repeatedly disrupted by bomb scares, and the same month the Cheka uncovered a conspiracy by several thousand officers, possibly backed by the British, to overthrow the Soviet government. In fact, the British were actively plotting against the Soviets,

76 For elaboration of the events of the revolution of 1917 and an analysis of the Bolsheviks' victory, see chapters 4 and 5.

77 Report of the Menshevik Central Committee to the Second International, July 1918, in Vladimir N. Brovkin (ed. and trans.), *Dear Comrades: Menshevik Reports on the Bolshevik Revolution and the Civil War* (Stanford: Hoover Institution Press, 1991), p. 106.

employing the mysterious adventurer and spy Sidney Reilly and fellow agent Robert Bruce Lockhart, and they soon sent troops into the north of Russia. Meanwhile the German Army moved eastward after the breakdown of the initial armistice, threatening the capital and precipitating the government's flight to Moscow. By the late spring of 1918 the Czech legions revolted in the Urals, and the Soviets were faced with full-blown civil war and armed foreign intervention.

Despite their qualms about terror, the more radical wing of the pro-peasant party, the Left SRs, joined the Bolsheviks in government in early December, about the same time that the Military-Revolutionary Committee that had directed the October coup was replaced by the infamous Cheka (the Extraordinary Commission for the Struggle with Counterrevolution and Speculation). The new People's Commissar of Justice was a prominent leader of the Left SR party, Isaac Steinberg, who for the next half-year served as a principal watchdog and constraint on the Cheka and those chafing to unleash mass terror. Within days of taking office, he issued a decree reviewing the arrests of people held by the revolutionary tribunals. For Lenin and his Cheka chief, Felix Dzerzhinskii, this was a severe challenge, and Steinberg followed with a series of further attempts to call the Cheka to account. In these first few months, while their opponents decried what they called "terror," in fact the Bolsheviks did not engage in much violence. But hundreds of newspapers, including socialist ones, were closed; some prominent opponents were detained; and steps were taken to put down armed action against the regime. There were incidents of popular retribution and rampant crime in the city. In his speeches Zinoviev singled out the Right SRs as guilty of terrorism, and early in January the Petrograd Soviet resolved that any violence from "the bourgeoisie and its servants, the Right SRs" would be answered with mass terror.[78] Armed Red Guards recruited from factories patrolled the streets. Untrained and unsupervised, they often overreacted, and people died. On January 5 and again on the 11th, they were deployed when demonstrators attempted to show their support for the opening of the Constituent Assembly. In the bloodiest incident (January 11), twenty-one people were killed. At the same time the yawning chasm between the masses and the liberals was brutally revealed when two of the most prominent members of the Kadet party, Fedor Kokoshkin and Andrei Shingarev,

---

78 Rabinowitch, *The Bolsheviks in Power*, p. 100.

were murdered in their hospital beds by embittered Baltic sailors. Lenin reacted with shock, but he decided not to pursue the case when shipmates of the culprits resisted their punishment.

The overwhelming worker support for the Bolsheviks that characterized the first months of the new regime rapidly began to dissipate in the new year. A Menshevik report on the situation in Central Industrial Region noted,

> Mass unemployment and famine cause disillusionment in Bolshevik socialism, and the latest events, such as the disbanding of the Constituent Assembly and the shootings at the demonstration in its defense, caused a number of mass protests and made many, even among those sympathetic to the Bolsheviks, have second thoughts. They are beginning to listen willingly to the speeches of the Mensheviks, who were not allowed to speak only a short time earlier. *Only the soldiers* are quite satisfied with the Bolshevik regime, although their numbers in the cities have diminished. (But this does not prevent them from playing the same role in the soviets.) Streaming into the villages, they disband local zemstvos and terrorize the peasant population, thus becoming a new base of Bolshevik power, this time in the villages.[79]

The Bolsheviks were forced to face the uncomfortable fact that there was significant disaffection among workers and a drift toward other socialist parties. The very base of Bolshevik strength was eroding, and the Soviet leaders calculated that their government faced an existential danger that required curtailing workers' democracy, relying on the loyalty (and ferocity) of the Red Guards, and limiting the ability of oppositional parties to operate openly. Fear of counterrevolution and anxiety about the disunity of their own party and supporters encouraged the Bolsheviks to allow, even instigate, violent reprisals against opponents and rivals.

As Arno Mayer and many others have noted, for the Bolsheviks the French models were a template for state terror. Just a month after the October takeover, Trotsky answered the wariness of the Left SRs about the application of censorship, arrests, and the use of force by declaring: "There is nothing immoral in the proletariat finishing off a class that is

---

79 Brovkin (ed. and trans.), *Dear Comrades*, p. 67.

collapsing . . . You wax indignant at the naked terror which we are applying against our class enemies. But let me assure you that in one month's time at the most, it will assume more frightful forms, modeled after the terror of the great French revolutionaries. Not the fortress [of Peter and Paul] but the guillotine awaits our enemies." To which the Left SR Sergei Mstislavskii pointedly retorted that, for socialist revolutionaries, the Bolsheviks seemed "entrapped in purely bourgeois forms of political revolution."[80]

During the long crisis over Brest-Litovsk, the Bolsheviks were faced with the gravest danger to their government, not only from the Germans but from the reluctance of people to join their forces to defend Soviet Power.[81] The Provisional Executive Committee of the Sovnarkom, without discussion by the whole government, issued a proclamation, "The Socialist Fatherland is in Danger," that "encouraged shooting common criminals and counterrevolutionaries at the scene of their crime."[82] Left SRs protested this extension of Cheka terror, while the Cheka used the document as a permit to carry out executions. Prisoners were routinely shot; Red Army soldiers, Red Guards, and anarchists carried out their own summary justice. "Petrograd's hospitals received piles of bodies picked up on the street. Frequently, the killers made off with the victims' clothing."[83] Still there were dissenting voices and efforts to restrain the bloodshed. Uritskii, head of the Petrograd Cheka, opposed the shootings, as did Nikolai Krestinskii, Commissar of Justice in the Sovnarkom of the Petrograd Commune, and the Left SR Prosh Proshian, Commissar for Internal Affairs. There were struggles within the Cheka between those favoring a more violent policy and those opposing. Terror alternated with amnesty. When some party members moved to dissolve the Petrograd Cheka, Dzerzhinskii telegraphed Zinoviev from Moscow to object. Even Zinoviev, who was usually one of the loudest proponents of terror, spoke of the necessity "for Soviet power to renounce its previous methods of struggle against political opponents" and "not to treat them in ways that were customary in all imperialist and monarchist states" (April 29, 1918). Yet, on

---

80   Keep (ed. and trans.), *The Debate on Soviet Power*, p. 178.
81   Rabinowitch, *The Bolsheviks in Power*, p. 186.
82   Ibid., p. 187.
83   Ibid., p. 221.

May 9, Red Army soldiers fired on a demonstration of workers in Kolpino outside Petrograd, wounding several and killing a union official.[84]

The Right SRs decided in May 1918 to call for the overthrow of the Bolshevik government, and to work with the Allies to that end. The Mensheviks, however, refused to collaborate either with the Allies or the Germans and opted for a political, rather than armed, struggle against Lenin's authority. Yet the Bolsheviks saw little distinction among "those who are not with us," and treated them all as if they "are against us." They manipulated local soviet elections, closed newspapers of opposition parties, and arrested their rivals.[85] On June 14, 1918, the Bolshevik majority expelled the Mensheviks along with the Right SRs from the All-Russian Central Executive Committee of Soviets (VTsIK), the legislature chosen by the congress of soviets. Two days later, the Soviet government that eight months earlier had abolished the death penalty (a move Lenin had disapproved), reintroduced it.

The leader of the moderate socialist Menshevik party, Iulii Martov, wrote to a comrade in Germany "immediately after [this] small Bolshevik coup d'état":

> With our expulsion from the soviets, the very foundation of the Soviet constitution is destroyed because the soviets have ceased to represent all the workers. In those places where we are in the majority, the soviets will be liquidated. This decree summarizes the process that has been going on everywhere during the last few months. Everywhere the workers demanded new elections to those soviets that were elected before the October coup. The Soviets [the government] have stubbornly resisted this demand. As a result, struggle over this question often escalated to workers' strikes and the suppression of workers' demonstrations by armed forces (Tula, Yaroslavl, etc.).

He noted that the Bolsheviks had the support of factory committees, but, like Bolshevized soviets, these refused "to hold new elections and likewise

---

84   William G. Rosenberg, "Russian Labor and Bolshevik Power after October," *Slavic Review* XLIV, 2 (Summer 1985), pp. 232–3.

85   For examples of how Bolsheviks dealt with opponents and oppositional parties winning elections to soviets, see Brovkin (ed. and trans.), *Dear Comrades*, pp. 66–93.

have been turned into a hired bureaucracy . . . This is what our Paraguayan communism looks like."[86]

The inroads that rival socialists made among workers and in elections to the soviets were met by the Bolsheviks with crude repression. Historian Vladimir N. Brovkin argues, "The Bolsheviks resorted to dictatorial measures not because they were powerful but because they saw the growing threats to their hold on power."[87] In his view "the Bolsheviks needed and wanted a civil war," for it made it "much easier to justify the use of armed force to crush open rebellion," to use the "drastic measures" necessary to keep the party in power, and enforce party unity. "Civil war gave Bolsheviks a chance to win back militarily what they were losing in the ballot box."[88] He presents the civil war as Bolsheviks against workers. The party used conscripted workers and peasants to defeat rebellious workers, intellectuals, merchants, and the other socialist parties. The Bolshevik victory is largely accounted for by their opponents' disunity, which allowed them "to defeat their enemies one at a time," as well as their "systematic mass terror."[89] Brovkin's focus on the Mensheviks' considerable support among workers in some key cities—though not in others—fails to appreciate the gravitation over time of significant numbers of workers, recruited peasants, and others making the principled or simply pragmatic choice to side with the Bolsheviks. While he oversimplifies Bolshevik calculations and plays down the party's support, he makes a powerful point that the Bolsheviks were willing to use any means at their disposal to hold on to power and reduce the influence of their opponents. For Lenin, politics worked within the logic of war.

On July 6, 1918, the Left SRs in Moscow assassinated the German Ambassador Count Wilhelm Mirbach. That same day, SRs launched an anti-Soviet uprising in the Volga town of Iaroslavl'. These events marked what Rabinowitch calls "the suicide of the Left SRs," the actions that precipitated the elimination of the Left SRs from the Soviet government and from the highest political circles, and the formation of a one-party government that would last for the next seven decades. The road to terror descended sharply. Yet even when on June 20, the popular commissar

---

86   Letter of Iu. O. Martov to A. N. Stein, June 16, 1918, ibid., pp. 96–7, 101.

87   Vladimir N. Brovkin, *The Mensheviks After October: Socialist Opposition and the Rise of the Bolshevik Dictatorship* (Ithaca: Cornell University Press, 1987), p. xvii.

88   Brovkin (ed. and trans.), *Dear Comrades*, p. 7.

89   Ibid., p. 11.

V. Volodarskii (Moisei Goldshtein) was assassinated, Uritskii held the Cheka back from reprisals or taking hostages. When Lenin heard of Petrograd's mild reaction to the killing, he angrily cabled:

> We heard only today in the CC [Central Committee] that in Piter, workers wanted to respond to the killing of Volodarskii with mass terror and that you (not you personally, but the Piter Chekists or Pekists [Petrograd Committee men]) held them back.
>
> I protest decisively.
>
> We are compromising ourselves: we threatened, even in the resolutions of the Soviet of Deputies, mass terror, and when it comes to that *we hold back* the revolutionary initiative of the masses, which is completely in the right.
>
> This is in-tol-er-able!
>
> The terrorists will consider us rags. The time is one of extreme warfare [*arkhivoennoe*]. It is essential to encourage this energy and the massive quality of the terror against the counterrevolutionaries, especially in Piter, which sets a *decisive* example.[90]

Trotsky spoke in Petrograd whipping up enthusiasm for stronger measures, and a local congress of soviets at the very beginning of August resolved that "Soviet power must insure the safety of the rear [by] maintaining a close watch over the bourgeoisie [and] instituting a policy of mass terror toward it . . . Our motto is mass armament of workers and the concentration of all forces for a life or death military attack on the counterrevolutionary bourgeoisie."[91]

Much of the violence by Bolsheviks in the first year took place far from Petrograd, in the provinces, where local officials dealt harshly with capitalists and aristocrats and clamped down hard on oppositional parties. At first isolated acts of revenge were taken by armed groups, against criminals, "speculators" (traders who overcharged their customers), and people identified as *burzhui* (bourgeois), but in general there were few pogroms against the better-off or other ethnic groups. Once active fighting broke out between Soviet and anti-Soviet forces in the summer of 1918, however,

---

90 Lenin to Zinoviev, June 26, 1918, in V. I. Lenin, *Polnoe sobranie sochineniia* (Moscow: Izdatel'stvo politicheskoi literatury, 1970), p. 106. (Henceforth, *PSS.*)

91 Rabinowitch, *The Bolsheviks in Power*, p. 324.

violence against civilians escalated. The most prominent victims of Red terror in the early days of the Civil War were the last tsar, Nicholas II, his wife, Aleksandra, and their children and servants. They had been under house arrest in the Urals city of Ekaterinburg, when on the night of July 16, 1918, local Bolsheviks, afraid that the imperial family would fall into the hands of advancing anti-Soviet forces, and with the sanction of top party leaders in Moscow, took the family and their servants into the basement of the Ipatev house and shot them. The executioners then hacked the bodies with swords and threw them into a pit.

On the morning of August 30, a military cadet, Leonid Kannegisser, shot and killed Uritskii to avenge the death of a friend, ironically eliminating the principal opponent of mass terror in the city. That same evening Lenin addressed Moscow workers, ending his speech with the words: "For us there is one alternative: victory or death." As he was leaving the hall, he was shot twice, allegedly by the Right SR Fanny Kaplan. Zinoviev, the head of the Petrograd Soviet, hysterically called for terror. He declared that the counterrevolution had raised its head, that two important party officials had been murdered, and that it was time to take appropriate measures. He proposed that workers be allowed to deal with the intelligentsia as they wish, right on the streets. Elena Stasova was appalled by Zinoviev's words, and when other comrades sat in stunned silence, she dared to take the floor and offer her opinion that he had spoken out of panic. The "boss of Petrograd" bolted from the room in anger, only to return in his overcoat prepared to go directly to the Putilov works to mobilize the workers. The other members of the Petersburg Committee resolved that instead of stirring up the workers, three-person commissions, the *troiki*, would ferret out "the former officers and other counterrevolutionary elements."[92]

Petrograd leaders rejected Zinoviev's proposal, but from Moscow, Iakov Sverdlov, the chairman of the All-Russian Central Executive Committee of the Soviets, called for a "massive red terror against the bourgeoisie and its agents." On September 2, the anniversary of the Terror of the French Jacobins, the hesitation ended and systematic terror began in Soviet Russia. Between 500 and 1,300 people were shot in Petrograd and 6,000 arrested in reprisal for the murder of Uritskii. Officials of the tsarist regime and wealthy people were the prime targets. Among those executed were four former tsarist ministers. However, few

---

92   E. D. Stasova, *Stranitsy zhizni i bor'by* (Moscow: Gosizpolit, 1957), pp. 100–1.

SRs—members of the party that had initiated assassinations of Soviet officials—were killed. Violence and terrorism, both ubiquitous in the revolution, now metastasized into terror. Terrorism and terror were tactical choices made by revolutionary actors—choices made "in the heat of battle," perhaps, but adopted consciously, clearly, deliberatively. As Peter Holquist put it, "Terror was not some unstructured, indiscriminate slaughter; nor was it a spontaneous, terrible retribution by peasants for past Cossack abuses. Terror was policy—organized, sanctioned, and conducted by officially established institutions."[93]

The nature and targets of the terror had changed significantly in the late summer of 1918. Martov reported that the Menshevik party had been effectively annihilated in Soviet Russia.

> Everything is destroyed: the press, the organization and so forth. Unlike czarist times, it is impossible to "go underground" to do any fruitful work because not only do the gendarmes, street sweepers, and the like keep an eye out for unreliability, but a segment of ordinary citizens (Communists and those with vested interest in the Soviet regime) regard denunciation, surveillance, and shadowing not only as proper but as the fulfillment of their supreme duty.

The earlier upsurge in worker opposition to Bolshevism had favored the more moderate socialist parties, but the collapse of industry and growing hunger led to workers leaving the cities for the countryside. "The *workers'* movement seemed to disappear. The masses of workers who remained at the factories lost hope that industry could be saved, turned their backs on the 'opposition,' which had previously expressed their discontent, and threw themselves into total apoliticism and unending indifference."[94] Economic collapse along with terror enforced by the Red Guards destroyed any coherent working-class opposition. Raw armed power had effectively been used against a democratic alternative to Bolshevik dictatorship. The Bolsheviks did not play fair; they did not respect the very rules of democratic politics that they had defended up to October 1917.

The Menshevik party split: the Left followed Martov as a loyal opposition

---

93 Holquist, *Making War, Forging Revolution*, p. 182.
94 Letter of Iu. O. Martov to A. N. Stein, October 25, 1918, in Brovkin (ed. and trans.), *Dear Comrades*, pp. 124–5.

to Bolshevism, renouncing armed struggle but continuing to organize workers against the dictatorship whenever possible; the Right moved toward the Right SRs and advocated an armed response to the Soviets. Other Mensheviks simply left the party and politics, emigrated, or joined the Communists and worked in Soviet institutions. The political struggle between the Bolsheviks and their opponents shifted by the fall, from individual terrorism and sporadic, isolated revolts against occasionally applied state terror, to organized warfare between rapidly mobilized armies (as well as less formally constituted partisan groups) and a state terror more systematically deployed. The nature of the enemy changed. "This is getting worse and worse," Martov went on, "because an ever-greater role in the anti-Bolshevik struggle is being played by all sorts of officers' and cadets' units, with sympathies ranging from Kornilovite at best to monarchist at worse."[95]

The civil and nationalist wars that raged for the next three years can be divided into three distinct periods. The first year of Bolshevik power up to the end of the world war in November 1918 was marked by the initial organization of the hostile camps, the first wave of foreign intervention, and loosely formed armies engaged in both partisan and regular warfare. From the Armistice to November 1919, General Denikin in the south, Admiral Aleksandr Kolchak in Siberia, and General Nikolai Iudenich in the Baltic presented potentially serious threats to the survival of the Soviet state. The Communists, as the Bolsheviks now called themselves, softened some of their earlier policies, at least for a time, and tried to build a broader base for their regime, somewhat curbing the terror and the policy of requisitioning of peasant grain. By mid-November 1919 the White forces had been broken, and advancing Soviet troops endured a long year of mopping up the remnants of anti-Bolshevik forces while moving beyond ethnic Russia into the peripheries. The last White armies left, along with the British and the French, late in 1920, and the most violent wars ended early in 1921–22 with the conquest of Georgia, the peace treaty with Poland, and the final Red campaigns. These subdued the massive peasant revolts in Tambov province and elsewhere, and the Muslim rebels known as Basmachi in Central Asia.

Counterrevolution and Intervention
Foreign military intervention prolonged the civil wars. Through 1918 Moscow faced two principal internal threats: in the south of Russia from

---

95   Ibid., p. 125.

the Volunteer Army, made up of former tsarist officers and heavily dependent on the local Don Cossacks; and from the west where the Germans
forced the Bolsheviks to abandon Ukraine, the bread-basket of tsarist
Russia. By April the Germans had overthrown the nationalist Ukrainian
parliament, the Rada, which was too radical for them, and installed General
Pavlo Skoropadsky as hetman. Both the Cossack counterrevolution in the
south and the anti-Bolshevik movements in Ukraine might have been eliminated had the Germans not come to the rescue, occupying Rostov-na-Donu
in early May. General Krasnov, the newly-elected ataman of the Don
Cossacks, allied himself with the Germans, declared "an independent
democratic republic" in the Don region, abolished all institutions and laws
of the revolution, and restored the *ancien régime* as much as possible. In
Ukraine as well, the counterrevolution, backed by the Germans, tried to
restore the old order. Skoropadsky appointed a cabinet made up of
Kadets—the liberal party that had once been highly anti-German, but
which now wanted an end to radical social reform and the kind of democracy that had led to anarchy and the collapse of the nation. Supported
primarily by large landlords who opposed the Rada's projected land reform,
the German-backed government lost the sympathies of Ukrainian peasants, disappointed by the failure to break up the noble estates. Many drifted
over to the Bolsheviks or joined anarchist bands.

Where they conquered, the Whites established a military dictatorship,
often assisted by liberal politicians who acted as administrators. Fortunately
for the Bolsheviks, their enemies could not unite. The Cossack ataman
General Krasnov refused to subordinate himself to Denikin, and Denikin,
who preferred the Allies, could not accept Krasnov's pro-German attitude.
When Denikin decided to campaign in the North Caucasus, Krasnov acted
on his own and attempted, unsuccessfully, to take Tsaritsyn on the Volga.
Had he succeeded, the anti-Bolsheviks in the south would have been able to
link up with those in the east.

The White opposition to Bolshevism was geographically and politically
fragmented. Born a peasant, General Denikin was more sensitive to the
social discontents that had led to the revolution than most of his fellow
officers. Highly suspicious of the liberals and moderate socialists who had
failed in 1917 to contain the radical impulses from below, he did not share
the more typical view of White generals that the revolution was simply a
conspiracy of the Jews. Prepared to rely on their own men, the remnants of
the nobility and some of the urban middle classes, and foreign assistance,

the White leaders made few concessions to the interests of the peasants and did little to prevent their men from plundering villages or committing anti-Semitic outrages. Some favored a program of restoring the tsarist order, while others accepted the political changes after the February Revolution. When General Wrangel beat back the Reds in Crimea, he treated the region as captured enemy territory, pillaging, raping women, and even murdering children. Once the area was secured, the new governor issued a decree reinstating all the laws of Russia before February 1917. This White counter-revolution shared few values with the anti-Bolsheviks on the Volga and in Siberia who were promoting the Constituent Assembly.

Besides the democratic and socialist opposition and the White restorationists, Moscow had to contend with a full-scale Allied intervention beginning in the late spring of 1918, when former prisoners of war and deserters from the Austro-Hungarian Army who wanted to fight on the side of the Allies formed a Czechoslovak army inside Russia. By March they numbered 40,000, and the Bolsheviks perceived their growing numbers as a potential threat. Lenin ordered the Czechoslovaks to be evacuated along the Trans-Siberian railroad to Vladivostok on the Pacific. As they moved eastward through the Urals into Siberia, however, the Czechoslovaks overthrew local soviets, and Moscow ordered that they be disarmed. People's Commissar of War Trotsky ordered that "every armed Czechoslovak on the railway be shot on the spot." When the Czechoslovak troops reached Omsk, the "capital" of western Siberia, anti-Bolshevik groups joined them and formed a West Siberian Commissariat, headed by a Right SR, as an anti-Soviet government. This new center of opposition identified not with the reactionary Cossack generals of the Don, but with more democratic elements. In Samara on the Volga a government, called Komuch (Committee of Members of the Constituent Assembly), was established with the purpose of restoring Russia's elected parliament. Opposed by factory workers and with little enthusiasm from the surrounding peasantry, Komuch depended on the Czech forces, which expanded their authority to Simbirsk, Kazan, and Ufa. Given its fragility, the SR government resorted to repression and arrests to maintain power. Here the Czechoslovaks, accidental actors caught in the midst of civil war, played the same role as the Germans and Allies elsewhere in Russia. Though they were never strong enough to destroy the Soviet regime and create an unchallenged anti-Bolshevik authority, their assistance sufficed to prop up the SRs and the Whites for a time and establish several independent power centers throughout the former Russian empire.

By fall 1918, Britain, France, the United States, Japan, Germany, France, Rumania, and Ottoman Turkey all had troops in Russia, along with Finnish, Polish, Czechoslovak, and Serbian soldiers. The Germans created and backed anti-Soviet governments in Belorussia, Ukraine, Lithuania, Latvia, Estonia, and Finland. Imperial Germany was on the way to realizing its goal of a *Mitteleuropa*: German dominance in the center of Europe, with parts of the former Russian Empire as client states. Germans not only advanced into the Don region, where they helped the Cossacks to drive out the Soviet troops, but also occupied the Crimean peninsula and sent an expeditionary force to Georgia, which declared its independence on May 26. The British secured a base at Arkhangelsk in the north, and in August they briefly occupied Baku in the south. In September the Turks took Baku, overthrowing the local socialists, and eventually installing a dependent Azerbaijani government. Americans joined British, French, and Serb troops at Murmansk, and the Japanese sat in Vladivostok. But like the Whites, the imperial powers were also not united. Their principal concern was winning the world war. Lenin told his beleaguered comrades that "the final solution depends on the outcome of the vacillations of the two hostile groups of imperialist countries—the American [–Japanese] conflict in the Far East and the Anglo–German in Western Europe." Caution and patience were essential to a successful outcome. "We must remain at our post until the arrival of our ally, the international proletariat, for this ally," he assured his readers, "is sure to arrive."[96]

The Red Army and Its Supporters

The Civil War was not only a war of armies but of ordinary people who had to choose in whose ranks to serve, whether to hold their positions under fire or desert. In the flush of the October Revolution the Soviet government had replaced the old Army with a socialist militia, abolishing all ranks and titles and forming a volunteer army with elections of officers by the rank and file. Just over 100,000 men joined the new force. When Trotsky took over as Commissar of War in March 1918, the only battle-ready military units on which the Soviet government could rely were the 35,000 Latvian riflemen commanded by Colonel Jukums Vācietis. A few units of the former tsarist army backed the Bolsheviks in the first armed

---

96 Lenin's report on foreign policy, May 14, 1918, in V. I. Lenin, *PSS*, XXXVI, pp. 340–1.

clashes with the Whites, but the old army was rapidly disintegrating, as hundreds of thousands of soldiers "voted with their feet" and left the front for home. The Red Guards that had distinguished themselves in October 1917 numbered only 4,000 in Petrograd and another 3,000 in Moscow. They were a ragtag militia at first, able to enforce Bolshevik rule in cities but far from an effective military force. Martov had a particularly harsh view of the Red fighters. "In fact, the Red Army recruits come not so much from the ranks of the proletariat as from its scum and from other vagabond elements replenished with déclassé elements of the demoralized old army. These recruits do their job for the sake of good pay and a full stomach at a time of general unemployment and famine."[97]

From these meager forces, Trotsky began the hard work of fashioning a Red Army of five million men over the next two and a half years. At first he relied on a volunteer army filled with revolutionary enthusiasts, but by the summer of 1918 he began drafting in industrial workers. He soon began to reverse the radical democratization of the military that had taken place after the October insurrection, ending the election of officers and instilling iron discipline in the ranks and among officers by the liberal use of threats and capital punishment. He ordered deserters, if caught, to be shot. Trotsky recruited former tsarist officers, and as early as April 1918, he introduced "political commissars" into the army to keep an eye on the officers. Lenin himself was wary of the so-called "military specialists" who had served before the revolution, until Trotsky informed him that the Red Army had no less than 30,000 former tsarist officers. Over three-quarters of the whole command and administration of the Red Army was made up of such "specialists" in the early years, though that percentage would fall to a third by the end of the Civil War. As the army ranks expanded, the "class" composition of the army changed, as the bulk of the fighting men no longer came from the workers but from the peasantry.

Russia's civil wars were both conventional wars fought by regular armies and irregular wars fought by guerrillas, insurgents, and peasant and anarchist bands. The two kinds of war affected each other, and civil war, Kalyvas argues, produces its own "civil war violence," the violence committed intentionally toward non-combatants. Civil war is particularly brutal and brutalizing for the civilian population, because it is a war

97 Brovkin (ed. and trans.), *Dear Comrades*, p. 109.

in which the field of battle is society itself.[98] Kalyvas breaks down the
processes by which brutalization leads to increased violence in civil wars:
"unremitting exposure to violence, removal of social controls, decline of
the cost of violent activity, rise in prominence of people with a propensity
for violence, and the unlearning of peaceful skills and learning of new
violent skills, resulting in the creation of vested interests in the use of
violence."[99] Each side in the Civil War required loyalty from its population; each side wanted followers and to prevent defectors. Collaborators
if not willing supporters were sufficient. But at the same time, neither side
had much to offer in material benefits. The fighting destroyed the economy, already damaged in the world war and revolution. Coercion and
terror were means to the end of enforced loyalty. As Kalyvas mentions,
"political actors would rather be disliked but feared than liked but not
feared when their rival is feared."[100] Violence was the easy means to create
fear. Lenin operated as if he understood but regretted these Machiavellian
principles. In one of his most sanguinary moments he wrote:

> Comrades! The uprising of the five kulak districts should be **merci-
> lessly** suppressed. The interests of the **entire** revolution require this,
> because now "the last decisive battle" with the kulaks is under way
> **everywhere**. One must give an example.
> 1. Hang (hang without fail, so **the people see**) **no fewer than one
>   hundred** known kulaks, rich men, bloodsuckers.
> 2. Publish their names.
> 3. Take from them **all** the grain.
> 4. Designate hostages . . .
>   Do it in such a way that for hundreds of versts around, the people
>   will see, tremble, know, shout: **they are strangling** and will strangle
>   to death the bloodsucker kulaks.
>   Telegraph receipt and **implementation**.
>   Yours, Lenin
>   Find some truly hard people.[101]

---

98 Kalyvas, *The Logic of Civil Wars*, p. 54.

99 Ibid., pp. 55–6.

100 Ibid., p. 114.

101 Richard Pipes (ed.), *The Unknown Lenin: From the Secret Archive* (New
Haven and London: Yale University Press, 1996), p. 50 (bold text in original).

The harsh lesson was that terror could establish the preliminary conditions after which loyalty would follow, and with loyalty would come acceptance, acquiescence to the state's authority and legitimacy, rather than raw force.

To win the war, both sides had to win support for, or at least the acquiescence in, the right of their side to rule—and rule exclusively. They may have desired active, committed supporters, but more often they had to settle for collaborators, people who would act as supporters but without attitudinal commitment to the cause. "The primary concern of the vast majority of the peasantry," writes Orlando Figes,

> was not to get itself involved in the civil war any more than it had to. The peasants were willing to fight against the landowners in their own localities; they formed their own peasant brigades; and they were even ready to fight for the Red Army, as long as it was seen to be defending the revolution in their own locality. But the peasants came to see the civil war increasingly as an alien political struggle between the socialist parties.102

A huge problem for all sides was defection. Desertion rates for the Red Army were "astronomical." Figes writes, "By late 1919 there were an estimated 1.5 million Red Army deserters in Russia. On some fronts up to 80 percent of the enlisted soldiers were registered as deserters during the harvest period."103 Many peasant soldiers left for their farms; others were concerned about their families; still others were upset at the shortages of supplies in the army. Only in 1920 did political reasons for deserting become more frequent, as peasants joined Green movements against the Soviet regime.104 The man who built the five-million-man Red Army believed there was only one way to create such an effective fighting machine:

102　Figes, *Peasant Russia, Civil War: The Volga Countryside in Revolution, 1917–1921* (Oxford: Oxford University Press, 1989), p. 175.

103　Ibid., p. 316. Joshua A. Sanborn takes issue with Figes's estimates. In the first two weeks of September 1919, 16,364 men deserted from the Red Army, but 97,420 rejoined or were captured in the same period. Sanborn, *Drafting the Russian Nation: Military Conscription, Total War, and Mass Politics 1905–1925* (DeKalb, IL: Northern Illinois University Press, 2003), p. 49.

104　Figes, *Peasant Russia, Civil War.*, pp. 317–20.

An army cannot be built without reprisals. Masses of men cannot be led to death unless the army command has the death penalty in its arsenal. So long as those malicious tailless apes that are so proud of their technical achievements—the animals that we call men—will build armies and wage wars, the command will always be obliged to place the soldiers between the possible death in the front and the inevitable one in the rear.[105]

"And yet," he goes on, "armies are not built on fear."[106] Inspiration, pride, Trotsky's own speeches, as well as competent commanders were all cited as elements that forged the army and made victory possible.

Terror, of course, was only one weapon in the Bolshevik arsenal. Propaganda and concessions to their opponents, negotiation and compromise also were used. In February 1919, Martov wrote a series of letters on what he perceived to be a Bolshevik turn toward moderation.

During the last two months [December 1918, January 1919], Soviet power has clearly been trying to embark on the path of reforms in its domestic policy. A whole series of factors have played a role in this sudden change. It seems that the experience of carrying through the policy of the Red Terror to its logical end had the most direct effect on this turnaround in attitude. When "up there" they found out how local authorities in the provinces (including the former capital, now Zinoviev's patrimony) applied directives from the center on summary justice in regard to "counterrevolutionaries" and on taking hostages, even the fearless people's commissars were embarrassed. In addition, they must have learned from the reports of Rakovskii, Ioffe, and other diplomatic representatives what indignation this bloody bacchanalia caused among the working masses abroad.[107]

The Cheka, he went on, had turned from "saviors" into "sovereigns" (*spasiteli, poveliteli*). "The question as to whether torture was useful was debated as easily as if the editors of [the *Courier of the Extraordinary Commissions*] were ancient Persians or Chinese." Chekists had become

---

105 Leon Trotsky, *My Life* (New York: Pathfinder Press, 1970), p. 411.
106 Ibid.
107 Brovkin (ed. and trans.), *Dear Comrades*, p. 138.

so powerful and independent that one agent claimed, "If we so please, *we can shoot even the Communists*."[108] Adopting a softer policy, the Soviet government declared an amnesty and freed oppositionists; the powers of the Cheka were curtailed; Mensheviks were readmitted into the Central Executive Committee of the Soviets, and their newspapers reappeared (temporarily). Moderate Bolsheviks like Leonid Krasin seemed to be winning the internal debates, and Foreign Commissar Giorgii Chicherin accepted the Allies' invitation to all belligerents in the civil war to meet on the Turkish island of Prinkipo.

Some historians have argued that the Bolsheviks' concessions to the loyal opposition were a cynical policy: when the country was in danger, they reached out for allies. Indeed Karl Radek specifically called for internal peace given the external threat. On the other hand, the Menshevik Rafael Abramovich noted that it was when danger was greatest that the Bolsheviks relapsed into terror against internal opponents.[109] But such easy equations cannot be made, for episodes of terror coincided with perceptions of internal as well as external danger. By the end of March 1919, the "soft line" came to an end, and Social Democrats and Socialist Revolutionaries once again were arrested. The Mensheviks were caught between criticizing Bolshevik policies and supporting the struggle against the White counterrevolution. Despite the official sanction from Moscow to allow the Mensheviks to operate openly, local Bolsheviks thwarted central party policy and continued to restrict or repress their activities. Even when Mensheviks enthusiastically supported the Red Army, Tula Bolsheviks put obstacles in their way to prevent workers from defecting to their rivals.[110] A report by Mensheviks in Bryansk confirmed that Bolshevik terror made organizing the workers impossible, even though the Mensheviks had managed to turn workers away from sympathy toward Denikin or indifference to the revolution back to supporting it. Both Bolsheviks and Mensheviks pushed for evacuating local industries if Denikin threatened the city, but the workers wanted to preserve their factories and jobs.[111] In 1920 Mensheviks supported the Reds in their war with Poland, and, as a Menshevik leader reported, "The *Burgfrieden*

---

108 Ibid., pp. 138–9 (italics in original).
109 Rafael Abramovich to Pavl Akselrod, May 30, 1920, in ibid., p. 197.
110 Brovkin (ed. and trans.), *Dear Comrades*, pp. 186–8.
111 Ibid., pp. 189–91.

[social peace] muffled the fear of our strengthening and suppressed the growing wrath against us."[112]

In the spring of 1919, the civil war entered a particularly difficult and destructive phase as the economy staggered toward complete collapse and White armies moved close to victory. In the east Kolchak launched a spring offensive and took Ufa. Iudenich advanced in the Baltic region, and Denikin's army, over 150,000 strong, took Tsaritsyn on the Volga and moved northward toward Moscow. The anti-Semitic partisan leader Nikifor Grigoriev, who had fought with the Reds, now turned against them. Only in the fall of 1919 were Trotsky's forces able to turn the tide. Most of the foreign interventionists began to pull out of Russia, while Soviet troops stopped the White campaign toward Petrograd, captured Kolchak, mopped up their enemies in Ukraine, and drove Wrangel out of Crimea.

In this chapter, violence is a dependent variable, something to be explained; but violence in the civil wars often operated at the same time as an independent variable, as the cause and accelerator of different forms of violence. Once it breaks out or is employed, violence itself transforms the situation. Developments that were unthinkable before become possible. Certain borders are drawn, others are transgressed; identities harden; emotions intensify; motivations shift. Both Reds and Whites engaged in terror, though each targeted different victims as the terror took on a class character. The Reds often shot captured officers or turned on the upper classes; the Whites took revenge on ordinary soldiers, Communist Party members, and Jews. Red Army men were instructed to treat the ordinary population well, but such orders were often not obeyed. While some Bolsheviks tried to limit terror to "the leading actors of the White Guard camp," their superiors often over-ruled them. In September 1919, with the Whites closing in from several directions, the Cheka arrested about 1,000 Kadets and their supporters, accusing them of belonging to a National Center that was planning an uprising against the Soviets. At the end of the month the Cheka executed sixty-seven of the imprisoned leaders. After a bomb attack by anar-chists and Left SRs on Moscow party headquarters, Dzerzhinskii unleashed a massive terror on Kadets, aristocrats, and former tsarist

112 Ibid., p. 195.

officials, executing prisoners and hostages. In these same years, 1918–19, the Cheka set up forced labor and concentration camps for opponents of the regime, the first islands in what would be known as the Gulag Archipelago. As the Bolshevik commander Martyn Latsis put it, the "meaning of civil war is kill that you may not be killed."[113]

> We are not carrying out war versus individuals. We are exterminating the bourgeoisie as a class. We are not looking for evidence or witnesses to reveal deeds or words versus the Soviet power. The first question we ask is to what class does he belong, what are his origins, upbringing, education or profession? These questions define the fate of the accused. This is the essence of the Red Terror.

The Whites and Their Supporters

> Both the Volunteer Army and the Bolsheviks did a mass of unclean deeds; and in the final analysis one was no better than the other.
>
> V. I. Vernadskii[114]

White armies had only as much power as they could muster at the point of a gun. Peasants and townspeople might cheer the Whites as they entered their villages and towns, but they soon turned away and refrained from actively supporting them. Many Ukrainians and other non-Russians feared Denikin, who promised to restore a single, united "Great Russia," more than they feared the Reds, who offered a program of "national self-determination." Like the Reds, the Whites and their sympathizers also engaged in mass violence against civilians, carrying out cold-blooded executions of Communists and workers. As early as December 1917, when White forces put down a pro-Bolshevik uprising in Rostov, they

---

113   Cited in Joshua Sanborn, "The Terror of War and Revolution," unpublished paper presented at the AAASS Convention, Boston, MA, December 4, 2004. See also *Dva goda bor'by na vnutrennom fronte* (Moscow: Gosudarstvennoe izdatel'stvo, 1920); *Chrezvychainaia komissii v bor'be s kontrrevoliutsiei* (Moscow, 1921); O. V. Budnitskii, *Rossiiskie evrei mezhdu krasnymi i belymi* (Moscow: Rosspen, 2006); and Willard Sunderland, *The Baron's Cloak: A History of the Russian Empire in War and Revolution* (Ithaca: Cornell University Press, 2014).

114   From his unpublished diary; cited in Kendall Bailes, "Natural Scientists and the Soviet System," in Diane P. Koenker, William G. Rosenberg, and Ronald Grigor Suny (eds.), *Party, State, and Society in the Russian Civil War* (Bloomington and Indianapolis, IN: Indiana University Press, 1989), p. 286.

turned their guns on the defeated workers. A certain Colonel Drozdovskii regretted that "we live in a terrible time, when man is becoming an animal"; as for the Bolsheviks, "these unbridled hooligans understand only one law: an eye for an eye, a tooth for a tooth." And in a revision of the *lex talionis*, he added: "But I would propose two eyes for one, and all teeth for one." Eventually, anyone associated with the Communist Party or participating in a local soviet was subject to the death penalty. General Wrangel formed a regiment of Red Army prisoners after ordering their 370 commanders to be shot. Though army units were relatively selective in their killing, popular movements allied to the Whites engaged in far more indiscriminate violence. In the summer of 1918, a Bolshevik-led government in the oil-producing city of Baku, which had not exercised any terror during their three months in power, peacefully left office after losing a crucial vote in the soviet. Later, when the famous Twenty-Six Baku Commissars fled the city as the Turkish army approached, they were captured by anti-Communists in Turkestan, brutally cut down, and hastily buried in the desert.[115] In Ukraine in 1919, bands of Cossacks or peasants broke into Jewish houses to rape, rob, and kill thousands, as they identified Jews with the hated Soviet regime.[116]

In August 1919, a workers' delegation from the Kuban region, then under General Denikin's authority, complained about the lack of freedoms and the effects of repression that paralleled similar protests from their comrades in Soviet territory. Press freedom had been severely curtailed, so that only right-wing newspapers could be published.

> The death penalty has become an everyday occurrence. Quite often executions are held without trial on the pretext of "an attempt to flee." Not infrequently, arrests and even executions have been conducted out of self-interest or revenge. There have been mass pogroms in a number of cities (Ekaterinoslav, Kremenchug, Elisavetgrad, and others) incited by baiting [minorities] and fueling national chauvinism.[117]

---

115 Ronald Grigor Suny, *The Baku Commune, 1917–1918: Class and Nationality in the Russian Revolution* (Princeton: Princeton University Press, 1972).

116 On the pogroms of Jews during the Civil War, see Oleg Budnitskii, *Russian Jews Between the Reds and the Whites, 1917–1920*, trans. Timothy J. Portice (Philadelphia: University of Pennsylvania Press, 2011).

117 Brovkin (ed. and trans.), *Dear Comrades*, p. 183.

White Terror, claims the late historian of the Whites, Viktor G. Bortnevski "was logically produced by a White political system of military dictatorship which tried to compete with the Bolshevik 'proletarian dictatorship.'"[118] Over time, a disorganized but vicious policy of retaliation became a more systematic punitive-repressive policy, sanctioned by broad laws that condemned to death anyone who was a member of the Bolshevik party or had aided it to come to power. With the military setbacks at the end of 1919 and into the beginning of 1920, there was "a significant increase in the severity and activities of the punitive-repressive organs. In practice, all controls and limitations on the activities of these organs were lifted. This prompted massive popular discontent in territories under White control and contributed to the military and political successes of the Reds."[119]

The Whites celebrated terror no less than many Bolsheviks. Generals Kornilov and Markov urged the Volunteer Army on with cries of "Take no prisoners. The more terror, the more victories."[120] Some Whites tried to justify the terror as incidental rather than systematic, unplanned, the work of "bad apples" at lower levels. N. V. Savich, one of Denikin's aides, wrote that

> The activities of the military commanders in those times became increasingly brutal; the troops summarily shot all of the Red commanders who fell into their hands. However, these acts were mostly perpetrated by only some units, who were often commanded by lower-rank officers, and were not the results of directives from above, but were in fact, contradictory to those directives. These were exceptions to the rule and deviations from the norm of behavior. Unfortunately, while these acts were exceptions, they were nevertheless frequent exceptions.[121]

Even the White dictator of Siberia, Admiral Kolchak, at his trial before the Irkutsk Military Revolutionary Committee, attempted to justify the massacres his forces carried out. When Kolchak questioned his detachment commanders about reported atrocities, they answered, according to him: "We are fighting Bolsheviks—what has been done to us we shall do too, as there is no other guaranty that we all shall not have our throats

---

118 Viktor G. Bortnevski, "White Administration and White Terror (The Denikin Period)," *Russian Review* LII, 3 (July 1993), p. 366.
119 Ibid.
120 Ibid., p. 356.
121 Ibid., p. 364

cut. We shall struggle in the same way as our adversary struggles against us." Kolchak's interrogator asked: "When facts of arbitrary arrests, searches, and shootings were established, were any measures taken to bring the guilty to justice?" Kolchak replied, "Such occurrences never left any foundation for bringing persons to justice—it was impossible to find out who had committed the crime and when."[122]

Some historians have claimed that the White Terror was a temporary measure, to be used for a limited time, while the Red Terror was something more permanent, a strategy toward a political purpose. Bolsheviks saw terror as a legitimate means to reconstruct the world, while the Whites saw terror as "repressive violence" to re-establish a previous status quo.[123] Red Terror was revolutionary; White Terror was conservative, restorative. But, as Joshua Sanborn points out,

> in the case of the Jews, we see not only the development of terror practices (like hostage-taking, decimation, mass retribution, mass deportation, rape, robbery, and sadistic, spectacularly cruel violence), but of the social intent. Most notably, efforts on the part of Ianushkevich's Stavka to gather material on Jewish behavior in the army stressed that commanders were to gather this to prove all the "harm" that Jews posed to the army and to the nation. Given the tone and exclusionary fantasies of both prewar and wartime anti-Semitic discourse, we see in the Jewish terror a facet of White Terror that cannot simply be seen as a method of military dictatorship, a requirement of wartime emergency, or even the most brutal of counter-insurgency strategies. These were processes that were justified by the war atmosphere, but whose vision extended well into the post-war period. As a result, the White Terror, like the Imperial Army's Terror campaign from 1914–1917, was revolutionary in its Terror against Jews, and who knows, might have taken this kernel even further had they prevailed in the Civil War.[124]

---

122 Testimony of Kolchak, 136–7; cited in Sanborn, "Terror in War and Revolution," p. 6.

123 Holquist mentions that scholars traditionally have seen the White terror as "arbitrary and non-instrumental," while the Red terror was ideological, centralized and systematic. He disputes this dichotomy. "Violent Russia," p. 646.

124 Sanborn, "Terror in War and Revolution," pp. 11–12.

Indeed, it is not simply by coincidence or accident that Red and White terror look alike, that both sides employed similarly horrific methods in their struggle to win the war and destroy the Other. The logic of civil war led both sides to use violence, not only in pitched battles of army against army, but also in their attempts to control populations in the absence of overwhelming force or positive support; to obtain information and prevent information reaching the enemy; to discourage defections, and to mobilize people to fight for their side and not for their enemies.

The Costs of the Russian Civil Wars

Although full figures for the extent of Red or White terror in the early years of Soviet Power are elusive, historians have given various estimates. Official Soviet accounts claim only about 13,000 killed by the Red Terror from 1918 to 1920, but Western historians have estimated between 50,000 and 140,000. Figures for the White terror are even more difficult to come by because the White forces fell under different administrations, and much of the violence on the anti-Bolshevik side was carried out by undisciplined forces operating independently of the more disciplined White forces. According to the best estimates, bands allied with Simon Petlura, who emerged as a major leader of independent Ukraine in 1918–19, committed 40 percent of anti-Jewish atrocities during the Civil War; another 25 percent were carried out by other Ukrainian forces; non-Ukrainian White armies, primarily Cossacks, were responsible for 17 percent; while units of the Red Army accounted for 8.5 percent. Estimates of Jews killed range from 35,000 to 150,000, with a shared consensus of about 50,000.[125] If, by terror, one means only the violence outside of armed conflict turned against civilians and prisoners by state or military authorities, then Red terror probably exceeded White terror. But, if one includes the violence by anti-Soviet popular movements and the pogroms against Jews, the numbers killed by the opponents of the Bolsheviks surpass those cut down by the Reds.

To understand the turn to terror by the Bolsheviks, the Red Terror of the Civil War years must be placed in two contexts: the context of what went before (World War I), and the context of what was going on at the time (the White Terror, foreign intervention, peasant rebellion, a relatively weak state, an unwillingness on the part of the Bolsheviks to

---

125   Holquist, "Violent Russia," pp. 646–7.

relinquish power, and their ambitious political program). The logic of violence in the Russian Revolution might be expressed in the following way: a minority party seized power in a hostile environment, in the midst of war and social dislocation. Unwilling to consider giving up power, even to a party (the Right SRs) that received a greater plurality of votes in the Constituent Assembly elections, the Bolsheviks resorted to their superior support among the armed population in order to stay in power, prevent the restoration of the *ancien régime*, and provoke an international revolution. Violence was the only means to those ends. Yet it was not primarily the Red Terror that led to their ultimate victory. That was enabled by the weakness and division among their enemies, the lack of will of the foreign interventionists to sustain their military effort, the strategic advantages of holding central Russia, and the support of workers and, ultimately, of much of the peasantry (who preferred the Bolsheviks, who had given them the land in 1917, to their opponents who would take it back). Add to these factors the Bolsheviks' alliances with significant elements among the non-Russian peoples, and their effectiveness to create a viable state apparatus and a five-million-man Red Army. Two cases from the South Caucasus provide counter-examples to the Bolshevik dictatorship's choices. In Menshevik Georgia, Marxist socialists came to power, but with majority support in the country. There they were able to construct a democratic government without significant use of terror, though they did use force and violence in campaigns against Abkhaz and Osetin minorities and repression against local Communists. With the backing of the population, faced by relatively weaker enemies, the Georgian Mensheviks were able to avoid mass terror and maintain democracy. The Baku Bolsheviks, however, were less fortunate. Stepan Shahumian and his comrades willingly gave up power when they lost their majority in the city soviet, but when they then tried to leave the city, they were captured by anti-Bolshevik forces and summarily executed in the deserts of Turkmenistan.

As Maxim Gorky reported in a famous quotation, Lenin was troubled by the realization that revolution required violence, and worried about having to employ such methods. In a conversation, Lenin told M. F. Andreeva, "What else can we do, dear M. F.? We have no alternative but to fight. Do we find it hard? Of course we do! You think it is not hard for me? It is, and very hard too. But look at Dzerzhinsky. He is beginning to look like nothing at all. There is nothing to be done about it. It is better to suffer than to fail."[126] Gorky, at first an opponent of Bolshevik methods, later reconciled himself to the use of violence: "The duty of true-hearted leaders of the people is superhumanly difficult. A leader who is not in some degree a tyrant is impossible. More people, probably, were killed under Lenin than under Thomas Münzer; but without this, resistance to the revolution of which Lenin was the leader would have been more widely and powerfully organized."[127] "I often used to speak with Lenin about the cruelty of revolutionary tactics and life," he remembered. "'What do you want?' he would ask in astonishment and anger. 'Is it possible to act humanely in a struggle of such unprecedented ferocity? Where is there any place for soft-heartedness or generosity? We are being blockaded by Europe, we are deprived of the help of the European proletariat, counter-revolution is creeping like a bear on us from every side. What do you want? Are we not right? Ought we not to struggle and resist? We know that what we want can only be achieved by ourselves.' "[128]

From anarchy through violence the Bolsheviks founded a state, established their own monopoly over the legitimate possession of the instruments of violence, and brought a brief respite between the revolutionary and civil war years and the cataclysm of Stalin's revolution from above. The ambitions of both Reds and Whites were directed toward building states and societies that only a minority of the population was ready to accept. The Reds were set on constructing a state that would eventually

---

126 Maxim Gorky, *Days with Lenin* (originally published in Russian, Moscow: Centrizdat, 1931); translated by C.W. Parker-Arkhangelskata; first published in the United States about 1930; republished by Red Star, 2014, RedStarPublishers.org), p. 36.

127 Ibid., p. 23.

128 Ibid., p. 29. For all his sympathy for the Bolshevik Revolution and the Communist movements, Eric J. Hobsbawm recognizes the connection between ideology and unlimited war. "What gave this terror an unprecedented inhumanity," he writes, "was that it recognized no conventional or other limits. It was not so much the belief that a great end justifies all the means necessary to achieve it (though it is possible that this was Mao Tse-Tung's belief), or even the belief that the sacrifices imposed on the present generation, however large, are as nothing to the benefits which will be reaped by the endless generations of the future. It was the application of the principle of total war to all times. Leninism, perhaps because of the powerful strain of voluntarism which made other Marxists distrust Lenin as a 'Blanquist' or 'Jacobin,' thought essentially in military terms, as his own admiration for Clausewitz would indicate, even if the entire vocabulary of Bolshevik politics did not bear witness to it. 'Who whom?' [*Kto kovo*, who will overtake whom] was Lenin's basic maxim: the struggle as a zero-sum game in which the winner took, the loser lost all." *The Age of Extremes: A History of the World, 1914–1991* (Vintage Books: New York, 1996), p. 391.

eliminate the bourgeoisie and capitalism and create the conditions for socialism; the Whites wanted to restore a social order already in ruins. The great majority of the population, the peasantry, had their own ambitions, and wavered in their loyalties from Red to White to Green. The greatest violence occurred when the Reds or the Whites were most insecure. As they conquered and pacified, the use of violence abated, and along with coercive power discursive power could be employed. Much of the terror in the Civil War, on both sides, was directed at real enemies, and was considered by both Whites and Bolsheviks justified as wartime measures against a ruthless enemy that was itself engaged in ferocious terror. Terror was strategic, instrumental, sanctioned and given meaning by political ideology, but also was propelled by powerful emotions like fear, anger, hatred, vengeance, and resentment, as well as a sense of retribution and justice. Your adversaries were not simply those shooting at you but also various populations constructed as "enemies." For the Whites, they were the Jews. For the Bolsheviks, they were not only the old ruling classes, but moderate socialists (Mensheviks and SRs) as well. Enemies were symbolic and potential as well as actual. How enemies are imagined always plays a part in the construction of dangerous Others. Sometimes, they were imagined as redeemable; at other times they were seen as indelible existential threats that had to be physically eliminated. The victory of the Bolsheviks was inconceivable without the use of the weapons of war, and in the context of the Russian civil wars, without the repressive violence of the Red Terror. Yet, at the same time, Communists successfully persuaded people of their vision and carefully, deliberately, built a state while at war. Lenin and the Bolsheviks not only accepted that the omelet of social revolution required the breaking of eggs, they also concluded that to hold power in the midst of civil war and social breakdown it was necessary to institutionalize the egg-smashing instruments.

A Postscript on State Terror under Stalin

A central contention of this chapter is that the violence of the revolution should be distinguished from the violence of the Stalinist years, that violence in war is fundamentally different from violence in peace. Violence in conditions of anarchy or near anarchy, where sovereignty and the nature of the state are contested, is different from violence directed by a constituted sovereign state against large numbers of the population over which it rules (its own people or a colonized population or a people in an occupied territory), in an effort to radically transform the social and political structure. The connections between these two tragic episodes need to be refined and specified in ways that essentialist arguments from personality, ideology, discourse, or conceptions of modernity fail to do.

The top-down violence of the Stalinist years requires its own elucidation—and will be examined elsewhere. Consider the range of explanations that have been offered by scholars. In her analysis of the Stalinist Great Terror, the founder of the "totalitarian school," Hannah Arendt, shows how emotion was used instrumentally by modern dictatorial regimes. Terror was employed, not only to eliminate enemies, but to cow the people, a means to rule through fear. As Arendt put it,

> a fundamental difference between modern dictatorships and all the other tyrannies of the past is that terror is no longer used as a means to exterminate and frighten opponents, but as an instrument to rule masses who are perfectly obedient. Terror as we know it today strikes without any preliminary provocation, its victims are innocent even from the point of view of the persecutor ... We are dealing ... with the arbitrariness by which victims are chosen, and for this it is decisive that they are objectively innocent, that they are chosen regardless of what they may or may not have done. [129]

In his discussion of the Stalinist terror, Arno Mayer contrasts the externalization of the revolution in France—the war against Europe from 1792 through the Napoleonic period—with the internalization of violence in the Soviet 1930s. Rather than an explanation, this is a suggestive description of differences between the two revolutions. In France, the devouring of the revolution's own children occurred at a moment of war and radicalization; it was passionate and excited; but in Russia the revolution had cooled. The revolutionary years were far behind, and Stalin's Great Terror was calculated and deliberate. Behind the mass killings lay fear and insecurity, produced both by the foreign environment and domestic difficulties, but fear, that most rational of emotions, only added to a mentality and purpose that Stalin and his closest comrades already possessed. The systematic killings aimed at a political end, though Mayer is unsure of what this was.[130]

---

129 Arendt, *The Origins of Totalitarianism*, p. 6.
130 Mayer, *The Furies*, pp. 660–2.

Some historians have generally explained the Terror of the 1930s in relation to the personal pathology of the chief himself. Stalin and his fellow Stalinists were simply violent men, willing to sign away the lives of hundreds of thousands of people to preserve the order they had built in the USSR and themselves at the top of that order. But other explanations, some of which argue from effect to cause, include:

- Stalin wanted to create a new elite loyal to himself and to his form of state socialism (A. J. Unger, Sheila Fitzpatrick).
- War and terror had socialized Soviet humans to become violent, to develop a habit of violence.
- Bolshevik ideology, and Marxism itself, not only allowed but exalted violence. The very doctrine of class struggle legitimized its use, first against class enemies and then against others.
- The excessive or surplus repression of Stalinism was necessary to achieve a particular form of autocracy in the face of a natural tendency toward oligarchy or more popular participation (Moshe Lewin, Herbert Marcuse).
- Real isolation and danger, both domestic and foreign, created an environment in which violence appeared to be an effective, even indispensable, tool of self-defense. In a world in which you are surrounded by enemies, paranoia is close to rationality.
- There really were enemies out there: saboteurs, fascists, Trotskyites, Zinovievites (Stalinist view).

Less specifically stemming from the context of the 1930s, broader explanations include:

- Human beings are simply violent creatures; it is in their nature, and once restraints are removed, as in revolutions or absolutist dictatorships, violence is likely to occur. We are hardwired to kill—at least men are!
- Violence creates group stability and solidarity. Once bound together by violence, the rulers constitute a community with greater internal loyalty. A gang mentality develops.
- Violence works; it is more effective than democratic rule in controlling a divided, rapidly changing society. Some degree of conformity, acquiescence in the governing class, can be achieved by violence and the fear that Terror induces.

- Violence trumps moderation. In certain kinds of political competition, moderates are outflanked by militants; options narrow; and those willing to use violence emerge on top (as with the Mafia).
- Violence is provoked by humiliation, by assaults to self-esteem and personal dignity.
- Modernity reinforces the efficacy of violence. Projects to create utopian societies require violence to overcome traditional habits, and remake humans in a new way.

In this chapter, I have tried to show how the specific context of the revolution and civil war combined with particular actors and their emotional and cognitive dispositions to make the use of terror highly likely. Here, all five of the "cons of history"—context, conjuncture, contingency, contradiction, and confusion—played a role. This historicized explanation, however, must be distinguished from the normative question of rationalization or justification of violence and terror. Although the humanitarian rules of war are usually suspended for internal conflicts, insurgencies, and "wars against terrorism," the practice of terror cannot be neatly segregated from questions of morality and justification. Historians reluctantly enter this treacherous territory, and yet their work often addresses the normative. Even if one accepts that a certain degree of violence was necessary for victory, and therefore justified in the minds of the perpetrators, the widespread terror employed or allowed by the Reds and the Whites can still be condemned as excessive and disproportionate.

How can violence and terror be justified? By its ends, for nothing but ends justify means; however, if the means make it impossible to reach the ends, or so taint the ends that they cease to be worthy or desired, then those means are inappropriate and are not justified by the ends. In real-world politics we do break eggs because we want omelets. Even great philosophers, and revolutionaries themselves, have expressed both enthusiasm for violence and distress about its use. Thomas Jefferson, Immanuel Kant, and Georg Wilhelm Hegel all defended the violence of the French Revolution as necessary to achieve human liberation. The exemplary revolutionary Rosa Luxemburg, on the other hand, who would lose her life at the hands of men far more excited by violence and death than she, rightly feared the consequences when revolutions make a virtue of necessity. Other revolutionaries, among them Trotsky and Lenin, worked hard to justify revolutionary violence. Isaac Steinberg, having served as People's

Commissar of Justice in Lenin's Sovnarkom, contrasted revolutionary violence, which in his view was "defensive, unavoidable, and necessary," from revolutionary terror, which he abhorred as "aggressive and provocative." For him, revolutionary violence arose from "righteous anger against the old order and passion for the new world," while terror came from "rage, hatred, and vengeance." The former targets "proven enemies," the latter is indiscriminate and without scruples.[131] The dilemma, of course, is that revolutionaries who remain humane and abjure terror, like Rosa Luxemburg or (my own favorite) Stepan Shahumian, are crushed by counterrevolutionaries willing to use terror. Revolution is war, and war requires using lethal force against enemies willing to use lethal force against you. But even the rules of war do not allow any means to be used. Terrorism and revolutionary terror are particularly noxious, unpredictable, and consequential forms of violence. Their inherent perversions carry on beyond their limited use, infecting the perpetrators while destroying the victims. The state terror under Stalin not only has no moral justification but also cannot be justified politically or strategically—except that it allowed a brutal man to achieve total power—for ultimately it weakened the Soviet regime, both in the short and longer term, nearly cost the Soviet Union its victory in the coming war, and eliminated the flexibility and creativity that might have kept the polity and ideology from petrification. Stalinism, like other episodes of mass killing in the twentieth century, among them the Armenian Genocide, the Holodomor in Ukraine, and the Holocaust, needs historians to provide textured, evidence-based, persuasive explanations, but that exercise should in no way diminish the moral outrage against colossal inhumanity.

Eggs and omelets have been repeatedly used as a metaphor to justify violence and terror. The Soviet dissident Vladimir Bukovsky once quipped that he had seen the broken eggs, but no one he knew had ever tasted the omelet.[132] There are those who believe that it was a waste of eggs to make such an impossible, utopian omelet, and others who believe in the omelet but not the breaking of eggs. My own view is that there are some omelets

---

131 Ibid., pp. 87–8; see Steinberg, *Gewalt und Terror in der Revolution* (Berlin, 1931).

132 Courtois (ed.), *The Black Book of Communism*, p. 19.

that are worth broken eggs, but, as anyone making breakfast knows, first one should make sure that all the ingredients are to hand and remember that eggs must be broken delicately, not smashed so that yolks, whites, and shells all get cooked together. Finally, all breakfast makers, as well as those who take up the sword of revolution or war, should take heed: eggs once scrambled can never be unscrambled.

Index

Jean Christophe (Rolland), 67
Jefferson, Thomas, 300
Jews, 57, 58, 69, 113, 155, 166, 172, 173, 230, 252, 254, 281, 289, 291, 293, 294, 297
  See also anti-Semitism
Jones, Gareth Stedman, 25, 104, 239
Jones, LeRoi, 12
journalism, as occupying ideological
  frontline, 64–5
Jowitt, Kenneth, 118
July Days, 198, 201, 223, 230, 236, 270

Kadet party, 199, 209, 210, 229, 236, 264, 272, 281, 289. *See also* Constitutional
  Democrats (Kadets)
Kahler, Miles, 143
Kaiser, Robert, 65
Kaledin, Aleksei, 271
Kalyvas, Stathis, 250, 267, 268, 284–5
Kamenev, Lev, 257
Kannegisser, Leonid, 278
Kant, Immanuel, 300
Kaplan, Fanny, 278
Karamzin, Nikolai, 160, 171
Karpovich, Michael, 92, 93
Katkov, Mikhail, 170
Kautsky, Karl, 252–3
Kavelin, Konstantin, 169
Keenan, Edward, 97
Keep, John L. H., 186, 200, 201, 202–4
Kennan, George, 55, 56, 63, 71–2
Kent, Rockwell, 68
Kerblay, Basile, 91
Kerensky, Alexander, 193, 194, 196, 197, 198, 200, 202, 209, 210, 271
Kerner, Robert, 62
Kesdekian, Arax, 4–5
Khlevniuk, Oleg, 109
Khodarkovsky, Michael, 146
Khomiakov, Aleksei, 167
Khrushchev, Nikita, 7, 20, 78, 84, 95
King, Jeremy, 141n44
Kipling, Rudyard, 138
Kireevskii, Ivan, 167
Kistiakivskyi, Bohdan, 175
Kivelson, Valerie, 145
Kliuchevskii, Vasilii, 160
Koenker, Diane P., 186, 206–8, 228, 233, 234, 236, 237, 238, 239, 245
Koestler, Arthur, 69, 120
Kokoshkin, Fedor, 272
Kolakowski, Leslek, 8
Kolchak, Aleksandr, 280, 292–3

Komuch (Committee of Members of the
  Constituent Assembly), 282
Konovalov, Aleksandr, 191, 235, 236
Kornilov, Lavr, 196, 198, 199, 210, 236, 271, 292
Korsch, Karl, 20
Kotkin, Stephen, 115, 116
Krasin, Leonid, 288
Krasnov, Petr, 271, 281
Kremlinology, 95
Krestinskii, Nikolai, 274
Kuhn, Thomas, 27

labor history, 18, 102–5, 243
Labrousse, Ernest, 215
Ladau, Ernesto, 26n18
Laitin, David D., 43, 44
Landes, Joan B., 216
language, growing interest in and attention
  to, 26
Lansing, Robert, 57
Lapidus, Gail, 111
Laqueur, Walter, 220–1
Lasch, Christopher, 54
Latsis, Martyn, 269, 290
L'Echo de Paris, 57
Lee, Andrea, 65
Lefebvre, Georges, 215, 216
Left Socialist Revolutionaries (SRs), 199, 272, 273, 274, 276, 289
Leites, Nathan, 75
Lenin, Vladimir, 1, 2, 20, 68, 99, 137n34, 142, 197, 198, 200, 226–7, 248, 252, 256, 257, 264, 265, 269, 278, 286, 295–6, 300
Leninist/Leninism, 4, 14, 66, 77, 91, 93, 100, 101, 105, 106, 119, 120, 121, 122, 137, 142, 198, 203, 217, 218, 219, 230, 248, 253, 256, 258, 259, 264, 266
Lenin's Last Struggle (Lewin), 91
Leon Trotsky: Portrait of a Youth (Eastman), 66
Lermontov, Mikhail, 162
Leroy-Beaulieu, Anatole, 55, 56
Lévi-Strauss, Claude, 20
Lewin, Moshe, 86, 90–2, 105–6, 108, 115–16
Lewis, Sinclair, 62
liberal-moderate socialist coalition, 209n57
liberal modernization theory, 12, 81–2, 85
Lieberman, Victor, 130–131n24
A Life for the Tsar (opera), 165
Lindblom, Charles E., 38
Lippmann, Walter, 57, 71
Lipset, Seymour Martin, 82

Index